UNDERSTANDING
CHILDREN *with*
AUTISM SPECTRUM
DISORDERS

Michelle R. Haney

Berry College

UNDERSTANDING CHILDREN *with* AUTISM SPECTRUM DISORDERS

Educators Partnering with Families

Los Angeles | London | New Delhi
Singapore | Washington DC

Los Angeles | London | New Delhi
Singapore | Washington DC

FOR INFORMATION:

SAGE Publications, Inc.
2455 Teller Road
Thousand Oaks, California 91320
E-mail: order@sagepub.com

SAGE Publications Ltd.
1 Oliver's Yard
55 City Road
London EC1Y 1SP
United Kingdom

SAGE Publications India Pvt. Ltd.
B 1/I 1 Mohan Cooperative Industrial Area
Mathura Road, New Delhi 110 044
India

SAGE Publications Asia-Pacific Pte. Ltd.
3 Church Street
#10-04 Samsung Hub
Singapore 049483

Acquisitions Editor: Diane McDaniel
Editorial Assistant: Megan Koraly
Production Editor: Laura Stewart
Copy Editor: Amy Rosenstein
Typesetter: C&M Digitals, Ltd.
Proofreader: Joyce Li
Indexer: Wendy Allex
Cover Designer: Karine Hovsepian
Marketing Manager: Terra Schultz
Permissions Editor: Adele Hutchinson

Copyright © 2013 by SAGE Publications, Inc.

All rights reserved. No part of this book may be reproduced or utilized in any form or by any means, electronic or mechanical, including photocopying, recording, or by any information storage and retrieval system, without permission in writing from the publisher.

Library of Congress Cataloging-in-Publication Data

Haney, Michelle R.
Understanding children with autism spectrum disorders : educators partnering with families / Michelle R. Haney.

p. cm.

Includes bibliographical references and index.
ISBN 978-1-4129-8246-7 (pbk.)

1. Autism spectrum disorders in children. 2. Autistic children—Education. 3. Autistic children—Family relationships. I. Title.

RC553.A88H353 2013
618.92'85882—dc23   2012017342

12 13 14 15 16 10 9 8 7 6 5 4 3 2 1

BRIEF CONTENTS

TABLE OF CONTENTS

PREFACE

This book developed from my search for a comprehensive yet engaging textbook I could use in my own classroom teaching students and professionals beginning to learn about the complex and fascinating research in Autism Spectrum Disorder (ASD). *Understanding Children With Autism Spectrum Disorders: Educators Partnering With Families* is an introductory textbook that presents the significant body of research and theory in the field of autism within the larger context of understanding the unique sociocultural dimensions of individuals with ASD and their families.

As awareness about ASD increases and prevalence rates of ASD soar, there is a need for all educators and professionals working with children with ASD and their families to understand a wide range of topics associated with ASD. The goals of this text are to introduce educators and other professionals to the complexity and diversity of children with ASD, the wide range of interventions and processes for making decisions about choosing interventions, teaming with parents to provide optimal educational opportunities, and the personal/professional growth that is likely to take place during such a journey. Although the text provides a research-based overview of autism within a theoretical framework that addresses key issues for both children and adults with ASD, the text emphasizes diagnosis, intervention, and support issues most germane to families with children and adolescents. This book is significantly different from others on the market because of the organizing theme recognizing the necessity of collaboration with families to effectively meet the needs of children with ASD. In addition, this book integrates a discussion of sociocultural characteristics of families.

This is an introductory text primarily targeting preservice teachers, advanced undergraduate students in psychology or preprofessional programs, and students in graduate-level education programs. The text is intended to serve as a core text for a semester- or quarter-long introductory college-level course about ASD and would also be appropriate as a supplementary text in a course about developmental disabilities or a more general course about disabilities. Given the unprecedented prevalence rates of ASD in children, the increasing efforts of advocates to ensure that children with ASD receive appropriate educational support, and the trend toward inclusion and noncategorical teacher credentialing, education programs across the nation are increasingly adding courses that explicitly address ASD. This text will also be attractive to a wider audience of students from a variety of disciplines, including speech-language pathology, occupational therapy, nursing, pediatrics, school administration, psychology, and counseling (particularly school psychology and school counseling).

The text fills an important niche in the cadre of autism textbooks for three primary reasons:

1. Families as partners for collaboration to formulate learning goals, implement interventions, and assess learning skills. Educators are best able to address learning goals when they partner with families to create collaborative supportive teams. Parents are a critical information source about their child. Parents have known the child the longest, seen their child across time and settings, and are invaluable in planning effective and meaningful educational and therapeutic programs. Furthermore, families can greatly enhance the progress toward achieving goals through generalization of skills, support through modeling and rewards, and suggestions for program maintenance when glitches are discovered.

2. Sociocultural dimensions of family as the framework for exploring issues surrounding autism and collaborating with families. Research shows the importance of family involvement in school for a child's success. The strengths and needs of any child cannot be comprehensively understood without understanding the child within the context of the family. Planning the most appropriate services for the child with autism is dependent on understanding the child's role in the family, the manner in which other family members relate to the child and his or her needs, the child's perception of themselves within the family context, the social-cultural history of the family, and other aspects of the family dynamics.

   Some types of disabilities, such as intellectual disabilities, cerebral palsy, severe visual and hearing impairments, are associated with easier access to community resources and an earlier diagnosis, resulting in a different trajectory of family needs. Exceptionalities such as autism are not associated with easily observed physical or cognitive deficits and may be diagnosed later in childhood. Children with these exceptionalities often have less access to community resources. Furthermore, those within and outside of the family may deny the neurological basis of these exceptionalities and instead blame parenting practices, educational opportunities, and the motivations of the child.

   Some disorders cause a greater degree of disruption within the family or limitation of the family's ability to travel and engage in activities in public. These issues are important to consider when working with children and families, as they can affect quality of life of all family members, the family's willingness to engage in a team approach with educators, and choosing goals that address real-life concerns and needs.

3. Strong pedagogical supports to help students make connections between research, theory, and real-life practices, including case studies, reflection and discussion questions, recommendations for further readings, and key vocabulary for each chapter.

- Each chapter opens with a list of bulleted learning objectives highlighting key concepts.
- Each chapter includes Chapter Reflection features relevant to the chapter's topic. This feature includes a wide range of interviews of parents, teachers, advocates, and researchers in the field of ASD. Follow-up reflection and discussion questions are provided.
- At the end of each chapter, five to six discussion questions help students apply research and theory. Several questions integrate featured information presented in highlighted section.
- A list of recommended readings and websites follows each chapter.
- A chapter summary is provided at the end of each chapter.
- A glossary of terms frequently used in the research and practice involving ASD.
- Objectives are identified in each chapter addressing the Knowledge and Standards for Teachers as established by the Council for Exceptional Children's Division of Autism and Developmental Disabilities.

Our understanding of ASD continues to change as we learn more about factors such as the neurobiology, genetics, environmental influences, and sociocultural influences that underlie this disorder. However, many issues remain constant. Families and children will always benefit from educators and other support providers that provide current information and resources in a manner that is respectful and empowers individuals and their families to make informed choices. It is my hope that this book will help those working with individuals who have autism and their families collaborate more effectively across settings and throughout the life span.

ACKNOWLEDGMENTS

I can no other answer make, but, thanks, and thanks.

William Shakespeare (*Twelfth Night*, Act 3, Scene 3)

This writing project was my response to a perceived need for an integrated and engaging textbook for students and professionals beginning to learn about the complex and fascinating research in ASD. First, I must thank my enthusiastic Berry College students for inspiring me to write this book to provide a meaningful resource for teaching a course in ASD. I would like to especially thank my graduate research assistant, Samantha Bell, and psychology student lab assistants Erica Radford, Hailey Purvis, Hillary Gann, and Haley Gresham, who were always willing to review chapters, check references, and other very helpful support tasks. Thanks to my father, Ted Rosen, who inspired me to pursue research and clinical work aimed at reducing barriers and promoting quality of life for individuals with developmental disabilities across the spectrum. I would also like to acknowledge that my year of sabbatical was a gift from Berry College and without which completion of this writing project would have been significantly more difficult. Appreciation and thanks to my incredible faculty secretary, Glenda Helms, who took care of many daily work details so I could devote more time to writing and my colleagues in the psychology department, who encouraged me to pursue this project. Love and reality checks from my husband, Shane, and our dear children, Lucy and Alex, inspired me to continue a focus on the importance of the family in life and in research. Many times while writing this book, I have also reflected upon my years working with educators, school psychologists, administrators, parents, and, of course, children with ASD. Thanks are due to those individuals in the Cobb County, Georgia, school system, and especially the Hawthorne Program, for impacting my life in such a profound way. My great appreciation goes to the many individuals who shared their stories and their experiences with me during interviews for this book. It is my hope that your life experiences are honored as a means of teaching future educators and other professionals about supporting children with ASD and their families. In particular, I would like to thank Eustacia Cutler for her encouragement and generosity in sharing her wisdom and life experiences with me over the course of several phone interviews. I would also like to offer thanks to the reviewers who generously provided valuable feedback about book chapters along the way. Reviewers for this book included the following:

Misty Ballew, Ed.D., Lipscomb University

Jonna Bobzien, Old Dominion University

Dr. Jan Charone-Sossin, Pace University

Francine L. Dreyfus, Pace University

Ruth B. Eren, Ed.D., Southern Connecticut University

Cheryl Fielding, University of Texas – Pan American

Cathy Gaylon Keramidas, West Virginia University

Jennifer A. Kurth, Northern Arizona University

Susan Longtin, Brooklyn College

Jennifer McFarland-Whisman, Marshall University

Kim Schulze, St. Cloud University of Louisville

Ellin Siegel, Ph.D., University of Nebraska – Lincoln

Thomas J. Simmons, University of Louisville

Dr. John J. Wheeler, Tennessee Technical University

Acknowledgment and thanks are due to Wesley H. Dotson and Charryse Fouquette Luckey for their contributions to the chapter on Applied Behavior Analysis. I wish these talented individuals all the best in their clinical work and research.

I would like to offer thanks to Neil Salkind for his years of encouragement and feedback during every stage of this project. Also, SAGE editor Diane McDaniel and editorial assistant Megan Koraly have been a pleasure to work with, and I heartily thank them for their encouragement and support with this book! Thank you, Diane, for giving me this opportunity to consolidate information in a manner that I hope will promote understanding and inspire students to careers in the field of ASD. There is so much more work to be done!

SECTION I

THE EVOLVING UNDERSTANDING OF AUTISM SPECTRUM DISORDER

Section I, "The Evolving Understanding of Autism Spectrum Disorder," begins with a chapter on the historical evolution of understanding autism as a spectrum disorder and the impact on the family. Chapter 2 highlights the diagnostic systems currently used to define Autism Spectrum Disorder (ASD), core deficits, and comorbid conditions frequently associated with ASD. Chapter 3 explores the biological issues and etiology of autism.

CHAPTER 1

HISTORICAL OVERVIEW OF AUTISM AND THE ROLE OF THE FAMILY

In this chapter, you will learn about:

- The significance of a historical perspective for understanding ASD.
- The treatment of mental illness and developmental disability before autism was recognized as a disorder.
- The evolution of the *Diagnostic and Statistical Manual of Mental Disorders (DSM)* and its impact on identifying autism.
- The impact of psychological paradigms on understanding ASD.
- Theories explaining the significant rise in prevalence rates.

CHAPTER REFLECTION: Interview With Eustacia Cutler

Author.

Ms. Cutler is an internationally renowned speaker and advocate for families raising children with ASD. In 1949, her 2-year-old daughter, Temple Grandin, was diagnosed with autism, then thought to be a form of infant schizophrenia. Though children with autism were often institutionalized, Ms. Cutler chose to raise Temple herself, seeking out—each step along the way—the few

(Continued)

(Continued)

but rare intervention services. Today, Temple Grandin holds a doctorate degree in Animal Science and has written many books about her experiences as a successful individual with ASD.

Author: How was autism understood when Temple was a child?

Ms. Cutler: Freudian thinking dominated the '50's understanding of autism, declaring it to be a psychosocial disorder. Not until Bernard Rimland's groundbreaking book in 1965 was it finally recognized as bioneurological.

A revealing example was an experience I had in 1962 researching a television documentary on so-called "disturbed children." A top psychiatrist took me to a ward. I'll never forget those doors opening onto a huge room filled with silent children, each alone, each repeating obsessively a minute and meaningless behavior ritual. Seeing my shock, the psychiatrist said: "Please don't write about autism. We don't know what it is, we don't know what to do about it. You will only hold out hope and there is none." At that time Temple had been

mainstreamed for the better part of 10 years.

Author: What advice do you share with mothers raising children with autism?

Ms. Cutler: Autism involves the trauma of lost identity, for both child and mother. A baby needs a mother to know she's a baby, but a mother needs a baby to know she's a mother. When that exchange is lost, both mother and baby are at sea. I studied identity at Harvard under Erik Erikson, the psychoanalyst who first recognized the crucial role it plays in our lives. He put his mark on me.

I always urge mothers to have some outside activity "so you won't lose your sense of self." Preferably it should be something that has nothing to do with autism. I worked in a theater. They knew I had children, but nothing more. Not only did theater work give me respite from the daily stress of autism, it also renewed my confidence in evaluating what was going on.

Ms. Cutler used her experiences with theater to create a family atmosphere that provided inclusive opportunities for Temple.

Ms. Cutler: When people ask: "What did you do together as a family?" I say, "We put on plays." When my children saw me perform, they, too, wanted to perform. Temple's love of addressing autism societies probably springs from her very early love of performing. Since family plays also included other children, it helped integrate Temple into the neighborhood.

To learn more about Ms. Cutler's experiences raising Temple, read her beautifully written memoir *A Thorn in My Pocket: Temple Grandin's Mother Tells the Family Story* (Cutler, 2004).

AUTISM AS A DISTINCT DISORDER

Leo Kanner

The first case studies describing children with autism were published in 1943. Leo Kanner, an American psychiatrist, described a disorder he called "Early Infantile Autism" as distinctly different from schizophrenia in his 1943 paper "Autistic Disturbances of Affective Contact." In this seminal paper, Kanner documents 11 case studies of children "whose condition differs so markedly and uniquely from anything reported so far, that each case merits—and, I hope, will eventually receive—a detailed consideration of its fascinating peculiarities" (p. 217). Kanner's work was first published in English and became very influential in the United States. In fact, Kanner's descriptions and reflections are so perceptive that they continue to be relevant to contemporary observations, questions, and concerns about children with autism today.

Johns Hopkins University.

Leo Kanner (1894–1981) was an Austrian-born psychiatrist and considered the first child psychiatrist in the United States. He was the first psychiatrist to describe case studies of children with autism in his seminal paper "Autistic Disturbances of Affective Contact" in 1943.

Hans Asperger

A year after Kanner's publication of the case studies, Hans Asperger published his second doctoral thesis about a similar disorder, which was titled "Autistic Psychopathology in Children" (Asperger, 1944/1991). Both Kanner and Asperger were born in Austria and educated in Vienna, but Kanner immigrated to the United States in 1924 (Frith, 1991). Although there is no evidence that the two had ever met, both Kanner and Asperger had been exposed to research by Eugen Bleuler about childhood schizophrenia that incorporated the term "autistic" to describe extreme social withdrawal sometimes observed in individuals with schizophrenia (Frith, 2003).

CHAPTER REFLECTION: Independent Discoveries

It is remarkable that these two scientists, who seemingly knew nothing about one another's work, published papers about a population so similar and used the same term, "autistic," to describe these children. There are other examples in history of scientists working independently on groundbreaking discoveries uncovered very close in time. In fact, instances of multiple independent discoveries are a relatively common phenomenon in science (Merton, 1961).

Asperger's Syndrome

The influence of Kanner's paper spread rather quickly in the United States and other parts of Europe. However, Asperger's paper, written in German, remained unknown in most of Europe or the United States until an English translation by Lorna Wing (1981) brought international attention to his work. At that time, Wing (1981) suggested the name "Asperger's Syndrome" replace the term "autistic psychopathy." This change in nomenclature was both to honor Asperger for his insightful work and to avoid possible confusion of the word "psychopathy" with sociopathic behavior. Ultimately, "Asperger's Syndrome" was adopted by the two most widely used systems for diagnosing developmental and mental disorders: the International Classification of Diseases, 10th Revision (ICD-10) and the *Diagnostic and Statistical Manual of Mental Disorders, Fourth Edition, Text Revision (DSM-IV-TR)*.

Kanner and Asperger: A Comparison

Both Kanner and Asperger described children with unusual behavioral characteristics. Furthermore, both recognized this to be a developmental disorder with deficits in socialization and language development. Kanner and Asperger provided clinical descriptions, diagnostic analyses, and predictions of future trends that were extraordinary in their accuracy based on what is known about autism today. For instance, both Kanner and Asperger noted a higher prevalence in boys, recognized autism to be a developmental disability (although Asperger noted diagnosis of autistic psychopathy as unlikely before age 3), and noted the propensity for comorbidity with other disorders. Although Asperger described a population of children with higher functioning skills, both Kanner and Asperger described similar core deficits including socialization, communication (verbal and nonverbal), and imagination (also discussed in terms of repertoire of interest and behavior). These core deficits served as scaffold for the development of diagnostic criteria for both autism and Asperger's Syndrome. The resulting "triad of core deficits" provides the framework of contemporary diagnostic criteria for Autism and Asperger's Syndrome in the *DSM-IV-TR* and the ICD-10. Diagnostic characteristics of Autism and Asperger's Syndrome will be discussed further in Chapter 5.

HISTORICAL CONCEPTUALIZATION OF AUTISM

CHAPTER REFLECTION: Historical Reflection

Ms. Cutler's (see "Chapter Reflections: Interview With Eustacia Cutler") described mental health professionals in the 1950s and 1960s as having profoundly different views about autism compared with our current understanding of ASD. Beliefs are greatly impacted by the time period in which you live.

Question: Do you think your attitude about educating children with social and communication difficulties would be the same if you were a teacher 50 years ago? How about 100 years ago?

Tracing the history of society's understanding of developmental disorders, mental illness, and specifically autism from the 1800s to modern times brings context to our current definition of ASD. A historical overview provides valuable perspective. Changes over time bring new theories, research tools, and perspectives that can build on previous knowledge and sometimes dramatically change our current understanding.

As an educator, you may be surprised how many "new" ideas are in fact dressed-up versions of past practices. Here are some reasons why history matters in education:

History helps us make informed decisions about practices that impact the future.

Consider George Santayana's (1905) famous cautionary remark that "those who cannot remember history are condemned to repeat it" (p. 284). Even if sociocultural forces seem poised to prevent contemporary society from viewing autism as we did in centuries past, understanding the history of autism can help us choose a bit more wisely with the advantage of hindsight. Understanding the past is an important tool for predicting how we will continue to understand autism.

Through an understanding of history, we learn how things are connected and how ideas came to be.

History also offers us insights and context for *why* we currently behave and believe as we do. Remnants of past practices, folk beliefs, and stereotypes linger within popular culture. If you have any doubts about the significance of media depictions, consider the impact of the movie *Rain Man* on popular culture. In this 1988 movie, Dustin Hoffman plays Raymond Babbitt, an autistic savant who is institutionalized because of a lack of independent living skills, yet has a remarkable ability to quickly memorize lists of rote information. Winning four Oscars, the movie *Rain Man* was the first time many people were exposed to the term "autism." Several decades later, this movie continues to influence popular culture's understanding of autism. For instance, autism, as depicted by *Rain Man*, is parodied by the popular media on shows such as *The Simpsons* and *Heroes,* and even captured in newly coined terms such as the rapper Jay-Z's self-described "rainman flow" (Abrantes, 2009). Although currently there is a well-established consensus within the medical, clinical, and research communities that only a minority of individuals with autism is represented by the character Raymond Babbitt, the stereotype of the person with ASD as a savant remains (Murray, 2006).

Changes in how scientific and clinical communities conceptualize autism have tremendous impact on families.

In the past, parents of children with autism were told that their children had a psychotic disorder that could only be addressed by professionals within an institutional residential setting with psychoanalysis the primary intervention. Parents were not involved in treatment or educational decisions and were considered incapable of supporting their children with autism.

The history of autism also includes a prolonged period where professionals considered autism to be caused by cold and unresponsive parents (particularly mothers) who were unkindly considered "refrigerator parents." In these cases, parents were encouraged to subject themselves to lengthy sessions of psychoanalysis to help them become better parents. A legacy of parental blame followed this period of understanding autism. Our current understanding of autism as a biological disorder also impacts families. For instance, future implications of a genetic etiology may include genetic counseling and routine prenatal screening for parents with a family history of autism.

AUTISM THROUGHOUT THE AGES

Although names describing individuals with ASD change over time, likely there have been people with ASD throughout human history. There are a few retrospective investigations about individuals who lived before autism was identified as a unique disorder. In these cases, a postmortem diagnosis is made based on historical documents indicating behaviors consistent with a contemporary diagnosis of autism. For instance, in *Autism in History: The Case of Hugh Blair of Borgue*, Houston and Frith (2000) construct a fascinating case study of a young man who appears to have autism living during the mid-1700s in Edinburgh. Likewise, Waltz and Shattock (2004) constructed several case reports of individuals with autism who lived in London during the 19th century.

CHAPTER REFLECTION: Origin of Term "Autism"

Derived from the Greek pronoun "autos" or "he himself," the term "autism" was coined by Eugen Bleuler in 1910 to describe extreme withdrawn behavior associated with some types of schizophrenia (Parnas, Bovet, & Zahavi, 2002).

Question: Can you recall instances in the media or personal conversations when autism has been confused with a mental illness? How is autism different from a mental illness such as schizophrenia?

It took decades after the publication of Kanner's paper before autism and childhood schizophrenia were considered separate disorders. Consider how closely the following description of a subgroup of children with schizophrenia in 1956 resembles our current definition of ASD. Bender (1956), a renowned psychiatrist for treating childhood schizophrenia, describes one of his case studies: "He is repressed, inhibited, withdrawn, often mute and incapable of adequate object relationships...does not respond to stimulation although he may be hypersensitive" (p. 499). A striking example of the transition from childhood schizophrenia to autism is the name change of one of the premier autism journals from *Journal of Autism and Childhood Schizophrenia* to *Journal of Autism and Developmental Disorders* in 1979.

TREATMENT BEFORE AUTISM WAS RECOGNIZED AS A UNIQUE SYNDROME

A clear definition of autism as a condition distinct from mental illness was not available until the 1940s. However, history reveals how people with atypical behavior have been treated across the ages (not well!). It is likely that people with severe to moderate autism were grouped together with those with mental illness and mental retardation (intellectual disabilities). The history of society's treatment of both mental illness and intellectual disability provides insight as to how those with ASD were likely treated. Unfortunately, there is a sad story to tell when considering the history of society's treatment of those with atypical behavior and special needs.

The Middle Ages: Inhumanity Toward Those With Disabilities

During the Middle Ages, inhumanity marked the treatment of individuals with mental illness and developmental disabilities. At that time, a prevailing belief was that individuals with disabilities were morally inferior. Any "weakness of will" was considered inherently immoral (as suggested by the writings of Thomas Aquinas). In many cases, those with behavior that deviated from the socially sanctioned norm were thought to be possessed by the devil or thought to be a witch. In fact, a common resource for addressing atypical behavior was the document *Malleus Maleifacarium (The Witch Hunter)* written in 1487 as a guide to diagnosing and punishing witches.

Treatment and punishment were hard to differentiate as both often resulted in physical pain and/or death. In any case, physicians generally did not treat diseases of the "mind." Thus, rather than "treatment" or "education" individuals with significantly atypical behavior were often locked away in institutions with very poor conditions and/or physically abused as punishment for their "inferiority."

The Enlightenment: A Clinical Approach

At the end of the 16th century, Philippe Pinel instituted a more humane and clinical approach to supporting those with mental illness, including removing chains, talking with patients, and categorizing disorders (Gerard, 1997). The end of the 17th century was known as the period of "Enlightenment" in Europe, during which mental and developmental disorders were more commonly seen as organic rather than a failure of will or sin. In 1812, the first American psychiatrist, Benjamin Rush, published a textbook about "diseases of the mind." Thus, during the late 1700s, atypical behavior was starting to be viewed as a concern to be treated rather than punished.

Institutions for Individuals With Disabilities

Prior to the 1900s, it was generally considered the family's responsibility to care for individuals who were unable to care for themselves (Houston & Frith, 2000). The emergence of state-run institutions for those with mental illness or other special needs emerged in Europe in the early 1900s. One of the most

Wikimedia Commons

Bethlem Hospital is depicted in "The Madhouse," one of William Hogarth's sequence of paintings called *A Rake's Progress* (1732–1733).

noteworthy (and infamous) was Bethlem. Later known as "Bedlam," (2012), this facility was known for the horrendous conditions in which the inmates lived. Likely there were individuals with ASD residing in these state-run institutions. In fact, Rimland, a prominent researcher and advocate in the field of autism, reported uncovering records of a boy with characteristics suggesting ASD institutionalized at Bedlam (1964). Also at this time in history, Dorothea Dix tirelessly advocated for more humane treatment of institutionalized people, particularly those with mental illness in the United States.

PSYCHOANALYSIS AND MOTHER-BLAMING

In his paper "Autistic Disturbances of Affective Contact," Kanner expressed ambivalence about the cause of autism. Although Kanner's observation that autism occurred during early development supported a biological origin, his remarks about the parents in his case studies foreshadowed the devastating trend of parent-blaming that followed. Negative impressions of parents (particularly mothers) are woven into several case studies. For instance, Kanner (1964) writes:

> His mother brought with her copious notes that indicated obsessive preoccupation with details and a tendency to read all sorts of peculiar interpretations into the child's performances. The mother, supposedly a college graduate, a restless, unstable, excitable woman, gave a vague and blatantly conflicting history of the family background and the child's development. (pp. 225–226)

Today, we recognize that parents of children with disabilities are often overwhelmed and stressed. Recognizing a parent's need for support is an important step in helping the child and the entire family.

**CHAPTER REFLECTION: Kanner's
Perception of Mothers**

What if Kanner's descriptions were of a parent attending a teacher conference? Today parents are encouraged to bring documentation of their children's behavior and development to enhance the accuracy of evaluations and outcomes of education, social, and medical decisions. Rather than a sign of obsessive behavior, detailed family, developmental, and medical histories are used to better plan for a child's education.

Reflection Question: Consider some other ways you might interpret the observations about parent behavior described by Kanner.

Based on the small sample of cases brought to his clinic, Kanner suggested that autism was associated with high socioeconomic class. Current research does not support Kanner's observations about increased prevalence of ASD within families with higher socioeconomic status (Ozonoff & Rogers, 2003). ASD occurs within all socioeconomic and ethnic groups. However, there is disparity in regard to receiving early diagnosis and treatment. This topic is addressed further in Chapter 3.

It is important to consider the time period during which Kanner received his clinical training. Psychiatric training in the early 1900s emphasized a detached, "cool and formal" approach to working with families. Despite his harsh depiction of parents and false conclusion regarding the relationship between social class and ASD, Kanner's case studies were incredibly observant and relevant to our current understanding of ASD.

PSYCHOANALYSIS AS A TREATMENT FOR AUTISM

For decades after Kanner first describe autism, professionals in the field of psychiatry and mental health believed that parents caused autism in their child because of cold and neglectful parenting practices. This belief stemmed from the most prominent (and for a time only) theory of personality development and psychological therapy, psychoanalysis. Psychoanalysis is a complex theory based on the belief that unconscious forces impact a significant

Sigmund Freud created and pioneered psychoanalysis as a treatment for mental illnesses and other atypical behaviors. © Life photo archive.

degree of human behavior and that personality development is most significantly impacted by early parenting practices. Thus, social forces (primarily parenting during the early part of childhood) were considered responsible for an individual's personality and later behaviors.

Extending Freud's Work: Treating Children

Sigmund Freud's daughter, Anna Freud, extended her father's work with adults to treating mental and behavioral disorders in children, and specifically addressed autism in children. Other influential psychoanalysists, such as Margaret Mahler, further expanded the theory of psychoanalysis as an explanation for autism. Mahler placed mothers at center stage in her theory of ego development and autism. Mahler writes:

> Early infantile autism develops, I believe, because the infantile personality, devoid of emotional ties to the person of the mother, is unable to cope with the external stimuli and inner excitations, which threaten from both sides his very existence as an entity. (1952, p. 297)

Mahler's theory combined the only acceptable theory of personality development at the time, psychoanalysis, with insightful observations about infants showing "no anticipatory posture at nursing, no reaching-out gestures, and no specific smiling response."

Bettelheim: The Champion of Mother-Blaming

Unfortunately, Mahler's ideas spurred several decades of professionally sanctioned "mother-blaming" into the 1970s. An outspoken leader in this regard was Bruno Bettelheim. Like Kanner and Asperger, Bettelheim was born in Austria. He became a prominent child psychiatrist after escaping from a concentration camp in Nazi Germany and immigrating to the United States (Pollack, 1997). Bettelheim coined the term *refrigerator mothers* to denote emotionally distant mothers. This notion that emotionally frigid mothering caused autism in children was extremely influential and outlined in his popular 1967 book, *The Empty Fortress: Infantile Autism and the Birth of Self.*

Thus, for decades after the introduction of Kanner's case studies, parents in the United States and much of Europe were blamed for their child's autism. Parents were often encouraged to institutionalize their child and considered by professionals incapable of effectively caring for their child. Sometimes parents underwent years of psychoanalysis in hopes of treating suspected psychopathology responsible for their "neglectful and harmful" parenting styles. History reveals that psychoanalysis was not only cruel and harmful to families of children with autism, but also unsuccessful in treating autism.

Bettelheim coined the term *refrigerator mother* to describe emotionally distant parenting practices that resulted in autism in young children. ©Otto Froehlich.

DEBUNKING THE MYTH OF THE "REFRIGERATOR MOTHER"

As the psychological tide turned from psychoanalysis and toward other perspectives such as behaviorism, cognitive psychology, and neuro/biopsychology, other theories about the etiology of autism emerged. Today it is believed that autism is likely a genetic, and certainly a biological disorder, often present at birth (discussed in Chapter 2). Although much work remains to be done to fully understand these factors, there is consensus within the medical, psychological, and scientific research community that autism is not caused by parenting practices.

Bernard Rimland is credited, in large part, for debunking the myth of autism as an emotional disorder caused by bad parenting. In 1964, Rimland, a research psychologist and father of a son with autism, published *Infantile Autism: The Syndrome and Its Implications for a Neural Theory of Behavior.* This influential book presented a convincing rationale asserting that autism was a cognitive disorder with neurobiological origins.

THE LEGACY OF PSYCHOANALYSIS AND ASD

It is difficult to fully capture the negative impact Freudian psychoanalysis has had on families, as parents struggled to understand autism and find support for their children. Yet, the advent of psychoanalysis as a treatment for mental and behavioral disorders challenged the prevailing belief that people with atypical behavior were either morally deficient or possessed by evil spirits.

Despite the harm often caused to families, psychotherapy ushered in a momentous positive change from past practices of dealing with atypical behavior. The advent of psychotherapy paved the way for legitimizing mental and behavioral disorders as appropriate topics to study scientifically and treat clinically, as opposed to punishing, castigating, and hiding away from society. Furthermore, Freud's theory of psychoanalysis made an undeniable impact on the way future generations of physicians, mental health professionals, and social service support providers would approach their work, especially with regard to the case study. Lastly, Freud's theory, although theoretically flawed, provided an important precedent for the study of child development, the treatment of childhood psychopathology, and the recognition of the critical role of parenting.

THE IMPACT OF SOCIETY'S CHANGING VIEWS ABOUT CHILDHOOD ON UNDERSTANDING AUTISM

Children as Little Adults

Over the years, mainstream notions about child development and the role of parents have changed dramatically. Prior to the 19th century, there was little documentation, not to mention diagnosis, of childhood psychopathology (Stone, 1973). Although it was believed that children were not susceptible to mental illness, children were otherwise considered "little adults" in that they had all the same traits as adults, but with less stamina and strength.

"Spare the Rod, Spoil the Child"

During the Middle Ages, the Christian doctrine of "original sin" significantly influenced child rearing in Europe. It was believed that children were born essentially selfish and lacking in morality. Parents were held responsible for assisting their children with religious instruction to reach salvation. This instruction often included the use of corporeal punishment (hence the phrase,

"Spare the rod, spoil the child"). Some families today choose parenting styles based on similar themes.

Children as Innately Good

In the mid-1700s, the view of childhood was greatly impacted by the philosopher Jean-Jacques Rousseau, who advocated that children were born "good" rather than as a blank slate or innately sinful. The innate goodness view suggested that parents should provide a protective and nurturing environment for development.

Tabula Rasa: *Children Born "Blank Slates"*

During the 1800s, there was a growing awareness that children had needs different from adults and required specialized care. John Locke's empiricism, a philosophical approach asserting that all is acquired through experience, reigned during the 17th century. His term *tabula rasa* (children were thought to be born a "blank slate") reflected the predominant view of childhood at that time. Once again, parents were considered paramount to shaping children into responsible citizens.

This philosophy of childhood allowed for some optimism for procuring positive outcomes. For instance, in the famous study of the "Wild Boy of Aveyron," Itard (1801/1962) attempted to rehabilitate a feral child found in the woods through intense educational intervention. In fact, some researchers suggest that the "Wild Boy of Aveyron" represents an early case study of a child with autism (Frith, 2003). This belief that environment (or "nurture") can significantly impact development was revived in the late 1960s with B. F. Skinner's theory of operant conditioning, leading to the development of many important interventions for autism.

Formal Study of Childhood as a Distinct Period of Development

Finally, in the 19th century scientists become truly focused on the empirical study of child development and recognition of childhood as a period of development distinctly and qualitatively different from adulthood. You may not think of Charles Darwin as a child psychologist. However, Charles Darwin was one of the first researchers to document child development, based on daily observations of his own children through his "baby biographies" (Lamb, Bornstein, & Teti, 2002).

Likewise, Jean Piaget also studied his own children to define benchmarks for understanding cognitive development during childhood. Piaget's influential theory of cognitive development (1954/1981), built on work done by Arnold Gesell (1928), Stanley Hall (1904), and others, provided a baseline for comparing the typical (sometimes referred to as "normal") development of cognition from infancy through adolescence. Thus, Piaget's stages of cognitive development coupled with the development of childhood tests such as the Binet to assess and document cognitive ability, allowed for a clearer understanding of both typical and atypical development in childhood. The body of work emerging from this period helped clarify expectations for typical development during childhood. Understanding typical development is key to identifying and helping children with atypical development.

CHAPTER REFLECTION: Considering Your Own Beliefs About Parenting and Childhood

The parents you work with may have perceptions about parenting and childhood very different from your own. Recognizing this can help you better connect with families and understand their preferences for certain types of interventions and supports.

Question: As you read about the history of society's view of childhood and parenting, consider which paradigm best fits with your own beliefs.

CODIFICATION OF MENTAL DISORDERS AND FORMALIZED DEFINITIONS OF AUTISM

The advent of the formal study of child development coupled with the psychological testing movement provided the climate for a codified diagnostic system. In the United States, the "bible" of diagnosing disorders such as ASD is the

DSM. We are currently in the 4th edition with a text revision, so it is currently referred to as the *DSM IV-TR.* The international diagnostic classification system for diagnosing autism and related disorders is the ICD, currently in its10th edition. Historically the *DSM* and the ICD have been fairly well aligned. Other systems for diagnosing ASD are discussed in Chapter 2.

Early Attempts to Categorize Types of Disability

Long before the publication of the *DSM-I* (in 1952), attempts were made to categorize types of disorders. For instance, William Cullen advocated for a distinction between physical and mental disorders in the late 18th century. Another important distinction was made in the mid-19th century between mental retardation and mental illness. These distinctions are very important to our current understanding of ASD. Even today, there are misperceptions of that ASD is a mental illness or that all children with ASD have low intellectual ability.

Omission of Autism From DSM-I and DSM-II

Autism did not appear as a disorder in either the first (*DSM-I,* 1952) or the second (*DSM-II,* 1968) *DSM.* Though considered a rare disorder, autism was diagnosed clinically using other sources such as Kanner's case studies. The *DSM-I* considered children with behavioral characteristics of autism to have "schizophrenic reaction type." Likewise, in the United Kingdom, the term "childhood schizophrenia," based on criteria from Creak's Nine Points, described our contemporary definition of ASD (Boucher, 2009). Creak's Nine Points, described impairment of emotional relationships, deficits in intellectual functioning, lack of personal awareness, preoccupation with particular objects, resistance to change, abnormal response to perceptual stimuli, anxiety, atypical speech development, and atypical motor development (Creak, 1961).

DSM-III Introduces Autism as a Distinct Disorder

The *DSM-III* (1980) was a significant change from the previous *DSMs.* In fact, the publication of the *DSM-III* revolutionized the manner in which mental disorders were conceptualized and treated (Mayes & Horwitz, 2005). Prior to the *DSM-III*, psychoanalysis was the primary theoretical framework for treating all kinds of mental disorders. However, a number of pressures from insurance companies, government policy and research agencies, and professional lobbying groups pushed for the *DSM-III* (American Psychiatric Association [APA], 1980) to provide a more empirical system for demonstrating effectiveness. The outcome was a diagnostic manual that provided a medical framework for conceptualizing mental disorders in the same way one would diagnose a physical illness. Symptoms were provided for diagnosis rather than the previous focus on the underlying cause. This was of great benefit to research psychologists and psychiatrists who could now operationally define disorders such as autism in a manner that allowed for replication.

The *DSM-III* was the first *DSM* to include autism as a distinct diagnostic category. Building upon Kanner's original work, Michael Rutter and colleagues (1971) contributed significantly to formulating a "triad of core deficits" on which the *DSM's* criteria for autism is based. Rutter and Bartak (1971) proposed that autism was a type of cognitive/language disorder with abnormal interpersonal relationships (extreme withdrawal), delays in speech and language development, and ritualistic compulsive behaviors that occurred before 30 months of age. Informed by growing awareness of autism and research publications about autism, autism was finally included in the *DSM* within the category "infantile autism" (*DSM-III* in 1980). The *DSM-III* focused on atypical language development as a key component to the diagnosis of infantile autism.

Inclusion of Asperger Disorder in DSM-IV

A year after the publication of the *DSM-III*, Lorna Wing's English translation of Asperger's case studies was received with great interest by clinicians and researchers in English-speaking countries, particularly within the United States. Asperger's work, along with other research in the field, resulted in a modified definition of autism that placed greater emphasis on impairment in communication as opposed to language in the next revision of the *DSM* (*DSM-III-Revised*, 1987). However, the diagnostic category Asperger's Syndrome was not included in the *DSM* until the fourth revision (*DSM-IV*) in 1994. Table 1.1 summarizes the changes in the diagnosis of autism from the *DSM* to the *DSM IV-TR*.

Table 1.1   Evolution of *DSM's* Characterization of Autism From 1952 to Current Version

DSM *(1952) and* DSM-II *(1968)*	DSM-III *(1980)*	DSM-III-R *(1987)*	DSM-IV *(1994)*	DSM-IV-TR *(2000)*
Heavily influenced by psychoanalysis/ focus on etiology (cause) rather than diagnosis	Embraces Medical Model/ subsequent versions less interested in etiology—focus is on diagnosis and treatment issues	Embraces Medical Model	Embraces Medical Model	Embraces Medical Model
Schizophrenic reaction, childhood type	Infantile Autism	Autistic Disorder	Autism and Asperger's Syndrome are under the category of Pervasive Developmental Disabilities (along with Rett Syndrome, Childhood Disintegrative Disorder, and Pervasive Developmental Disorder, Not Otherwise Specified (PPD-NOS))	Autism and Asperger's Syndrome are under the category of Pervasive Developmental Disabilities Provides more details about Asperger's Syndrome

THE NEW ZEITGEIST

Another significant change in psychological perspectives was *behaviorism.* Behaviorism is the paradigm that considers psychology the science of changing behaviors through objective methods. The term *behaviorism* was coined by John Watson in his classic paper "Psychology as the Behaviorist Views It" (1913). By 1930, behaviorism was accepted throughout mainstream psychology, particularly in the United States.

The *neobehaviorists* expanded the behaviorist perspective resulting in an explosion of research and later application to a wide range of clinical and educational interventions. One of the most prolific of the neobehaviorists, B. F. Skinner, carefully developed the theory of operant conditioning based on research with animals (namely pigeons and rats) on which the many variants of applied behavior analysis are based (discussed in Chapter 7).

At the time behaviorism began to take off in applied efforts, the United States was in the midst of the Great Depression. In the past, poverty was associated with moral ineptitude. American psychologists such as Galton and other leaders of the eugenics movement held the attitude that the wealthy class was genetically superior (both intellectually and morally) and justly deserved economic advantages they enjoyed.

However, in the 1930s more Americans experienced poverty than ever before. The stock market crash resulted in fortunes lost by families that could not recall experiencing poverty. Thus, poverty and harsh environmental circumstances were understood, perhaps better than ever before in the United States, as something distinct from class, ability, or ethnicity. In an effort to bring the United States out of the Great Depression, Roosevelt instituted the New Deal, infusing governmental aid to alleviate the culture of poverty. An era of optimism surrounded these policies with the hope that changes in environmental conditions would allow people to regain their financial stability. Extending this view to behaviorism is the belief that changing environmental conditions results in predictable behavior changes.

Although behaviorism does not attempt to explain what causes autism, behaviorism has stimulated a tremendous amount of empirical research regarding intervention and educational support. Furthermore, unlike psychoanalysts, behaviorists viewed parents as partners in planning, data collection, and implementing interventions. Parents were considered valuable resources for helping change problematic behaviors associated with autism.

In large part, this change was due to the efforts of O. Ivar Lovaas, who in the mid-1960s pioneered the application of operant conditioning (known as applied behavior analysis) to teaching children with autism. Applied behavior analysis, or ABA, offered interventions options that did not exist before. ABA was used to successfully replace maladaptive behaviors (such as self-injury or aggressive behaviors) with behaviors that were less harmful and helped the individual fit into mainstream society, increase attention and focus to support learning, and learn adaptive skills that fostered independence.

COGNITIVE PSYCHOLOGY AND AUTISM

During the 1960s, there was a growing dissatisfaction with the subject matter and methodology of behaviorism, which excluded the study of mental processes such as attention, perception, memory, and thought. Cognitive psychology reclaimed the subject matter of mind and thought, long associated with psychoanalysis, but retained the scientific method of investigation championed by the behaviorism and the natural sciences. The cognitive revolution (or cognitive renaissance as referred to by contemporary cognitive psychologists) was an explosion of research that addressed a diverse array of concepts, such as information processing (Neisser, 1967), artificial intelligence (see Wagman, 1993), eyewitness testimony (Loftus & Palmer, 1974), and linguistics (e.g., Noam Chomsky and Steven Pinker). The resulting research and theoretical frameworks generated were extremely important to modern-day understanding of ASD.

Cognitive research has led to investigations of differences in perception, memory, and theory of mind between children with autism and their typically developing peers. This work has led to much theorizing about the etiology of autism, generated specific types of interventions and educational strategies, and resulted in the recognition of individual strengths in areas such as memory and visual spatial skills.

Today, cognitive psychology and cognitive neuroscience continue to flourish as influential scientific paradigms. Contributions from cognitive scientists significantly impacted our understanding of ASD in many ways that will be discussed throughout this book.

HUMANISTIC PSYCHOLOGY AND EMPOWERMENT

Like the cognitive perspective, humanistic psychology was a reaction against the prevailing paradigms of the time (early 1960s), psychoanalysis and behaviorism. The focus of humanism was on individual and subjective experience rather than empirical investigations that were central to both behaviorism and later cognitive psychology. Further, clinical work and research based on humanistic psychology addressed aspects of the person as a whole (rather than as a group of behaviors) in an effort to facilitate a personally meaningful and enriched existence (Schultz & Schultz, 1987).

Although there is not a direct connection between the humanistic movement and specific treatments for or theoretical constructs exploring the etiology of ASD, humanism is central to the parent advocacy and self-advocacy movements that have greatly impacted the visibility of autism, opportunities for inclusion in schools and other community domains, and legal initiatives to provide additional support for services and research. The humanistic perspective contributed to the development of a host of parent support/advocacy groups.

International, national, and grassroots local support groups not only provide parents with a community of support and knowledge about ASD, but also serve as a powerful medium for shaping public policy and popular culture awareness about issues such as prevalence, early intervention, and the controversial immunization–autism connection. In fact, parents involved in these types of support groups often develop strong coping skills that help to buffer the enormous stress associated with parenting a child with autism, and often become advocates on behalf of all children with autism and their families (Pottie & Ingram, 2008; Ryan & Cole, 2009). Furthermore, parent advocacy has been critical for securing inclusive educational opportunities for children with ASD.

COMING FULL CIRCLE: THE DECADE OF THE BRAIN AND THE HUMAN GENOME PROJECT

With advances in scientific technology and knowledge, the biological perspective has been the prevailing paradigm since the late 1980s. In fact, psychological paradigms such as cognitive psychology and behaviorism have merged into domains (unimaginable to either behaviorists or cognitive psychologists of years past) such as cognitive neuroscience and behavioral neuroscience.

The Decade of the Brain

Two international collaborative efforts to understand human biology and raise public awareness about this research mark the current zeitgeist of the biological perspective. On January 1, 1990, President George W. Bush, proclaimed 1990–2000 to be the Decade of the Brain (1990). Efforts to stimulate, highlight, and celebrate research understanding the structure and function of the human brain reflect current trends of contemporary psychology and psychiatry. Advances in neuroimaging and other technology allow for researchers to better understand the structure of the brain and investigate the relationship between structures of the brain and behaviors impacted by autism (such as communication), as well as with other cognitive skills (such as attention, memory, planning, and problem solving).

The Human Genome Project

Another tremendous influence on research efforts to understand autism from a biological perspective was the Human Genome Project, a 13-year endeavor to map out the entire sequence of human chromosomes. Arguably one of the greatest scientific achievements of our generation, the Human Genome Project was completed ahead of schedule in 2003 as the result of international scientific collaboration in an effort to make available this valuable knowledge before competing private organizations could patent this knowledge (National Human Genome Research Institute, 2009).

CHAPTER REFLECTION: The Ethics of Genetic Research and Autism

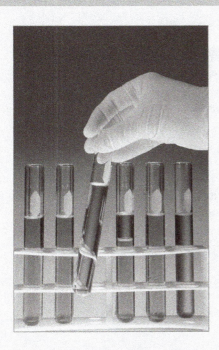

An important, and interesting, aspect of the Human Genome Project was the development of the Ethical, Legal, and Social Implications (ELSI) program. Anticipating the potential discoveries of genes associated with an array of diseases and syndromes, James Watson, a leader of the Human Genome Project and codiscoverer of the structure of DNA, strongly advocated for a mechanism to address ethical, legal, and social implications of knowledge about the human genome (Collins, Morgan, & Patrinos, 2003). The ELSI was an unprecedented undertaking that integrated a concentrated focus on ethical and social implications of science alongside groundbreaking scientific investigations. These efforts led to the passing of federal legislation (Genetic Information Nondiscrimination Act, 2008) to protect individuals and families against discrimination based on their genetic information (Collins, Morgan, & Patrinos, 2003). Thus, if ever we arrive at a time of routine genetic screening of infants, or possibly the fetus, for indicators of ASD, there will be a precedent for providing protection for those individuals against a lifetime of potential discrimination.

Inspired by the incredible success and potential of the Human Genome Project, the National Alliance for Autism Research (NAAR) kicked off the Autism Genome Project in 2004. A collaboration between public and private sectors, the Autism Genome Project involves scientists from 19 countries investigating genes and gene variants contributing to the expression of ASD (Autism Genome Project, 2009). Echoing the current biological focus of understanding the etiology of autism is the controversial debate about the relationship between autism and vaccinations (specifically thimerosal, a mercury-based preservative traditionally used in many childhood vaccinations and discussed more in Chapter 3).

CONTEMPORARY UNDERSTANDING OF ASD

Today, it is widely believed that autism is a developmental disorder likely caused by genetic factors. The integration of neuroscience with cognitive psychology, behaviorism, and cognitive behaviorism has led to an exciting and powerful new paradigm for understanding autism. Results from genetic research and investigations of brain–behavior connections refine our understanding of the etiology of autism.

Advances in research can be used to provide earlier screening, resulting in earlier intervention. In addition, increasingly sophisticated research may lead to psychopharmacological interventions targeting specific types of autism to facilitate successful interventions or prevent the characteristic expression of the disorder. Research about our current understanding of biological issues and the etiology of ASD is explored in Chapter 2.

PREVALENCE: AUTISM ON THE RISE

CHAPTER REFLECTION: Prevalence Increases in ASD

When people find out you are taking a course about Autism Spectrum Disorders, they are likely to ask, "Why are the rates of individuals diagnosed with autism increasing at such a high rate? Does this represent a *real* increase in the number of cases, or something else? What is the cause of these reported increases?" Not surprisingly, these are the same questions parents ask when they find out their child has ASD.

Question for Reflection: What are some of the theories you have heard explaining the increase in cases of ASD? Which theories are most compelling to you and why?

Current Prevalence Rate

Although there are many theories to explain this alarming increase in prevalence rates of ASD, the true reason is likely a multifaceted combination of many theories. A 2009 prevalence study estimated that 1 in 91 (approximately 1%) children in the United States had ASD (Kogan et al., 2009). In 2009, the Centers for Disease Control and Prevention (CDC) reported similar increases in its monitoring data (CDC, 2009b), and report an overall prevalence rate of 1 in 110 children (CDC, 2009b). The most current data about prevalence rates of ASD in the United States at the time of this book's publication reflect even greater increases. On March 28, 2012, the CDC released a report citing estimates of 1 in 88 children having ASD in the United States (CDC, 2012).

Other trends from prevalence data indicate that, on average, boys are four to five times more often diagnosed with ASD than girls and that ASD exists across racial, ethnic, and socioeconomic groups in the United States (CDC, 2009a, 2012).

Table 1.2 Prevalence Changes of Autism Spectrum Disorders

Identified Prevalence of Autism Spectrum Disorders ADDM Network 2000-2008 Combining Data From All Sites				
Surveillance Year	Birth Year	Number of ADDM Sites Reporting	Prevalence per 1,000 Children (Range)	This Is About 1 in X Children
2000	1992	6	6.7 (4.5-9.9)	1 in 150
2002	1994	14	6.6 (3.3-10.6)	1 in 150
2004	1996	8	8.0 (4.6-9.8)	1 in 125
2006	1998	11	9.0 (4.2-12.11)	1 in 110
2008	2000	14	11.3 (4.8-21.2)	1 in 88

Source: From the Centers for Disease Control and Prevention. Autism Spectrum Disorders (ASDs) website: http://www.cdc.gov/ncbddd/autism/data.html.

Explaining Increases in ASD

Changes in diagnostic criteria

One theory explaining increases over time, considers the changes in diagnostic criteria. Before the *DSM* included a definition of autism, diagnosis was based on Kanner's original description of severely autistic individuals. Likewise, only individuals with more severe characteristics were diagnosed as having autism before the recognition of Asperger's Syndrome.

Prior to the 1980s (before Asperger's Syndrome was recognized), prevalence rates were estimated as 0.4 to 0.5 children to every 1,000 (Lotter, 1967; Rutter, 2005), and prevalence rates based on the *DSM-III* (which had a stricter criteria for diagnosing autism than later versions of the *DSM*) were similar (Burd, Fisher, & Kerbeshian, 1987; Ritvo et al., 1989). In 2000, the CDC conducted a prevalence study of ASD using established monitoring sites across the United States. At that time using *DSM-IV* criteria, average prevalence rates were estimated to be 6.7 per 10,000 (or 1 in 150 children), with some differences across states (CDC, 2007). Thus, prevalence studies based on the *DSM-IV*, which had more inclusive diagnostic criteria, indicated significant increases in autism. Increases in prevalence rates may be attributed, in part, to changes in diagnostic criteria that provided a wider spectrum for identifying ASD.

Increased awareness

Prevalence increases may be impacted by the well-organized ASD awareness-raising campaigns. Increasingly, medical, educational, community advocacy, and governmental groups have concentrated efforts to raise awareness about identifying children at risk for developmental disabilities and provide services for young children. For instance, the federal government provides incentives for states receiving educational funding to participate in "project child find" to locate children at risk for disabilities (Part C of the Individuals with Disabilities Education Act, 1997). Likewise, the National Research Council published recommendations about educating children with ASD (2001); the American Academy of Pediatrics issued a policy statement about screening young children for developmental disabilities (Council on Children with Disabilities, 2006); and the National Advisory Child Health and Human Development Council identified a national goal of newborn and prenatal screening for developmental disabilities (Mental Retardation and Developmental Disabilities [MRDD] Branch NICHD, 2005).

Advances in diagnostic tools

Advances in early identification of ASD may also contribute to increased prevalence rates. For instance, research has identified early signs of autism such as lack of nonverbal social communication skills. Examples of nonverbal social communication observed in typically developing infants are joint attention (jointly attending to an object or person with the child), pointing, social smiling, responding to caregiver's voice, and eye contact. Thus, we no longer have to wait until a child fails to develop appropriate language skills before carefully considering ASD. In addition, psychometrically sound screening instruments are now available for identifying children with ASD before age 3 (such as the Checklist for Autism in Toddlers, the Early Screening for Autistic Traits Questionnaire, and the Social Communication Questionnaire). Early diagnosis and intervention is discussed in Chapter 5.

Actual Increases in Cases of ASD

Currently, there are large-scale studies investigating the relationship between exposure to environmental factors such as medications, alcohol, and infection and ASD (American Academy of Pediatrics, 2012; Institute of Medicine, 2008). Although empirical research fails to support a causal relation between childhood immunizations and ASD (see Immunization Safety Review Committee, 2004 for a thorough analysis of controlled epidemiological studies), many parents and advocacy groups strongly believe there is a direct link between Measles-Mumps-Rubella vaccination (MMR) and the onset of autism in some children. More specifically, these groups have focused on the preservative, thimerosal, which contains ethylmercury, as causing ASD. Advocacy efforts led to federal legislation that removed thimerosal from childhood vaccinations in the United States in 2001.

Surveillance research is beginning to emerge, tracking prevalence trends in cohorts of children who were less likely to have exposure to thimerosal because of legislation limiting its use. This research indicates a continuous rise in cases of ASD, despite reduced exposure to thimerosal as compared with earlier generations of children (i.e., Schechter & Grether, 2008). Despite this research, many parents feel strongly that immunizations caused their child's ASD. Regardless of the cause, parents who believe their child's ASD was triggered by the MMR immunization experienced a devastating loss as they helplessly witnessed the regression of skills in their young child. Sensitivity to this profound loss is critical to establishing a trusting collaborative relationship with parents.

TEACHING TIPS

- Misconceptions about the *cause* of ASD can be traced to our beginning understanding of the disorder. As an educator working with individuals with ASD and their families, embrace opportunities to correct such misperceptions when you hear them from colleagues, friends, and even the media.

- You may be asked by other teachers, administrators, friends, or parents about increases in the prevalence of ASD. Acknowledge that a significant component of these increases appear caused by changes in diagnostic criteria, increased awareness, and advances in diagnostic tools. However, be sensitive to concerns that changes in the environment or other toxins may contribute to increases in ASD.

- Remember that understanding history is the key to repeating mistakes of the past. Consider reading or rereading some of the classics of the autism literature to recall how individuals with ASD and their families (particularly mothers) were treated in the past (i.e., books by Temple Grandin, Eustacia Cutler, Bernard Rimland, and Catherine Maurice; also Houston and Frith [2000], *Autism in History: The Case of Hugh Blair of Borgue*). An important take-home message from these autobiographies is the importance of collaborating with parents and individuals with ASD in establishing educational goals, choosing interventions, and transition planning.

SUMMARY

Kanner (1943) and Asperger (1944) independently described cases of children with autism, establishing a new disorder distinct from mental illness or intellectual disability. The emergence of diagnostic classifications systems, such as the *DSM*, provided opportunities for clinicians and researchers to more accurately identify and investigate autism. Based on Freudian psychoanalysis, the notion of poor parenting practices causing autism was advocated by prominent therapists. Other psychological paradigms challenged psychoanalytic perspectives, including behaviorism, cognitive psychology, humanistic psychology, and biopsychology.

There is much speculation surrounding the dramatic increases in prevalence rates of ASD. Increased prevalence rates are likely associated with many factors, including changes in diagnostic criteria over time, increased awareness of ASD, and advances in early diagnostic tools. Researchers continue to investigate the relationship between environmental factors and ASD as contributing to real increases in prevalence. Although research does not support a clear connection between childhood immunizations and ASD, many parents and advocacy groups believe that vaccinations and the mercury-containing preservative, thimerosal, caused ASD in some children. Teachers must strive to respect parents' beliefs about ASD while maintaining an empirical approach to evaluating claims about ASD.

DISCUSSION AND REFLECTION QUESTIONS

1. The current definition of ASD is remarkably similar to Kanner's original description of autism. Why do you think Kanner's original case studies have stood the test of time, and what might that tell us about ASD?

2. Over time, different scientific paradigms have greatly impacted the role played by parents in supporting children with ASD. How might issues of our time impact the role of parents in supporting children with ASD? How is this different from your grandparents' generation?

3. What lessons have we learned from the history of treating children with developmental and intellectual disabilities? Are there lessons still to be learned from this historical review?

4. How might you respond to a parent who believes that her son's ASD was caused by childhood vaccinations? Consider finding a point at which you can respect her beliefs, but move forward together in providing support for her child.

RECOMMENDED FURTHER READINGS AND INTERNET SOURCES

Further Readings

Asperger, H. (1991). *Autistic psychopathy in childhood*. In U. Frith (Ed. and Trans.), *Autism and Asperger syndrome* (pp. 37–92). London: Cambridge University Press. (Original work published 1944)

Cutler, E. (2004). *A thorn in my pocket*. Arlington, TX: Future Horizons.

Frith, U. (2003). *Autism: Explaining the enigma* (2nd ed.). Oxford, UK: Blackwell Publishing.

Grinker, R. R. (2007). *Unstrange minds: Remapping the world of autism*. New York, NY: Basic Books.

Kanner, L. (1943). Autistic disturbances of affective content. *Nervous Child, 2,* 217–250.

Institute of Medicine. (2008). *Autism and the environment: Challenges and opportunities for research* [Workshop proceedings]. Washington, DC: National Academies Press.

Nadesan, M. H. (2005). *Constructing autism: Unraveling the 'truth' and understanding the social*. Abingdon, UK: Routledge.

Rimland, B. (1964). *Infantile autism: The syndrome and its implications for a neural theory of behavior*. New York, NY: Appleton-Century-Crofts.

Internet Sources

Centers for Disease Control and Prevention. (2012). Centers for Disease Control and Prevention. Autism Spectrum Disorders. Retrieved from http://www.cdc.gov/ncbddd/autism/data/html.

National Institute of Child Health and Human Development. (n.d.). *State of the science in autism: Communication/social/emotional development*. Bethesda, MD: Author. Retrieved from http://www.nichd.nih.gov/publications/pubs/sos_autism/sub7.cfm.

National Research Council. (2001). *Educating children with autism*. Washington, DC: The National Academies Press. Retrieved from http://www.nap.edu/openbook.php?isbn=0309072697. (Free download)

REFERENCES

Abrantes, G. (2009). *Jay-Z calls his way with words the 'rain man flow'*. Retrieved from http://newsroom.mtv.com/2009/08/28/jay-z-rain-man/.

American Academy of Pediatrics. (2012). *Prevalence of autism spectrum disorders*. Retrieved from http://www.aap.org/en-us/about-the-aap/aap-press-room/pages/Prevalence-of-Autism-Spectrum-Disorders.aspx?nf.

American Psychiatric Association. (1952). *Diagnostic and statistical manual of mental disorders* (1st ed.). Washington, DC: Author.

American Psychiatric Association. (1968). *Diagnostic and statistical manual of mental disorders* (2nd ed.). Washington, DC: Author.

American Psychiatric Association. (1980). *Diagnostic and statistical manual of mental disorders* (3rd ed.). Washington, DC: Author.

American Psychiatric Association. (1987). *Diagnostic and statistical manual of mental disorders* (3rd ed., Text Rev.). Washington, DC: Author.

American Psychiatric Association. (2000). *Diagnostic and statistical manual of mental disorders* (4th ed., Text Rev.). Washington, DC: Author.

Asperger, H. (1944). Die 'aunstisehen Psychopathen' im Kindesalter. *Archiv für Psychiatrie und Nervenkrankheiten,117*, 76–136.

Asperger, H. (1991). *Autistic psychopathy in childhood*. In U. Frith (Ed. and Trans.), *Autism and Asperger syndrome* (pp. 37–92). London: Cambridge University Press. (Original work published 1944)

Autism and mental retardation: A study of the early social communication. *Archives de Pediatrie, 14*(3), 234–238.

The Autism Genome Project Consortium. (2007). New insights into autism from a comprehensive genetic map. *Nature Genetics, 39*, 319–328.

The Autism Genome Project. (2009). *About the AGP*. Retrieved from http://www.autismgenome.org/about/about.htm.

Baron-Cohen, S. (1995). *Mindblindness: An essay on autism and theory of mind*. Cambridge, MA: MIT Press.

Baron-Cohen, S., Leslie, L. M., & Frith, U. (1985). Does the autistic child have a theory of mind? *Cognition, 21*, 37–46.

Encyclopædia Britannica. (2012). *Bedlam*. Retrieved from http://www.britannica.com/EBchecked/topic/58154/Bedlam.

Bender, L. (1956). Schizophrenia in childhood: Its recognition, description, and treatment. *American Journal of Orthopsychiatry, 26*, 499–506.

Boucher, J. (2009). *The autistic spectrum: Characteristics, causes, and practical issues*. Thousand Oaks, CA: Sage.

Burd, L., Fisher, W., & Kerbeshian, J. (1987). A prevalence study of pervasive developmental disorders in North Dakota. *Academy of Child and Adolescent Psychiatry, 26*, 700–703.

Bush, G. H. (1990). *Presidential proclamation 6158*. Retrieved from http://www.loc.gov/loc/brain/proclaim.html.

Centers for Disease Control and Prevention. (2007). CDC surveillance summaries. *Morbidity and Mortality Weekly Report, 56*. Retrieved from http://www.cdc.gov/mmwr/pdf/ss/ss5601.pdf.

Centers for Disease Control and Prevention. (2009a). *Autism spectrum disorders*. Retrieved from www.cdc.gov/ncbddd/autism/data/html.

Centers for Disease Control and Prevention. (2009b). CDC surveillance summaries. *Morbidity and Mortality Weekly Report, 58*. Retrieved from http://www.cdc.gov/mmwr/preview/mmwrhtml/ss5810a1.htm.

Centers for Disease Control and Prevention. (2012). Prevalence of autism spectrum disorders—Autism and developmental disabilities monitoring network, 14 sites, United States, 2008. *Morbidity and Mortality Weekly Report, 61*. Retrieved from http://www.cdc.gov/Features/CountingAutism/.

Collins, F. S., Morgan, M., & Patrinos, A. (2003). Viewpoint: The Human Genome Project: Lessons from large-scale biology. *Science, 300*(5617), 286–290.

Council on Children with Disabilities, Section on Developmental Behavioral Pediatrics,

Bright Futures Steering Committee, Medical Home Initiatives for Children with Special Needs Project Advisory. (2006). Identifying infants and young children with developmental disorders in the medical home: An algorithm for developmental surveillance and screening. *Pediatrics, 118*(1), 405–420.

Creak, M. (1961). Schizophrenic syndrome in childhood: Progress report of a working party. *Cerebral Palsy Bulletin, 3,* 501–504.

Cutler, E. (2004). *A thorn in my pocket.* Arlington, TX: Future Horizons.

Frith, U. (1991). Asperger and his syndrome. In U. Frith (Ed. and Trans.), *Autism and Asperger syndrome.* New York, NY: Cambridge University Press.

Frith, U. (2003). *Autism: Explaining the enigma* (2nd ed.). Malden, MA: Blackwell Publishing.

Genetic Information Nondiscrimination Act. Public Law 110-233, 122 Stat. 881 (2008). Retrieved from http://www.gpo.gov/fdsys/pkg/PLAW-110publ233/pdf/PLAW-110publ233.pdf.

Gerard, D. L. (1997). Chiarugi and Pinel considered: Soul's brain/person's mind. *Journal of the History of the Behavioral Sciences, 33*(4), 381–403.

Gesell, A. (1928). *Infancy and human growth.* Oxford, UK: Macmillan. Retrieved from PsycINFO database.

Hall, G. S. (1904). *Adolescence: Its psychology and its relations to physiology, anthropology, sociology, sex, crime, religion, and education* (Vols. 1–2). New York, NY: Appleton.

Houston, R. A., & Frith, U. (2000). *Autism in history: The case of Hugh Blair of Borgue.* Malden, MA: Blackwell Publishing.

Immunization Safety Review Committee. (2004). *Immunization safety review: Vaccinations and autism.* Washington, DC: The National Academies Press.

Individuals with Disabilities Education Act Amendments of 1997. Part C. 105-17.

Institute of Medicine. (2008). *Autism and the environment: Challenges and opportunities for research* [Workshop proceedings]. Washington, DC: National Academies Press.

Itard, J. M. G. (1962). *The wild boy of Aveyron.* (G. Humphrey & M. Humphrey, Eds. and Trans.). New York, NY: Appleton-Century-Crofts. (Original work published 1801 and 1806)

Kanner, L. (1943). Autistic disturbances of affective content. *Nervous Child, 2,* 217–250.

Kanner, L. (1964). *A history of the care and study of mental retardation.* Springfield, IL: Charles C. Thomas.

Kogan, M. D., Blumberg, S. J., Schieve, L. A., Boyle, C. A., Perrin, J. M., Ghandour, R. M., . . . van Dyck, P. C. (2009). Prevalence of parent-reported diagnosis of autism spectrum disorder among children in the US. *Pediatrics, 124*(5), 1395–1403.

Lamb, M. E., Bornstein, M. H., & Teti, D. (2002). *Development in infancy: An Introduction.* Mahwah, NJ: Lawrence Erlbaum Associates.

Loftus, E. F., & Palmer, J. C. (1974). Reconstruction of automobile destruction: An example of the interaction between language and memory. *Journal of Verbal Learning and Verbal Behavior, 13,* 585–589.

Lotter, V. Epidemiology of autistic conditions in young children: I. Prevalence. *Social Psychiatry, 1,* 124–137.

Lovaas, O. I. (1981). *Teaching developmentally disabled children: The ME book.* Baltimore, MD: University Park Press.

Lovaas, O. I. (1987). Behavioral treatment and normal educational and intellectual functioning in young autistic children. *Journal of Consulting and Clinical Psychology, 55*(1), 3–9.

Lovaas, O. I. (2003). *Teaching individuals with developmental delays: Basic intervention techniques.* Austin, TX: Pro-ED.

Mahler, M. (1952). On child psychosis and schizophrenia: Autistic and symbiotic infantile psychosis. *The Psychoanalytic Study of the Child, 7,* 286–305.

Mayes, R., & Horwitz, A. (2005). DSM-III and the revolution in the classification of mental illness. *Journal of the History of Behavioral Sciences, 41*(3), 249–267.

Mental Retardation and Developmental Disabilities (MRDD) Branch NICHD. (2005, June).

Report to the National Advisory Child Health and Human Development Council. Washington, DC: U.S. Department of Health and Human Services.

Merton, R. K. (1961). Singletons and multiples in scientific discovery: A chapter in the sociology of science. *Proceedings of the American Philosophical Society, 105,* 470–486.

Murray, S. (2006). Autism and the contemporary sentimental: Fiction and the narrative delete fascination of the present. *Literature and Medicine, 25*(1), 24–45.

National Research Council. (2001). *Educating children with autism.* Washington, DC: The National Academies Press. Retrieved from http://www.nap.edu/openbook.php?isbn=0309072697.

Neisser, U. (1967). *Cognitive psychology.* New York, NY: Appleton-Century-Crofts.

Ozonoff, S., & Rogers, S. (2003). From Kanner to the millennium. In S. Ozonoff, S. Rogers, & R. Hendren (Eds.), *Autism spectrum disorders: A research review for practitioners.* Arlington, VA: American Psychiatric Publishing.

Parnas, J., Bovet, P., & Zahavi, D. (2002). Schizophrenic autism: Clinical phenomenology and pathogenic implications. *World Psychiatry, 2*(3), 131–136.

Piaget, J. (1981). *Intelligence and affectivity: Their relationship during child development* (T. A. Brown & C. E. Kaegi, Eds. and Trans.). Oxford, UK: Annual Reviews. Retrieved from PsycINFO database. (Original work published in 1954)

Pollack, R. (1997). *The creation of Doctor B: A biography of Bruno Bettelheim.* New York, NY: Touchstone.

Pottie, C. G., & Ingram, K. M. (2008). Daily stress, coping, and well-being in parents of children with autism: A multilevel modeling approach. *Journal of Family Psychology, 22*(6), 855–864.

Rimland, B. (1964). *Infantile autism: The syndrome and its implications for a neural theory of behavior.* New York, NY: Appleton-Century-Crofts.

Ritvo, E. R., Freeman, B. J., Pingree, C., Mason-Brothers, A., Jorde, L., Jenson, W. R., . . . Ritvo, A. (1989). The UCLA-University of Utah epidemiologic survey of autism: Prevalence. *American Journal of Psychiatry, 146,* 194–199.

Rutter, M. (2005). Incidence of autism spectrum disorders: Changes over time and their meaning. *Acta Paediatr, 94,* 2–15.

Rutter, M., & Bartak, L. (1971). Causes of infantile autism: Some considerations from recent research. *Journal of Autism and Childhood Schizophrenia, 1,* 20–32.

Ryan, S., & Cole, K. R. (2009). From advocate to activist? Mapping the experience of mothers of children on the autism spectrum. *Journal of Applied Research in Intellectual Disabilities, 22*(1), 43–53.

Santayana, G. (1905). *Life of reason: Reason in common sense* (Vol. 1). London: London Constable.

Schechter, R., & Grether, J. (2008). Continuing increases in autism reported to California's Developmental Services System. *Archives of General Psychiatry, 65*(1), 19–24.

Schopler, E. (1987). Specific and nonspecific factors in the effectiveness of a treatment system. *American Psychologist, 42*(4), 376–383.

Schultz, D. P., & Schultz, S. E. (1987). *A history of modern psychology.* Orlando, FL: Harcourt-Brace.

Stone, M. H. (1973). Child psychiatry before the twentieth century. *International Journal of Child Psychotherapy, 2,* 264–308.

Wagman, M. (1993). *Cognitive psychology and artificial intelligence: Theory and research in cognitive science.* Westport, CT: Praeger Publishers.

Watson, J. B. (1913). Psychology as the behaviorist views it. *Psychological Review, 20,* 158–177.

Watson, J. B. (1930). *Behaviorism* (Rev. ed.). New York, NY: Norton.

Waltz, M., & Shattock, P. (2004). Autistic disorder in nineteenth-century London. Three case reports. *Autism, 8*(1), 7–20.

Wing, L. (1981). Asperger's syndrome: A clinical account. *Psychological Medicine, 11*(1), 115–129.

U.S. Office of Special Education Projects. (n.d.). *IDEA child find project.* Retrieved from http://www.childfindidea.org.

CHAPTER 2

CURRENT UNDERSTANDING OF AUTISM SPECTRUM DISORDER

In this chapter, you will learn about:

- The concept of autism as a spectrum disorder.
- The triad of core deficits associated with Autism Spectrum Disorder (ASD).
- Classification systems used for defining ASD.
- Other disorders that frequently coexist with ASD.

CHAPTER REFLECTION: Interview With Catherine Rice, Ph.D.

Dr. Rice is a behavioral scientist at the National Center on Birth Defects and Developmental Disabilities at the Centers for Disease Control and Prevention (CDC), and diagnostic associate for the Emory Autism Center. She has conducted numerous studies investigating prevalence rates of autism throughout the country.

How have we come to view autism as a spectrum disorder?

Over the years, the concept of autism has definitely changed. Originally, it was conceptualized as a specific and severe form of the disorder with nonverbal or echolalic language and an intellectual disability. Until 1980, there was limited

(Continued)

(Continued)

guidance about the criteria for autism. In the 1970s, Michael Rutter put together criteria for describing autism. However, the focus was more on the classic autism prototype.

Then in late 1970s and 1980s, we began to really see the concept of the spectrum emerge. Lorna Wing's description of subtypes of autism, including *active but odd, passive, aloof, and overly formal* (Wing, 1997), contributed to the idea of autism as a spectrum disorder. Furthermore, Lorna Wing translated into English Hans Asperger's writings about children with high-functioning autism, leading to our current understanding of Asperger's Syndrome.

In the 1990s, people started to think more about subtypes of autism. The *Diagnostic and Statistical Manual of Mental Disorders (DSM)* category of Pervasive Developmental Disability (and atypical autism in the International Classification of Diseases [ICD]) and inclusion of Asperger's Syndrome also moved us toward thinking about autism on a continuum. As the diagnosis of autism became more codable and specific, we began to see an increase in the prevalence of autism. This was also impacted by the introduction of autism into federal education law (Individuals with Disabilities Education Act [IDEA]) in the early 1990s.

How have changes in the conceptualization of autism impacted prevalence rates of autism?

These changes in autism criteria happened in a relatively short amount of time, so at the time there was not good data to show us how these diagnostic changes impacted prevalence changes. However, since then we have seen increases in prevalence rates of autism coincide with changes in diagnostic criteria. However, what we are not seeing is the leveling out that would be expected. We would expect autism rates to increase quickly and then level out. But we are not seeing the flattening out in prevalence rates of autism, and that is where it gets tricky.

Our concept of autism and the diagnostic criteria definitely explains *some* of the increase, but not all of it. Data indicate continuing increases in prevalence across different data collection sites. Autism is so diverse and complex. For instance, in some areas across the country, we see an increase in rates of autism with intellectual disability. If expansion in awareness and diagnostic changes were the only reasons for increases, you might expect to see increases mostly in rates of the milder forms of autism, those higher functioning children without intellectual disabilities.

In the early 1990s, we did see this. Prevalence data indicated a big decrease in the proportion of children getting diagnosed with autism that also had intellectual disabilities (from 60% to 40%) and then it leveled off. So now when we see higher rates of autism with intellectual disabilities in some sites across the country, it lends support to the notion that there is *no single explanation* to account for the patterns in our data.

Do you think our current classification systems, DSM-IV-TR *and* ICD-10 *are able to capture the complexity of the autism spectrum as we understand it today?*

In addition to the need for criteria to address young children and adults, our biggest challenge is how to draw the line between what is truly a disorder and what are features of the disorder but not necessarily a disability. Sometimes the term "Broader Autism Phenotype" (BAP) is used to capture individuals who function pretty well independently, yet have a sort of autism personality profile. BAP describes a set of characteristics such as atypical language, communication, and social skills, similar to features of autism, that do not meet diagnostic criteria for autism.

If we cannot really characterize and understand what that line is, it is difficulty to clearly understand changes in prevalence as the concept of autism broadens. I hope the *DSM* will focus on this.

How do disorders that seem to fall on the autism spectrum relate to ASD?

What is so challenging about autism is that it is not one single thing. You can pull out a piece of autism and say, "This is a learning disability because there is a scattering of skills." You can pull out unusual attention and find characteristics of ADHD. You can consider the significant deficits in communication and say there is a communication disorder.

But what we are saying with autism is that in addition to these pieces, which may be pulled out in their own right as a disability, these difficulties cluster together and stand out as a core cluster of deficits. Furthermore, autism involves a fundamental deficit of social awareness that you don't see in these other disorders.

I think it makes sense that people say there is an overlap between autism and these other disorders. Is the overlap etiological [due to a similar cause]? We don't know. We do need to determine what the individual person is struggling with and how to address their deficits.

© Catherine Rice.

AUTISM AS A SPECTRUM DISORDER

The ribbon with puzzle pieces has been used as an international symbol to demonstrate support for solving the puzzle of ASD.

The current definition of ASD is very similar to Kanner's original description of infantile autism in 1943. Currently clinicians, educators, and researchers recognize a "triad" of core deficits that underlie a diagnosis of ASD. However, individuals with ASD express a diverse range of functioning on each of these core deficits. You may have heard the folksy but ever-so-true saying, "If you met one person with autism, you have met one person with autism." This colloquial remark reflects the widely held understanding that autism is a "spectrum" disorder. The concept of a continuum or spectrum reflects the wide range of strengths and weaknesses within the population of ASD. For instance, individuals with ASD may have cognitive ability (as assessed by standardized intelligence tests) ranging from intellectually disabled (70 or below, sometimes called "mentally retarded") to gifted (130 or above). In addition, some people with ASD are essentially nonverbal (but may communicate with sign language or assistive technology) while others are quite loquacious with a highly developed and often specialized vocabulary. Individuals with ASD may express interest in socialization with peers and enjoy many types of social interactions while others exhibit extreme aloofness and preference for being alone.

Over time, the conceptualization of autism as a "spectrum" disorder has become common in clinical and research circles. For instance, on the Web page of the National Institute of Mental Health (NIMH) and the Centers for Disease Control and Prevention (CDC) "Autism Spectrum Disorder" is used as the heading to describe Pervasive Developmental Disorders (CDC, 2009; NIMH, 2012). However, the most frequently used classification systems for diagnosing autism at the time of this book's publication (*DSM-IV-TR* and ICD-10) do not use the concept of a spectrum in the definition of autism.

The understanding of autism as a spectrum disorder was inspired by an analysis of children who exhibited core deficits of autism in Camberwell, London (Wing & Gould, 1979). In analyzing these core deficits, including socialization, communication, and imagination, Wing and Gould discovered a wide continuum of severity. In particular, they noted much variation in cognitive ability level and language skills among children who exhibited the core deficits associated with a diagnosis of autism. Later, Wing (1981) coined the term "autistic spectrum disorder." Although the concept of autism falling on a "continuum" expresses the wide range of skill levels individuals express in each deficit area, the concept of a "spectrum" reflects the unclear boundaries between subtypes of autism (Boucher, 2009). Research from genetic studies investigating genetic liability for autism (certain genetic features or combinations of genes putting one at risk for ASD) lends empirical support to the idea of autism as a spectrum disorder (Bregman, 2005).

THE TRIAD OF CORE DEFICITS

Regardless of where one falls on the spectrum, all individuals with ASD have a triad of core deficits, including significant deficits as compared with their same-age peers in socialization, communication, and behaviors/interests. Likewise, all classification systems define autism as a disorder that begins early in development (onset before age 3) characterized by the triad of core deficits. The triad of core deficits include socialization, communication (both verbal and nonverbal), and restricted, repetitive, and stereotyped patterns of behaviors and interests.

Commercially available standardized assessment tools allow for the reliable diagnosis of core deficits by age 3, and research is currently focusing on even earlier diagnosis in the first 2 years of life (Luyster et al., 2005). In fact, research indicates that deficits in social communication can be identified early in the first year of life based on recognition of familiar faces, engagement in social imitative games and social smiles, social referencing, and joint attention (Bregman, 2005).

Figure 2.1   Triad of Core Deficits

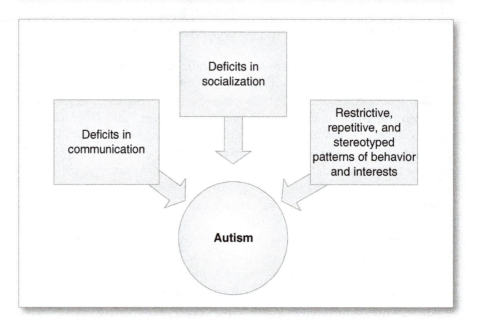

Social Development

The *DSMIV-TR* (American Psychiatric Association [APA], 2000, p. 70) describes social deficits of autism as qualitative impairments in the use of nonverbal behaviors such as eye gaze and body posture, a lack of appropriate peer relationships, deficits in spontaneous attempts to share enjoyment, interests, and achievement with others, and deficits in social or emotional reciprocity (the "give-and-take" of relationships).

Social communication is arguably the key factor in differentiating autism from other developmental disabilities (Berument et al., 2005; Matson et al., 2003; National Institute of Child Health and Human Development, 2006; Viellard et al., 2007). In fact, some researchers theorize that social communication is the *key* core deficit underlying autism (i.e., Baron-Cohen, 1995; Lord, Rutter, DiLavore, & Rissi, 2002).

Analysis of data about past behavior to explain current behavior is called retrospective. Retrospective studies involving parent interviews and analysis of home movies created before the child was diagnosed with ASD indicate early impairments in the development of skills associated with social engagement (Gamliel & Yirmiya, 2009). Some of the earliest indicators that a child might have ASD involve atypical development of social communication skills such as joint attention (Charman, 2003; Dawson et al., 2004) and social referencing (Dawson et al.). Joint attention is coordinated by the infant and is the basis of engaging in shared experiences involving behaviors such as gazing and pointing (Dawson et al.). Social referencing involves referring to others to gather information about events (Dickstein & Parke, 1988). In addition, typically developing children engage in symbolic and pretend play by approximately 18 months of age (Santrock, 2010). Failure to develop pretend and symbolic play in early childhood is another characteristic of ASD (Jarrold, 2003).

Early difficulties with joint attention, language development, imaginary play, and social reciprocity likely contribute to later problems developing peer relationships. Children with ASD experience difficulty initiating and sustaining peer interactions, and subsequently may experience more frequent rejection and alienation from peers. Furthermore, restricted and stereotyped interests and behaviors (i.e., only wanting to play with the train set), difficulty with transitions (i.e., transitioning from one game to another), and other atypical behaviors contribute to difficulties with developing peer relationships. Consequently, children, particularly those with high functioning cognitive skills, tend to experience higher rates of loneliness than their typically developing peers (Bauminger, Shulman, & Agam, 2003).

Overall, children with ASD demonstrate varying degrees of social interest and social development. However, most children with ASD appear to relate differently to others at an early age and often appear less skilled in social interactions and less motivated by social experiences than their typically developing peers (Heflin & Alaimo, 2007). Furthermore, these social skill deficits contribute to reduced peer interactions and thus less access to the richest source of social learning opportunity (Wolfberg, 2003).

Verbal and Nonverbal Communication

Nonverbal communication, such as facial imitation (Meltzoff & Moore, 1983), joint attention (Dawson et al., 2004), and eye contact (Phillips, Baron-Cohen, & Rutter, 1992) are some of the earliest forms of social communication. Individuals with ASD often have difficulty using facial expressions, body posture, and gestures to regulate social interactions, and tend to use nonverbal communication to request rather than to engage in a shared experience (Weatherby & Prizant, 2005). In addition, individuals with ASD tend to have difficulty initiating and maintaining age-appropriate peer relationships and spontaneously seeking enjoyment. Regardless of overall cognitive ability or

Table 2.1 Deficits in Social Development Expressed in the School Setting

These deficits are expressed on a continuum ranging from mild to severe. Elle is an 8-year-old child with a more severe form of ASD. Jackson is an 8-year-old child with ASD and high-functioning skills.

Qualitative impairments in the use of	Elle	Jackson
Nonverbal behaviors such as eye gaze and body posture	Does not make eye contact when teacher or peers are talking with her. Tends to use peripheral vision (looking out the corner of her eye) when interacting with someone. When the teacher describes and points to the classroom picture schedule on the wall, Elle's eye gaze does not follow in that direction.	Doesn't seem to pick up on the body language or nonverbal cues of his peers. For instance, if a peer shrugs or looks away in response to something Jackson is saying, Jackson just keeps on talking. Jackson does not modify his own behavior to better fit in with what his peers are interested in doing.
Appropriate peer relationships	Does not engage in cooperative play (goal-oriented social play) or imaginary play. When other children are playing in the classroom, Elle takes her preferred toy and moves to a corner of the room away from the other children. She is not interested in interacting with the teacher either.	Expresses a desire to be included in peer activities. However, when peers include him in games, he frequently gets frustrated because classmates are not following the rules to his specification. Because of frequent peer rejection, Jackson often stays around the teacher during free play and recess.
Spontaneous attempts to share enjoyment, interests, and achievement with others	Elle is enjoying lining up toy dolls during free play. A classmate sits beside her and tries to join her in the activity. Elle pushes her away and cries.	A classmate offers to share his favorite comic book with Jackson. Jackson informs him that he has already read the comic and that it has the weakest story line in the series.

verbal skills, individuals with ASD tend to have difficulty with social and emotional reciprocity, which involves navigating the give-and-take of social relationships. It is important to understand that many people with autism are interested in other people, although some are not. However, regardless of their degree of interest, all individuals on the autism spectrum experience impairments in socialization skills significantly below their same-age peers. For instance, a child with ASD may wish to join a group of children who are playing on the playground but lacks skills needed to enter the playgroup. Furthermore, if the child gains access into a playgroup, she may lack the subtle give-and-take of play (social reciprocity) required to maintain membership in the playgroup. On the other side of the spectrum, a young adolescent with ASD may avoid interacting with his peers altogether and prefer engaging in activities involving objects.

People with ASD generally have deficits in both verbal and nonverbal communication. Approximately one third of individuals with ASD have no functional speech (Bryson, 1996), and delay in the onset of spoken language is an indicator noted in the *DSM-IV-TR*. Individuals with ASD often have deficits in nonverbal communication such as accurately reading body language of others and using facial expression and types of body language to communicate with others. There is also a subgroup of individuals who demonstrate language loss, often after age 2 (Christopher et al., 2004).

Verbal communication deficits associated with ASD include difficulty initiating and/or sustaining conversation (a type of social communication deficit). Furthermore, individuals with ASD with verbal language may have an unusual quality to their language. For instance, the language may have a stilted or mechanical quality, an unusual pitch (e.g., may seem high pitch or raspy) or tone (e.g., may seem monotone), or be exceptionally loud or soft in volume. Individuals with ASD often use language in idiosyncratic way (such as describing food preference by shape or color, rather than taste) and interpret language in concrete manner (literal interpretation of comments such as "I blew up at her"). Language may be repetitive and stereotyped.

Some individuals demonstrate echolalia, the repetition of words or entire phrases seemingly out of context. Echolalia may be immediate (repeat words or phrases directly after hearing them) or delayed (may repeat a commercial or teacher direction days later in a different setting). Echolalia seems to serve a purpose in slowing down the processing of language, and in some cases may be used functionally. For instance, I recall working with a teacher who could not understand why a child repeated the same script (delayed echolalia) from a particular cartoon every day before lunch. After interviewing the child's parents, we learned that this child insisted on watching the same-recorded cartoon before his dinner each evening. His repetition of the cartoon dialogue before lunch at school indicated that he understood it was lunchtime and was ready for a meal. This example certainly underscores the importance of parent collaboration in teaching children with ASD!

Even children with ASD who have good vocabulary skills and no history of language delays demonstrate deficits in pragmatic language skills. Pragmatic

Table 2.2   Deficits in Communication Expressed in the School Setting

Qualitative impairments in	Elle	Jackson
Development of language skills	Elle did not begin to say words until 3 years of age. Although she is 8, her vocabulary skills are more like those of a 2-year-old.	Jackson began speaking in complete sentences at 20 months of age. His vocabulary skills are above those of his same-age peers. When he talks about his favorite topics, such as trains, he uses highly technical language. His speech is fast paced. He tends to speak in a louder-than-appropriate volume and with intonation that is flat and sounds somewhat robotic.
Difficulty initiating or sustaining conversation	Elle rarely initiates verbal interactions. She uses some functional vocabulary to elicit assistance. For instance, she will request snacks, drinks, time in the swing, and certain toys.	When Jackson tries to initiate conversations with peers or adults, he jumps right in and begins talking about trains. Generally, his topic of choice is not related to anything the person has been saying or doing. He does not pause to gauge the listener's response, pay attention to nonverbal cues, or ask questions of the listener. His teacher remarks that "It feels as if Jackson is *talking at* rather than *talking to* you."
Stereotyped and repetitive or idiosyncratic language	Elle frequently repeats things that are said to her (echolalia). For instance, her teacher says, "Good morning, Elle." Elle replies, "Good morning, Elle." Her word choice is sometimes odd. For instance, instead of asking for a cookie, she might say, "Elle want not a cracker."	Jackson tends to describe things in unusual ways.

language encompasses the social rules or conventions for communication. For instance, knowing when it is appropriate to use slang or to whom one can tell a personally revealing joke are examples of pragmatic language. People with ASD often need direct instruction and practice in the subtleties of pragmatic language that others seem to just pick up from observation.

Restricted, Repetitive, and Stereotyped Patterns of Behavior, Interests, and Activities

This third core deficit has also been described as an impairment of imagination (Wing, 1996), which captures the lack of pretend play characteristic of children with ASD. Kanner (1943) was the first to observe these behaviors in his original descriptions of children with autism. Restricted, repetitive, and stereotyped patterns of behavior, interests, and activities encompass behaviors that are often identified early by caregivers because of their odd appearance and age inappropriateness. These behaviors are unique among the core indicators of ASD because they represent atypical behaviors present in individuals with ASD as opposed to a lack of desirable behaviors such as language or social skills (Bishop, Richler, & Lord, 2006). Furthermore, these behaviors cause much stress for parents and caregivers (Gabriels et al., 2005).

Behaviors such as hand or finger flapping, body rocking, and other stereotyped motor mannerisms are easily observed and among the earliest characteristics of ASD identified as a concern by caregivers. These behaviors are sometimes called self-stimulatory behaviors or stereotypies (Heflin & Aliamo, 2007). Individuals with ASD may demonstrate restrictive interests or behaviors that are atypically intense in focus. For instance, a fourth grader may only read books or talk about maps for several months. Any free time, creative writing assignment, or opportunity for conversation centers around maps. Likewise, individuals with ASD may prefer objects to people and may appear more interested in parts than the whole (Heflin & Alaimo). This category of behaviors also includes rigid adherence to seemingly nonfunctional routines or rituals. For instance, an individual with ASD may insist on a particular route to school or work. If there is a roadblock or traffic jam and an alternate route is taken, he may be unable function at work or school because of intense anxiety or perhaps have a temper tantrum. Often this rigidity is associated with intense discomfort and/challenging behaviors when routines are disrupted.

Although restricted, repetitive, and stereotyped patterns of behavior, interests, and activities are often present in typically developing young children (Evans et al., 1997; Thelen, 1979) and older individuals with other types of disabilities (Frith, 2003), research indicates that these behaviors are more pronounced in individuals with ASD and occur throughout the life span (Bishop, Richler, & Lord, 2006). These restricted, repetitive, and stereotyped patterns of behavior are likely related to the sensory abnormalities (such as preoccupations with certain noises, spinning objects, or tactile sensations) reported by individuals with ASD and their caregivers (e.g., Grandin & Scariano, 1986; Williams, 1999). Likewise, sensory abnormalities in visual, hearing, and touch appear more pronounced

Table 2.3   Restricted, Repetitive, and Stereotyped Patterns of Behavior, Interests, and Activities in the School Setting

Qualitative impairments in	Elle	Jackson
Preoccupation with one or more stereotyped and restricted pattern of interest that is atypically over-focused or intense	During free play or choice of classroom activities, Elle has only two activities she prefers. She always chooses to swing in the classroom swing or line up dolls across the play mat. Even when new toys are introduced, she prefers the same two activities.	Jackson is fascinated with trains. He collects books about trains, model trains, train maps, and collects facts about trains. When asked to write a story, chose book to read, or do a project, he always chooses a theme involving trains.
Seemingly unreasonable adherence to specific and nonfunctional routines or rituals	Elle sits in the second desk in the first row of the classroom. If that desk is moved or her things are placed in a different desk, Elle has a temper tantrum.	Jackson becomes very agitated if the daily schedule is changed. On Monday, lunch was an hour early to accommodate a class assembly. Jackson put his head on his desk while the students were lining up for lunch and was visibly upset.
Stereotyped and repetitive motor behaviors (or stereotypies such as hand flapping)	When Elle is done with her classwork and other times during the day she flaps her hands back and forth until she is redirected by the teacher.	
Persistent preoccupation with parts of objects	When she is not lining up the dolls, Elle sometimes licks and sniffs them.	

within the population of individuals with ASD than among individuals with other types of developmental disabilities (Leekam et al., 2007), and are present throughout the life span (Crane, Goddard, & Pring, 2009).

Other Proposed Core Deficits

Joint attention

The discovery of joint attention, one of the earliest types of reciprocal social interactions, has allowed for the diagnosis and study of autism as early as 1 year of age. Joint attention develops between 6 to 12 months and involves the shared attention or experience with another individual, usually a caregiver (Charman, 2003). Recognition of joint attention allows for earlier interventions as well as explorations in new types of interventions to help develop skills such as shared attention. Joint attention appears critical to the development of more complex social interactions, and may be a preliminary step to developing theory of mind.

Theory of mind

Theory of mind (TOM) refers to understand the mental state of someone else and in a sense "engage in a form of mind reading" (Durand, 2005, p. 92). TOM is often tested using the "false belief task" (Wimmer & Permer, 1983). The finding that individuals with autism seem to lack TOM, sometimes called "mindblindness" (Baron-Cohen, 1985) is thought to be a core deficit associated with later difficulties with social development. The weak central coherence theory is another compelling theory about the etiology of autism stemming from a cognitive perspective.

Theory of weak central coherence

TOM may not explain all aspects about the unique cognitive profile of individuals with autism. When given certain tasks, such as putting together puzzles or abstract designs, most people demonstrate a cognitive style that allows for the integration of information to form a whole or gestalt. A cognitive style reflecting central coherence allows one to use some information to make judgments about the greater picture. However, Happe and Frith (2006) found that individuals with autism tend to focus on details or local features of the environment at the expense of seeing the whole. They called this a local processing cognitive style and suggested that a weak central coherence explains additional information about how people with autism process information. The weak central coherence theory seems to account for a trend of strengths on performance oriented tasks involving visuospatial skills in people with ASD (Shah & Frith, 1993).

Individuals with ASD may focus on details and fail to perceive the whole image, or *gestalt*. This processing cognitive style suggests a weak central coherence.

CLASSIFICATION SYSTEMS FOR DEFINING ASD

Although there are several different classification systems for defining and diagnosing autism and other disorders falling within the autism spectrum, most of the classification systems address the three core deficits and describe the onset of these deficits early in development. Four of the most commonly used classification systems are described below. The most widely used classification system within the United States for diagnosing autism and other developmental disorders is the *Diagnostic and Statistical Manual of Mental Disorders (DSM),* published by the American Psychiatric Association. The International Classifications of Diseases (ICD), published by the World Health Organization (WHO), closely aligns with the *DSM* and is used by the medical professional in Europe and many other countries. Within the United States, public schools determine eligibility for special education services based on defining criteria outlined in the Individuals with Disabilities Education Act (IDEA). Published by the National Center for Infants, Toddlers, and Families, the 0–3 Infant Diagnostic Classification System addresses the need for a classification system integrating developmental issues of infants and children ages 0 to 3.

Diagnostic Statistical Manual of Mental Disorders, *Fourth Edition, Text Revision*

The evolution of the *DSM* is discussed in Chapter 1. The most current edition at the time this book is being written is the *Diagnostic and Statistical Manual of Mental Disorders, Fourth Edition, Text Revision (DSM-IV-TR;* APA, 2000), with the development of fifth edition *(DSM-V)* under way. There was little focus within the clinical or research community on diagnosing autism and related disorders in infants and young children at the time the *DSM-IV* was being developed (C. Lord, personal communication, May 25, 2010; Volkmar, Chawarska, & Klin, 2008). However, it is likely that the *DSM-V* will better address diagnostic issues of infants and young children given the tremendous amount of research generated about early identification and diagnosis of ASD since the publication of the *DSM-IV* (C. Lord, personal communication, May 25, 2010).

The *DSM-IV* describes an umbrella of related developmental disorders, called Pervasive Developmental Disorders (PDD). Characteristics of these disorders appear early in development and occur across developmental domains (pervasive in nature). Both autistic disorder and Apserger's disorder fall under the category of PDD. In the upcoming *DSM-V*, a single spectrum is likely to replace the PDD construct (APA, 2009).

For a diagnosis of autistic disorder, delays or abnormal functioning in the development of social interaction, language used in social communication, and/ or symbolic or imaginative play must be apparent prior to age 3. In addition, the child must present at least six characteristics from three sets of criteria. More specifically, at least two characteristics from the *impairment in social interactions* criteria, at least one characteristic from the *impairment in communication* criteria, and at least one characteristic from the repetitive and *stereotypic patterns of behaviors, interests, or activities* criteria. The criteria are described as *qualitative impairments* indicating that diagnosis using the *DSM* is based on descriptions, rather than requiring measurements or a particular numerical score.

Asperger's Syndrome, another type of PDD, was added for the first time in the *DSM-IV* and remained unchanged in the *DSM-IV-TR*. The *DSM* states that a child cannot meet both the criteria for Asperger's Syndrome and autistic disorder (or any other PDD). Typically, children with Asperger's Syndrome are identified later than those with autistic disorder. Other differences include a lack of developmental delays in the onset of language development and less stringent criteria for diagnosis. In fact, many individuals with Asperger's Syndrome demonstrate strengths in vocabulary knowledge and some types of verbal skills. Yet, social communication remains a hallmark of the disorder. Another difference between the disorders is that individuals with Asperger's Syndrome must present age-appropriate cognitive development, self-help skills, and general adaptive behavior skills (aside from socialization). Conversely, a high percentage of individuals who meet the criteria for autistic disorder demonstrate significant delays in cognitive development and adaptive behavior skills (Rice, 2007). However, distinguishing between high-functioning autism and Asperger's Syndrome is controversial and may be more clearly addressed in the *DSM-V*.

Pervasive Developmental Disorder, Not Otherwise Specified (PDD-NOS), sometimes called *atypical autism,* is a disorder with many characteristics of autism, yet does not meet the criteria for autism under the *DSM* diagnostic system. For instance, a child may present atypical language development and impaired social skills, yet these deficits were not observed until later in childhood. Other lower incidence disorders (occur less often) that fall under the PDD category include Rett disorder and childhood disintegrative disorder (CDD).

Both CDD and Rett disorder are devastating disorders where children demonstrate a dramatic loss of skills, resulting in severe cognitive and physical disability. Although CDD affects significantly more males (Frombonne, 2002), Rett disorder is only identified in females. Both disorders involve seemingly normal development followed by significant regression in developmental skills. Regression associated with CDD is usually first apparent at about age 2, while in Rett disorder regression tends to become apparent at about 5 years of age (APA, 2000).

The regression seen in CDD and Rett disorder is different from that typically observed in regressive autism. For instance, regression in autism is often observed earlier than that in either Rett disorder or CDD (Osterling & Dawson, 1994). In addition, children with regressive autism generally do not lose adaptive or motor skills (Luyster et al., 2005). Children with Rett disorder and CDD demonstrate significant regression in all developmental domains (APA, 2000).

International Classification of Diseases

The International Classification of Diseases (ICD-10; WHO, 1992) is published by the World Health Organization and is widely used in Europe and other countries. Disorders falling within the autism spectrum are described in the section on Mental and Behavioral Disorders. This section of the ICD-10 was developed to align with the *DSM* to promote consistency across diagnostic systems. Like the *DSM-IV-TR*, the ICD-10 uses the category of pervasive developmental disorders to include disorders that are pervasive in nature and occur early in childhood. Childhood autism is aligned with the *DSM-IV-TR* diagnosis of autistic disorder, and Asperger's Syndrome with Asperger's disorder. The ICD-10 describes delays in motor skill development and motor clumsiness as possible features of Asperger's Syndrome. In the ICD-10 the term "atypical autism" is comparable with the *DSM-IV-TR* diagnosis of PDD-NOS.

Individuals with Disabilities Education Act

The Individuals with Disabilities Education Act (IDEA; 2004) is federal legislation that dictates eligibility criteria for special education as well as the processes for determining eligibility and services for children with special needs within public schools. In 1990, autism was added as a category of special education eligibility under IDEA (Knoblauch & Sorenson, 1998). Prior to 1990, children with an ASD may have received special education services through the behavior disorder, learning disability, intellectual disability, or other health-impaired category of special education within the public schools. Although each state, local school district, and school interprets the federal criteria and creates regulations based on IDEA, schools must comply with the tenets of IDEA to obtain federal funding.

Unlike the *DSM* or ICD, IDEA does not offer criteria for making a diagnosis. Rather, IDEA provides criteria by which eligibility for special education is judged by the multidisciplinary team that includes parents. Furthermore, IDEA

Table 2.4 Definition of Autism Under the Individuals with Disabilities Education Act (2004)

- A developmental disability significantly affecting verbal and nonverbal communication and social interaction, generally evident before age 3 that adversely affects a child's educational performance. Other characteristics often associated with autism are engagement in repetitive activities and stereotyped movements, resistance to environmental change or change in daily routines, and unusual responses to sensory experiences.
- Autism does not apply if a child's educational performance is adversely affected primarily because the child has an emotional disturbance.

provides a single category of autism. However, it is common practice within the public schools to consider other diagnoses within the autism spectrum, such as Asperger's disorder and PDD-NOS, to be included under the "autism" eligibility category of special education.

The 0–3 Infant Diagnostic Classification System

A significant body of research has targeted diagnosis and intervention of ASD in infants and young children since the publication of the *DSM-IV-TR*. However, the *DSM-IV-TR* was published before much of this research was available and the focus on early intervention was not where it is today. The 0–3 Infant Diagnostic Classification System, published by Zero to Three, offers diagnostic options that are developmentally appropriate for infants and young children (Evangelista & McLellan, 2004). Under the category of Disorders of Relating and Communicating, children under the age of 3 may be diagnosed with multisystem developmental disorder, which is associated with delays in language, social development, motor planning, and sensory processing.

COEXISTENCE OF ASD WITH OTHER DISORDERS

Many other disorders share features of ASD and are sometimes considered to be "on the autism spectrum." As noted in the interview with Dr. Rice, it is unknown whether these common features are due to a similar genetic cause. In addition, there are other disorders frequently diagnosed along with ASD

(Gillberg & Billstedt, 2000). The diagnosis of two or more clinical disorders, known as comorbidity, can impact the course of the disorder as well as the efficacy of interventions (Deprey & Ozonoff, 2009).

A prevalence study of children in metropolitan Atlanta, Georgia, revealed 63% of children diagnosed with autism also had a coexisting clinical condition (Yeargin-Allospp et al., 2003). Although the *DSM-IV-TR* prohibits a diagnosis of autism with some types of related disorders (such as ADHD), the current version *(DSM-V)* is likely to remove this restriction.

There are several genetic disorders frequently associated with ASD, including fragile X syndrome and tuberous sclerosis (discussed in Chapter 3, "Biological Issues and Etiology of Autism Spectrum Disorder"). Many other medical conditions and clinical disorders are often *comorbid* with ASD. Some of the most frequently occurring comorbid conditions are described below, including Attention Deficit Hyperactive Disorder (ADHD), intellectual disabilities, seizure disorders, sleep disorders, and certain psychiatric conditions.

ASD and Attention Deficit Hyperactivity Disorder

Although the *DSM-IV-TR* rules out a diagnosis of Attention Deficit Hyperactivity Disorder (ADHD) when a child has an autistic disorder, difficulty with attention and overactivity are described as common for children

Table 2.5   Criteria for Diagnosing Attention Deficit Hyperactive Disorder (ADHD)

- Observed characteristics associated with ADHD documented by age 7.
- Behaviors documented include significant difficulties with sustain attention, over activity, and behaving impulsively.
- Some of these symptoms observed in at least two different settings (such as home and school).
- These observed behaviors are apparent for at least 6 months. The behaviors are developmentally inappropriate for the individual's chronological age.
- These observed behaviors negatively impact functioning in the individual's life which may include social, school, occupational, or self perception.

Source: Adapted from: American Psychiatric Association. (2000). *Diagnostic and statistical manual of mental disorders* (4th ed. Text Revision). Washington, DC: Author.

with ASD (Goldstein & Schwebach, 2004). In fact, current estimates indicate that 20% to 50% of children with ASD also meet the diagnostic criteria for ADHD (Rommelse et al., 2010). Lack of impulse control and self-regulation associated with ADHD may exacerbate behavioral and learning difficulties characteristic of ASD (Goldstein & Schwebach; Raymaekers et al., 2007). Furthermore, a study by Frazier et al. (2001) indicated that children meeting the *DSM-IV-TR* criteria for both a PDD and ADHD had more significant impairments, including higher rates of hospitalization.

ASD and Intellectual Disabilities

It is important to remember that not all children with ASD have cognitive impairments. In fact, many children with ASD obtain cognitive ability scores significantly above their same-age peers. Furthermore, assessment of the cognitive ability of children with ASD is often challenging because of deficits in communication, social development, and transitioning to new tasks and settings and a cognitive profile of scattered strengths and weaknesses may underestimate an overall ability potential (discussed further in Chapter 6). Likewise, not all individuals with an intellectual disability have ASD. Individuals with intellectual disabilities may have relative strengths in social and communication skills that are uncharacteristic of ASD.

However, many individuals with ASD also have an intellectual disability. The *DSM-IV-TR* (APA, 2000) states, "Approximately 75% of children with Autistic Disorder function at the retarded level" (p. 67). More recent prevalence studies indicate lower rates ranging from 0.41 (Centers for Disease Control and Prevention, 2009) to 0.68 (Yeargin-Allsopp et al., 2003).

CHAPTER REFLECTION: Decreases in Autism With Intellectual Disability

In the interview with Dr. Rice, she described prevalence research revealing a trend toward a decrease in the proportion of children diagnosed with both autism and an intellectual disability over time. This decrease in ASD and intellectual ability may be associated with more sophisticated diagnostic tools as

(Continued)

(Continued)

well as a broader definition that includes disorders such as Asperger's Syndrome.

Question: How might this trend impact our expectations about academic achievement and inclusion for students with ASD?

Dr. Rice: Individuals with more severe behaviors associated with ASD are more likely to also have an intellectual disability (Matson & Shoemaker, 2009). Furthermore, individuals with both an intellectual disability and ASD are likely to require more educational and other supports. In addition, these individuals are less likely to have functional verbal skills, and are at increased risks for seizure disorders and other medical conditions (Ballaban-Gil & Tuchman, 2000; Klinger, O'Kelley, & Mussey, 2009). Interestingly, the gender difference of boys outnumbering girls in prevalence of ASD is drastically reduced in cases of dual diagnosis of both ASD and an intellectual disability (Yeargin-Allsopp et al., 2003).

Table 2.6   Intellectual Disability as Defined by IDEA and the *DSM-IV-TR*

Both IDEA and the *DSM-IV-TR* define an intellectual disability (called mental retardation in the *DSM-IV-TR*) as including the following:

- Scores on a standardized test of intelligence 2 standard deviations or more below the mean (generally this is a score of 70 or below). *Best practice requires scores on two different intelligence tests document significantly below-average cognitive ability.*
- Significantly below-average ability on assessments of adaptive functioning. *Adaptive functioning addresses independent functioning skills associated with communication, self-care, daily living, and socialization skills.*
- Onset apparent before age 18. *This is developmental disorder that is not acquired later in development.*
- IDEA requires significantly below-average academic achievement as indicated by standardized tests of achievement and school performance.

Source: Adapted from: American Psychiatric Association. (2000*). Diagnostic and statistical manual of mental disorders* (4th ed. Text Revision). Washington, DC: APA.

Table 2.7   *DSM-IV-TR* Severity Levels of Intellectual Disability

The *DSM-IV* (APA, 2000, p. 46) further classifies severity level based on scores of intellectual ability:

  Mild 50–55 to approximately 70

  Moderate 35–40 to 50–55

  Severe 20–25 to 35–40

  Profound below 20 or 25

Source: Adapted from: American Psychiatric Association. (2000). *Diagnostic and statistical manual of mental disorders* (4th ed. Text Revision). Washington, DC: APA.

Note: There is a movement away from the use of intelligence test scores and toward considering levels of supports needed to characterize an intellectual disability (Turnbull, Turnbull, & Wehmeyer, 2010). This change may be reflected in the DSM-V.

ASD and Seizure Disorders

There is a high rate of seizure disorders within the population of individuals with ASD. This is especially true when there is also an intellectual disability present (Amiet et al., 2008; Hara, 2007). In addition, girls with ASD are at increased risk for developing epilepsy (Amiet et al.). Likewise, children with regressive autism may be at increased risk of developing epilepsy, which involves chronic seizure activity (Tuchman & Rapin, 1997).

Current prevalence estimates indicate that approximately 36% children with ASD also have diagnoses of epilepsy (Hara, 2007). Onset of epilepsy often occurs at two peak times: before age 5 and again during adolescence (Barbaresi, Kats, & Voigt, 2006). Chapter 3 discusses strategies for teachers to monitor medication and procedures associated with seizure disorders.

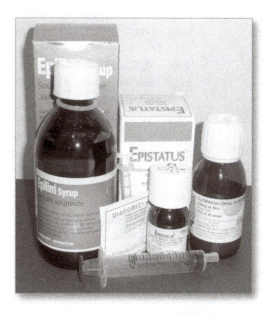

Anticonvulsant drugs are often used to treat seizure disorders. Many individuals with ASD also have seizure disorders, such as epilepsy.

ASD and Sleep Disorders

Many parents report that their children with ASD experience difficulty falling asleep and staying asleep (Schreck & Mulick, 2000). Problems with sleep not only potentially impact the child's ability to learn and behavior (Stores & Wiggs, 1998), but are disruptive to the entire family—particularly the child's caregivers (Hoffman et al., 2005). Furthermore, while unsupervised, children may get hurt or even leave the home during the night.

Sleep disorders are frequently identified in children with ASD (Herring et al.,1999). In an investigation of parent-reported sleep problems in their children with ASD, Schreck et al. (2004) found that fewer hours of sleep predicted increased symptoms of autism such as stereotypic behaviors and social skill difficulties. In a related study, Hoffman et al., (2005) identified other sleep-related difficulties predictive of problematic behaviors.

ASD and Psychiatric Disorders

People with ASD are at increased risk of having mental health difficulties, particularly mood disorders such as depression. Among the mood disorders, depression is most frequently identified in individuals with high-functioning ASD (Brereton, Tonge, & Einfeld, 2006). However, depression may be more difficult to assess in individuals with lower abilities who are likely to have poorer communication skills.

Anxiety disorders frequently are diagnosed in individuals with ASD and may be associated with difficulties predicting future outcomes and responses of others. In addition, the perception of feeling overwhelmed by sensory stimulation may contribute to feelings of panic and generalized anxiety. Psychiatric disorders and ASD is discussed further in Chapter 5 within the context of assessment and diagnosis.

TEACHING TIPS

• Even as diagnostic definitions are revised, core deficits of ASD remain the same. Regardless of an individual's level of functioning, teaching supports should address social communication and restrictive, repetitive, and stereotyped behaviors, interests, and activities. Furthermore, each child on the autism spectrum has a unique profile of strengths and weaknesses as well as interests and preferences.

• Remember that autism is a *spectrum disorder*. Thus, although interventions should be selected based on the use of evidence-based practices, what works for one child might not work for another. Even children with very similar scores on standardized tests may require different goals, academic placements, and intervention strategies.

• Individuals with ASD often have comorbid conditions such as depression, anxiety, seizure disorders, and other medical conditions. Be sure to carefully check with school records and confirm with parents other comorbid conditions that may impact the child's functioning at school. Frequent communication with parents helps ensure that teachers are aware of new diagnoses or changes in a child's medical condition, medications, or other treatment regiments outside of the school day.

SUMMARY

Autism is currently conceptualized as a spectrum, reflecting the diverse range in which characteristics of the disorder may be expressed. Although the concept of autism as a spectrum disorder differs from previous frameworks, there is a consistent triad of core deficits underlying the disorder. The three core deficits are socialization, communication, and restricted, repetitive, and stereotyped patterns of behaviors and interests. Other proposed core deficits include deficits in the development of joint attention, theory of mind, and weak central coherence. Both joint attention and theory of mind are related to social development. Weak central coherence explains deficits in cognitive skills, such as drawing conclusions.

There are several classification systems used to diagnose and understand autism and other disorders on the autism spectrum. One of the most widely used is the *DSM-IV-TR*; APA, 2000). The *DSM-IV-TR* describes autistic disorder as a type of pervasive developmental disability. Disorders sharing the core deficits of ASD include Asperger's Syndrome, PDD-NOS, Rett disorder, and CDD. Other diagnostic systems are available in the ICD-10 and IDEA. The Infant Diagnostic Classification System addresses the need for a classification system integrating developmental issues of infants and children ages 0 to 3.

Some of the most frequently occurring comorbid conditions are ADHD, intellectual disabilities, seizure disorders, sleep disorders, anxiety disorders, and mood disorders.

DISCUSSION AND REFLECTION QUESTIONS

1. What might be some concerns about conceptualizing autism as part of a continuum of related difficulties?

2. Are there clear boundaries between ASD and what constitutes "normal" human behavior?

3. Why is it important for different classification systems (such as the *DSM*, ICD, and IDEA) to be aligned? How does this impact both the ability of professionals to meet the needs of children with ASD and efforts within the research community?

4. Describe some of the frequently occurring disorders that are comorbid with ASD.

5. Consider additional information you might need to collect from parents, background records, and so on to best support a child in your classroom who has a seizure disorder or an anxiety disorder in addition to ASD.

RECOMMENDED FURTHER READINGS AND INTERNET SOURCES

American Academy of Pediatrics. (2009). *The prevalence of autism spectrum disorders.* Retrieved from http://pediatrics.aappublications.org/content/124/5/1395.abstract.

American Psychiatric Association. (2000). *Diagnostic and statistical manual of mental disorders* (4th ed., Text Rev.). Washington, DC: Author.

Frith, U. (2003). *Autism explaining the enigma* (2nd ed.). Malden, MA: Blackwell Publishing.

National Institute of Child Health and Human Development. (2006). *State of the science in autism: Communication/social/emotional development.* Bethesda, MD: Author. Retrieved from http://www.nichd.nih.gov/publications/pubs/sos_autism/sub7.cfm.

National Research Council. (2001). *Educating children with autism.* Washington, DC: The National Academies Press. Retrieved from http://www.nap.edu/openbook.php?isbn=0309072697. (Free download)

REFERENCES

American Psychiatric Association. (1994). *Diagnostic and statistical manual of mental disorders* (4th ed.). Washington, DC: Author.

American Psychiatric Association. (2000). *Diagnostic and statistical manual of mental disorders* (4th ed., Text Rev.). Washington, DC: Author.

American Psychiatric Association. (2009). *Report of the* DSM-V *Neurodevelopmental Disorders Work Group.* Retrieved from http://www.psych.org/MainMenu/Research/DSMIV/DSMV/DSMRevisionActivities/DSM-V-Work-Group-Reports/Neurodevelopmental-Disorders-Work-Group-Report.aspx.

Amiet, C., Gourfinkel-An, I., Bouzamondo, A., Tordjman S., Baulac, M., Lechat, P., et al. (2008). Epilepsy in autism is associated with intellectual disability and gender. Evidence from a meta-analysis. *Biological Psychiatry, 64,* 577–582.

Ballaban-Gil, K., & Tuchman, R. (2000). Epilepsy and epileptiform EEG: Association with autism and language disorders. *Mental Retardation and Developmental Disabilities Research Reviews, 6,* 300–308.

Barbaresi, W. J., Katusic, S. K., & Voigt, R. G. (2006). A review of the state of the science for pediatric primary health care clinicians. *Archives of Pediatric and Adolescent Medicine, 160,* 1167–1175.

Baron-Cohen, S. (1995). *Mindblindness: An essay on autism and theory of mind.* Cambridge, MA: MIT Press.

Bauminger, N., Shulman, C., & Agam, G. (2003). Peer interaction and loneliness in high-functioning children with autism. *Journal of Autism and Developmental Disorders, 33*, 489–507.

Berument, S. K., Starr, E., Pickles, A., Tomlins, M., Papanikolauou, K., Lord, C., & Rutter, M. (2005). Pre-linguistic autism diagnostic observation schedule adaptive for older individuals with severe to profound mental retardation: A pilot study. *Journal of Autism and Developmental Disorders, 35*(5), 821–829.

Bishop, S. L., Richler, J., & Lord, C. (2006). Association between restricted and repetitive behaviors and nonverbal IQ in children with autism spectrum disorders. *Child Neuropsychology, 12*, 247–267.

Boucher, J. (2009). *The autistic spectrum: Characteristics, causes and practical issues.* London: Sage.

Bregman, J. D. (2005). Definitions and characteristics of the spectrum. In D. Zager (Ed.), *Autism spectrum disorder: Identification, education, and treatment* (3rd ed., pp. 3–39). Mahwah, NJ: Lawrence Erlbaum Associates.

Brereton, A. V, Tonge, B. J., & Einfeld, S. L. (2006). Psychopathology in children and adolescents with autism compared to young people with intellectual disability. *Journal of Autism and Developmental Disorders, 36*, 863–870.

Bryson, S. (1996). Brief report. Epidemiology of autism. *Journal of Autism and Developmental Disabilities, 26*, 165–167.

Centers for Disease Control and Prevention. (2009). CDC surveillance summaries. *Morbidity and Mortality Weekly Report, 58*. Retrieved from http://www.cdc.gov/mmwr/preview/mmwrhtml/ss5810a1.htm.

Charman, T. (2003). Why is joint attention a pivotal skill in autism? *Philosophical Transactions of the Royal Society B: Biological Sciences, 16*, 315–324.

Christopher, J. A., Sears, L. L., Williams, P. G., Oliver, J., & Hersh, J. (2004). Familial, medical, and developmental patterns of children with autism and a history of language regression. *Journal of Developmental & Physical Disabilities, 16*(2), 163–170.

Crane, L, Goddard, L., & Pring, L. (2009). Sensory processing in adults with autism spectrum disorders. *Autism: The International Journal of Research & Practice, 13*(3), 215–228.

Dawson, G., Toth, K., Abbott, R., Osterling, J., Munson, J., Estes, A., & Liaw, J. (2004). Early social attention impairments in autism: Social orienting, joint attention, and attention to distress. *Developmental Psychology, 40*, 271–283.

Dickstein, S., & Parke, R. D. (1988). Social referencing in infancy: A glance at fathers and marriage. *Child Development, 59,* 506–511.

Deprey, L., & Ozonoff, S. (2009). Assessment of comorbid psychiatric conditions in autism spectrum disorders. In S. Goldstein, J. A. Naglieri, & S. Ozonoff (Eds.), *Assessment of autism spectrum disorders* (pp. 290–318). New York, NY: Guilford Press.

Durand, V. M. (2005). Past, present, and emerging directions in education. In D. Zager, (Ed.), *Autism spectrum disorders: Identification, education, and treatment* (3rd ed., pp. 89–109). Mahwah, NJ: Lawrence Erlbaum Associates.

Evans, D. W., Leckman, J. F., Carter, A., Reznick, J. S., Henshaw, D., King, R. A., & Pauls, D. (1997). Ritual, habit and perfectionism: The prevalence and development of compulsive like behaviour in normal young children. *Child Development, 68*(1), 58–68.

Evangelista, N., & McLellan, M. J. (2004). The Zero to Three diagnostic system: A framework for considering emotional and behavioral problems in young children. *School Psychology Review, 33,* 159–173.

Frazier, J. A., Biederman, J., Bellordre, C. A., Garfield, S.B., Geller, D.A., Coffey, B. J., & Faraone, S.V. (2001). Should the diagnosis of attention deficit/hyperactivity disorder be considered in children with pervasive developmental disorder? *Journal of Attention Disorders, 4*, 203–211.

Frith, U. (2003). *Autism: Explaining the enigma* (2nd ed.). Malden, MA: Blackwell Publishing.

Frombonne, E. (2002). Prevalence of childhood disintegrative disorder. *Autism, 6,* 149–157.

Gabriels, R. L., Cuccaro, M. L., Hill, D. E., Ivers, B. J., & Goldson, E. (2005). Repetitive behaviors in autism: Relationships with associated clinical features. *Research in Developmental Disabilities, 26,* 169–181.

Gamliel, I., & Yirmiya, N. (2009). Assessment of social behaviors in autism spectrum disorders. In S. Goldstein, J. A. Naglieri, & S. Ozonoff (Eds.), *Assessment of autism spectrum disorders* (pp. 138–170). New York, NY: Guilford Press.

Gillberg, C., & Billstedt, E. (2000). Autism and Asperger syndrome: Coexistence with other clinical disorders. *Acta Psychiatrica Scandinavia, 102,* 321–330.

Goldstein, S., & Schwebach, A. J. (2004). The comorbidity of pervasive development disorder and attention deficient hyperactivity disorder: Results of a retroactive chart review. *Journal of Autism Development Disorder, 34,* 329–339.

Grandin, T., & Scariano, M. (1986). *Emergence: Labeled autistic.* Novato, CA: Arena.

Happe, F., & Frith, U. (2006). The weak coherence account: Detail-focused cognitive style in autism spectrum disorders. *Journal of Autism and Developmental Disorders 35,* 5–25.

Hara, H. (2007). Autism and epilepsy: A retrospective follow-up study. *Brain Development, 29,* 486–490.

Heflin, L. J., & Alaimo, D. F. (2007). *Students with Autism Spectrum Disorder.* Upper Saddle River, NJ: Pearson.

Herring, E., Epstein, R., Elroy, S., Iancu, D. R., & Zelnik, N. (1999). Sleep patterns in autistic children. *Journal of Autism and Developmental Disorders, 29,* 143–147.

Hoffman, C. D., Sweeney, D. P., Gilliam, J. E., Apodaca, D. D. Lopez-Wagner, M. C., & Castillo, M. M. (2005). Sleep problems and symptomology in children with autism.

Focus on Autism and Other Developmental Disabilities, 20, 194–200.

Individuals with Disabilities Education Act, 20 U.S.C. §§ 1400 et seq (2004).

Jarrold, C. (2003). A review of research into pretend play in autism. *Autism, 7,* 379–390.

Kanner, L. (1943). Autistic disturbances of affective content. *Nervous Child, 2,* 217–250.

Klinger, L. G., O'Kelley, S. E., & Mussey, J. L. (2009). Assessment of intellectual functioning in autism spectrum disorder. In S. Goldstein, J. A. Naglieri, & S. Ozonoff (Eds.), *Assessment of autism spectrum disorders* (pp. 209–252). New York, NY: Guilford Press.

Knoblauch, B., & Sorenson, B. (1998). IDEA's definition of disabilities. *ERIC Clearinghouse on Disabilities and Gifted Education, ERIC Digest E560.* Reston, VA: ERIC.

Leekam, S. R., Nieto, C., Libby, S. J., Wing, L., & Gould, J. (2007). Describing the sensory abnormalities of children and adults with autism. *Journal of Autism and Developmental Discord, 37,* 894–910.

Lefer, O. T., Folstein, S. E., Bacalman, S., Davis, N. O., Dinh, E., Morgan, J., . . . Lainhart, J. E. (2006). Comorbid psychiatric disorders in children with autism: Interview development and rates of disorders. *Journal of Autism and Developmental Disorders, 36,* 849–861.

Lord, C., Rutter, M., DiLavore, P., & Rissi, S. (2002). *Autism Diagnostic Observation Schedule (ADOS).* Los Angeles, CA: Western Psychological Services.

Luyster, R., Richler, J., Risi, S., Hsu, W. L., Dawson, G., Bernier, R., . . . Lord, C. (2005). Early regression in social communication in autism spectrum disorders: A CPEA study. *Developmental Neuropsychology, 27,* 311–336.

Matson, J., & Shoemaker, M. (2009). Intellectual disability and its relationship to autism spectrum disorder. *Research in Developmental Disabilities, 30,* 1107–1114.

Matson, J. L., Mayville, E. A., Lott, J.D., Bielecki, J., & Logan, R. (2003). A comparison of social and adaptive functioning in persons with psychosis, autism, and severe or profound mental retardation. *Journal of Developmental and Physical Disabilities, 15*(1), 57–65.

Meltzoff, A. N., & Moore, M. K. (1983). Newborn infants imitate adult facial gestures. *Child Development, 54,* 702–709.

National Institute of Child Health and Human Development. (2006). *State of the science in autism: Communication/social/emotional development.* Bethesda, MD: Author. Retrieved from http://www.nichd.nih.gov/publications/pubs/sos_autism/sub7.cfm.

National Institute of Mental Health. (2012). Autism Spectrum Disorders (Pervasive Developmental Disorders). Retrieved from http://www.nimh.nih.gov/health/topics/autism-spectrum-disorders-pervasive-developmental-disorders/index.shtml.

Osterling, J., & Dawson, G. (1994). Early recognition of children with autism: A study of first birthday home videotapes. *Journal of Autism and Developmental Disorders, 24,* 247–257.

Phillips, W., Baron-Cohen, S., & Rutter, M. (1992). The role of eye contact in goal detection: Evidence from normal infants and children with autism or mental handicap. *Development and Psychopathology, 4,* 375–383.

Raymaekers, R., Antrop, I., van der Meere, J. J., Wiersema, J. R., & Roeyers, H. (2007). HFA and ADHD: A direct comparison on state regulation and response inhibition. *Journal of Clinical and Experimental Neuropsychology, 29,* 418–427.

Rice, C. (2007, February 9). Prevalence of autism spectrum disorders—Autism and Developmental Disabilities Monitoring Network, 14 Sites, United States, 2002. *MMWR. Surveillance Summaries, 56,* 12–28.

Rommelse, N. J., Franke, B., Geurts, H. M., Hartman, C. A., & Buitelaar, J. K. (2010). Shared heritability of attention-deficit/hyperactivity disorder and autism spectrum disorder. *European Child & Adolescent Psychiatry, 19,* 281–295.

Santrock, J. W. (2010). *Children* (11th ed.). New York, NY: McGraw Hill.

Schreck, K.A., & Mulick, J. A. (2000). Parental reports of sleep problems in children with autism. *Journal of Autism and Developmental Disorders, 30,* 127–135.

Schreck, K. A., Mulick, J. A., & Smith, A. F. (2004). Sleep problems as possible predictors of intensified symptoms of autism. *Research in Developmental Disabilities, 25,* 57–66.

Shah, A., & Frith, U. (1993). Why do autistic individuals show superior performance on the Block Design task? *Journal of Child Psychology and Psychiatry, 34,* 1351–1364.

Stores, G., & Wiggs, L. (1998). Abnormal sleep patterns associated with autism: A brief review of research findings, assessment methods and treatment strategies. *Autism, 2,* 157–170.

Thelen, E. (1979). Rhythmical stereotypies in normal human infants. *Animal Behaviour, 27,* 699–715.

Tuchman, R. F., & Rapin, I. (1997). Regression in pervasive developmental disorders: Seizures and epileptiform electroencephalogram correlates. *Pediatrics, 99,* 560–566.

Turnbull, H. R., Turnbull, A., & Wehmeyer, M. (2010). *Exceptional lives: Special education in today's schools* (6th ed.). Upper Saddle River, NJ: Merrill/Prentice Hall.

Viellard, M., Da Fonseca, D., De Martino, S., Girardot, A.-M., Bastard-Rosset, D., Duverger, H., . . . Poinso, F. (2007). Autism and mental retardation: A study of the early social communication. *Archives de Pediatrie, 14*(3), 234–238.

Volkmar, F. R., Chawarska, K., & Klin, A. (2008). Autism spectrum disorders in infants and toddlers. An introduction. In K. Chawarska, A. Klin, & F. R. Volkmar (Eds.), *Autism spectrum disorders in infants and toddlers: Diagnosis, assessment, and treatment* (pp. 1–22). New york, NY: Guilford Press.

Weatherby, A. M., & Prizant, B. M. (2005). Enhancing language and communication development in Autism Spectrum Disorders: Assessment and intervention guidelines. In D. Zager (Ed.), *Autism Spectrum Disorders: Identification, education, and treatment*

(3rd ed., pp. 327–359). Mahwah, NJ: Lawrence Erlbaum Associates.

Williams, D. (1999). *Autism and sensing: The unlost instinct*. London: Jessica Kingsley Publishers.

Wimmer, H., & Perner, J. (1983). Beliefs about beliefs: Representation and constraining function of wrong beliefs in young children's understanding of deception. *Cognition, 13*, 41–68.

Wing, L. (1996). *The autism spectrum*. London: Constable.

Wing, L. (1997). The autistic spectrum. *Lancet, 13*, 1761–1766.

Wing, L. (1981). Asperger's syndrome: A clinical account. *Psychological Medicine, 11(1)*, 115–129.

Wing, L., & Gould, J. (1979). Severe impairments of social interaction and associated abnormalities in children: Epidemiology and classification. *Journal of Autism and Childhood Schizophrenia, 9*, 11–29.

Wolfberg, P. J. (2003). *Peer play and the autism spectrum*. Shawnee Mission, KS: Autism Asperger Publishing Company.

World Health Organization. (1992). *International classification of diseases: Diagnostic criteria for research* (10th ed.). Geneva, Switzerland: Author.

Yeargin-Allsopp, M., Rice, C., Karapurkar, T., Doernberg, N., Boyle, C., & Murphy, C. (2003). Prevalence of autism in a US metropolitan area. *JAMA, 289*, 49–55.

CHAPTER 3

BIOLOGICAL ISSUES AND ETIOLOGY OF AUTISM SPECTRUM DISORDER

In this chapter, you will learn:

- The significance of understanding Autism Spectrum Disorder (ASD) as a neurobiological disorder to families and educators.
- Atypical development of brain structures and neural development associated with ASD.
- Contemporary theories about the causes of ASD.
- Possible interventions linked to biological theories.

CHAPTER REFLECTION: A Mother's Perspective on Regressive Autism

Douglas Atkins

Christie, a mother of two, has been a leader in her community establishing parent support groups and advocacy work on behalf of families with children with ASD. Her son, Douglas, was diagnosed with ASD as a young child. Christie feels that changes in Douglas' diet greatly impacted his presentation of ASD.

Douglas was more than 4 weeks premature and had to stay 21 days in the Neonatal Intensive Care Unit due to respiratory distress, before we were able to take him home. He had been on several

(Continued)

(Continued)

rounds of antibiotics—so his immune system was shot.

Until about 15 months, we had no problems feeding Douglas. Two weeks after his 15-month immunizations, we started to see odd behaviors. For one thing, Douglas slept for about 24 hours after the immunization, ran a fever, and was highly irritable when awake. Following the shots, Douglas engaged in new and concerning behaviors such as looking at us through his peripheral vision, lining up his toys during play, and biting kids in the nursery.

For a child born almost 5 weeks early, we felt his milestones were pretty much on track until about 15 weeks. However, around 18 months he began shutting all of the doors and emptying all of the shelves. But, Douglas didn't fit the "stereotype" of autism. He was cuddly, not cold or distant.

His language was not coming in like it should have been. Douglas learned

nouns pretty easily, but that was it. His pediatrician was not concerned. We finally convinced him to refer Douglas for a hearing test. It turned out that Douglas had fluid in his ears. He had a history of many ear infections. The doctor put tubes in his ears to drain the fluid. After that he had an explosion of new nouns, but no verbs, adjectives, etc. Douglas had two sets of tubes over the years, and was sick all the time.

The turning point for us was when my cousin told me about a doctor who treated hyperactive children by addressing things like yeast. I decided to write him a detailed letter including all of Douglas' medical history documenting his chronic ear infections and treatment with antibiotics. He connected me with two other individuals who have helped so much. Both individuals got back to me and our support was in place. There was a huge difference in Douglas when we began to address yeast and other issues in his diet.

It is important for teachers of children with ASD to develop rapport with parents that includes updates on significant medical concerns. This helps the teacher better understand the child's behavior and support parents in documenting behaviors that might be associated with a medical condition. Teachers also serve as a resource for helping parents find answers to questions about ASD.

Teachers are among the professionals with whom parents work the closest. Because of perceptions of the teacher as an "expert" in ASD and limited opportunities to talk with medical personnel, parents may ask their child's teacher questions associated with biological issues. For instance, parents may ask teachers about the cause of ASD, how ASD affects their child's brain and learning, the use of medical interventions, and genetic implications of ASD. Although teachers should not provide medical advice, it is important for teachers working with children with ASD to have an understanding of key issues and research findings in the field of ASD.

Advances in our understanding of the neurobiology and genetics associated with ASD are rapid and exciting. Although teachers may not be able to answer every question a parent may raise (which is true for any professional), they can guide parents to appropriate resources. Keeping abreast of advances in the field of ASD allows teachers to better address parent questions, evaluate new therapies and claims about ASD, and pinpoint sources that can best address concerns that might arise.

NEUROBIOLOGY AND DEVELOPMENT: QUESTIONS PARENTS MAY ASK

Parents May Ask: Did I Cause My Child to Have ASD?

Parents may wonder if they somehow caused their child's ASD. This is one question teachers shouldn't hesitate to answer and assure parents that child-rearing practices *do not* cause ASD. Today there is consensus within the scientific community that ASD is a neurobiological disorder not caused by child-rearing practices.

Historically, parents were blamed for causing their child's autism as described in Chapter 1. ASD is currently understood as both a neurobiological and a developmental disorder. Current research reveals many differences between the neurobiology of individuals with ASD, and other individuals, including differences in brain structure, cellular growth (synaptogenesis), neurotransmitters, and myelination. The term developmental disorder indicates that ASD occurs early in development, possibly early in fetal development.

Diagnostic criteria, such as the *Diagnostic and Statistical Manual of Mental Disorders, Fourth Edition (DSM-IV)* (American Psychiatric Association [APA], 2004) and International Classification of Diseases, 10th Revision (ICD-10) (World Health Organization [WHO], 1993), stipulate that characteristics of ASD are apparent (either by current functioning or retrospective information) before age 3. Evidence that ASD is a biological and developmental disorder comes

Matt Kalber

Autism wasn't considered a biological disorder until the mid-1960s with the publication of Rimland's book *Infantile Autism: The Syndrome and Its Implications for a Neural Theory of Behavior* (1964). Rimland is pictured second from the left.

primarily from four lines of research. These include family and twin studies, research at the cellular level reflecting early developmental irregularities, research investigating differences in brain structure and localized function of individuals with ASD, and research within the field of genetics. Other compelling lines of research investigate problems with neural connectivity, synapse formation, and plasticity as underlying deficits associated with ASD (Boucher, 2009; Coleman, 2005; Steyaert & De La Marche, 2008).

It is widely believed that ASD has a wide range of phenotypes (expression of the disorder) with many different possible etiologies (causes of the disorder). Individuals with diseases associated with ASD, such as tuberous sclerosis, fragile X syndrome, Williams syndrome, and congenital rubella, are said to have syndromic ASD, while those with no identifiable medical disorder associated with ASD are said to have nonsyndromic (or idiopathic) ASD. However, both syndromic and nonsyndromic ASD are neurobiological in origin and likely genetic.

Parents May Ask: Is ASD a Genetic Disorder?

Parents may wonder if having a child with ASD suggests that their other children might have characteristics of ASD. The answer is that having a child with ASD is associated with a higher likelihood that siblings will also have ASD or other learning difficulties, as compared with families that do not have children with ASD. Families having one child with ASD are 3 to 6 times more likely to have a child with ASD than a family without ASD (Rutter, 2005; Rutter, Silberg, & Simonoff, 1999). Further evidence of genetic etiology (genetic cause of ASD) comes from twin studies of children with ASD. Monozygotic twins (identical twins who share the same genetic material) have a 60% to 70% likelihood of both twins having ASD (concordance rate), while dizygotic twins (fraternal twins, have genetic material comparable to siblings) have a 5% concordance rate (Rutter; Steyaert & De La Marche, 2008).

Thus, increased shared genetic material results in a higher concordance rate of ASD. Furthermore, siblings of children with ASD are more likely to have mild developmental delays, such as language problems, compared with siblings of typically developing children (Ritvo, Freeman, Mason-Brothers, & Ritvo, 1985). However, many families that have both a child with ASD and other children who do not appear to have any learning or developmental difficulties. Males are our four times as likely as females to have ASD (Fombonne, 2005), offering further support for a biological, and more specifically genetic, etiology.

Parents May Ask: How Does ASD Impact My Child's Brain Development?

Irregularities at the cellular level and during early brain development

ASD is considered a Pervasive Developmental Disorder. Thus, developmental difficulties are apparent in many domains (pervasive across several domains of functioning). The pervasive nature of the disorder is also reflected by atypical cellular and neurological development. Children with ASD appear to have atypical development at the cellular level, which is likely to impact many aspects of brain development.

Irregularities early in development reflected by impairments at the cellular level suggest neurological difficulties likely to impact many (if not all) areas of the brain. In behavioral terms, that is what we find. Impairments in socialization, communication, and unusual behaviors reflect atypical development across many domains. For instance, the cellular arrangement in the frontal and temporal lobes of individuals with ASD is smaller, more numerous, and more densely packed than in the brains of individuals without ASD (Volker & Lopata, 2008). These cells are formed during the earliest phases of brain development, suggesting a disorder with developmental origins.

ASD has been described as a disorder of growth regulation (Akshoomoff, Pierce, & Courchesne, 2002). During normal early brain development, the brain is both losing and gaining. These changes occur throughout life, but at a faster rate during infancy than any other time during the life span. In early in infancy our brains have an abundance of neurons, branches (axons), and connections (synapses). Programmed cell death and pruning (cell death related to environmental experiences) are important parts of brain maturation (Kolb & Whishaw, 1996). Likewise, infancy is a time of tremendous cell and synaptic growth in the brain. Research from brain imaging studies and postmortem studies (donated brains of deceased individuals with ASD) reveal atypical brain growth during early development.

Some of the earliest observations associated with atypical brain development involved observations of an abnormally large head circumference (macrocephaly) in children later diagnosed with ASD as well as in their first-degree relatives (Courchesne, Carper, & Akshoomoff, 2002). In young children, head circumference appears to be an accurate reflection of brain volume (Courchesne, Redcay, & Kennedy, 2004). From infancy to approximately age 2, children with ASD appear to have a greater amount of cerebral grey and white matter than infants without ASD (Courchesne, Redcay, & Kennedy). However, later in childhood this trend is not apparent. In fact, after age 2 there are no longer significant differences in head circumference between children with ASD and children without developmental disorders (Courchesne, Redcay, & Kennedy).

Irregularities in brain structure and localized function

Advances in neuroimaging technology allow for the investigation of how the brains of individuals with ASD differ from those of individuals without ASD. In addition, neuroimaging technology such as functional magnetic resonance imaging (fMRI), magnetic resonance spectroscopy, and single-photon emission computed tomography, reveal how brains of individuals with ASD function differently than other brains when involved in specific tasks such as talking, thinking, and reading.

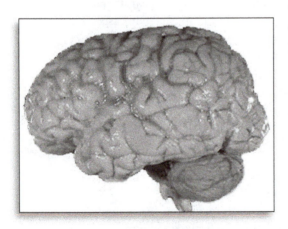

Abnormalities in the cerebellum, sitting at the base of the brain, are the most consistent findings of brain abnormalities in ASD reported in research literature.

This image is a work of the National Institutes of Health, part of the United States Department of Health and Human Services.

The cerebellum and ASD

ASD appears to impact all major areas of the brain, including the cerebellum, the cerebral cortex, the limbic system, the brain stem, and the corpus callosum (Akshoomoff et al., 2002; Hardan et al., 2009). An increasing number of studies indicate that individuals with ASD have atypical cerebellar development (Akshoomoff et al.; Bauman &

Kemper, 2005; Tiemeier et al., 2010). Abnormalities in the cerebellum are the most consistent finding of brain structural abnormalities in the research literature (Stanfield et al., 2008). The cerebellum (Latin for "little brain" as it resembles the two hemispheres of the cerebral cortex) is the structure at the base of the brain. Considered part of the hindbrain, the cerebellum is associated with the vestibular system and coordinates movement, balance, and equilibrium. In addition, the cerebellum is associated with cognitive processes such as certain types of learning and memory and even emotional function (Tiemeier et al.).

CHAPTER REFLECTION: From the Lab to the Classroom, What Are the Implications of Deficits in Cerebellar Functioning?

The cerebellum is associated with aspects of vestibular functioning such as balance, coordination, timing, and posture. Children with ASD often use their body in ways that appear odd. Although some children with ASD have good gross motor skills, they may engage in odd behaviors such as touching the walls as they walk down the hall, walking on their tiptoes, or holding their hands or arms at an odd angle. These behaviors may be associated with atypical cerebellar development. Likewise, many children with ASD enjoy activities that stimulate cerebellar functioning, such as jumping on a trampoline, swinging, and rolling. These activities are sometimes incorporated into a behavioral plan (used as a reward in learning activities) or even as part of sensory integration therapy (discussed later in the chapter). The cerebellum also processes aspects of language, attention, and memory.

The amygdala and ASD

Another area of the brain that appears significantly affected by ASD is the amygdala, an almond-shaped collection of nuclei located beneath the temporal lobe. The amygdala is part of the limbic system, which is associated with

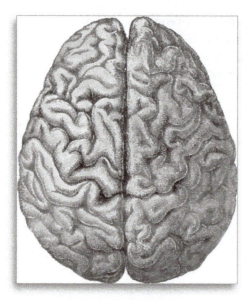

ASD has been associated with atypical development in many areas of the brain.

motivation and emotion, and is particularly involved in emotional responses of fear and aggression.

When the amygdala is stimulated in animal studies, the animal becomes aggressive or fearful depending on the area stimulated (Aggleton & Passingham, 1981; Passer & Smith, 2004). Humans with amygdala lesions demonstrate behavioral characteristics of ASD, such as impaired social judgment (Baron-Cohen et al., 2000) and damage to the amygdala in humans is associated with atypical eye contact (Gamer & Büchel, 2009; Spezio, Huang, Castelli, & Adolphs, 2007), a common feature of ASD.

The amygdala of individuals with ASD appears to be both structurally and functionally different. Postmortem studies (using brains of deceased individuals) indicate greater than typical cell density in the amygdalas of individuals with ASD (Bauman & Kemper, 1994; Rapin, 1998). Research using functional magnetic resonance imaging (measures change of blood flow associated with a region of the brain) indicates that individuals with ASD have decreased amygdala volume and fail to use the amygdala when processing pictures of faces (Akshoomoff et al., 2002). Some studies find that children with ASD demonstrate the pattern of greater than average amygdala growth early in childhood, and decreased size and number of neurons later in development (Volker & Lopata, 2008).

Other evidence to support our understanding of ASD as a neurological disorder:

- Approximately 3 out of 4 individuals with autism also have lower cognitive functioning, which generally indicates some serious damage or dysfunction of the brain (Tsai, 2005). Thirty-three percent to 59% of individuals with ASD achieve scores below 70 on standardized intelligence tests, falling within the range of intellectual disability (Rice, 2007).

- Impairment in communication must be present for a diagnosis of ASD. Many children with ASD have delayed onset of speech, lifelong difficulties with functional verbal communication, or are nonverbal. Distinct portions of the brain are involved in expressive language and receptive language (Kolb & Whishaw, 1996). Likewise, damage to these specific regions of the brain result in significant difficulties with speech production, comprehension, or both (Tsai, 2005).
- Other neurological abnormalities (such as hypotonia, hypertonia, abnormal posture and gait, seizure disorders) are indicators of neurological impairment and often found in individuals with ASD (Tsai, 1999).
- There are several genetic syndromes that are associated with ASD. Refer to Abrahams and Geschwind (2008) for a review of genetic syndromes associated with ASD.

THE GENETICS OF ASD

CHAPTER REFLECTION: "If You Meet One Person With Autism, You Have Met One Person With Autism"

This is a popular saying among those working with people who have ASD. You have likely known more than one individual with ASD. Although they all demonstrate deficits impacting communication, social functioning, and repertoire of behaviors, consider how different those individuals were from one another. Autism is called a "spectrum" disorder because skills, overall functioning, and areas of deficits vary so widely. Individual differences are apparent among people with ASD, just like within the typically developing population. However, different types of ASD also appear associated with a wide range of genetic abnormalities we are just starting to understand.

Is There Just One Type of Autism?

Building upon the completion of the mapped human genome, geneticists are refining our understanding of the role that genes play in complex disorders such as ASD. Although only 10% to 20% of individuals with ASD have an identifiable genetic disorder, there is growing research to suggest that a variety of complex genetic-environment interactions are involved in ASD (Abrahams & Geschwind, 2008).

Today we understand ASD to be a heterogeneous disorder likely involving many different etiologies (Gregg et al., 2008). Geneticists often refer to the *autisms* (Abrahams & Geschwind) to convey the diverse etiologies that we are coming to understand. For the majority of cases of ASD, it is likely that multiple genes interact with other factor in very complex ways (Piggot, Shirinyan, Shemmassian, Vazirian, & Alarcón, 2009). In most cases, we have yet to identify a specific combination of genetic abnormalities associated with ASD. Yet, deletions, duplications, and inversions of genetic material on certain chromosomes have been associated with ASD. No single genetic disorder accounts for more than 1% to 2% of total cases of ASD. Thus, ASD is a neurobiological disorder involving many different genetic and neurological pathways.

Fragile X Syndrome

The most common genetic condition known to be associated with ASD is fragile X syndrome. Approximately 2% to 3% of individuals with fragile X syndrome also have ASD (Rutter, 2005). The name fragile X is due to the appearance under a microscope of a fragile-looking piece of material hanging from the X chromosome (The National Fragile X Foundation, 2009). Individuals with fragile X syndrome exhibit a wide range of symptoms and levels of functioning, from mild learning difficulties to intellectual disabilities.

Tuberous Sclerosis

Although quite rare, tuberous sclerosis is the most frequently occurring genetic disorder caused by a single gene associated with ASD. Tuberous sclerosis causes benign tumors to grow throughout the body, including within the brain, and is associated with a variety of physical and cognitive difficulties, including seizures, developmental delays, and ASD in many individuals with the disorder (Wong, 2005). ASD is most frequently identified in individuals with tuberous sclerosis who have intellectual disabilities, severe seizure disorders, or tubers in the temporal lobe (Bolton, Park, Higgins, Griffiths, & Pickles, 2002). Although only 1% to 4% of individuals with ASD have tuberous sclerosis, prevalence estimates suggest that anywhere from 16% to 50% of individuals with tuberous sclerosis have ASD (Wong).

The Search for Chromosomes and Candidate Genes Associated With ASD

Using multiplex families with autism, researchers are investigating specific genes that may be associated with ASD. The term "multiplex", refers to families with at least two siblings diagnosed with ASD (Tsai, 2005). Interestingly, the funding for much of this research has come from parent advocacy groups that effectively lobby the government and raise significant amounts of money to support research on the genetic basis of ASD.

Current research in cytogenetics (the study of chromosomes) suggests candidate genes that may put one at risk for ASD on several different chromosomes, including chromosomes 2, 7 (Rutter, 2005), 15 (Volkar & Lopata, 2008), 16 (Weiss et al., 2008), and 22

Source: © National Human Genome Institute. Date Posted: February 9, 2006 Sen. Harkin with Human Genome CD.

Senator Tom Harkin is pictured holding a CD-ROM containing the human genome. Spurred on by findings from the Human Genome Project and advances in molecular genetics, researchers are investigating specific genes that may be associated with ASD.

(Manning et al., 2004). After fragile X syndrome and tuberous sclerosis, the 15q11-13q region of chromosome 15 has the most common known genetic mutations (duplications and triplications) associated with ASD (Volker & Lopata). It is likely that susceptibility genes do not actually causes ASD, but interact with various factors to trigger the expression of the disorder (Rutter).

G-Banded Chromosomal and FISH Analyses

Research investigating the genetic underpinnings of ASD have led to enhancements in genetic screening for genetic disorders associated with ASD. In the past, genetic testing was largely done using a procedure called G-banded chromosomal analysis. Unique patterns of bands identify the location of genes on each of the 23 pairs of chromosomes. The G-banded chromosomal technique is limited to identifying relatively large pieces of genetic material that have been deleted or added to the chromosome.

Even more spectacular is the FISH analysis (fluorescence in situ hybridization) in which a fluorescent probe targets a DNA-specific region to detect if there is a deletion. FISH analysis revealed the most common microdeletion in humans, found on chromosome 22 (22q11). This microdeletion is frequently associated with a condition known as DiGeorge syndrome (Oskardóttir, Vujic, & Fasth, 2004). Fifty percent of those with this deletion also meet the diagnostic criteria for ASD (Vorstman et al., 2006). Genetic testing may be helpful in better understanding the etiology of some types of ASD.

Whole Gene Microarray

The whole gene microarray allows for the identification of even smaller details of DNA segments. The microarray creates a "molecular portrait" that can be compared with other samples of known disorders (Bioscience Corporation, 2009). Using the microarray technology, researchers have identified a microdeletion on chromosome 16 (16p11.2), which has been found in many of cases of ASD involving genetic screening (Weiss et al., 2008).

Genetic Screening and ASD

Increasingly, when ASD is suspected, genetic screening is recommended. As we better understand the relationship between genetic disorders and ASD, parents will be able to obtain increased clarity about the course of their child's disorder and target interventions most likely to be helpful for their child. Genetic screening is followed by genetic counseling to help parents understand the meaning of the test results. Genetic counseling often involves discussions about potential risks for reoccurring syndromes or genetic abnormalities for family planning. Furthermore, genetic screening allows for the identification of children with rare syndromes or genetic abnormalities to be invited to participate in research studies. The participation of these individuals in genetic research is vital for continual progress in understanding the etiology of ASD.

The American College of Medical Genetics recommends a tiered approach to genetic testing for ASD based on the family history, developmental history, and clinical features of the individual (Schaefer & Mendelsohn, 2008). Refer to the recommended readings at the end of the chapter to learn more about the role of genetic testing in diagnosing ASD.

It can be comforting to parents to have some answers regarding the source of their child's ASD. Many parents express dismay about the long periods of uncertainty during which health care providers sometimes dismiss parental concerns about atypical behaviors or embrace a "wait and see" approach. Genetic screening techniques allow for information about possible ASD very early in infancy or in some cases, even during pregnancy.

Genetic Screening and ASD: Cautions and Limitations

Individuals working directly with children with ASD may question the benefit of genetic screening to parents and children with ASD, particularly in light of the financial cost. They may wonder if knowing a child's ASD is caused by a microdeletion or associated with a genetic syndrome can inform the educational plan, predict the best type of speech-language program, or help identify a medication that will reduce challenging behaviors.

In addressing these questions, it is important to realize that our current understanding of the genetic implications of ASD is virtually in its infancy. Only a few decades ago, parenting, rather than genetics, was believed to cause ASD. Even so, in many cases understanding that a child has a specific genetic disorder can inform educational and other types of interventions. Furthermore, as we learn more about the genetic and molecular basis of ASD psychopharmacological interventions will be investigated to target specific genes and corresponding behaviors.

Regardless of the results of genetic testing, it is important that the individuality of each child be recognized. Parents yearn for teachers and others to understand their child as a unique individual rather than a syndrome or disorder. Even individuals with the same genetic disorder differ in relative strengths and weaknesses, expression of the disorder, life experiences, and personal interests/motivators. Knowing that a child has a specific disorder can provide insight, open doors for certain programs and areas of support, and offer some degree of comfort in terms of understanding the origins and course of the disorder. However, parents know their child as a unique member of their family *with* a disorder. Mutual respect and collaboration with families is dependent upon recognition of the child as an individual.

Currently there is no cure for ASD. Individuals are likely to experience characteristics of ASD throughout their lifetime. The significant amount of variation within ASD underscores the importance of understanding the person with ASD as an individual within the context of ASD.

ENVIRONMENTAL TOXINS AS TRIGGERS FOR ASD

CHAPTER REFLECTION: Respecting Parents' Beliefs About the Origin of Their Child's ASD

You have likely heard from parents or through the media stories describing how certain things in the environmental triggered a child to have ASD. Beliefs about the origin of ASD are important. A parent's willingness to embrace certain types of interventions and educational strategies may be associated with their beliefs about how a child came to have ASD.

Furthermore, the teacher's response to parents' statements and questions about the origin of their child's ASD is likely to impact future collaborative efforts. It is important that teachers respect parents' beliefs about the origin of their child's ASD. At the same time, teachers can offer parents information based on empirically supported research and help parents monitor their child's behavior when new therapies are introduced. Teachers can also help parents learn to make informed decisions about new interventions.

Neurobiological views on the etiology of ASD, such as atypical brain development and genetic disorders, have attracted a great deal of research interest. However, other views about the etiology of ASD abound. Likely certain environmental factors trigger ASD in individuals who are genetically susceptible. However, investigating interactions between genetics and environmental factors associated with the etiology of ASD is extremely complex and made more difficult by the heterogeneous nature of ASD and limitation in technology and pooling data (Altevogt, Hanson, & Leshner, 2009).

Efforts to publicize possible connections between environmental toxins and ASD were pioneered by the legendary physician Bernard Rimland in his search to treat his son's ASD. Theories abound suggesting that these environmental triggers may result in gastrointestinal disorders, immunological dysfunction, or other disorders underlying ASD.

Gastrointestinal Disorders and Dietary Interventions

You may have worked with children with ASD who have digestive difficulties. These difficulties not only raise questions about the etiology of ASD, but also provide obstacles for a child's ability to reach his potential. When a child has unresolved or chronic digestive problems, they may be unavailable for learning.

Reports of gastrointestinal (GI) difficulties including foul-smelling stool, diarrhea, and constipation in children with ASD led to the leaky gut theory of ASD (Wakefield et al., 2002). The leaky gut theory suggests that some children with ASD experience severe inflammation in the gut membrane, causing irregular metabolic pathways. The theory has also been linked to the measles, mumps, and rubella (MMR) vaccination controversy (vaccinations or preservatives in the vaccinations triggering the "leaky gut").

Gluten- and Casein-Free Diets

In the opening vignette, Christie Atkins describes her son's regressive autism and related medical problems. She describes improvements in Douglas's behavior following dietary interventions. Many parents report that specialized diets free of gluten (plant proteins found in wheat, barley, and rye) and casein (a protein in dairy products) are helpful in treating behaviors associated with ASD. Although peer-reviewed research has yet to establish a clear link between gluten or casein sensitivity and ASD, it is possible that children with ASD are more at risk for these types of metabolic disorders.

There are many anecdotal reports about the link between ASD and GI problems and small-scale studies investigating these claims. However, there are limited studies that include large samples and appropriate comparison groups with controls (Erickson et al., 2005). Based on available research, it does not appear that GI disorders occur at a greater frequency within the ASD population than within the general population. However, additional research is needed to better understand this issue given the significant number of parents that report GI distress within the ASD population.

The classroom teacher can help collect behavioral data for parents who are implementing special diets. They can also ensure that children are not given foods at school that parents feel negatively impact the child's digestive system. However, it is unlikely that changes in diet will "cure" characteristics associated with ASD. However, it is possible that dietary interventions can help the child feel better and allow them to benefit from educational and behavioral interventions.

Secretin

Secretin, a gastrointestinal hormone used to diagnose digestive difficulties, was first profiled as a treatment for autism after a case study described improvements in eye contact, language, sleep, and overall social functioning (Travis, 2001). Following this highly publicized case study, anecdotal claims and case reports testifying to the effectiveness of secretin in reducing behavioral characteristics of ASD led to large numbers of parents clamoring for this treatment for their child with ASD (Kaminska, Czaja, Kozielska, Mazur, & Korzon, 2002). Literature reviews of research involving GI difficulties and ASD describe several double-blind, placebo-controlled trials of single and multiple doses of secretin used to treat ASD (Erickson et al., 2005; Esch & Carr, 2004; Kern, Espinoza, & Trivedi, 2004). Based on these reviews, the effectiveness of secretin to reduce behavioral characteristics of ASD has not been empirically demonstrated using large-scale double-blind studies (Erickson et al.; Esch & Carr; Kern et al.; Scahill & Martin, 2005).

The Need to Address GI Difficulties

At this time, the extent to which GI disorders are associated with ASD is unclear (Erickson et al., 2005; Pavone & Ruggieri, 2005). However, it is clear that children with ASD sometimes experience GI discomfort. When children with ASD experience GI pain (or other discomforts), they may be unable to communicate this experience. Instead, they may demonstrate puzzling behaviors such as strange body posturing, rocking, and head banging. These behaviors are sometimes addressed through behavioral interventions without consideration of their function. Although behaviors that put an individual at risk of hurting himself or others must be dealt with immediately, these behaviors might be indicative of GI distress or other medical conditions.

Individuals trained in applied behavioral analysis (ABA) use functional behavior analysis to identify *why* a behavior is occurring before implementing an intervention plan. Information such as determining factors immediately preceding the target behavior (antecedent) and immediately following the target behavior (consequence) can help identify if the behavior is done to escape something aversive, gain something desirable, or for some other reason such as expressing frustration or pain (ABA is discussed more fully in Chapter 7).

Regardless of whether or not food allergies or food intolerances cause ASD, GI problems can cause extreme discomfort in children. Pain clearly impedes many aspects of development and learning. Although there lacks a consensus in the empirical literature demonstrating the effectiveness of specialized diets in reducing behaviors associated with ASD (Pavonne & Ruggieri, 2005), there are numerous books and websites with parent testimony asserting the ability of these diets to reduce symptoms of ASD. In addition, prominent individuals within popular culture, such as Jenny McCarthy, share highly publicized personal stories of their own children being cured of autism using dietary interventions (McCarthy, 2007).

Known Environmental Toxins That Negatively Impact Early Development

There is strong clinical evidence, as well as experimental animal studies, demonstrating the negative impact of environmental toxins on early development, particularly involving lead and mercury, which both cross the placenta during pregnancy when brain structures are forming (Hubbs-Tait, Nation, Krebs, & Bellinger, 2005). There are many environmental toxins proposed as possible triggers of ASD, including exposure to thalidomide (routinely administered to pregnant women to reduce nausea during pregnancy in the late 1950s), Pitocin (a synthetic version of the hormone oxytocin used to induce pregnant women into labor), and prenatal exposure to drugs such as cocaine and alcohol (see Evers, Novotny, & Hollander, 2003, for a review). The most highly contentious of possible environmental triggers is the measles, mumps, and rubella (MMR) vaccine.

The MMR Vaccination and ASD

Parents of children with ASD and the scientific community often collaborate to advance shared agendas regarding identification and treatment of individuals with ASD. Parents of children with ASD have been very effective in developing communities and forums to share their experiences and ideas. These advocacy groups are effective in both lobbying and public awareness efforts. Thus, when parents partner with the scientific community, great advances in research, legal precedents, and interventions result. However, there are times when they are not in agreement. Arguably, the area of greatest contention between the medical/research community and parent/advocacy groups is the association between the MMR vaccination and ASD.

There is a strong consensus within the international scientific and medical community that exposure to mercury (found with the preservative thimerosal traditionally used in the MMR vaccination) is not responsible for increased prevalence rates of ASD (Doja & Roberts, 2006; Fombonne, Zakarian, Bennett, Meng, & McLean-Heywood, 2006; National Academy of Sciences, 2004). Although it is possible that subtypes of ASD are triggered by vaccinations, viruses, or other substances in the environment (Lainhart et al., 2002), the current consensus within the scientific community supports a neurobiological origin of ASD unrelated to thimerosal or vaccinations such as MMR. However, there is a growing concern among parents of young children that vaccinations, especially when several are given at one time, might be harmful to their young children.

Although it is critical to understand the current research, it is also important to respect parental beliefs about the origin of their child's ASD. Some parents recall significant regression in their young children following the administration of MMR vaccinations, culminating with a diagnosis of ASD. In fact, 1 in 3 children with ASD experienced developmental regression before age 3 (Rourke, 1998), known as autistic regression. If you are working with a parent whose child experienced autistic regression, they may be more likely to experience feelings of guilt and loss of their child's developmental status as compared with parents of other children with ASD (Davidovitch, Glick, Holtzman, Tirosh, & Safir, 2000).

Furthermore, parents of children with regressive autism are more likely to attribute their child's ASD to external causes, rather than to genetic predisposition (Goin-Kochel & Myers, 2005). This belief may impact parental choice of interventions, such as their willingness to try complementary and alternative medicine. Autistic regression is often associated with seizures and cognitive impairments (Goin-Kochel & Myers; Wiggins, Rice, & Baio, 2009), occur more often in boys, and is often associated with later medical problems such as eating/drinking, sleep, seizures, and atypical fear response (Wiggins, Rice, & Baio).

OTHER THEORIES ABOUT THE ETIOLOGY OF ASD

Immunological Dysfunction

CHAPTER REFLECTION: Can a Compromised Immune System Cause ASD?

In the opening vignette, Christie describes Douglas as having numerous infections as a baby and young child: *"He had been on several rounds of antibiotics—so his immune system was shot. . . . He had a history of many ear infections."*

Although not well understood, another theory explaining the etiology of ASD is that some children have a genetic predisposition making them susceptible to certain environmental triggers. When exposed to the trigger (exposure to certain viruses, specific foods, etc.), the child acquires ASD. Difficulties with immune functioning may reflect such a genetic predisposition.

The theory that a subgroup of ASD is associated with deficits in the immune system has a growing body of research support, yet lacks epidemiological research needed to fully understand the role of the immune system in the etiology of ASD (DelGiudice & Hollander, 2003; Tsai, 2005). Immunological dysfunction may involve depressed immune systems, maternal infection, autoimmune difficulties, or difficulties with immune regulation (DelGiudice & Hollander; Patterson, 2009; Tsai). Immune dysfunction is likely associated with a complex interplay of genetic predisposition and environmental factors (DelGiudice & Hollander) and is consistent with parent reports of GI problems, food allergies, asthma, and eczema.

However, research in the field of epigenetics may hold the key for answers about how and if such genetic predispositions (discussed in the box above) arise in autism (Schanen, 2006). Epigenetics is the process by which environmental triggers may "turn on" or "turn off" the expression of particular genes. Epigenetics may explain why one identical twin may have ASD, yet another develops typically. A project for mapping the human epigenome is under way. However, it looks to be a considerably more complex project than even the Human Genome Project. An article about epigenetics in *Time* magazine (Cloud, 2006) predicts, "When completed, the Human Epigenome Project (already under way in Europe) will make the Human Genome Project look like homework that 15th century kids did with an abacus."

Viral Infection

There are known diseases associated with ASD, the best known being congenital rubella (Evers, Novotny, & Hollander, 2003). Children with ASD caused by maternal rubella are most often severely impaired (Evers et al.). Other viral infections associated with ASD include the congenital cytomegalovirus (CMV), measles introduced prenatally, stealth viruses (derived from the herpes viruses), and varicella (chickenpox). However, the rates of cases of ASD associated with these viruses are quite small and do not prove causation.

INTERVENTIONS LINKED TO BIOLOGICAL THEORIES OF ASD

Psychopharmacological Treatments

Although there are no medical treatments to cure ASD (Rapin, 2002), psychopharmacological interventions are sometimes used to address specific behavioral concerns. Teachers can assist in determining if medication is warranted by

Psychopharmacological treatments are sometimes used to address specific behavioral concerns or comorbid conditions associated with ASD. However, there are no known interventions that can *cure* ASD.

documenting the severity and pattern of target behaviors (Scahill, 2008). Psychopharmacological interventions are frequently used to address comorbid (or co-occurring) conditions such as aggression, self-injurious behavior, overactivity, seizure activity, and sleep difficulties. Psychopharmacological are less likely used to address core deficits of ASD such as language and communication (Findling, 2005). In addition, medications are sometimes helpful in addressing emotional difficulties such as anxiety and depression (Novotny & Hollander, 2003).

Mood disorders and SRIs

There is a high rate of comorbidity between ASD and mood disorders such as depression and anxiety (Leyfer et al., 2006). This appears especially true for individuals with average or above-average cognitive skills, possibly because of increased self-awareness of social difficulties and opportunity for interactions with typically developing peers (Wing, 1992; Vickerstaff, Heriot, Wong, & Dossetor, 2007). It can be difficult to accurately assess mood disorders in individuals with limited language skills (Leyfer et al.). Since social communication is a core deficit of ASD, information from teachers and parents is particularly important in making accurate diagnoses of a mood disorder (Gadow, DeVincent, & Schneider, 2008).

Selective serotonin reuptake inhibitors (SSRIs) are frequently used to address depression as well as compulsive/repetitive behaviors in individuals with ASD (Novotny & Hollander, 2003; West, Brunssenn, & Waldrop, 2009). Abnormal levels of serotonin appear implicated in ASD (Chugani, 2002; Chugani et al., 1999; Novotny & Hollander). SSRIs, including fluoxetine (Prozac), sertraline (Zoloft), and paroxetine (Paxil), seem to prevent certain nerve cells in the brain from reabsorbing serotonin, which is associated with elevated mood (Mayo Foundation for Medical Education and Research, 2009). Side effects associated with SSRIs may include irritability, impaired sleep, reduced appetite, agitation, hyperactivity (McDougle, Stigler, & Posey, 2003), and appear more frequently in children with ASD than in other children receiving these medications (West, Brunssen, & Waldrop).

Risperidone for aggressive, self-injurious, and repetitive behaviors

Risperidone, an atypical antipsychotic medication, is sometimes prescribed to reduce aggressive, self-injurious, or excessively repetitive behaviors (Read & Rendall, 2007; West & Waldrop, 2006). Risperidone is used for moderate to severe aggressive or self-injurious behaviors that are ongoing and severely impact quality of life (Scahill, 2008). Side effects associated with risperidone may include weight gain, anxiety, and fatigue (Moussavand & Findling, 2007; Read & Rendall).

Other medications sometimes used to address emotional and behavioral concerns in children with ASD include antianxiety medications, anticonvulsants, beta-blockers, opiate blockers, sedatives, and psychostimulant medications. For a review of common medications used to treat ASD, refer to Moussavand and Findling (2007) and Sweeney, Forness, and Levitt (1998).

Treating Seizure Disorders

Many individuals with ASD experience seizures, which vary in severity and frequency. Seizure disorders often begin either before age 5 or after age 10 (Volkmar & Nelson, 1990), and more often in individuals with intellectual disabilities (Goin-Kochel & Myers, 2009; Wiggins, Rice, & Baio, 2009; Tuchman, 2003). Children who experienced autistic regression also appear more at risk for seizure disorders (Goin-Kochel & Myers, 2009; Tuchman, 2004; Wiggins et al.). Chronic seizure activity indicates a diagnosis of epilepsy and often requires medical intervention. Antiepileptic drugs, used to treat seizure disorders, are often administered during the school day and may result in side effects such as sluggishness, impaired concentration and memory, drowsiness, weight gain, irritability, anxiety, and aggression. Antiepileptic drugs are sometimes used to treat mood disorders as well (Palermo & Curatolo, 2004).

Teachers working with children known to have a history of seizure activity should work with parents and school administration to develop a seizure management plan. Although some seizures are short and appear as brief lapses in attention (petit mal seizures), others involve motor activity (simple partial seizure) and possibly loss of consciousness (as in the case of complex partial seizures).

Contrary to some conventional wisdom, individuals having seizures should never be restrained or have objects placed in their mouths. Instead, ensure that they are away from furniture or objects on which they might injure themselves. If possible, individuals should be turned to their side to ensure they have unrestricted airway. After a seizure, individuals are often exhausted and may require a clean change of clothing. Care should be taken to provide privacy and reassurance. The Epilepsy Foundation of America provides recommendations for emergency aid on its website (http://www.epilepsyfoundation.org/about/firstaid).

Administering and Monitoring Medications at School

It is critical that teachers closely monitor children taking medications. This information helps identify side effects and assist physicians in adjusting dosage or selecting a more appropriate medication. Furthermore, it is important to understand the school policy regarding storage and administration of medications. Although some schools are fortunate enough to have school nurses to aid with this procedure, increasingly schools do not have nursing support (McCarthy, Kelly, & Reed, 2000).

Whenever possible, educators are encouraged to provide parents with ongoing documentation of a child's behavior while taking medications. It is important that medication regiments are documented and copies given to key personnel. Tips for developing a medication protocol appear in Tables 3.1. Tables 3.2 and 3.3 address medicine documentation and storage at school. More detailed guidelines are available from the American Academy of Pediatrics' Counsel on School Health (2009).

Table 3.1   Tips for Administration of Medication in the Schools

- Incorporate policies for administering medications into ongoing teacher and support staff training.
- Maintain student confidentiality.
- Accurate and timely administration and documentation of medications is essential.
- Require a written medication form signed by both the prescribing physician and child's guardian.
- Store prescription medications in secure locations (locked if possible). Refrigeration may be necessary.
- Frequent communication with parents is important to share changes in behaviors or other observations about medication use at school.
- Document missed dosages or other errors in medication routines.
- Be aware of possible side effects and possible emergency procedures.

Table 3.2   Example Documentation Chart for Administering Medications at School

Child's name	
Date and time medication administered	
Name of medication	
Name of individual administering medication	
Was child compliant or noncompliant when taking medication?	
Changes/Noteworthy behaviors (note how long after taking medication changes observed)	

Table 3.3   Checklist for Storing Medications at School

- ✓ Name of medication (use a separate form for each medication)
- ✓ Time(s) medications are to be administered
- ✓ Where is medication stored, does it require refrigeration?
- ✓ Can medication be self-administered by the child?
- ✓ Does the medication need to be taken with food or water?
- ✓ Description of possible side effects
- ✓ Name and phone number of guardians
- ✓ Name and phone number of prescribing physician

COMPLEMENTARY AND ALTERNATIVE MEDICINE

Many parents of children with ASD consider using interventions that have limited supporting empirical research and are thus considered "complementary" or "alternative." It is possible that in time an integrated analysis based on high-quality empirical research will support some of these treatments. When parents raise questions about such treatments, teachers can offer available information about what is currently known, as well as strategies for evaluating available research.

Candida Yeast

Some clinicians note a greater than typical degree of candida, a yeastlike fungus, in children with ASD, which may be related to immune system difficulties and possibly associated with exposure to antibiotics, viruses, or other environmental toxins (Kidd, 2002). Antifungal medications are sometimes used to treat symptoms of ASD in cases of yeast overgrowth. However, research regarding the effectiveness of this treatment, as in many types of complementary and alternative medicine (CAM), is sparse and inconclusive (Pavone & Ruggieri, 2005; Steyaert & De La Marche, 2008). Yet, anecdotal reports from parents and clinicians are compelling and warrant further investigations marked by scientific rigor.

Vitamins

The use of vitamins to treat psychological disorders can be traced to the 1950s when first used to treat schizophrenia. It is theorized that vitamin supplements might serve to impact neurotransmitters, such as serotonin. Rimland pioneered efforts to investigate vitamins C and B6, and dimethylglycine as treatments for ASD (Rimland, Callaway, & Dreyfus, 1978; Rimland, 2002). Others have built on this research (i.e., Dolske, Spollen, McKay, Lancashire, & Tolbert, 1993; Gilberg & Coleman, 2000). However, there is limited research using double-blind randomized methodology and available studies include small samples sizes (Cartwright & Power, 2003; Pavonne & Ruggieri, 2005).

Many individuals with ASD have a limited repertoire of foods they eat because of food intolerances and allergies (Kidd, 2002). Thus, inclusion of vitamin supplements may be warranted to ensure appropriate nourishment. However, parents should understand that vitamins in large doses can be toxic. As with all supplements, natural or otherwise, parents should be advised to consult with their child's pediatrician or medical caregiver before beginning a new treatment.

Detoxification of Mercury (Chelation)

Some believe that exposure to heavy metals, such as mercury, early in development is a contributing cause to ASD (Kidd, 2002). Chelation, which has been used to treat individuals in cases of severe lead poisoning, introduces molecules that bond to specific metals in the body (Metz, Mulick, & Butter, 2007). However, the use of chelation to treat neurodevelopmental disorders such as ASD has not been approved by the FDA and has been associated with several deaths in adults (Cartwright & Power, 2003; Centers for Disease Control and Prevention, 2006).

Sensory-Integration Therapy

Although the effectiveness as an intervention for developmental disabilities is not supported by empirical research (Miller, Schoen, James, & Schaaf, 2007; Polatajko, Kaplan, & Wilson, 1992; see Smith, Mruzek, & Mozingo, 2007, for a review of this literature), sensory integration therapy is considered fairly mainstream within the educational and clinical communities. Sensory issues in the ASD population are well documented and many anecdotal and case reports speak to the importance of addressing these difficulties. Issues associated with sensory difficulties will be further addressed in Chapter 8.

CHAPTER REFLECTION: The Allure of Pseudoscience

Some advertised therapies to "treat" ASD are based on pseudoscience, which undermines the scientific process and often is rooted in ulterior motives such as personal gain. Because of the uncertainties associated with ASD and pervasive nature of the disorder, parents of children with ASD are often targets of those promoting therapies based on pseudoscience.

Pseudoscience falsely purports to be based on scientific principles. Appealing to emotions, basing claims on distrust/disbelief of established scientific evidence, avoiding testing its claims, and relying on subjective experience for validation raises the red flags of pseudoscience (Coker, retrieved December 19, 2009 from https://webspace.utexas.edu/cokerwr/www/index.html/distinguish.htm).

Application: *Perform a Web search for "treatments for autism" and choose an intervention with which you are unfamiliar. Using the criteria discussed above (more extensive criteria are available at the website listed above under "Science vs. Pseudoscience"), critique the treatment.*

The Future of CAM to Treat Children With ASD

There are many more CAMs available to parents than can be addressed in a short review. In the future some of interventions we consider to be "complementary and alternative" may become more mainstream and first-line treatment. Thus, the desire of parents to pursue CAMs and their beliefs about the effectiveness of these treatments should not be dismissed. However, making decisions about interventions based on empirical science should be the standard.

Teachers can assist parents in investigating research about treatments and evaluating the risk–benefit ratio associated with particular treatments. Teachers can be helpful in collecting information for parents about the behavior of the child at school, to assist in monitoring the effectiveness of a CAM. Jacobson, Foxx, and Mulick (2007) present a framework for helping parents make a "data-based decision" by setting up a simple experimental design. Teacher observations and behavioral ratings are particularly helpful if they are "blind" to when the treatment actually begins. However, it is often helpful for school personnel to be aware of any new treatment regiments (including diet changes) parents implement because they may impact learning.

TEACHING TIPS

• ASD is a neurobiological disorder that often is associated with atypical motor development. Consult with an Occupational Therapist regarding activities or environmental modifications that provide support for developing motor skills. Likewise, individuals with ASD often have unusual sensory interests, preferences, or aversions. Learn about each individual's preferences and aversions, and provide opportunities to engage in sensory activities (such as jumping on a trampoline, swinging on a swing) they find pleasurable. Furthermore, try to minimize and teach coping strategies to address sensory experiences considered aversive.

• Respect parents' beliefs about the cause of ASD for their child. Remember that collaboration is important to providing optimal support for the child, and collaboration is built on mutual trust. Affirm the parents right to express their beliefs, but assert the importance of choosing interventions based on empirical support (choosing *evidence-based practices* are further discussed in Chapters 6, 9, and 10).

• Assist parents in evaluating the effectiveness of medication or alternative treatments they have chosen to pursue by documenting performance, changes in behavior, and collecting frequent data about progress toward meeting individualized education program goals. Communicate to parents trends you find in your data, particularly with regard to changes observed since new treatments have been implemented by the parents or supports outside of the school.

SUMMARY

ASD is a neurobiological disorder that occurs early in development. Research indicates that ASD likely has a genetic basis. Converging evidence indicates a neurobiological origin of ASD, including twin and family studies, brain imaging research, and generic research. Parents have many different beliefs about the origin, or etiology, of their child's ASD. Although it is difficult to ascertain how a child came to have ASD, the beliefs parents hold about the etiology of ASD may impact their choice of interventions and willingness to collaborate with teachers. Assisting parents with identifying empirical research investigating interventions, respecting their beliefs about the cause of their child's ASD, and helping collect data about their child's behavior when new treatments are introduced contribute to a positive relationship that enables future collaborative efforts to support the child.

DISCUSSION AND REFLECTION QUESTIONS

1. How might genetic testing be used to better support families with young children who might have ASD? What are the potential risks of genetic testing?

2. Although brain scans are generally not used to diagnose ASD, how might they be used to better understand ASD and target educational supports?

3. Matthew is a 7-year-old with ASD. His parents are interested in trying a natural supplement they have heard will decrease behavioral outbursts. What advice might you give them as they grapple with this decision? Consider helping them make an informed decision, assisting in collaboration with other medical professionals, and helping parents collecting data to make informed decisions.

RECOMMENDED FURTHER READINGS AND INTERNET SOURCES

Further Readings

American Academy of Pediatrics, Council on School Health. (2009). Policy statement—Guidelines for the administration of medication in school. *Pediatrics, 124,* 1244–1251. Retrieved from http://www.pediatrics.org/cgi/content/full/124/4/1244.

Cohen, D., Sudhalter, V., Landon-Jimenez, D., & Keogh, M. A neural network approach to the classification of autism. *Journal of Autism and Developmental Disorders, 35,* 103–116.

Coleman, M. (Ed.). (2005). *The neurology of autism.* New York, NY: Oxford University Press.

Hollander, E. (Ed.). (2003). *Autism spectrum disorder.* New York, NY: Marcel Dekker.

Jacobson, J. W., Foxx, R. M., & Mulick, J. A. (2005). *Controversial therapies for developmental disabilities. Fad, fashion, and science in professional practice.* Mahwah, NJ: Lawrence Erlbaum Associates.

Many books are available that expand upon the theme of ASD as a biomedical disease first described by Bernard Rimland. Two noteworthy books parents are likely to read include *Healing the New Childhood Epidemics: Autism, ADHD, Asthma, and Allergies* by Kenneth Bock (2008), Ballantine Books, and *Changing the Course of Autism: A Scientific Approach for Parents and Physicians* by Bryan Jepson (2007), Sentient Publications.

Internet Sources

Autism Genome Project at http://www.autism genome.org/

Centers for Disease Control and Prevention. *Autism Spectrum Disorders* at http://www .cdc.gov/ncbddd/autism/research.html

Exploring Autism. *What Is Autism? Genetic Conditions Associated With Autistic Disorder* at http://www.exploringautism.org/autism/ evaluation.htm

Interagency Autism Coordinating Committee. *Strategic Plan for Autism Spectrum Disorder Research* at http://iacc.hhs.gov/strategic-plan

REFERENCES

Abrahams, B. S., & Geschwind, D. H. (2008). Advances in autism genetics: On the threshold of a new neurobiology. *National Review of Genetics, 9,* 341–355.

Aggleton, J. P., & Passingham, R. E. (1981). Syndrome produced by lesions of the amygdala in monkeys (*Macaca mulata*). *Journal of Comparative and Physiological Psychology, 95,* 961–977.

Akshoomoff, N., Pierce, K., & Courchesne, E. (2002). The neurobiological basis of autism from a developmental perspective. *Development and Psychopathology, 14,* 613–634.

Altevogt, B. M., Hanson, S. L., & Leshner, A. I. (2009). Autism and the environment: Challenges and opportunities for research. *Pediatrics, 121,* 1225–1229.

American Academy of Pediatrics, Council on School Health. (2009). Policy statement— Guidelines for the administration of medication in school. *Pediatrics, 124,* 1244–1251. Retrieved from http://www .pediatrics.org/cgi/content/full/124/4/1244.

Baron-Cohen, S., Ring, H. A., Bullmore, E. T., Wheelwright, S., Ashwin, C., & Williams, S. C. R. (2000). The amygdala theory of autism. *Neuroscience and Biobehavioral Review, 24,* 355–364.

Bauman, M. L., & Kemper, T. L. (2005). Neuroanatomic observations of the brain in autism: A review and future directions.

International Journal of Developmental Neuroscience, 23, 183–187.

Bauman, M., & Kemper, T. (1994). *The neurobiology of autism.* Baltimore, MD: Johns Hopkins University Press.

Bioscience Corporation. (2009). *Super array: Whole genome microarray vs. focused microarray.* Retrieved from http://www .sabiosciences.com/techsrc/microarray.html.

Bolton, P. F., Park, R., Higgins, N., Griffiths, P. D., & Pickles, A. (2002). Neuro-epileptic determinants of autism spectrum disorders in tuberous schlerosis complex. *Brain, 125,* 1247–1255.

Boucher, J. M. (2009). *The autistic spectrum: Characteristics, causes and practical issues.* Thousand Oaks, CA: Sage.

Cartwright, C., & Power, R. (2003). Alternative biological treatments for autism. In E. Hollander (Ed.), *Autism spectrum disorders* (pp. 347–367). New York, NY: Marcel Dekker.

Centers for Disease Control and Prevention. (2009). *Autism spectrum disorders.* Retrieved from http://www.cdc.gov/ncbddd/autism/research.html.

Chugani, D. C. (2002). Role of altered brain serotonin mechanisms in autism. *Molecular Psychiatry, 7*(Suppl 2), S16–S17.

Chugani, D. C., Muzik, O., Rothermel, R., Janisse, J. J., Lee, J., & Chugani, H. T. (1999). Developmental changes in brain serotonin synthesis in the dentatothalamocortical pathway in autistic boys. *Annals of Neurology, 42,* 666–669.

Coleman, M. (1994). Second trimester of gestation: A time of risk for classical autism? *Developmental Brain Dysfunction, 7,* 104–109.

Cartwright, C., & Power, R. (2003). Alternative biological treatments for autism. In E. Hollander (Ed.), *Autism spectrum disorders* (pp. 347–367). New York, NY: Marcel Dekker.

Centers for Disease Control and Prevention. (CDC). (2006, March). Deaths associated with hypocalcemia from chelation

therapy—Texas, Pennsylvania, and Oregon, 2003-2005. *Morbidity and Mortality Weekly Report, 55*(8). Retrieved from http://www.cdc.gov/mmwr/preview/mmwrhtml/mm5508a3.htm.

Cloud, J. (2010, January 6). Why your DNA isn't destiny. *Time.* Retrieved from http://www.time.com/time/magazine/article/0,9171,1952313,00.htm.

Courchesne, E., Carper, R., & Akshoomoff, N. (2003). Evidence of brain overgrowth in the first year of life in autism. *JAMA, 290,* 153–170.

Courchesne, E., Redclay, E., & Kennedy, D. P. (2004). The autistic brain: Birth through adulthood. *Current Opinion in Neurology, 17,* 489–496.

Davidovitch, M., Glick, L., Holtzman, G., Tirosh, E., & Safir, M. P. (2000). Developmental regression in autism: Maternal perception. *Journal of Autism and Developmental Disorders, 30,* 113–119.

DelGiudice, G., & Hollander, E. (2003). Immune dysfunction in autism. In E. Hollander (Ed.), *Autism spectrum disorders* (pp. 153–173). New York, NY: Marcel Dekker.

Doja, A., & Roberts, W. (2006). Immunizations and autism: A review of the literature. *Canadian Journal of Neurological Sciences, 33,* 341–346.

Dolske, M. C., Spollen, J., McKay, S., Lancashire, E., & Tolbert, L. (1993). A preliminary trial of ascorbic acid as supplementary therapy for autism. *Progress in Neuropsychopharmacology and Biological Psychiatry, 17,* 765–774.

Erickson, C. A., Stigler, K. A., Corkins, M. R., Pose, D. J., Fitzgerald, J. F., & McDougle, C. J. (2005). Gastrointestinal factors in autistic disorder: A critical review. *Journal of Autism and Developmental Disorders, 35,* 713–727.

Esch, B. E., & Carr, J. E. (2004). Secretin as a treatment for autism: A review of the evidence. *Journal of Autism and Developmental Disorders, 34,* 543–556.

Evers, M., Novotny, S., & Hollander, E. (2003). Autism and environmental toxins.

In E. Hollander (Ed.), *Autism spectrum disorders* (pp. 175–196). New York, NY: Marcel Dekker.

Findling, R. L. (2005). Pharmacologic treatment of behavioral symptoms in autism and pervasive developmental disorders. *Journal of Clinical Psychiatry, 66,* 26–31.

Fombonne, E. (2005). Epidemiology of autistic disorder and other pervasive developmental disorders. *Journal of Clinical Psychiatry, 66*(suppl 10), 3–8.

Fombonne, E., Zakarian, R., Bennett, A., Meng, L. Y., & McLean-Heywood, D. (2006). Pervasive developmental disorders in Montreal, Quebec, Canada: Prevalence and links with immunizations. *Pediatrics, 118,* 139–150.

Gadow, K. D., DeVincent, C., & Schneider, J. (2008). Predictors of psychiatric symptoms in children with an autism spectrum disorder. *Journal of Autism and Developmental Disorders, 38,* 1710–1720.

Gamer, M., & Büchel, C. (2009). Amygdala activation predicts gaze toward fearful eyes. *The Journal of Neuroscience, 29,* 9123–9126.

Gilberg, C., & Coleman, M. (2000). *The biology of autistic syndromes* (3rd ed.). Cambridge, UK: Cambridge University Press.

Goin-Kochel, R. P., & Myers, B. J. (2009). Congenital versus regressive onset of autism spectrum disorders: Parents' beliefs about causes. *Focus on Autism and Other Developmental Disabilities, 20,* 172–179.

Gregg, J. P, Lit, L., Baron, C. A., Hertz-Picciotto, I., Walker, W., Davis, R. A., Croen, L. A., Ozonoff, S., Hansen, R., Pessah, I. N., & Sharp, F. R. (2008). Gene expression changes in children with autism. *Genomics, 91,* 22–29.

Hardan, A., Pabalan, M., Gupta, N., Bansal, R., Melhem, N., Fedorov, S., Keshavan, M., & Minshew, N. (2009). Corpus callosom volume in children with autism. *Psychiatry Research: Neuroimaging Section, 174,* 57–61.

Hubbs-Tait, L., Nation, J. R., Krebs, N. F., & Bellinger, D. C. (2005). Neurotoxicants, micronutrients, and social environments. individual and combined effects on children's development. *Psychological Science in the Public Interest: A Supplement to Psychological Science, 6,* 57–120.

Kaminska, B., Czaja, M., Kozielska, E., Mazur, E., & Korzon, M. (2002). Use of secretin in treatment of childhood autism. *Medical Science Monitor, 8,* 22–26.

Kern, J. K., Espinoza, E., & Trivedi, M. H. (2004). The effectiveness of secretin in the management of autism. *Expert Opinion Pharmacotherapy, 5,* 379–387.

Kidd, P. M. (2002). Autism, an extreme challenge to integrative medicine. Part II: Medical management. *Alternative Medicine Review, 7,* 472–499.

Kolb, B., & Whishaw, I. Q. (1996). *Fundamentals of human neuropsychology* (4th ed.). New York, NY: W. H. Freeman.

Lainhart, J. E., Ozonoff, S., Coon, H., Krasny, L., Dinh, E., Nice, J., & McMahon, W. (2002). Autism, regression, and the broader autism phenotype. *American Journal of Medical Genetics, 113,* 231–237.

Leyfer, O. T., Folstein, S. E., Bacalman, S., Davis, N. O., Dinh, E., Morgan, J., . . . Lainhart, J. E. (2006). Comorbid psychiatric disorders in children with autism: Interview development and rates of disorders. *Journal of Autism and Developmental Disorders, 36,* 849–861.

Manning, M. A., Cassidy, S. B., Clericuzio, C., Cherry, A. M., Schwartz, S., Hudgins, L., Enns, G. M., & Hoyme, H. E. . (2004). Terminal 22q deletion syndrome: A newly recognized cause of speech and language disability in the autism spectrum. *Pediatrics, 114*(2), 451–457.

Mayo Foundation for Medical Education and Research. (2009, June 23). *Selective serotonin reuptake inhibitors (SSRIs)*. Retrieved from http://www.mayoclinic.com/health/ssris/MH00066.

McCarthy, A. M., Kelly, M. W., & Reed, D. (2000). Medication administration practices of school nurses. *Journal of School Health, 70,* 371–376.

McCarthy, J. (2007). *Louder than words: A mother's journal in healing autism.* New York, NY: Dutton.

McDougle, C. J., Stigler, K.A., & Posey, D. J. (2003). Treatment of aggression in children and adolescents with autism and conduct disorders. *Journal of Clinical Psychiatry,* 64(suppl 4), 16–25.

Metz, B., Mulick, J. A., & Butter, E. M. Autism: A late-20th century fad magnet. In J. W. Jacobson, R. M. Foxx, & J. A. Mulick (Eds.), *Controversial therapies for developmental disabilities: Fads fashions, and science in professional practice* (pp. 237–263). Mahwah, NJ: Lawrence Erlbaum Associates.

Miller, L. J., Schoen, S. A., James, K., & Schaaf, R. C. (2007). Lessons learned: A pilot study on occupational therapy effectiveness for children with sensory modulation disorder. *The American Journal of Occupational Therapy,* 61, 161–169.

Moussavand, S., & Findling, R. L. (2007). Recent advances in pharmacological treatment of pervasive developmental disorders. *Current Pediatric Reviews, 3,* 79–91.

National Academy of Sciences. (2004). *Immunization safety review: Vaccines and autism.* Washington, DC: The National Academies Press.

The National Fragile X Foundation. (2009). *Fragile X syndrome.* Retrieved from http://www.fragilex.org/fragile-x-associated-disorders/fragile-x-syndrome.

Novotny, S., & Hollander, E. (2003). Antidepressants and anticonvulsants/mood stabilizers in the treatment of autism. In E. Hollander (Ed.), *Autism spectrum disorders* (pp. 231–245). New York, NY: Marcel Dekker.

Oskardóttir, S., Vujic, M., & Fasth, A. (2004). Incidence and prevalence of the 22q11 deletion syndrome: A population-based study in western Sweden. *Archives of Diseases in Childhood, 89,* 148–151.

Palermo, M. T., & Curatolo, P. (2004). Pharmacologic treatment of autism. *Journal of Child Neurology, 9,* 155–164.

Passer, M. W., & Smith, R. E. (2004). *Psychology. The science of mind and behavior* (2nd ed.). New York, NY: McGraw Hill.

Patterson, P. H. (2009). Immune involvement in schizophrenia and autism: Etiology, pathology, and animal models. *Behavioural Brain Research, 204,* 313–321.

Pavonne, L., & Ruggieri, M. (2005). The problem of alternative therapies in autism. In M. Coleman (Ed.), *The neurology of autism* (pp. 173–200). New York, NY: Oxford University Press.

Piggot, J., Shirinyan, D., Shemmassian, S., Vazirian, S., & Alarcón, M. (2009). Neural systems approaches to the neurogenetics of autism spectrum disorders. *Neuroscience, 164,* 247–256.

Polatajko, H. J., Kaplan, B. J., & Wilson, B. N. (1992). Sensory integration treatment for children with learning disabilities: Its status 20 years later. *The Occupational Therapy Journal of Research, 12,* 323–341.

Rapin, I. (1998). Neurobiology of autism. *Annals of Neurology, 43,* 7–14.

Rapin, I. (2002). The autistic spectrum disorders. *New England Journal of Medicine, 347,* 302–303.

Read, S. G., & Rendall, M. (2007). An open-label study of risperidone in the improvement of quality of life and treatment of symptoms of violent and self-injurious behavior in adults with intellectual disabilities. *Journal of Applied Research in Intellectual Disabilities, 20,* 256–264.

Rice, C. (2007). Prevalence of autism spectrum disorders: Autism and developmental disabilities monitoring network, 14 sites, United States, 2002. *Morbidity and Mortality Weekly Report, 56,* 12–28.

Rimland, B. (2002). The use of vitamin B6, magnesium, and DMG in the treatment of autistic children and adults. In Shaw W. (Ed.), *Biological treatments for autism and PDD.* Lenexa, KS: The Great Plains Laboratory.

Rimland, B., Callaway, E., & Dreyfus, P. (1978). The effect of high doses of vitamin B6 on autistic children: A double-blind cross over study. *American Journal of Psychiatry, 135*, 472–475.

Rourke, B. P. (1998). Symposium: Asperger, Williams, and velocardiofacial syndromes: The NLD connection. *Clinical Neuropsychology, 12*, 266.

Ritvo, E. R., Freeman, B. J., Mason-Brothers, A., Mo, A., & Ritvo, A. M. (1985). Concordance for the syndrome of autism in 40 pairs of afflicted twins. *American Journal of Psychiatry, 142*, 74–77.

Rutter, M. (2005). Incidence of autism spectrum disorders: Changes over time and their meaning. *Acta Paediatrica, 94*, 2–15.

Rutter, M., Silberg, J., & Simonoff, E. (1999). Genetics and child psychiatry: II Empirical research findings. *Journal of Child Psychology and Psychiatry, 40*, 19–55.

Scahill, L. (2008). How do I decide whether or not to use medication for my child with autism? Should I try behavior therapy first? *Journal of Autism and Developmental Disorders, 38*, 1197–1198.

Scahill, L., & Martin, A. (2005). Psychopharmacology. In F. Volkmar, R. Paul, A. Klin, & D. Cohen (Eds.), *Handbook of autism and pervasive developmental disorders* (Vol. 2, 3rd ed., pp. 1102–1117). Hoboken, NJ: John Wiley & Sons.

Schaefer, G. B., & Mendelsohn, N. (2008). Clinical genetics evaluation in identifying the etiology of autism spectrum disorders. *Genetics in Medicine, 10*, 301–305.

Schanen, N. C. (2006). Epigenetics of autism spectrum disorders. *Human Molecular Genetics, 15*(2), 138–150.

Stanfield, A. C., McIntosh, A. M., Spencer, M. D., Philip, R., Gaur, S., & Lawrie, S. M. (2008). Towards a neuroanatomy of autism: A systematic review and meta-analysis of structural magnetic resonance imaging studies. *European Psychiatry, 23*, 289–299.

Smith, T., Mruzek, D. W., & Mozingo, D. (2007). Sensory integration therapy. In J. W. Jacobson, R. M. Foxx, & J. A. Mulick (Eds.), *Controversial therapies for developmental disabilities: Fad, fashion, and science in professional practice* (pp. 331–362). Mahwah, NJ: Lawrence Erlbaum Associates.

Spezio, M. L., Huang, P.Y., Castelli, F., & Adolphs, R. (2007). Amygdala damage impairs eye contact during conversations with real people. *The Journal of Neuroscience, 27*, 3994–3997.

Steyaert, J. G., & De La Marche, W. (2008). What's new in autism? *European Journal of Pediatrics, 167*, 1091–1101.

Sweeney, D. P., Forness, S. R., & Levitt, J. G. (1999). An overview of medications commonly used to treat behavioral disorders associated with autism, tourette syndrome, and pervasive developmental disorders. *Focus on Autism and Other Developmental Disabilities, 13*, 144–150.

Tiemeier, H., Lenroot, R. K., Greenstein, D. K., Tran, L., Pierson, R., & Giedd, J. N. (2010). Cerebellum development during childhood and adolescence: A longitudinal morphometric MRI study. *NeuroImage, 49*, 63–70.

Travis, J. (2001). The science of secretin. Will studies of rodent brains give new life to a controversial autism therapy? *Science News, 160*, 314–316.

Tsai, L. (1999). Psychopharmacology in autism. *Psychosomatic Medicine, 61*, 661–665.

Tsai, S. J. (2005). Is autism caused by early hyperactivity of brain-derived neurotrophic factor? *Medical Hypotheses, 65*, 79–82.

Tuchman, R. (2003). Treatment of seizures in children with autism spectrum disorders. In E. Hollander (Ed.), *Autism spectrum disorders* (pp. 265–272). New York. NY: Marcel Dekker.

Tuchman, R. (2004). AEDs and psychotropic drugs in children with autism and epilepsy. *Mental Retardation and Developmental Disabilities Research Reviews, 10*, 135–138.

Vickerstaff, S., Heriot, S., Wong, M., & Dossetor, D. (2007). Intellectual ability, self-perceived social competence, and depressive symptomatology in children with high-functioning autistic spectrum disorders. *Journal of Autism and Developmental Disorders, 37*, 1647–1664.

Volker, M. A., & Lopata, C. (2008). Autism: A review of biological bases, assessment, and intervention. *School Psychology Quarterly, 23*, 258–270.

Volkmar, F. R., & Nelson, D. S. (1990). Seizure disorders in autism. *Journal of the American Academy of Child and Adolescent Psychiatry, 29*, 127–129.

Vorstman, J. A., Morcus, M. E., Duijff, S. N., Klaassen, P. W., Heineman-de Boer, J. A., Beemer, F. A., . . . van Engeland, H. (2006). The 22q11.2 deletion in children: High rate of autistic disorders and early onset of psychotic symptoms. *Journal of the American Academy of Child and Adolescent Psychiatry, 45*(9), 1104–1113.

Wakefield, A. J., Puleston, J. M., Montgomery, S. M., Anthony, A., O'Leary, J. J., & Murch, S. H. (2002). Review article: The concept of entero-colonic encephalopathy, autism and opioid receptor ligands. *Ailmentary Pharmacology & Therapeutics, 16*, 443–674.

Weiss, L. A., Shen, Y., Korn, J. M., Arking, E., Miller, D. T., Ragnheidur F., . . . Daly, M. J. (2008). Association between microdeletion and microduplication at 16p11.2 and autism. *New England Journal of Medicine, 358*, 667–675.

West, L., Brunssen, S. H., & Waldrop, J. (2009). Review of the evidence for treatment of children with autism with selective serotonin reuptake inhibitors. *Journal for Specialists in Pediatric Nursing, 14*, 183–191.

West, L., & Waldrop, J. (2006). Risperidone use in the treatments for the core deficits and associated symptoms of autism in children. *Pediatric Nursing, 32*, 545–549.

Wiggins, L. D., Rice, C. E., & Baio, J. (2009). Developmental regression in children with an autism spectrum disorder identified by a population-based surveillance system. *Autism, 13*, 357–374.

Wing, L. (1992). Manifestations of social problems in high functioning autistic people. In E. Schopler & G. Mesibov (Eds.), *High-functioning individuals with autism* (pp. 129–142). New York, NY: Plenum Press.

Wong, F. (2005). Study of the relationship between tuberous sclerosis complex and autistic disorder. *Journal of Child Neurology, 21*, 199–204.

SECTION II

COLLABORATING WITH FAMILIES FOR DIAGNOSIS AND SETTING EDUCATIONAL GOALS

Section II, "Collaborating With Families for Diagnosis and Setting Educational Goals," begins with a discussion of sociocultural characteristics of families central to developing a collaborative relationship built on trust and mutual respect (Chapter 4). Chapter 5 discusses the process of data collection and appropriate assessments contributing to accurate diagnosis that informs educational planning. Chapter 6 highlights important issues integral to early intervention and the shared decision-making process in planning for educational success. Woven within each chapter are issues critical for partnering with families as part of a team to address educational and developmental concerns.

CHAPTER 4

COLLABORATING WITH AND SUPPORTING FAMILIES OF CHILDREN WITH ASD

In this chapter, you will learn about:

- Strategies for creating effective partnerships with families built on trust, collaboration, and authentic caring.
- The theoretical framework for understanding parent–teacher partnerships, including family systems theory, Bronfenbrenner's bioecological theory, and Vygotsky's social-cultural theory.
- Sociocultural characteristics of families and their children with ASD such as divorce, single-parent households, remarriage, and blended families.
- Factors contributing to a family-centered approach that builds on the strengths of families.
- Addressing the needs of siblings.

THE FAMILY AS A VALUABLE PARTNER

The Individuals with Disabilities Education Act (IDEA, 2004) mandates parent involvement in every phase of the special education process, including pre-referral, assessment, creating the educational plan, and monitoring progress. Parents of children with Autism Spectrum Disorder (ASD) are often assertive advocates who have overcome barriers to having their child identified as having ASD and have developed areas of expertise associated with ASD and their child (Stoner et al., 2005). The difficulty many parents report obtaining the initial diagnosis from medical professionals can impact their expectations about the teacher–parent relationship (Stoner et al.). Furthermore, ASD is a

Partnering with families requires establishing a relationship built on trust.

complex disorder with an unknown etiology that can add to the frustration parents often feel about understanding the disorder.

Partnering with families requires establishing a relationship built on trust. In addition, demonstrating competence, professionalism, and authentic caring require intentional skill development. Careful planning for conferences, inclusive practices during meetings, active listening skills, and conflict resolution skills are important for establishing trust and strengthening the family–school partnership.

An example of a promising practice for training teachers to collaborate with parents of children with ASD during educational planning is "the collaborative model for promoting competence and success" (COMPASS; Ruble, Dalrymple, & McGrew, 2010). COMPASS is a teacher training intervention that supports teachers consulting with parents to target three goals that have been identified as deficit areas during assessment. Teaching strategies are identified based on the outcome of the prioritized goals. In a study of 35 special education teachers of children with ASD, teachers trained in the COMPASS model had significantly better individualized education program (IEP) goal attainment of target objectives than teachers of children with ASD not trained in the model (Ruble et al.). Furthermore, high treatment fidelity was reported in the COMPASS-trained group.

Establishing Trust

Trust is the backbone of an effective family–school partnership (Angell, Stoner, & Sheldon, 2009; Hoy & Tschannen-Moran, 1990; Turnbull, Turnbull, & Wehmeyer, 2007). Although parents and educators may have different belief systems and expectations about the partnership, trust provides a framework to investigate differences and develop shared goals (Angell et al.). However, parents of children with ASD may enter into the teacher–parent relationship distrustful of school personnel (Marcus, Kunce, & Schopler, 2005). Often they have experienced barriers to obtaining a diagnosis accessing services for their child

(Stoner et al., 2005). Furthermore, a child with ASD often presents unique and significant stressors to all family members, particularly mothers (Kuhn & Carter, 2006). In particular, research suggests that mothers of children with ASD experience significant stressors related to the pervasive nature of the disorder, lack of information about interventions and the course of the disorder, and challenging behaviors sometimes associated with ASD (Osborne & Reed, 2009; Phetrasuwan & Miles, 2009). In fact, parents of children with ASD may experience greater levels of stress than parents of children with other developmental disabilities or special health care needs (Schieve, Blumberg, Rice, Visser, & Boyle, 2009).

Angell, Stoner, and Sheldon (2009) identify barriers to a trusting relationship as including a lack of perceived competence (teachers appearing to lack knowledge about their child's disability), a school climate lacking acceptance and warmth toward children with disabilities and their families, barriers to receiving services, and problems with the multidisciplinary team. An overarching component of establishing trust is ongoing and effective communication. Angell and colleagues state, "The importance of communication in the development of trust cannot be overemphasized" (p. 167). They describe effective communication as honest, frequent, and immediate (communicating emerging concerns immediately).

Table 4.1 Establishing Trust Within the Parent–School Partnership

- **Confidentiality**—Strive to maintain the family's confidentiality (Turnbull et al., 2007). Although personal family information can be important in documenting developmental history and other aspects of a child's functioning, be sure to honor a family's confidentiality to the greatest extent possible.
- **Reliability and Commitment**— Follow through with promises made to parents. Check to make sure that services and assessments have taken place within a reasonable time frame.
- **Communication**—Address problems as they arise, clearly clarify concerns and points made during interactions, practice good listening skills, and express yourself in a straightforward and candid manner (Angell et al., 2009; Hoy & Tschannen-Moran, 1990; Turnbull et al.).
- **Professional Competence**—Strive to learn about autism and interventions to address the child's identified needs. Investigate organizations, websites, books, or professionals with which you might consult or refer parent for additional information (Turnbull et al.). Parents perceive competent teachers as flexible and willing to try modifications or accommodations that may support their child (Angell et al.).

(Continued)

Table 4.1   (Continued)

- **Collaboration Within the School Team**—Trust in the school partnership is enhanced when parents perceive effective collaboration within the school multidisciplinary team (Angell et al.).
- **Equality and Respect**—Affirm that parents possess valuable knowledge and expertise about supporting their child (Angell et al.; Harte, 2009; Turnbull et al.). Make efforts to use inclusive language to encourage parents to voice concerns, contribute ideas, and share information.
- **Honor cultural differences**—Demonstrate sensitivity to cultural differences and reflect upon how the child's beliefs and values may differ from your own (Dyches, Wilder, Sudweeks, Oblakor, & Algozzine, 2004; Summers et al., 2005; Turnbull et al.).

Authentic Caring

Another significant component of trust is parents' perception that teachers demonstrate authentic caring. Angell and colleagues (2009) define authentic caring as "actions and behaviors that parents identified as genuine, voluntary, child focused, and benefitting children or the parents themselves" (p. 166). Parents perceive teachers as demonstrating authentic caring when teachers go beyond what is required by the system and treat their child as an individual.

THEORETICAL FRAMEWORK FOR FAMILY–EDUCATOR PARTNERSHIPS

As a teacher, understanding issues associated with families allows you to work more effectively with parents. Beliefs about child-rearing practices, disability, and interventions are a reflection of the family's cultural experience. Recognizing a belief as a cultural difference, rather than an attitude of indifference, allows the teacher to encourage parents to become more involved in their child's education.

Teachers are part of the interconnecting relationships of the child and the family. Let's consider three theories that address these complex relationships to facilitate the parent–teacher partnership.

Family Systems Theory

Each child in your class is part of a dynamic family system. All families are unique, and the characteristics of families change over time. Divorces, adoptions, births, deaths, and other transitions impact every member of the family. A child with ASD may place additional demands on parents. Recognizing the family as a system may help you identify resources or supports to alleviate stressors. Identifying supports for a sibling struggling academically, respite care so parents can have a date night, or a parent support group to help parents connect with social opportunities can have positive outcomes for the child sitting in your classroom.

Family systems theory was developed to explain the dynamic nature of the family (Minuchin, 1974; Satir, 1988). Family roles, boundaries and rules are components of the family system that can impact the parent–teacher relationship (Christian, 2006). Family systems theory helps explain how different family members may play certain roles. For instance, older siblings may serve as caretaker, a family member may serve as the peacemaker to negotiate conflict, or one parent may be more likely to interact with school personnel. The child with ASD has a family role as well. Their role is part of the intricate and fluid balance of the family system. Family roles are influenced by the culture in which the family lives or has lived.

Although the classroom teacher is not expected to play the role of a family therapist, understanding family systems theory provides a framework for conceptualizing the child within the family unit.

Some parents immediately express a willingness to collaborate with the school. Others seem to set up a barrier resisting collaboration. At times, closing boundaries can help families strengthen the family unit. Sometimes these

---

CHAPTER REFLECTION: Your Family System

When you were a child, did your parents ever change jobs, have to care for an ill family member, or go through a difficult time? Did you have a sibling who left home for college or needed extra support from your parents? Consider how stress placed on one member of your family impacted your own family system. Did family rules and individual roles become more pronounced and boundaries more closed, or was your family open to outside support?

boundaries help families unite and support each other. However, sometimes-closed boundaries prevent families from getting the support they need (Goldenberg & Goldenberg, 1996).

Hecimovic and Greogory (2005) describe characteristics for being an effective partner and support for families of children with ASD. These characteristics include respecting the uniqueness of the family system and communicating confidence in family members; praising families when they experience accomplishments; demonstrating empathy and sensitivity when working with families struggling to find appropriate interventions and meet goals; and being future-oriented and optimistic about the future. Overall, creating a family-centered support system is critical. Each member of the family, and the family system itself, impacts the development of the child with ASD. Likewise, the child with ASD impacts all members of the family. Consequently, supports that buffer the resiliency of the family system and its members facilitate the development of individuals with ASD (Symon, 2001). These supports can be introduced by outside systems, such as schools.

Supports to families can create opportunities for families to socialize and reduce isolation, attend meetings to participate in educational planning, and connect with advocacy groups to increase feeling empowered and optimistic. Integration of family–centered practices has been embedded into federal legislation guiding education of children with special needs.

Bronfenbrenner's Bioecological Theory

There are many other systems affecting the family. A framework for understanding these systems allows teachers a better understanding of the family and the interaction between family and school. The bioecological theory offers insight into developing special education interventions and strengthening the home-school partnership (Sontag, 1996). In fact, Bronfenbrenner advocated a family-centered approach to supporting children with special needs (Bronfenbrenner, 1975). Bronfenbrenner's bioecological systems theory (2004) describes nested levels in which the family system is nested, as depicted in Figure 4.1.

The level teachers might first consider is the microsystem, which involves day-to-day interactions. For example, a mother asks the teacher to work on independence in dressing at school. She describes morning battles involving picking out clothes and trying to get him to put them on. Her description of mother–son interaction is an example of a microsystem.

However, there is likely more to this story than meets the eye. Other systems may be impacting her concerns. For instance, difficulties getting dressed in the morning have resulted in the child being late to school many mornings. After

Figure 4.1   Bronfenbrenner's Bioecological Systems Theory

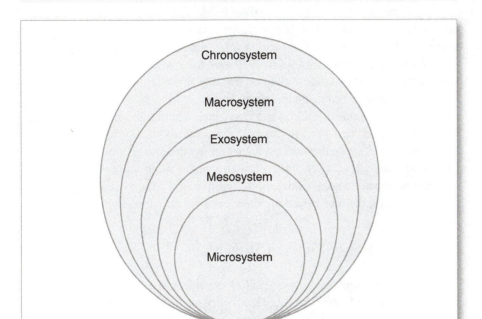

several weeks of this, the school contacts the mother to let her know that her son has been excessively tardy to school. They inform her that if this pattern continues they will make a referral to social services. This relationship between the mother and the school represents a mesosystem, which is a relationship between microsystems (school and family). The school–family mesosystem impacts the urgency she feels in addressing her son's compliance and independence with getting dressed. If the teacher understood this additional level, she could speak with the principal and ask for some leniency as they worked together on the shared goal of increasing dressing behaviors in the morning routine.

Furthermore, recent changes in the father's employment require him to travel more frequently. Thus, the father is now less available to help in the morning. The father's work is an example of an exosystem, or social setting not immediately impacting the child but influencing relationships. This additional information helps explain why the mother had not brought up these concerns earlier in the school year and why they are so pressing now.

In public schools, federal financial support is directly tied to student attendance. In these tough economic times, schools may feel pressure to come down hard on excessive absences and tardiness. In this case, the school's reaction to a child being tardy to school is influenced by a macrosystem, which is an institution or aspect of the greater culture that influences the microsystem. Helping the parents understand why the school is threatening to refer them to social services might ease feelings of persecution or distrust, and encourage the parents to meet with the principal to talk about this problem and set realistic goals. For instance, it might be acceptable to allow the child to come to school by 9:00 a.m. for 2 weeks while the teacher and parents work together with the child on dressing skills.

The last system in Bronfenbrenner's theory is the chronosystem, which describes the impact of sociohistorical changes over time. The mother may have become increasingly aware that parents can raise concerns about her child's educational goals because of increased awareness from autism advocacy groups and changes in special education laws over time. Furthermore, it is currently recognized that autism is a neurobiological disorder and that parents do not cause their child to have ASD. Thus, the time period in which one lives also impacts family decisions.

Vygotsky's Social-Cultural Theory

Vygotsky's social-cultural theory (1962) considers the impact of culture on learning and overall development. This theory has gained increasing popularity in education because, unlike many other theories of learning and development, it takes into account the cultural context of learning. Vygotsky (1962) believed that learning takes place within the context of relationships. Cultural tools for transmitting knowledge, such as writing, mathematics, music, and storytelling, are passed down through generations.

Vygotsky believed that learning is most effective when it takes place within a child's zone of proximal development. This zone captures a point at which the child can almost master a skill alone, but still requires some support. Adults who know the child well can scaffold an activity so that support is slowly reduced as the child gets closer to mastery (Rogoff, 1990). This is a useful concept for developing educational goals.

You might wonder if such a theory applies to a child who has weaknesses in social communication and low motivation for engaging in social relationships. Although children with ASD might not learn the same as other children, they are still impacted by the culture in which they live. For instance, the sequence of behaviors embedded in morning routines is intricately related to culture (get dressed, eat breakfast, brush teeth). An adult who knows a child's preferences and skill level is able to enhance learning by creating mediated learning opportunities. In fact, some interventions developed for children with ASD are based on social-cultural theory, such as floortime and other play-based therapies (Greenspan & Wieder, 1998; discussed in Chapter 10).

An awareness of how a child plays and how parents interact with the child during play can facilitate learning in the classroom. For instance, in a survey of 748 parents of children with ASD conducted by the National Autistic Society (2007), parents reported gains in basic academic skills when Thomas the Train pictures, toys, and stories were used to teach concepts such as colors and numbers. Parents reported using Thomas & Friends to develop language, social skills, and emotional regulation. Parents also provided mediated learning experiences to help their children with ASD develop parallel play (side-by-side play) with siblings using Thomas trains.

CHAPTER REFLECTION: Sandra Humphreys, a Parent-to-Parent Leader

Sandra is a Navigator Team Leader for her county. The statewide Navigator Team Project is managed by Parent to Parent of Georgia, the state's Parent Training and Information Center that is a federally funded program authorized under part D of IDEA. Sandra and her team have helped develop programs that provide monthly support meetings for parents of children with ASD and other disabilities, group outings for families, recreational programming such as "Challenger Sports" for children with special needs, and hosted trainings for families navigating the public school system's special education programs. She now works with Parent to Parent developing new teams in other counties throughout the state.

Author: *How did you get involved with Parent to Parent?*

Sandra: I began just advocating for my own daughter. When I retired, my daughter was 8, and I wanted to volunteer somewhere. I had been that isolated mom, focusing all my attention around my daughter, Emmie. Now I work systematically to help all children, which also helps my daughter. By volunteering my time to lead a Navigator Team, I have learned even the smallest effort can make big differences for many children.

Author: *What are some of the concerns that parents express at the monthly brainstorming meetings?*

Sandra: Our earliest goals were to address core issues such as the need for child care, recreation for our kids in the community, social needs of families and children, and parent educators to help understand

(Continued)

(Continued)

special education routines and laws. The top three goals continue to be (1) recreation, (2) socialization, and (3) education.

Author: *Describe the challenges you face in your role as leader of this parent-led support program?*

Sandra: Getting the word out to families that we are here and gaining their trust. It has been most difficult involving our underserved populations in the community. We would like to find a Spanish-speaking outreach worker and to have more African American families participate in our program.

Author: *What advice could you give to teachers working with parents?*

Sandra: When a parent speaks up with a question or comment, it is probably a bigger deal than you think! Many parents are afraid to voice their concerns or questions, so really pay attention to what they are asking or saying. Encourage parents to keep a journal of changes in medical or therapy regiments and to give all service providers a copy of the summary. Parents don't always know how to be good historians, and those working with their children often depend on them for background information. Encourage parents to attend support groups or workshops or join Navigator Team and become active in making changes that will support their child.

SOCIOCULTURAL CHARACTERISTICS OF FAMILIES AND THEIR CHILDREN WITH ASD

The Impact of ASD on the Family System

Children with ASD are not only students in a classroom, but members of a family. Every family is different, and understanding the sociocultural characteristics of a family is important in effectively collaborating with parents. Both family systems theory and Bronfenbrenner's theories predict that difficulties experienced by one member of the family will impact the entire family system.

There is a significant body of research describing high stress levels of families that have children with special needs, particularly when families include children with ASD. In fact, families of children with ASD appear to experience a greater degree of stress than families of children with other types of special needs (Bouma & Schweitzer, 1990; Higgins, Bailey, & Pearce, 2005; Weiss, 2002). There are likely many factors contributing to this high level of family stress associated with ASD, including difficulties getting the initial diagnosis, lack of consensus about the cause and prognosis, uneven profile of skills, pervasive nature of the disorder, tremendous out-of-pocket expenses for treatment, and lack of integrated support services to address ASD.

There is a significant body of research describing high stress levels of families that have children with special needs, particularly when families include children with ASD. The many demands placed on families are exacerbated by lack of resources.

When extra demands are placed on parents, multiple systems are impacted within and outside the family. Sometimes the stresses associated with raising a child with ASD interact with other characteristics of the spousal relationship resulting in marital discord. Marital discord is common in all types of families, but is exacerbated by additional stress to the family system. As parents have less time to devote to each other and themselves, issues such as family roles, resource limitations, and frustration are heightened.

Families of Divorce

The rate of divorce among families with children with ASD is not clear (Freedman et al., 2010; Hartley et al., 2010). Regardless of the frequency, marital stress and divorce introduces significant changes into all members of the family at many different levels (Rivers & Stoneman, 2003). Family changes associated with divorce may be particularly confusing and disturbing to a child with ASD. It is important that parents are able to put aside their differences to coparent and negotiate what is best for the children. For instance, visitation routines need to be strictly followed to introduce a level of predictability and stability into the noncustodial parent–child relationship. Likewise, a predictable pattern of activities during scheduled visitation may help provide comfort and smooth the transition.

Single-Parent Households

Children with disabilities more likely to live in single-parent household, primarily raised by their mother (Fujiura & Yamaki, 2000). Single-mother households, in particular, are more likely to live in poverty than other types of households (Fields, 2003). Most often, when parents divorce, the mother ends up with custody of the children. When families divorce, financial and emotional resources for addressing family needs are often significantly reduced (Boyd & Bee, 2010). In fact, in single-mother households the family income drops an average of 40% to 50% following a divorce (Bradbury & Katz, 2002).

When raising a child with ASD, cohabitating parents often decide to embrace traditional division of labor roles to address the intense caregiving responsibilities (Gray, 2002). Mothers returning to work following a divorce may find child care difficult to coordinate. Children with ASD may require specialized child care, which tends to be both expensive and difficult to find (Parish et al., 2008). Even mothers working prior to a divorce are likely to experience additional child care needs following divorce. Fathers with child custody are likely to experience similar difficulties. Often, single-parent families rely on extended family, particularly grandparents, for support with child care. Teachers can encourage the custodial parent to involve extended family members playing a key role in the child's care in educational meetings and planning.

Remarriage and Blended Families

Some parents decide to remarry. These new blended families introduce stepparents and sometimes stepsiblings into the family. With so many changes introduced into the family, all the children are likely to need extra time with their biological parents and extra patience and love as they adjust to their new family. These changes are likely to be especially hard for a child with ASD. Social stories might be a helpful strategy for creating a scripted, visual, and concrete story explaining the sequence of events that take place in the new family environment (social stories are discussed in Chapter 10). Consultation with the custodian parent would be helpful in capturing the routines altered by the new family such as dinnertime, bedtime, and getting ready for school in the morning. Teachers may consider asking the custodial parent if the stepparent might be included in meetings and goal planning. In any case, teachers should encourage stepparents to contact the school if they have specific questions about ASD.

The addition of stepsiblings provides increased opportunity for socialization. However, stepsiblings need to be provided with age-appropriate information about ASD, and rules about engagement for play, sharing personal items, arrangement of things in the house, and so on. Parents might be encouraged to lay down ground rules about how to prevent and address challenging behaviors for the family. It is especially important that a typically developing sibling (sibling without ASD) not be thrust into the position of caretaker and defender of her sibling with ASD. Siblings may find support from a sibling group for biological siblings and stepsiblings through local autism support chapters. Supports for siblings are discussed more later in the chapter.

There are many other types of family arrangements, and every family is unique. Taking time to understand the unique issues and changing dynamics of a child's family will help you better support the child in the classroom. Table 4.2 provides tips for working with all types of families experiencing transition or hardship.

Table 4.2 Supporting Children With ASD and Their Families During Significant Transitions

Sensitivity and support for the child with ASD in the classroom
Children in your classroom may need a "grace period" when these new transition occur, with somewhat lowered expectations.
Divorce or remarriage of parents may negatively impact the ability to focus and perform in the classroom setting for any child. However, the classroom routines are likely to be the one place of consistency in the child's life. Thus, a sensitive approach to continuing with educational goals is desired.
Social stories may be helpful in providing structure for understanding new home routines such as visiting the noncustodial parents or getting ready for school without the help of the other parent. Social stories are discussed in Chapter 10.
A functional behavior assessment (FBA) may also be helpful in determining what triggers new challenging behaviors, and the consequences of the behaviors to create behavior plans that helps the child manage behavioral difficulties at school. The FBA and related behavior management strategies are discussed in more detail in Chapter 7.

(Continued)

Table 4.2 (Continued)

Communication with both parents
Keep the channels of communication between school and parents open for both parents.
If one parent has sole custody of the child, request permission from that parent to communicate with the noncustodial parent. Include both parents in meetings and decision making when appropriate.
Share information about parent support groups so parents do not feel alone.
Be a resource for information by recommending books, websites, workshops, and referrals to other agencies for support.
Supports for siblings and stepsiblings
Assist parents in locating siblings support groups.
Help parents identify age-appropriate information about ASD for new stepsiblings.
With parent permission, consult with the siblings' classroom teachers to help them be aware of the new family transition and possible need for emotional support.
Financial issues
Single parents often experience a reduction in family income following a divorce. This can be especially devastating for a single mother who had been a stay-at-home mother to devote energy to the demands of child care. Teachers can be helpful in providing information about financial supports for which she may be eligible.
The school social worker is a good resource for helping parents understand how to apply for resources such as Medicaid, state children's health insurance programs, Supplemental Security Income (SSI), and Social Security Disability Income (SSDI).
The National Autism Association's Family First program offers resources for families experiencing marital stress, including small grants for marriage therapy.
The Helping Hands program of the National Autism Association also offers financial support to help defray costs of interventions for children with ASD for families experiencing significant financial hardship.
There may be additional sources within your state or local community. Local autism support groups may have more information about these supports.
Respite care
Encourage parents to learn about available **respite care** (a short-term child care service) and take advantage of it. They will be better parents to all of their children when they are able to take care of themselves and nurture other relationships.
Finding respite care can be time consuming and may not all meet the needs of the family. However, encourage parents to investigate available resources. Look for services that offer flexibility.
The United Cerebral Palsy association offers a "Respitality" program that includes families with children who have developmental disabilities. The Respitality program offers respite care as well as hospitality support, such as a 24-hour getaway, including hotel and meals donated by local businesses in the community. Availability of the Respitality program likely differs from state to state, but it is worth looking into!

What can the teacher do to help?

Generally teachers are not trained family therapist and should not work outside their boundaries of knowledge or training. However, recognition of a significant family transition that has taken place and empathy for the ramifications of these transitions can go a long way. The following are suggestions for supporting children and families that have had significant family transitions.

EMPOWERING FAMILIES OF CHILDREN WITH ASD

There is much research documenting the profound degree of caregiver stress associated with parenting a child with ASD (i.e., Gray, 2005; Hastings et al., 2005; Phelps, McCammon, Wuensch, & Golden, 2009). In fact, research indicates that caregivers of children with ASD experience greater degrees of stress than parents caring for children with other types of disabilities (Abbeduto et al., 2004; Grey, 2002; Schieve et al., 2007). However, despite experiencing a significant degree of caregiver stress, families have unique strengths that can be highlighted and integrated into educational planning. Identifying and building on family strengths and coping mechanisms can also be used to help parents cope with stress associated with caring for their child with ASD (Pottie & Ingram, 2008; Schieve et al.). When parents are empowered to cope with stress, identify their child's needs, and collaborate to plan for their child's education, there are significant benefits to the child's overall development (Dunst, 2002).

Recognizing and Building on Strengths in the Family System

Extended family and friends

Although grandparents may not fully understand ASD, often they offer unconditional love, assist with child care, and provide empathy and friendship (Hillman, 2007; O'Brien & Daggert, 2006).

However, intergenerational conflicts sometimes arise when grandparents draw upon biases about people with disabilities that existed during

Grandparents are often a source of support and guidance for families. These supports can mitigate stressors associated with caring for the needs of a child with ASD.

their youth (O'Brien & Daggert, 2006). Grandparents may lack knowledge about the diagnosis and symptoms of ASD (Margetts, Le Courteur, & Croom, 2006; Sandler, 1998). Furthermore, grandparents and other extended family may not fully understand the emotional and physical toll that caring for a child with ASD has upon the entire nuclear family (Hillman, 2007). When grandparents are integrated into school activities, meetings, planning sessions, and information/training opportunities, they can provide invaluable supports for the child with ASD and the entire family.

In some instances, grandparents are the primary caregivers. Grandparents caring for a child with ASD may need extra support from the school and community. Financial limitations, difficulty accessing necessary supports, and considerations of who will care for their grandchild when they die have been identified as concerns of grandparents caring for children with disabilities (Janicky, McCallion, Grant-Griffin, & Kolomer, 2000).

Spirituality and the family's religious community

Although public schools have the responsibility of separating matters of religion from public education, it can be helpful to recognize the support and strength some parents associate with their religion and religious community. Research indicates that some individuals find comfort in embracing their religion and spiritual practices during times of stress (Graham, Furr, Flowers, & Burke, 2001). In a study of 119 mothers of children with ASD, greater levels of maternal religious belief were associated with positive coping skill such as a higher self-esteem and a more optimistic life perspective (Ekas, Whitman, & Shivers, 2009). Furthermore, in a survey about the role of religion in families of children with autism, 66% of families reported personal prayer as a means of expressing their beliefs and seeking comfort (Coulthard & Fitzgerald, 1999). Some parents report experiencing a heightened sense of spirituality resulting from learning to cope with the day-to-day struggles associated with caring for their child with ASD (Ekas et al.).

Siblings

There is conflicting research regarding the effect of growing up with a sibling with ASD (Quintero & McIntyre, 2010; Rivers & Stoneman, 2003). However, sibling relationships are likely to impact all siblings in significant ways.

Typically developing siblings provide many benefits to their siblings with ASD. Siblings provide rich experiences with social interactions, model appropriate behaviors associated with play, provide companionship, and give opportunities to practice sharing (McHale, Sloan, & Simeonsson, 1986; Turnbull et al., 2006). In addition, siblings are likely to participate in some aspects of care for their sibling with ASD, with caregiving increasing as they age (Turnbull et al.). Siblings may act as a protector outside the home (Donnelly et al., 2000) and may provide their sibling with ASD inclusive social opportunities within the community to which they might not otherwise have access. Siblings may even take on the role of primary caregiver for their sibling with severe ASD when parents are no longer able to do so (Quintero & McIntyre, 2010).

Siblings of children with ASD often benefit from support to address conflicting feelings and emotions they may have about their sibling with ASD.

The impact of having a sibling with ASD on the typically developing sibling is complex and dependent on many factors, including severity of the ASD, individual characteristics, family supports, and degree of marital conflict between parents (Ferraioli & Harris, 2010).

Living with a sibling with ASD may promote development of interpersonal skills, nurturing skills (Howlin & Yates, 1990), and positive self-concept (Macks & Reeve, 2007). Furthermore, these early experiences may contribute to a desire to help others overcome adversity reflected in future career choices (Ferraioli & Harris, 2010). Siblings of children with ASD may also feel like a valued member of the family, as they are counted on to perform certain care duties for their siblings.

However, these positive experiences may come at a cost. Siblings of children with ASD may receive less parental attention and other family resources that are concentrated to meet the demands of caring for the sibling with ASD (Pilowsky, Yirmiya, Doppelt, Gross-Tsur, & Shalev, 2004) and may be exposed to significant levels of family stress (Henderson & Vanderberg, 1992). As they approach adolescence and increasingly value conformity to their peer groups, siblings of children with ASD may be embarrassed by the unusual behavior of their sibling and resent not being able to have friends spend the night or join in family activities (Ferraioli & Harris, 2010). In addition, they may feel burdened by caregiving demands and worry about how they might continue to care for their sibling when their parents are gone.

Addressing Needs of Siblings of Children With ASD

Age-appropriate education and information about ASD

It is important to recognize each sibling as a unique individual with strengths as well as needs (O'Brien & Daggert, 2006). Sometimes siblings of children with ASD lack information or have misinformation about their sibling's behaviors, the cause of ASD, and other aspects of ASD. For instance, young children may not understand the stereotyped and repetitive behaviors, and may become frustrated when they are rejected during play (Ferraioli & Harris, 2010). Likewise, opportunities to learn effective means of communication and social engagement with their siblings with ASD can help empower typically developing siblings (O'Brien & Daggert).

Social Support

Another source of sibling stress is feeling alienated from peers who they may perceive as not understanding the day-to-day experience of living with a sibling with ASD (Kaminsky & Dewey, 2002). Social support is important for all members of the family. Family support groups can help connect children and teens with peers who understand what it is like to have a sibling with ASD. The "Chapter Reflection: Sib Shops" box describes a program that connects children with siblings who have developmental disabilities with social support.

CHAPTER REFLECTION: Sib Shops

Sib Shops, created by Don Meyers and conducted all over the country, provide a forum for siblings of children with disabilities to connect with their peers and discuss meaningful topics such as feeling embarrassed by a sibling's behaviors and concerns about their sibling's long-term care needs. These events are described as fun programs that include games, cooking, and other recreational activities where kids can socialize with peers who also have siblings with disabilities. In addition, Sib Shops help parents and teachers better understand the needs of children and adolescents who have siblings with disabilities.

For more information, visit Sibling Support Project website at www.siblingsupport .org.

Quality Time With Parents

Although it is important to include siblings with ASD in family activities, at times typically developing siblings may need some time alone with their parents. Respite care can allow parents to attend special events with their typically developing peer, without concerns about drawing attention away from their special day. Making time to focus on each child's needs is important to the entire family system.

PARTNERING WITH FAMILIES FROM DIVERSE ETHNIC BACKGROUNDS

Every family should be considered as a unique system with individual strengths and needs. Thus, we must be careful to not stereotype families or family members based on ethnicity. However, families from cultural backgrounds different from the majority culture share some characteristics (Greder & Allen, 2007).

Table 4.4 highlights some important points to consider when working with families from diverse ethnic backgrounds. Educators are encouraged to learn as much as possible about individual families and their culture when partnering to support children.

Aspects of parenting beliefs and beliefs about disability are influenced by culture. For instance, families from collectivist orientations (such as many Latino and Asian cultures) may be less interested in independent skills, such as

Table 4.3 Tips for Helping Parents Support Their Typically Developing Child

- Teach parents how to introduce topics such as feeling embarrassed about their sibling's behavior or concerns about protecting their sibling.
- Help the child feel secure and safe.
- Accept fears, anger, and frustrations as natural. Offer unconditional love and make time to spend with each child.
- Emphasize that each child's needs are important and each child is an individual.
- Make sure caregiving demands of typically developing child for child with ASD are age appropriate and not overwhelming.

Adapted from O'Brien and Daggert (2006).

Table 4.4   Working Families From Diverse Backgrounds

- Recognize that families from cultural minorities straddle two worlds (known as biculturalism). They are members of their communities, yet retain a cultural identity that may not be understood or valued by the majority culture (Dauphinais, Charley, Robinson-Zañartu, Melroe, & Baas, 2009).
- Reflect upon the impact of historical power inequities. Institutionalized racism and inequity are a real part of family memories for many families from ethnic minority backgrounds (Blue-Banning et al., 2000; Harry, 1992). What appears to be disinterest in collaborating with the school, may actually be distrust of institutions, such as schools (Harry, 1992).
- Strive to understand roles of family members and extended family. Parents may defer to elders in the family, such as grandparents, in making important decisions.
- Make extra efforts to provide information in a language parents can understand. Inquire about literacy needs in private, rather than during conferences with a group of people. Parents cannot fully participate as partners in supporting their child if they do not have access to information (Klinger & Harry, 2006). Likewise, parents need to be able to communicate their questions, concerns, and wishes to the educational team.

dressing oneself, and more interested in their child following appropriate social protocols in public settings or being accepted by their family (Blue-Banning, Turnbull, & Pereira, 2002). These factors should be taken into consideration during educational planning.

SUMMARY

The family is a valuable partner working with educators and other team members to set goals, evaluate functioning, choose interventions, and plan for transitions. Establishing trust is key to creating and maintaining an effective family–school partnership. Trust is developed through ensuring confidentiality, being reliable and committed to following through with promises, engaging in good communication, demonstrating professional competence, integrating resources from the school team, treating parents equally and with respect, and honoring cultural differences. The family systems theory, Bronfenbrenner's bioecological, and Vygotsky's sociocultural theories provide theoretical framework for creating family-centered supports.

Teachers should learn about the family system to the extent possible. Characteristics such as low income, being a speaker of English as a second language, single-parent households, remarriage, and being a cultural or ethnic minority can place additional stressors on the family. Families that have children with special needs, particularly ASD, may benefit from information in obtaining supports for siblings, information about financial supports, and respite care (including after school and summer). Educators are encouraged to learn as much as possible about the culture of families when partnering to support their child.

TEACHING TIPS

• Incorporate a means of personal reflection into your weekly practice as an educator. For instance, in a journal consider the extent to which you were able to work toward building trust with the parents of children you support. Set goals for areas you need to strengthen, such as carrying through with promises made to families, effective communication with parents, professional competence (are there areas in which you could use additional training?), collaborating with the school team, demonstrating affirmation and respect for beliefs and preferences of parents, and honoring cultural differences.

• Work toward understanding the roles of family members and extended family. Make sure parents understand that they are welcome to invite extended family or friends to participate in IEP meetings and discussions.

• Determine if a parent requires information in a language other than English, or is unable to read, prior to a formal meeting such as an IEP. To the extent possible, ensure that parents have access to information about their child's progress, special education procedures, and so on, in the language and medium they can access.

DISCUSSION AND REFLECTION QUESTIONS

1. How might you work toward building a partnership built on trust with parents who had a bad experience working with their child's previous teacher?

2. When you talk with the child's previous teacher, she informs you that the parents are angry and argumentative during meetings. She feels that the parents blame the school for their child's ASD. Consider what you might do in preparing for the conference to help the parents feel included and prepared for the meeting? What steps can you take during the meeting to diffuse conflict and address parental concerns, while also meeting the goals of the meeting? Finally, how can you follow up with parental concerns and issues raised during the meeting to continue to build parental trust?

3. You have a child in your class with a sibling with ASD. This child is academically successful, yet seems socially withdrawn. How might you go about providing support for the sibling and linking resources with the family?

RECOMMENDED FURTHER READINGS AND INTERNET SOURCES

Further Readings

Carter, E. (2007). *Including people with disabilities in faith communities: A guide for service providers, families, and congregations.* Towson, MD: Paul H. Brookes.

Turnbull, A., Turnbull, R., Erwin, E., & Soodak, L. (2006). *Families, professionals, and exceptionality. positive outcomes through partnership and trust* (5th ed.). Upper Saddle River, NJ: Pearson Prentice Hall.

Internet Sources

Family Support America—Provides resources and links to programs that are family-centered. http://www.familysupportamerica .org

National Center for Culturally Responsive Educational Systems. www.nccrest.org/publications/ briefs.html

About.com: Autism—Provides websites linking resources about including people with autism in religious services within several different faiths. http://autism.about.com/od/coping withautism/p/spirituality.htm

Sibling Support Project. http://www.sibling support.org

REFERENCES

Abbeduto, L., Seltzer, M. M., Shattuck, P., Krauss, M. W., Orsmond, G., & Murphy, M. M. (2004). Psychological well being and coping in mothers of youths with autism, Down syndrome, or fragile X syndrome. *American Journal on Mental Retardation, 109,* 237–254.

Angell, M. E., Stoner, J. B., & Shelden, D. L. (2009). Trust in education professionals: Perspectives of mothers of children with disabilities. *Remedial and Special Education, 30,* 160–176.

Blue-Banning, M. J., Turnbull, A. P., & Pereira, L. (2000). Group action planning as a support strategy for Hispanic families: Parent and professional perspectives. *Mental Retardation, 38,* 262–275.

Blue-Banning, M. J., Turnbull, A. P., & Pereira, L. (2002). Hispanic youth/young adults with disabilities: Parents' visions for the future. *Research & Practice for Persons with Severe Disabilities, 27,* 204–219.

Bouma, R., & Schweitzer, R. (1990). The impact of chronic childhood illness on family stress: A comparison between autism and cystic fibrosis. *Journal of Clinical Psychology, 46,* 722–730.

Boyd, H., & Bee, D. (2010). *Developing child* (12th ed.). Boston, MA: Pearson.

Bradbury, K., & Katz, J. (2002). Are lifetime incomes growing more unequal? Looking at new evidence on family income mobility. *Regional Review 12,* 2–5.

Bronfenbrenner, U. (1975). *Influences on human development.* New York, NY: Holt.

Bronfenbrenner, U. (2004). *Making human beings human: Bioecological perspectives on human development.* Thousand Oaks, CA: Sage.

Coulthard, P., & Fitzgerald, M. (1999). God we trust? Organised religion and personal beliefs as resources and coping strategies, and their implications for health in parents with a child on the autistic spectrum. *Mental Health Religion and Culture, 2,* 19–33.

Christian, L. G. (January, 2006).Understanding families: Applying family systems theory to early childhood practice. *Beyond the Journal. Young Children on the Web.* Retrieved from http://www.naeyc.org/files/yc/file/200601/ChristianBTJ.pdf.

Dauphinais, P., Charley, E., Robinson-Zañartu, Melroe, O., & Baas, S. (2009). Home-school-community communication with indigenous american families. *Communiqué, 37,* 1–6.

Donnelly, J. A., Bovee, J., Donnelly, S. J., Donnelly, J. R., Donnelly, L. K., Donnelly, J. R., ... Callaghan, M. R. (2000). A family account of autism: Life with Jean-Paul. *Focus on Autism and Other Developmental Disabilities, 15,*196–201.

Dunst, C.J. (2002). Family centered practices: Birth through high school. *Journal of Special Education, 36,* 139–147.

Dyches, T. T., Wilder, L. K., Sudweeks, R. R., Oblakor, F. O., & Algozzine, B. (2004). Multicultural issues in autism. *Journal of Autism and Developmental Disorders, 34,* 211–222.

Ekas, N. V, Whitman, T. L., & Shivers, C. (2009). Religiosity, spirituality, and socioemotional functioning in mothers of children with autism spectrum disorder. *Journal of Autism and Developmental Disorders, 39,* 706–719.

Ferraioli, S. J., & Harris, S. (2010). The impact of autism on siblings. *Social Work in Mental Health, 8,* 41–53.

Fields, J. (2003). *America's families and living arrangements: 2003.* Current Population Reports, P20-553. Washington, DC: U.S. Census Bureau.

Freedman, B. H., Kalb, L., Zablotsky, B., & Stuart, E. (2010). *Relationship status among parents of children with autism spectrum disorders: A population-based study.* Paper presented at the International Meeting for Autism Research, Baltimore, MD.

Fujiura, G., & Yamaki, K. (2000). Trends in demography of childhood poverty and disability. *Exceptional Children, 66,* 187–199.

Goldenberg, I., & Goldenberg, H. (1996). *Family therapy: An overview* (5th ed.). Monterey, CA: Brookes.

Graham, S., Furr, S., Flowers, C., & Burke, M. T. (2001). Religion and spiritual beliefs in coping with stress. *Counseling and Values, 46,* 2–13.

Gray, D. E. (2002). Ten years on: A longitudinal study of families of children with autism. *Journal of Intellectual & Developmental Disability, 27,* 215–222.

Greder, K. A., & Allen, W. D. (2007). Parenting in color. Perspectives on parenting. In B. S. Trask & R. R. Hamon (Eds.), *Cultural diversity and families* (pp. 118–133). Thousand Oaks, CA: Sage.

Greenspan, S. I., Wieder, S., & Simons, R. (1998). *The child with special needs: Encouraging intellectual and emotional growth.* Reading, MA: Addison Wesley.

Harry, B. (1992). Restructuring the participation of African-American parents in Special Education. *Exceptional Children, 59,* 123–131.

Harte, H. A. (2009). What teachers can learn from mothers of children with autism. *Teaching Exceptional Children, 42,* 24–30.

Hastings, R. P., Kovshoff, H., Ward, N. J., Espinosa, F., Brown, T., & Remington, B., (2005). Systems analysis of stress and positive perceptions in mothers and fathers of pre-school children with autism. *Journal of Autism and Developmental Disability, 35,* 635–644.

Hecimovic, A., & Gregory, S. (2005). The evolving role, impact, and needs of families. In D. Zager (Ed.), *Autism spectrum disorders: Identification, education, and treatment* (3rd ed., pp. 111–142). Mahwah, NJ: Lawrence Erlbaum Associates.

Henderson, D., & Vanderberg, B. (1992). Factors influencing adjustment in families of autistic children. *Psychological Reports, 71,* 167–171.

Higgins, D., Bailey, S., & Pearce, J. (2005). Factors associated with functioning style and coping strategies of families with a child with an autism spectrum disorder. *Autism, 9,* 125–137.

Hillman, J. (2007). Grandparents of children with autism: A review with recommendations for education, practice, and policy. *Educational Gerontology, 33,* 512–527.

Howlin, P., & Yates, P. (1990). A group for the siblings of children with autism. *Communication, 24,* 11–16.

Hoy, W. K., & Tschannen-Moran, M. (1990). Five faces of trust: An empirical confirmation in urban elementary schools. *Journal of School Leadership, 9,* 184–208.

Individuals with Disabilities Education Act, 20 U.S.C. §§ 1400 et seq (2004).

Janicky, M. P., McCallion, P., Grant-Griffin, L., & Kolomer, S. R. (2000). Grandparent caregivers I: Characteristics of grandparents and the children with disabilities for whom they care. *Journal of Gerontological Social Work, 33,* 35–55.

Kaminsky, L., & Dewey, D. (2002). Psychosocial adjustment in siblings of children with autism. *Journal of Child Psychology and Psychiatry and Allied Disciplines, 43,* 225–232.

Klingner, J., & Harry, B. (2006). The special education referral and decision-making process for English language learners: Child study team meetings and placement conferences. *Teachers College Record, 108,* 2247–2281.

Kuhn, J., & Carter, A. (2006). Maternal self-efficacy and associated parenting cognitions among mothers of children with autism. *American Journal of Orthopsychiatry, 76,* 564–575.

Macks, R. J., & Reeve, R. E. (2007). The adjustment of non-disabled siblings of children with autism. *Journal of Autism and Developmental Disorders, 37,* 1060–1067.

Marcus, L., Kunce, I., & Schopler, E. (2005). Working with families. In F. Volkmar, R. Paul, A. Klin, & D. Cohen (Eds.), *Handbook of autism and pervasive developmental disorders* (pp. 1055–1085). New York, NY: John Wiley & Sons.

Margetts, J. K., Le Courteur, A., & Croom, S. (2006). Families in a state of flux: The experience of grandparents in autism spectrum disorder. *Child: Care, Health, and Development, 32,* 565–574.

McHale, S. M., Sloan, J., & Simeonsson, R. J. (1986). Sibling relationships of children with autistic, mentally retarded, and non-handicapped brothers and sisters. *Journal of Autism and Developmental Disorders, 16,* 399–413.

Minuchin, S. (1974). *Families and family therapy.* Cambridge, MA: Harvard University Press.

The National Autistic Society. (2007). *Making connections. A report on the special relationship between children with autism and Thomas & Friends.* Retrieved from http://www.nas.org.uk/nas/jsp/polopoly.jsp?d=368&a=14021.

O'Brien, M., & Daggert, J. A. (2006). *Beyond the autism diagnosis. A professional's guide to helping families.* Baltimore, MD: Paul H. Brookes.

Phelps, K.W., McCammon, S. L., Wuensch, K. L., & Golden, J. A. (2009). Enrichment, stress, and growth from parenting an individual with an autism spectrum disorder. *Journal of Intellectual & Developmental Disability, 34,* 33–141.

Phetrasuwan, S., & Miles, M. S. (2009). Parenting stress in mothers of children with autism spectrum disorders. *Journal for Specialists in Pediatric Nursing, 14,* 157–165.

Pilowsky, T., Yirmiya, N., Doppelt, O., Gross-Tsur, V., & Shalev, R. S. (2004). Social and emotional adjustment of siblings of children with autism. *Journal of Child Psychology and Psychiatry, 45*(4), 855–865.

Pottie, C. G., & Ingram, K. M. (2008). Daily stress, coping, and well-being in parents of children with autism: A multilevel modeling approach. *Journal of Family Psychology, 22,* 855–864.

Quintero, N., & McIntyre, L. L. (2010). Sibling adjustment and maternal well-being: An examination of families with and without a child with an autism spectrum disorder. *Focus on Autism and Other Developmental Disabilities, 25,* 37–46.

Rivers, J. W., & Stoneman, Z. (2003). Sibling relationships when a child has autism:

Marital stress and support coping. *Journal of Autism and Developmental Disorders, 33,* 383–394.

Rogoff, B. (1990). *Apprenticeship in thinking: Cognitive development in social context.* New York, NY: Oxford University Press.

Ruble, L. A., Dalrymple, N. J., & McGrew, J. H. (2010). The effects of consultation on individualized education program outcomes for young children with autism: The collaborative model for promoting competence and success. *Journal of Early Intervention, 32,* 286–301.

Sandler, A. G. (1998). Positive adaption in parents of adults with disabilities. *Education and Training in Mental Retardation and Developmental Disabilities, 33,* 123–130.

Satir, V. (1988). *The new peoplemaking.* Palo Alto, CA: Science and Behavior Books.

Schieve, L. A., Blumberg, S. J., Rice, C., Visser, S. N., & Boyle, C. (2007). The relationship between autism and parenting stress. *Pediatrics, 119,* 114–121.

Stoner, J. B., Bock, S. J., Thompson, J. R., Angell, M.E., Heyl, B. S., & Crowley, E. P. (2005). Welcome to our world: Parent perceptions of interactions between parents of young children with ASD and education professionals. *Focus on Autism and Other Developmental Disabilities, 20,* 39–51.

Summers, J. A., Hoffman, L., Marquis, J., Turnbull, A., Poston, D., & Nelson, L. L. (2005). Measuring the quality of family-professional partnerships in special education. *Exceptional Children, 72,* 65–81.

Symon, J. B. (2001). Parent education for Autism: Issues in providing services at a distance. *Journal of Positive Behavior Interventions, 3*(3), 160–174.

Turnbull, A., Turnbull, R. Erwin, E., & Soodak, L. (2006). *Families, professionals, and exceptionality: Positive outcomes through partnership and trust* (5th ed.). Upper Saddle River, NJ: Pearson Prentice Hall.

Turnbull, A., Turnbull, R., & Wehmeyer, M. L. (2007). *Exceptional lives. Special education in today's schools* (5th ed.). Upper Saddle River, NJ: Merrill/Prentice Hall.

Turnbull, H. R., Wilcox, B. L., & Stowe, M. J. (2002). A brief overview of special education law with focus on autism. *Journal of Autism and Developmental Disorders, 32,* 479–493.

Vygotsky, L. S. (1962). *Thought and language.* Cambridge MA: MIT Press.

Weiss, M. J. (2002). Hardiness and social support as predictors of stress in mothers of typical children, children with autism, and children with mental retardation. *Autism, 6,* 115–130.

CHAPTER 5

IDENTIFICATION AND THE DIAGNOSTIC PROCESS

In this chapter, you will learn about:

- Interventions and supports implemented by public schools prior to referral for diagnostic assessments.
- Screening and surveillance for Autism Spectrum Disorder (ASD) in infants and young children.
- Components of a nondiscriminative multifaceted evaluation.
- Assessments that support the diagnosis of ASD and educational planning, including assessments of intellectual ability and cognitive processes, emotional functioning, and academic skills.

TESTS DESIGNED FOR EARLY SURVEILLANCE AND SCREENING

The average age of diagnosis of autism for children is between 3 to 4 years (Mandell, Maytali, & Zubritsk, 2005; Zwaigenbaum et al., 2009), and 7 years for Asperger's Syndrome (Mandell et al., 2005). However, ASD can be reliably diagnosed at 2 years of age and in some cases as young as 15 to 18 months (Lord & Risi, 2000; National Research Council, 2001; Zwaigenbaum et al., 2005).

Screening and developmental surveillance tools are critical for identifying children with ASD during early childhood because early identification allows for early intervention (Boyd, Odom, Humphreys, & Sam, 2010; Robins, 2008). Early intervention is associated with better outcomes (Harris & Handleman, 2000). In particular, it is important that pediatricians and others offering primary care for infants and young children routinely utilize screening instruments designed to identify ASD in young children (Plauché

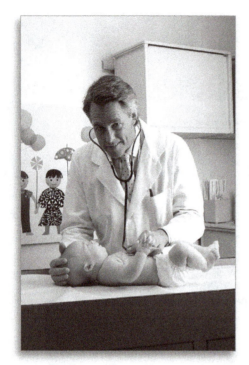

Today, pediatricians can use screening and developmental surveillance tools to identify children with ASD as early as 18 months of age and sometimes earlier.

Johnson, Myers, & The Council on Children with Disabilities, 2007). Without these standardized screening tools, young children with ASD may not be diagnosed until significantly older (Robins, 2008).

There are a growing number of instruments available for screening young children with ASD (Oosterling et al., 2009). The Modified Checklist for Autism in Toddlers (M-CHAT) is a popular screening tool for detecting characteristics of ASD in infants and toddlers 16 to 30 months of age (Robbins, Fein, Barton, & Green, 2001). The M-CHAT is a revision of the Checklist for Autism in Toddlers (CHAT; Baron-Cohen, Allen, & Gillberg, 1992), which was a nine-item questionnaire developed in the United Kingdom to screen for autism at 18 months (Bishop, Luyster, Richler, & Lord, 2008). The M-CHAT extends the age range and consists of 23-items in a dichotomous ("yes" or "no") addressing domains associated with ASD, including language, motor skills, social and emotional functioning, pointing/joint attention skills, and arousal modulation (Robbins et al., 2001). Preliminary research suggests good sensitivity (ability to detect characteristics of ASD) and specificity (ability to rule out other conditions such as language delay; Bishop et al., 2008; Kleinman et al., 2008).

Another version of the M-CHAT, the Quantitative Checklist for Autism in Toddlers (Q-CHAT), has recently been published to better target the upper range of young children from 18 to 24 months (Allison et al., 2008). The popularity of these screening instruments is likely because of the strong research literature supporting the instruments' psychometric properties, the ease of administering and scoring, and the fact that there is no charge for downloading and using the instruments and they are in several languages (i.e., MCHAT can be downloaded at http://www2.gsu.edu/~psydlr/Diana_L._Robins,_Ph.D..html).

For a thorough review of diagnostic issues and assessment instruments designed for infants and toddlers with ASD, refer to *Autism Spectrum Disorder in Infants and Toddlers* by Chawarska, Klin, and Volkmar (2008).

Table 5.1 Screening Instruments for ASD in Young Children

These instruments were not designed to diagnose ASD, but to screen for infants and young children at risk for ASD or other developmental disorders.

- **Infant Toddler Checklist**—For children 18 months and younger to broadly screen for communication delays, specifically targeting social communication (Wetherby, Brosnan-Maddox, Peace, & Newton, 2008).
- **Screening Tool for Autism in Two-Year-Olds (STAT)**—A 12-item interactive assessment investigating behaviors associated with ASD (Stone, McMahon, & Henderson, 2008).
- The Autism Observational Scale for Infants—Developed to monitor and screen for ASD in high-risk infants (6–18 months), such as those with siblings with ASD, by assessing developmental characteristics such as visual orienting and tracking, imitation, and sensory-motor development (Bryson, McDermott, Rombough, Brian, & Zwaigenbaum, 2008).

There are a growing number of empirically strong tools for diagnosing and screening for ASD.

CHAPTER REFLECTION: Early Surveillance and Screening by Pediatricians

In many cases, pediatricians are on the front line for early identification of ASD (Plauché Johnson et al., 2007). With proper surveillance and population-based screening, pediatricians can refer children to specialists that allow for early diagnosis of ASD and reduce the delay of providing services (Robbins, 2008).

Case Study: Surveillance Followed by Screening

Sammy's pediatrician routinely considers developmental concerns or risk factors associated with characteristics of ASD (surveillance). During today's visit, she notes that 18-month-old Sammy has not

(Continued)

(Continued)

met developmental milestones in emerging language skills, has an older sibling with ASD, and fails to respond to his name when called in the doctor's office. Based on this surveillance data, the pediatrician decides to administer a standardized screening instrument.

Surveillance procedures may not be enough to identify young children at risk for ASD. Robbins (2008) investigated 4,797 cases of toddlers screened with the M-CHAT. Of the 21 cases that received a diagnosis of ASD, only four had been identified through routine surveillance during well-child visits.

The American Academy of Pediatrics (AAP) recommends that pediatricians include autism-specific screening for all children at 18-months and again at 24-months old (AAP, 2006).

Case Study: Routine Screening at Critical Stage of Development

During Brianna's 18-month well-baby visit, her pediatrician administers the M-CHAT.

Brianna's mother responds to a series of questions from the M-CHAT regarding Brianna's language, motor skills, social development, and behavior. For instance, she indicated that Brianna did not seem interested in other children, rarely imitates others, does not look at things her parents point to, and seems oversensitive to noise. Based on the results of the M-CHAT, the pediatrician refers Brianna to an autism diagnostic center for a comprehensive evaluation.

Question: Should an ASD screening instrument be routinely administered to all children during the 18-month well-baby visit? Consider the cons (i.e., cost, time, incorrectly identifying a child with ASD) in light of the pros (i.e., early identification and services for child, parent supports, and education).

Children on the mild end of the spectrum, particularly those with no delays in early language development and good cognitive skills, may not receive a diagnosis until later. In the Chapter Reflection box, Becky Marks describes having her son, Carson, diagnosed with Asperger's Syndrome.

**CHAPTER REFLECTION: Interview
With Becky Marks, Mother of Carson**

When did Carson first get diagnosed with Asperger's Syndrome? I asked my pediatrician for a consultation because I had observed "red flags" that made me wonder if he was on the spectrum. Carson talked on time (in fact was early in developing language milestones), but lacked imaginative play. He had always been described by other caregivers as seeming like a "little man" rather than a child. Other red flags I observed included a fascination with objects like vacuum cleaners, hand flapping more than usual for his age, and more interest in interacting with adults rather than with children. Carson mostly spent time with other adults and had limited interactions with other children. His in-home child care provider, who watched Carson and an 11-year-old home-schooled child, thought Carson was "delightful." So, no one ever suggested he might be on the autism spectrum.

My pediatrician had never asked me questions about these types of characteristics. So I asked for a consultation to share my concerns with her.

How did it go? She was a good listener, which is really important for parents. I brought all my documents, and laid it all out for her. She had me complete a questionnaire—screening for ASD. It was the University of Cambridge's Questionnaire. After she scored it she said, "It looks like Asperger's Syndrome."

Did she follow up with recommendations? Yes, she was helpful. She suggested two places to pursue psychological evaluation and formal diagnosis. She also suggested I contact an Occupational Therapist and gave me a referral.

Overall, teachers and doctors who are good listeners are the most important. Ongoing communication between parents and teachers is always necessary! I also learn a lot from doing my own research, through books and articles. I am a teacher, and I like learning all I can on my own.

RESPONSE TO INTERVENTION

In most instances, when a child appears to have characteristics of ASD, a phase of prediagnostic (sometimes called "pre-referral") supports are implemented in the school setting, prior to a formal evaluation. In many school systems across the United States, a systematic tiered approach called Response to Intervention (RTI) is used to provide educational support within general education before considering special education services.

Purpose of RTI

Using this approach, empirically validated interventions are implemented within the general education classroom (VanDerHeyden & Snyder, 2006). The child's progress is monitored and a decision is made as to continue monitoring the child's progress, try a different and sometimes more intensive empirically validated strategy, or make a referral to determine eligibility for special education services (Hoover & Patton, 2008; Turnbull, Turnbull, & Wehmeyer, 2007). Although RTI offers school systems a systematic framework for providing early supports, research is needed to determine the appropriateness for using RTI to identify ASD (Allen, Robins, & Decker, 2008).

It is important that teachers help parents understand the goals of pre-referral strategies for their child. Pre-referral procedures, such as RTI, can be used to provide early screening and support to children at risk. In addition, these data collected have the potential to enhance diagnosis and inform decisions about service delivery (Barnet et al., 2006). The broad-spectrum design of RTI is potentially useful in identifying and targeting social and academic needs for young children with ASD who have challenging behavior (Barnett et al.). Barnett and colleagues (2006) note that RTI has the potential to prevent misdiagnosis of children with ASD by providing a system of functional classification that describes specific behaviors and the extent to which they are modified by particular interventions.

Data Collection and the Multidisciplinary Team

During all phases of the preassessment and the assessment process, the multidisciplinary team must work together to collect information, evaluate data, and determine the next step. Parents are a vital part of this team. The multidisciplinary team may include individuals from a variety of backgrounds who are knowledgeable about the child's development. These team members will include the classroom teacher, the parents (or child's legal guardian), a special education teacher, and a school administrator. Multidisciplinary teams have the potential to provide a holistic understanding of the child's potential, current functioning, and learning needs. Furthermore, a multidisciplinary team brings multiple perspectives and skills to the development of interventions addressing the child's learning needs (Goodlin-Jones & Solomon, 2003).

Parents are a vital member of the multidisciplinary team during all phases of assessment.

THE DATA COLLECTION PROCESS

In addition to data collected from screening instruments and other standardized tests, parents and teachers contribute important information about a child's background history, current functioning, and response to targeted interventions.

Table 5.2 Other Members of the Interdisciplinary Team

- The **school psychologist** generally writes a psychoeducational report based on a battery of tests and interviews. Often skilled in developing and assessing individualized educational program (IEP) goals.
- The **speech-language pathologist** may conduct a speech and language assessment. Results from these evaluations may support the development of goals for speech/language therapy as well as other IEP goals implemented within the classroom setting. These goals may address articulation, expressive language, receptive language, and pragmatic language (use of language within the context of social interactions).
- The **occupational therapist** may conduct assessments of fine motor skills and sensory integration functioning. Supports the development of these skills by offering individual therapy as well as consultation with regular and special education teachers.

The Role of Teachers in the Data Collection Process

Data such as student work samples and classroom anecdotal observations represent a "slice of life" that can provide additional information to better understand a student's academic, behavioral, and social needs. Teachers also participate in more formal data collection or ongoing progress monitoring such as structured observations, standardized behavior rating scales, or testing students on skills acquired following interventions.

The Role of the Parents in the Data Collection Process

Parents contribute critical information to diagnostic process, such as background history, frequency and intensity of behaviors outside the school setting and over time, and generalization of skills outside the school setting. Parents can also provide valuable context for understanding a child's behavior.

Data collected from parents not only assist with accurate diagnosis, but also inform the selection and refinement of interventions. For instance, parents may provide information about the effectiveness of an Applied Behavior Analysis (ABA) program implemented within the home. Information about the antecedents (things that occur prior to the behavior), target behavior (such as frequency or intensity), and consequences (what happens following the behavior, such as receiving attention) can support the development of interventions that target emerging skills at school. ABA as an intervention for children with ASD is discussed in Chapter 8. In addition, structured interviews and parent rating scales are useful in better understanding a child's current level of functioning across settings. Examples of intervention programs that are directly linked to ongoing assessments are the Treatment and Education of Autistic and related Communication-Handicapped Children (TEACCH) program (discussed in Chapter 6) and the Social Communication, Emotional Regulation, and Transactional Support model (SCERTS; discussed in Chapter 10).

COMPONENTS OF A NONDISCRIMINATIVE MULTIFACETED EVALUATION

The federal law governing special education in the United States stipulates that schools use nonbiased and multifactored assessments to determine if a child is eligible for special education services (IDEA, 2004).

CHAPTER REFLECTION: Factors to Be Considered When Conducting a Nonbiased Multifactored Assessment

- Does the test discriminate based on gender, race, culture, or native language?
- Can the test be administered in the child's native language?
- Is the assessment conducted by individuals trained to administer and interpret the tests?

- Are decisions about a child's diagnosis, eligibility for special education, and/or placement in an educational setting based on a comprehensive multifaceted assessment rather than a single test result?

In addition to being nonbiased, a multifaceted assessment includes information from multiple sources and across developmental domains and settings (Goodlin-Jones & Solomon, 2003). Thus, information should be gathered using a variety of assessment tools appropriate for the child's developmental level with input from those who know the child best, including teachers, parents, and other caregivers.

Each child with ASD is unique, and assessments should be tailored to specific needs and concerns. For instance, children with severe language deficits may require an evaluation of nonverbal communication skills and assessments for assistive technology needs; and children with skills significantly below their same-age peers may require assessments of adaptive behavior to evaluate independent functioning. Furthermore, functional behavioral assessments (FBA; discussed in Chapter 7) may be helpful to address the needs of children with challenging behaviors.

At a minimum a comprehensive psychoeducational evaluation to provide a diagnosis and support educational planning should include the following:

- Diagnostic assessment tools designed to identify autism or other disorders on the autism spectrum
- Assessment of cognitive ability addressing both verbal and nonverbal skills
- Assessment of language skills
- Assessment of social-emotional functioning
- Assessment of academic or emerging academic skills

ASSESSMENTS OF CHILDREN AGES 0–3 AND INDIVIDUALS WITH SEVERE IMPAIRMENTS

Assessments of young children are likely to include structured observation and observations in natural settings, activities assessing developmental skills (such as play), and interviews with caregivers. Testing involving standardized question-answer or paper-pencil types of tasks is often difficult or impossible with young children (National Research Council, 2001). Likewise, when evaluating older children with significant impairments (particularly children with very low expressive and receptive language skills), assessments are likely to focus more on developmental skills rather than academic-oriented assessments. In these instances, information from teachers and caregivers play a significant role in obtaining an appropriate diagnosis.

The following types of data collection techniques are often included in assessments of all children with ASD, but are particularly important when evaluating young children (0–3) or older children and adolescents with more severe disabilities.

Interview, Surveys, and Behavior Checklists With Caregivers and Teachers

Interviews with parents, teachers, and other caregivers are always an important part of a psychoeducational evaluation. However, when conducting assessments with young children, especially involving developmental disabilities, these interviews are critical. Interviews with parents and other caregivers usually provide opportunities to learn about the child's developmental history, including prenatal development, birth history, and ages at which the child met developmental milestones (Bishop et al., 2008; Shriver, Allen, & Matthews, 1999). Concerns about sleep, diet, and other medical issues are also addressed. The interview may include questions about the child's family history of ASD or other developmental disorders (Chawarska & Bearss, 2008).

Some interviews are informal, and others are structured with specific questions and scoring procedures. For instance, the Ages and Stages Questionnaire, Second Edition (ASQ; Bricker & Squires, 1999) is an example of a structured questionnaire that elicits information from caregivers about language, personal-social, fine and gross motor, and cognitive development.

> **CHAPTER REFLECTION: Assessing Adaptive Behaviors in Young Children or Children With Severe Disabilities: The Vineland Adaptive Behavior Scale-II**
>
> **The Vineland Adaptive Behavior Scale-II** (VABS-II; Sparrow, Balla, & Cicchetti, 2005) is a comprehensive and widely used interview conducted with both teachers and caregivers (Chawarska & Bearss, 2008). The VABS-II provides information about independent functioning and skills important for everyday living (Chawarska & Bearss; Sparrow et al.), including information about communication, daily living skills, socialization, motor skills, and maladaptive behavior. This instrument can be used for very young children as well as older individuals with developmental disabilities (standardized for use with ages 0–90).
>
> Although the VABS-II does not provide a diagnosis of ASD, it does provide information about everyday functioning that can be helpful in educational, vocational, and transitional planning. Furthermore, significantly below average adaptive behavior may indicate an intellectual disability (mental retardation). However, there are several other criteria that must be met for a diagnosis of an intellectual disability, including cognitive ability scores of 70 or below, below-average functioning across developmental domains such as language and social development, and a history of developmental delays (American Psychiatric Association, 2000).

Teacher interviews provide information about the child's behavior and overall functioning within the school setting, in comparison to same-age (and often typically developing) peers. Teachers provide information about the child's relative social, behavioral, and academic functioning within the classroom. Teachers can also provide information about the child's daily routine. It is helpful to allow parents, caregivers, and teachers the opportunity to answer open-ended questions such as, "Do you have any concerns about this child's development?"

Teachers and caregivers may also complete behavior checklists and rating scales that allow for a quantifiable score comparing a child's behavior and daily functioning to children of the same age. Rating scales offer the advantage of providing objective information about a child's behavior across settings and time (Merrell, 1999).

Review of Records

In addition to interviews, a careful review of educational and medical records provides valuable information. A review of the child's medical and educational history can provide perspective and context for current functioning. ASD is a developmental disorder in which deficits in communication/language, social development, and behavior are apparent by age 3. Thus, documentation of developmental delays, skill regression, and atypical sequence of development assist with making an appropriate diagnosis of ASD.

Observations

Observations provide additional support to corroborate other assessment data and help clarify issues of current functioning. Some observations are informal, and others are structured in which the examiner records information about the rate, frequency, or intensity of a behavior in a particular setting. It is especially important to observe a child across a variety of settings including structured (such as an academic setting or storytime at the library), social (playground or a play date), and during independent play opportunities (environment with age-appropriate attractive toys).

Assessing Developmental Level

The Psychoeducational Profile, Third Edition (PEP-3) was developed to assess developmental skills in children 6 months to 7 years with ASD (Goodlin-Jones & Solomon, 2003; Hall, 2009). Subtests of the PEP-3 address developmental abilities, including expressive and receptive language, fine and gross motor, and visual-motor imitation as well as maladaptive behaviors (Schopler, Lansing, Reichler, & Marcus, 2005).

Another widely used test assessing developmental level is the Bayley Scales of Infant and Toddler Development, Third Edition (Bayley-III; published by PsychCorp). The Bayley provides estimates of developmental functioning up to 42 months and assesses adaptive behavior, cognition, language, motor skills, and social emotional development. Three of the scales (Cognitive, Language, and Motor) involve direct interaction with the child, and the others are based on observations and caregiver/teacher reports.

Another popular test for use with young children suspected of having ASD is the Mullen Scales of Early Learning (MSEL, 1995), which provides developmental age equivalents in gross and fine motor, visual reception, and receptive and expressive language skills for children from birth to 68 months. The age equivalents are useful to assess developmental skills of older children with severe developmental disabilities (Goodlin-Jones & Solomon, 2003).

ASSESSMENT TOOLS DESIGNED FOR DIAGNOSING ASD

There are an increasing number of tests designed to assist with the diagnosis of ASD. These instruments are standardized on populations of children that have been diagnosed with ASD. Among the available instruments, three of the most frequently used assessment instruments include the Childhood Autism Rating Scale, Second Edition (CARS2; Schopler, Reichler, & Renner, 1988), the Autism Diagnostic Interview-Revised (ADI-R; Rutter, Couteur, & Lord, 2003), and the Autism Observation Schedule (ADOS; Lord et al., 1999; Allen, Robins, & Decker, 2008). For a comprehensive overview of available screening and diagnostic tools for ASD, refer to *Assessment of Autism Spectrum Disorders* (Goldstein, Naglieri, & Ozonoff, 2009).

Childhood Autism Rating Scale, Second Edition

The CARS is one of the most widely used assessment tools for supporting the diagnosis of autism (Allen, Robins, & Decker). The CARS originated as a clinical tool developed by North Carolina's TEACCH program (Schopler, Reichler, DeVellis, & Daly, 1980). Currently in its second edition, the CARS2 is an interview with caregivers and teachers appropriate for children ages 2 and older. The CARS includes 15 items rated on a 7-point scale completed by an interviewer and provides ratings of mild autism, moderate autism, severe autism, or nonautism. Best practice resources (such as Thomas & Grimes, 2002) consider the CARS a screening tool insufficient for diagnosing ASD. Training videos are available for administration and scoring through the publisher (Western Psychological Services, www.wpspublish.com).

The "Gold Standard" in ASD Assessment

The Autism Diagnostic Observation Scale and the Autism Diagnostic Interview-Revised

When used together, the Autism Diagnostic Observation Scale (ADOS; Lord, Rutter, DiLavore, & Risi, 1999) and Autism Diagnostic Interview-Revised

(ADI-R; Rutter et al., 2003) are considered the "gold standard" in autism diagnosis and research best practice (Lord & Corsello, 2005; Luyster et al., 2009). Administration of both the ADOS and ADI-R require specialized training. The publishers recommend attending training workshops for use of ADOS in both clinical and research settings (Western Psychological Services, 2010). There is an impressive literature incorporating the ADOS and ADI-R into a wide range of autism research. These instruments were designed for assessment for ages 18 months and older.

The ADI-R is a semistructured interview designed to provide information contributing to a diagnosis of ASD for children and adults. Based on the diagnostic criteria of the *Diagnostic and Statistical Manual of Mental Disorders, Fourth Edition, Text Revision (DSM-IV-TR)* and the International Classification of Diseases, 10th Revision (ICD-10), the ADI-R includes a series of structured questions in three primary areas: reciprocal social interaction, communication and language, and restricted/stereotyped and repetitive interests and behavior (Rutter et al., 2003).

The ADOS is a standardized assessment tool that includes parent/caregiver interviews and an interactive assessment procedures that provides a context for assessing characteristics of ASD (Rice, 2009). In addition, the ADOS-Toddler Module for Children is under development to better identify ASD in infants and toddlers less than 30 months with a nonverbal mental age of at least 12 months (Luyster et al., 2009).

Table 5.3   The Autism Diagnostic Observation Schedule (ADOS)

✓ Assesses social interaction, verbal and nonverbal communication, and play or imaginative use of materials.

✓ Includes three different modules to account for different levels of language skills (nonverbal to single words, limited phrase speech, and verbally fluent).

✓ Provides an interactive context to elicit behaviors associated with ASD. For instance, the "birthday party" subtest includes a doll, toy cake, and toy candles to create an authentic opportunity for eliciting symbolic and functional play.

✓ Provides a classification of ASD or "Nonspectrum."

✓ Helps identify supports needed for educational planning.

Source: Adapted from Rice, C. (October 8 & 9, 2009). Autism Diagnostic Observation Schedule. Clinical ADOS Workshop. Atlanta, GA.

CHAPTER REFLECTION: Interview With Dr. Catherine Lord

Dr. Lord is a Senior Research Scientist and Director of the University of Michigan Autism and Communication Disorders Center. Her research contributions in the field of ASD are many, including longitudinal studies of children with ASD and development of the ADOS.

How has the ADOS contributed to accurately diagnosing ASD?

The ADOS not only standardizes how people assess ASD, but allows professionals to communicate more effectively about characteristics of ASD. In addition, when we created the ADOS, we didn't expect it to be such a clinically useful tool for demonstrating functional levels to parents and school teams. Parents or teachers observing the administration of the ADOS can observe how a child responds in a situation that is pleasant and fun, but not providing too much help for the child. For instance, we can say to parents, "Your child is really good at requesting, but did not demonstrate pretend play." So clinically, it is like a way to have a common ground with parents and teachers.

What changes do you anticipate in the future for diagnosing ASD?

I think we are going to consider autism as a spectrum disorder (ASD). We know autism is a behavioral disorder with many different types of neurobiological origins. Likely, the focus will be on two dimensions: social communication and repetitive behaviors and interests. But first, language level and chronological age will be considered. I think we need to try to get people to think about the child's developmental level first. Assessments will also consider severity level.

Are you working on other instruments to assess ASD?

Currently, we are working on a standardized measure of spontaneous language. We are creating tasks that are fun for kids but that the examiner follows within a semistructured module. These are tasks that make kids want to talk. The examiner then evaluates the audiotaped language for grammar, pragmatics, content, etc. We are also investigating measures for diagnosing ASD in children with limited language skills.

ASSESSMENT OF INTELLECTUAL ABILITY AND COGNITIVE PROCESSES

Intellectual Assessment: The Challenge of Measuring Intellectual Potential

A comprehensive psychoeducational assessment usually includes a measure of intellectual ability. An assessment of intellectual ability can inform decisions about educational goals and educational placements (Filipek et al., 1999). In addition, tests of intellectual ability provide information about severity of symptoms and prognosis of acquiring skills (Filipek et al.; Goodlin-Jones & Solomon, 2003).

Current research indicates that 33% to 59% of individuals with ASD achieve scores below 70 on standardized intelligence tests, falling within the range of intellectual disability (Rice, 2007). In some states, documentation of intellectual disability allows access to additional resources outside the school system unavailable to individuals with only a diagnosis of ASD. Thus, scores from assessments of intellectual functioning may be used to support a comorbid (or co-occurring) diagnosis of intellectual disabilities. Conversely, there remains a social stigma associated with below average cognitive ability (Markova, 2004).

Despite the potential benefits of understanding a child's ability level, it can be difficult to accurately estimate cognitive potential in individuals with ASD. This is particularly true when a child has limited language or social-communication skills and low motivation to engage with the test examiner (Filipek et al., 1999; Handleman & Delmolino, 2005). Tests of cognitive ability often require precise responses, efficient cognitive processing (working quickly to achieve the correct answer), and prolonged one-on-one engagement with the test examiner. Thus, clinical judgment based on experience working with children with ASD is critical to interpreting tests of intellectual ability for children with ASD (Filipek et al.). Furthermore, clinicians and educators should be aware that ability testing may underestimate the true potential of individuals with ASD (Filipek et al.).

General intelligence, or overall ability level, is not considered a stable construct until age 7 (Sattler, 2008). Tests providing a developmental level are often used, rather than a traditional "intelligence test," when evaluating young children or children with severe disabilities.

The intellectual ability of children is often assessed using standardized tests of intelligence such as the Wechsler Intelligence Test, the Stanford-Binet Intelligence Scales, or the Differential Abilities Test (Handleman & Delmolino, 2005). The most widely used is the Wechsler Intelligence Scale for Children-Fourth Edition (WISC-IV); Mayes & Calhoun, 2008; Flanagan & Kaufman, 2004). The WISC-IV provides a Full Scale Score along with four Index Scores, including Verbal Comprehension, Perceptual Reasoning, Working Memory, and Processing Speed. An experienced examiner will choose instruments that best address the functioning of the child being assessed. A comprehensive discussion of cognitive instruments is not possible within the scope of this chapter. However, interested readers are referred to Jerome Sattler's (2008) *Assessment of Children: Cognitive Foundations.*

Individuals with ASD sometimes demonstrate an uneven profile of scores on subtests of intelligence tests (Handleman & Delmolino, 2005; Joseph, Tager-Flusberg, & Lord, 2002). For instance, overall ability score may be below average, yet individual subtests may indicate higher functioning. For some individuals with ASD (particularly those with language difficulties), scores on subtests involving nonverbal or perceptual reasoning (such as tasks that involve puzzles and creating abstract designs with blocks) may be significantly higher than tasks involving verbal comprehension (Filipek et al., 1999; Lincoln, Searcy, Jones, & Lord, 1995). Conversely, individuals with high-functioning autism or Asperger's Syndrome may present a profile of higher scores on tasks of verbal comprehension, but relatively poorer performance on nonverbal subtests (Klin, Volkmar, Sparrow, Cicchetti, & Rourke, 1995) and tasks involving working memory and processing speed (Mayes & Calhoun, 2008).

Assessment of Cognitive Processes

Although not necessary for a diagnosis of autism, assessments of cognitive processes may provide additional information about how a child learns contributing to more effective interventions (Goodlin-Jones & Solomon, 2003). Evaluations of cognitive processes are generally conducted by a school psychologist, neuropsychologist, or other licensed psychologist with specialized training and are most useful for individuals with high-functioning skills accessing academic curriculum.

Assessments of cognitive processes such as attention, memory, executive functioning, and perspective taking can help the multidisciplinary team better understand how a child with ASD learns.

Attention

Children with high-functioning ASD often have good ability to sustain attention. However, attention difficulties may manifest when they are asked disengage visual attention and shift to a new task (Bryson, 2004).

A suspected core deficit of ASD is an overfocus on extraneous details at the expense of the big picture (or "missing the forest for the trees," Goodlin-Jones & Solomon, 2003, p. 73). Known as impaired or weak central coherence (Happé & Frith, 1996), this perceptual cognitive style helps explain why children with ASD sometimes have difficulty gleaning the meaning from a reading passage or lesson in spite of their memory for specific information related to the assignment (Happé, 1994).

For those children with ASD who seem to experience difficulty with sustained attention, behavior-rating scales addressing inattention, impulsivity, and overactivity are sometimes used. Behavioral ratings are recorded across time and setting by multiple evaluators (such as teachers and parents). These tools can be used address the possibility of a comorbid condition such as Attention Deficit Hyperactivity Disorder (ADHD). Examples of frequently used behavior rating scales include the Conners Rating Scale, Third Edition (Conners, 2008), the Behavior Assessment System for Children, Second Edition (BASC II, Reynolds & Kamphaus, 2009), and the Achenbach Child Behavior Checklist (CBCL, Achenbach & Rescorla, 2001). In addition, a functional behavioral assessment may reveal that rather than poor attention skills, the child has low motivation and lack of interest in the task.

Perspective Taking (Theory of Mind)

Theory of Mind (TOM), coined by Premack and Woodruff (1978), is the understanding that others bring a unique perspective to problem-solving situations based on their experiences and knowledge. In addition, TOM enables one to form hypotheses about what others are thinking to anticipate the behavior of others. Children typically develop TOM been 3 to 5 years of age (Flavell, 2000). However, even adolescents and adults with ASD seem to experience difficulty with tasks that rely on TOM for accurate problem solving. Some researchers believe that difficulty with TOM is a core deficit of ASD and directly related to deficits with social communication skills (i.e., Baron-Cohen, Leslie, & Frith, 1985; Happé, 1994). The "Chapter Reflection: Evaluating Theory of Mind: The False Belief Task" box describes a false belief task, sometimes used to evaluate TOM.

CHAPTER REFLECTION: Evaluating Theory of Mind: The False Belief Task

The Sally/Anne scenario is an example of a **false belief task.**

Sally is playing with a doll in the playroom. Before Sally leaves the room, she puts the doll to bed in the dollhouse. Naughty Anne enters the playroom, hides the doll in a basket, and leaves the playroom. Then Sally comes back into the room to play with her doll. Where does she look for the doll?

– Children older than 5 understand that Sally does not know that Anne has hidden the doll in the basket. They know that Sally will look where she left the doll—*in the dollhouse.*

– Younger children and children who do not have TOM don't take into consideration that Sally does not have access to the same information that they have. Thus, they respond that Sally looks *in the basket.*

Source: Based on the original Sally and Anne task by Wimmer, H., & Perner, J. (1983). Beliefs about beliefs: Representation and constraining function of wrong beliefs in young children's understanding of deception. *Cognition, 13*, 103–128.

Executive Functioning

Executive functioning, associated with the prefrontal cortex of the brain (Santrock, 2008), is used to describe many higher-level skills that are necessary for learning and being successful in school. In fact, the prefrontal lobe is described as the "CEO of the brain" (Goldberg, 2001). Although the prefrontal lobes are not fully mature until late adolescence/early adulthood (Goldberg), emerging executive functioning skills becoming increasing important for academic success for school-aged children and adolescents.

Table 5.4 Executive Functioning Difficulties Associated With ASD

- Difficulty disengaging attention and shifting to something else in the environment.
- Mental inflexibility—tendency toward rigid routines and behaviors; difficulty adjusting to transitions or new routines
- Difficulty planning and organizing
- Lack of self-monitoring

Like individuals with damage to their prefrontal cortex, individuals with ASD often have deficits in executive functioning skills (Ozonoff, 1995). Although executive functioning is not a term often used in educational settings, understanding aspects of executive functioning may provide insight into creating interventions providing structure and support to promote learning.

ASSESSMENT OF ACADEMIC SKILLS OR ACADEMIC READINESS

Understanding a child's academic skills, strengths, and interests provides information critical for setting goals and selecting intervention strategies.

Information about a child's current academic skills is essential for setting educational goals. Often children with ASD have marked strengths in certain academic areas relative to others. In addition, they may do well on tasks involving rote memory but have more difficulty on tasks requiring more abstract reasoning such as inference, analogy, or prediction. Understanding a child's relative strengths and interests allows for the creation of interventions that are motivating and promote learning.

For children with near age-appropriate academic skills, traditional standardized achievement tests such as the Wechsler Individual Achievement Test for Children-Third Edition (WIAT-III; Wechsler, 2009) or the Woodcock-Johnson Test of Achievement-Third Edition (Woodcock, McGrew, & Mather, 2001) are often used. The Bracken Test of Basic Concepts (Bracken, 1998) is helpful for younger or older children with lower skills to identify academic readiness and basic concept skills.

CHAPTER REFLECTION: Difficulties with Written Expression and Children With ASD

It is important to assess written expression skills in high-functioning children with ASD. Many high-functioning children with ASD experience significant difficulty expressing their thoughts in writing (Mayes & Calhoun, 2008). This appears associated with both weaknesses in grapho-motor skills associated with handwriting as well as weaknesses with executive functioning skills such as planning and organization. Thus, these children often experience high levels of frustration and anxiety, as well as low motivation, when presented with writing assignments and written exams. To help children with ASD better demonstrate their knowledge and develop their writing skills, the following strategies may be helpful.

– Provide instruction and practice in keyboarding skills. Allow the use of a computer whenever possible when engaged in writing tasks.

– Offer assistance with note-taking such as the use of guided notes or a copy of the teacher or a peer's notes.

– Consider offering an oral exam to students when a written exam is part of test material, if testing for knowledge rather than writing skills.

– Emphasize quality over quantity of writing on written expression assignments.

ASSESSMENT OF EMOTIONAL FUNCTIONING

Individuals with ASD are at risk for experiencing clinically significant levels of mood disorders (Deprey & Ozonoff, 2009; Klim et al., 2000). In fact, depression is the most common psychiatric condition diagnosed in individuals with ASD (Ghaziuddin, Ghaziuddin, & Greden, 2002; Howlin, 1997). Furthermore, individuals with ASD who also have a seizure disorder (Hermann, Seidenberg, & Bell, 2000) or family history of depression (Ghaziuddin & Greden, 1998) at an increased risk for depression. Thus collecting information about family and medical history is helpful in assessing a risk for depression. Early detection of depression is essential for promoting optimal long-term outcomes for individuals with ASD (Ghaziuddin et al.).

In a study by Delong and Dwyer (1988), individuals with Asperger Syndrome were found to have higher rates of bipolar disorder, a mood disorder with periods of clinical depression and periods of mania, as compared to the typical population. Individuals with ASD may demonstrate a wide range of symptoms associated with depression such as irritability, social withdraw, sadness, suicidal ideology, and oppositional or aggressive behavior (Ghaziuddin et al., 2002).

Research suggests that anxiety disorders are also comorbid (occurring together) psychiatric conditions frequently occurring within the ASD population (Deprey & Ozonoff, 2009; Klin et al., 2000) and treatment is available for individuals with ASD (Leyfer et al., 2006). In particular, obsessive compulsive disorder (reoccurring and intrusive thoughts causing anxiety reduced by performing rituals that are often unrelated to the obsessive thought) and specific phobias (debilitating fears of specific objects or situations) are common anxiety disorders found in children with ASD (Leyfer et al.). Symptoms of anxiety appear to increase with age for individuals with ASD (Gadow, DeVincett, Pomeroy, & Azizian, 2004).

Accurate diagnosis of psychiatric conditions in individuals with ASD has significant implications for choice of interventions and maintaining high quality of life. Both mood disorders and anxiety experienced by individuals with ASD significantly impact the ability to function successfully (Klin, 2000). Furthermore, behavioral and pharmacological interventions are available to treat psychiatric disorders once diagnosed.

Diagnosing conditions such as mood or anxiety disorders in ASD can be difficult for several reasons. Many of the assessment tools used for diagnosis are self-report interviews requiring expressive and receptive language skills. Since approximately half of individuals with ASD are functionally nonverbal (Leyfer et al., 2006) and many others demonstrate marked difficulties with expressive verbal skills, traditional tests addressing emotional functioning may not be appropriate. In addition, the ability to identify, reflect upon, and describe emotional difficulties is often difficult for individuals with ASD. Furthermore, symptoms of mood and anxiety disorders sometimes appear different within the context of ASD (Deprey & Ozonoff, 2009).

CHAPTER REFLECTION: Symptoms of Depression and ASD

Individuals with ASD may not express symptoms typically experienced by people with depression. For instance, individuals with depression and ASD may lack intense feelings of guilt because of the abstractness of the emotion. In addition, changes in sleep and eating habits may not be apparent because of the rigidity and need for sameness (Deprey & Ozonoff, 2009). Increased incidents of challenging behaviors (i.e., tantrums and noncompliance), increased social withdrawal, and reduced rates of time spent in preferred activities compared with baseline behaviors contribute to an accurate diagnosis of depression for individuals with ASD (Deprey & Ozonoff).

Question: If you suspect that a child with ASD in your class is experiencing depression, how might you collect information to contribute to an accurate diagnosis?

Assessments of emotional functioning of individuals with ASD often include interviews with caretakers and teachers, observations, and standardized behavior rating scales designed to identify characteristics of depression and anxiety. However, there is limited research regarding the effectiveness (validity) of these assessment instruments for use with individuals with ASD (Leyfer et al., 2006).

The Autism Comorbidity Interview-Present and Lifetime Version (ACI-PL, Leyfer et al., 2006) is a semistructured interview for caregivers of children with ASD. The ACI-PL distinguishes core features of autism from psychiatric disorders such as mood and anxiety disorders. Although not specifically designed for diagnosis of individuals with ASD, other instruments commonly used to evaluate social-emotional functioning in children with ASD include the following:

- The Schedule for Affective Disorders and Schizophrenia for School Aged Children (K-SADS-IVR; Ambrosini, 2000)
- The Diagnostic Interview schedule for Children (Shaffer, Fisher, & Lucas, 2004).
- The Behavioral Assessment System for Children (BASC-2; Reynolds & Kamphaus, 2009)

For readers interested in more detailed information about these tests and others designed to assess social and emotional difficulties in children, see Reynolds and Kamphaus (2003). Social development in ASD is more fully addressed in Chapter 10.

OTHER TYPES OF ASSESSMENTS

Assessment of Speech and Language

Communication is a core deficit in individuals with ASD (American Psychiatric Association, 2000). In many cases, a speech-language pathologist conducts a thorough evaluation of both verbal and nonverbal social-communication skills.

Evaluating the extent to which children are able to communicate provides a baseline for choosing tools and strategies that can promote the development of communication skills. Building communication skills is discussed in Chapter 9.

Even individuals with high-functioning ASD who did not experience delays in language experience difficulties with pragmatic language. Pragmatic language is the verbal and nonverbal communication used to convey social norms and convention and is critical for building relationships. For instance, successful social interactions require the ability to read nonverbal cues such as rolling of the eyes, a disinterested body posture, or tone of voice. In addition, pragmatic language involves understanding social conventions for particular situations (such as the use of formal vs. informal greetings and the use of slang in the appropriate setting and context). Most children pick up pragmatic language skills through daily social interactions. However, individuals with ASD often need direct instruction and extensive practice with these skills in natural settings.

A speech/language evaluation may also address speech concerns, such as unusual prosody (rhythm, intonation), pitch, or volume. This information may be used to determine eligibility for speech/language therapy as well as supporting the educational planning of children with ASD.

The psychoeducational evaluation conducted by the psychologist addresses communication as well. Information from parent and teacher interviews, observations, and other tests such as tests of intelligence, achievement, development, and adaptive behavior can provide information about current functioning. Parent information is especially important for documenting atypical language development. An example of a parent interview tool addressing language functioning is the Social Communication Questionnaire (SCQ; Rutter, Bailey, & Lord, 2003). The SCQ is a screening tool for children ages 4 and older based on items from the Autism Diagnostic Interview-Revised (ADI-R) addressing social communication skills such as expressing empathy and peer relationships.

Table 5.5   Speech and Language Difficulties Associated With ASD

- Echolalia—Repeating back certain words or phrases after spoken by another person or heard from another source (i.e., television) that seems out of context
- Limited or lack of language (verbal and/or nonverbal)
- Repetitive or narrowly focused content of language
- Difficulty with pragmatics, or understanding the social aspect of language such as body language, nuances in language, interpreting tone, and volume
- Speaking with an unusual prosody (may sound robotlike or use a sing-song voice) or pitch (unusually high or low)
- Difficulty with volume control

Assessment of Gross and Fine Motor Skills

Motor skills are sometimes an area of strength in children with ASD. However, particularly in children with Asperger's Syndrome, fine motor skills may be poor (Mayes & Calhoun, 2008). Weaknesses in fine motor skills are associated with handwriting difficulties as noted above. Tests that provide developmental age equivalents and tests of adaptive behavior generally address some aspects of fine motor functioning. Medical records, observations, and teacher–parent interviews can provide additional information about motor skill development. If there are concerns about fine motor skills development (skills involving small motor movements in hands such as writing, cutting, buttoning, working with puzzles and blocks), a referral for an evaluation by an occupational therapist may be warranted. Likewise, if there are concerns about gross motor functioning (large motor skills involved in walking, running, jumping, and throwing), a referral to a physical therapist may be warranted. Furthermore, physical education teachers trained in adaptive physical education can help modify recreational and motor skill building activities to include children with significant motor difficulties.

Assessment of Maladaptive or Atypical Behaviors

All children demonstrate challenging behaviors at times. However, the frequency, intensity, and age appropriateness of these behaviors dictate the extent to which the behaviors are atypical. Maladaptive behaviors may include aggression, self-stemming or perseverative behaviors, and self-injurious behaviors. When these behaviors significantly impact the safety of the child or others, or significantly interfere with the child's ability to function, the child may be referred to behavioral specialist who conducts assessments to create a baseline level of the behaviors and set goals for interventions. Strategies for addressing challenging behaviors through applied behavior analysis are discussed in Chapter 7.

At times, challenging behaviors may be associated with medical concerns such as pain (Carr & Owen-DeSchryver, 2007). Thus, a referral

Temple Grandin, daughter of Eustacia Cutler (interviewed in Chapter 1), is a gifted woman with ASD who eloquently describes the challenges of experiencing intense sensory sensations and how she has coped with these difficulties.

to the child's pediatrician may also be warranted. Information about when the challenging behaviors became problematic and a functional behavioral assessment (FBA) documenting under what conditions the behavior is most likely to occur can help physicians determine if there might be a medical cause.

Assessment of Sensory Issues

First-person anecdotal information (i.e., Grandin, 1995, 1996) suggests that people with ASD often experience distress associated with sensory experiences that are well tolerated by others. Furthermore, research suggests that many children with ASD experience higher rates of sensory difficulties than their typically developing peers (Watling, Deitz, & White, 2003). Children with ASD may demonstrate both hypersensitivities (i.e., overly sensitive to certain sounds, type of physical contact, or textures) and hyposensitivities (i.e., seems not to notice people in the room, high tolerance for pain; Johnson & Myers, 2007).

Sensory issues are not routinely assessed using standardized instruments in psychoeducational evaluations. However, often behavior rating scales and interviews include questions about sensory issues. Furthermore, sensory concerns can be addressed during an occupational therapy and/or ABA assessment. In addition, sensory concerns should be addressed by a medical evaluation. The key issue is the extent to which unusual sensory experiences impact behavior and impede the child's ability to learn. Although sensory processing disorder is not described in the *DSM-IV-TR*, a diagnosis of sensory processing disorder or regulatory-processing sensory disorder is sometimes made by an occupational therapist or developmental pediatrician.

The decision to include interventions addressing sensory issues on the child's IEP is made by the IEP team, which includes the parents. Interventions to address these concerns may involve modifications to the environment (such as soft lamps rather than fluorescent lighting, cutting the tags out of clothing), scheduling lunch or other activities in environments with controlled noise levels, and vestibular activities (such as jumping or swinging). These types of interventions are further discussed in Chapter 8.

Sensory integration therapy, designed to help the child organize sensory stimuli by exposure to increased and reduced levels of sensory stimuli (Scott, Clark, & Brady, 2000), is offered by some public schools. However, the effectiveness of sensory integration therapy is not well documented (Baranek, 2002; Dawson & Watling, 2000; Leong & Carter, 2008; National Research Council, 2001; Stephenson & Carter, 2009). Conversely, a stronger research literature supports the use of behavioral interventions, such as sensory extinction and replacement techniques, to address some types of sensory difficulties (Scott et al., 2000). For instance, Devlin, Leader, and Healy (2009) found that a behavioral intervention based on an FBA was more effective in reducing self-injurious behavior than sensory-integration therapy.

It is important to note that many individuals with ASD report finding sensory interventions helpful. Likewise, parents and teachers report a reduction in challenging behaviors following interventions based on sensory integration techniques (such as weighted vests and brushing). Thus, much work is needed in this area to better understand the contributions of sensory integration therapy to reducing sensory difficulties. Regardless of the interventions used to address sensory difficulties, the experience of unusual sensory perceptions appears to be a significant problem for many individuals with ASD.

Assessments addressing sensory processing can be helpful in determining sensory issues that are distressful or distracting. Individuals with ASD present unique profiles of sensory issues. Thus, an individual with ASD may have none or some sensory difficulties and with varying levels of intensity. The Evaluation of Sensory Processing (ESP; Parham & Ecker, 2002) is an instrument designed to assess sensory processing across all sensory domains in children ages 2 to 12.

Table 5.6   Examples of Sensory Difficulties Associated With ASD

- Over- or underarousal
- Limited eye contact and/or use peripheral vision during social interactions
- Aversion to change or novelty
- Atypical sensory exploration (such as licking or sniffing nonfood objects)
- Sensory aversions (such as smells, fabric textures, food textures, certain sounds)
- Heightened desire for sensory stimuli
- Unusual posture

Table 5.7   Behaviors That May Be Triggered by Sensory Difficulties

- Tantrums
- Rocking back and forth
- Self-injurious behaviors
- Repetitive behaviors (i.e., opening and closing doors)
- Refusal to wear certain clothes, eat certain foods, brush teeth, bathe, have nails/hair cut, play with sand, clay, or other "messy" materials

• As a member of the multidisciplinary assessment team, be sure to include observations of the child across time and settings (i.e., during individual seat work time, during classwide group activities, lunch, recess) and to include evaluated work samples to demonstrate current functioning in reading, language, mathematics, fine motor skills, and so on. Be sure to include the things the child *can* do or *does particularly well* in your anecdotal notes to share with the team. A comprehensive assessment should include information about *both weaknesses and strengths.*

• Document observations and anecdotal notes about the child's social interactions with peers and adults, classroom stimuli that the child find's aversive, and activities/objects that the child find particularly motivating. As the classroom teacher, you can often provide valuable information that may not be accessible through a standardized test. Thus, the quality of your observations are critical to providing the best picture of the child's current functioning.

• During the assessment process, classroom teachers may be asked to complete several standardized rating scales about the child's behavior, adaptive living skills, communication skills, and social-emotional functioning. Generally, you will be asked to consider the child being evaluated in comparison to typically developing children in the class. If you have questions about how to complete the rating scale, it is important that you ask the school psychologist or other professional who asked you to complete the rating scales. The data obtained from your ratings will contribute to important decisions made. Thus, it is your responsibility to provide the most accurate responses possible.

Screening and surveillance for characteristics of ASD in young children is critical to early identification and intervention. Screening tools, such as the M-CHAT, allow for early identification and intervention. A pre-referral phase of supports is often implemented within public schools when ASD is suspected in school-aged children. A systematic tired approach, RTI, may be implemented to monitor the effects of educational supports.

Once a child has been referred for a psychoeducational evaluation within the public schools, a multidisciplinary team works together to collect and interpret data from a wide range of sources. Parents and teachers play a key role in the data collection process. Federal law dictates that evaluations are both nondiscriminative and multifaceted, considering the child's cultural background and language and evaluating skills across time and domains. Special consideration should be made when testing very young children and those with severe impairments.

A comprehensive psychoeducational evaluation provides important information to make an accurate diagnosis, choose optimal educational placements and interventions, and set appropriate educational goals. The ADOS ADI-R are considered the "gold standard" in ASD assessment and contribute to an accurate diagnosis of ASD. An assessment of intellectual ability is an important aspect of the psychoeducational evaluation. However, depending on language functioning, ability potential may be difficult to assess using standardized tests of intelligence. Furthermore, the assessment of academic functioning and cognitive processes such as attention, perspective taking, and executive functioning in high-functioning individuals with ASD may support the development of appropriate educational supports. Addressing social and emotional functioning provides additional information about educational needs and allows for the identification of individuals at risk for comorbid psychiatric conditions such as mood or anxiety disorders.

Assessments of language functioning, motor skills, atypical behaviors, and sensory concerns provide important information about a child's overall functioning and needs. Individuals with specialized training, such as speech-language pathologists, occupational therapists, and applied behavioral therapists, often contribute additional assessment information in these domains.

DISCUSSION AND REFLECTION QUESTIONS

1. Describe the role of the classroom teacher as part of the multidisciplinary team contributing to a nondiscriminative and multifaceted evaluation.

2. What are some of the challenges to consider when evaluating young children and individuals with severe impairments? How might these challenges be addressed?

3. How do specialized diagnostic tools designed to evaluate ASD, such as the ADOS, contribute to choosing optimal interventions?

4. Explain the key domains to be addressed when evaluating a child with characteristics of ASD.

5. Why might a speech-language pathologist or an occupational therapist be called upon to conduct additional information, and how is this related to the diagnosis of ASD?

6. Why is it important to evaluate emotional functioning in individuals with ASD? How are psychiatric conditions, such as depression and anxiety, sometimes expressed differently in individuals with ASD?

RECOMMENDED FURTHER READINGS AND INTERNET SOURCES

Further Readings

American Academy of Pediatrics, Council on Children with Disabilities, Section on Developmental Behavioral Pediatrics. (2006). Identifying infants and young children with developmental disorders in the medical home: An algorithm for developmental surveillance and screening. *Pediatrics, 118,* 405–420.

Chawarska, K., Klin, A., & Volkmar, F. R., (2008). *Autism spectrum disorders in infants and toddlers: Diagnosis, assessment, and treatment.* New York, NY: Guilford Press.

Goldstein, S., Naglieri, J. A., & Ozonoff, S. (2009). *Assessment of autism spectrum disorders.* New York, NY: Guilford Press.

Lord, C., Rutter, M., DiLavore, P., & Risi, S. (1999). *Autism diagnostic observation schedule (ADOS).* Los Angeles, CA: Western Psychological Services.

Internet Sources

Sensory Processing Disorder Foundation website: Provides information about SPD, how it is diagnosed, and treatments. http://www.spd network.org/about-sensory-processing-disorder.html

University of Michigan Autism and Communication Center website: Describes ongoing research involving the development and use of assessment tools for ASD. http://www .umaccweb.com

REFERENCES

Achenbach, T. M., & Rescorla, L. A. (2001). *Manual for the ASEBA school-age forms & profiles.* Burlington, VT: University of Vermont, Research Center for Children, Youth, & Families.

Allen, R. A., Robins, D. L., & Decker, S. L. (2008). Autism spectrum disorders: Neurobiology and current assessment practices. *Psychology in the Schools, 45*(10), 905–917.

Allison, C., Baron-Cohen, S., Wheelwright, S., Charman, T., Richler, J., Pasco, G., & Brayne, C. (2008). The Q-Chat (Quantitative Checklist for Autism in Toddlers): A normally distributed quantitative measure of autistic traits at 18–24 months of age: Preliminary report. *Journal of Autism and Developmental Disorders, 38,* 1414–1425.

Ambrosini, P. J. (2000). Historical development and present status of the schedule for affective disorders and schizophrenia for school-age children (K-SADS). *Journal of the American Academy of Child and Adolescent Psychiatry, 39,* 49–58.

American Academy of Pediatrics, Council on Children with Disabilities, Section on Developmental Behavioral Pediatrics. (2006). Identifying infants and young children with developmental disorders in the medical home: An algorithm for developmental surveillance and screening. *Pediatrics, 118,* 405–420.

American Psychiatric Association. (2000). *Diagnostic and statistical manual of mental disorders* (4th ed., Text Rev.). Washington, DC: Author.

Baranek, G. T. (2002). Efficacy of sensory motor interventions for children with autism. *Journal of Autism and Developmental Disorders, 32,* 397–322.

Baron-Cohen, B., Allen, J., & Gillberg, C. (1992). Can autism be detected at 18 months? The needle, the haystack, and the CHAT. *The British Journal of Psychiatry, 161,* 839–843.

Baron-Cohen, S., Leslie, A. M., & Frith, U. (1985). Does the autistic child have a "theory of mind'? *Cognition, 21,* 37–46.

Barnett, D. W., Elliott, N., Wolsing, L., Bunger, C. E., Haski, H, McKissick, C., & Vandeer Meer, C. D. (2006). Response to intervention for young children with extremely challenging behaviors: What it might look like. *School Psychology Review, 35,* 568–582.

Bayley, N. (2006). *Bayley scales of infant and toddler development.* San Antonio, TX: The Psychological Corporation.

Bishop, S. L., Luyster, R., Richler, J., & Lord, C. (2008). Diagnostic assessment. In K. Chawarska, A. Klin, & F. R. Volkmar (Eds.), *Autism spectrum disorders in infants and toddlers: Diagnosis, assessment, and treatment* (pp. 23–49). New York, NY: Guilford Press.

Boyd, B. A., Odom, S. L., Humphreys, B. P., & Sam, A. M. (2010). Infants and toddlers with autism spectrum disorder: Early identification and early intervention. *Journal of Early Intervention, 32,* 75–98.

Bracken, B. A. (1998). *The Bracken Test of Basic Concepts.* San Antonio,TX: Psych Corps.

Bricker, D., & Squires, J. (1999). *The Ages and Stages Questionnaire (ASQ-3): A parent-completed child monitoring system* (3rd ed.). Baltimore, MD: Brookes.

Bryson, L. R. (2004). Impaired disengagement of attention in young children with autism. *The Journal of Child Psychology and Psychiatry, 45,* 1115–1122.

Bryson, S. E., McDermott, C., Rombough, V., Brian, J., & Zwaigenbaum, l. (2008). The Autism Observation Scale for Infants (AOSI): Scale development and reliability data. *Journal of Autism and Developmental Disorders, 38,* 731–738.

Carr, E., & Owen-DeSchryver, J. (2007). Physical illness, pain, and problem behavior in minimally verbal people with developmental disabilities. *Journal of Autism and Developmental Disabilities, 37,* 413–424.

Chawarska, A., & Bearss, K. (2008). Assessment of cognitive and adaptive skills. In K. Chawarska, A. Klin, & F. R. Volkmar, (2008). (Eds.), *Autism spectrum disorders in infants and toddlers: Diagnosis, assessment, and treatment* (pp. 50–75). New York, NY: Guilford Press.

Chawarska, K., Klin, A., & Volkmar, F. R. (2008). *Autism spectrum disorders in infants and toddlers: Diagnosis, assessment, and treatment.* New York, NY: Guilford Press.

Conners, C. K. (2008). *Conners comprehensive behavior rating scale manual.* Toronto, Canada: Multi-Health Systems.

Dawson, G. D., & Watling, R. (2000). Interventions to facilitate auditory, visual, and motor integration in autism: A review of the evidence. *Journal of Autism and Developmental Disorders, 30,* 415–421.

Delong, R. G., & Dwyer, J. T. (1988). Correlation of family history with specific autistic subtypes: Asperger's syndrome and bipolar affective disease. *Journal of Autism and Developmental Disorders, 18,* 593–600.

Deprey, L., & Ozonoff, S. (2009). Assessment of comorbid psychiatric conditions in autism spectrum disorders. In S. Goldstein, J. A. Naglieri, & S. Ozonoff (Eds.), *Assessment of autism spectrum disorders* (pp. 290–318). New York, NY: Guilford Press.

Devlin, S., Leader, G., & Healy, O. (2009). Comparison of behavioral intervention and sensory-integration therapy in the treatment of self-injurious behavior. *Research in Autism Spectrum Disorders, 3,* 223–231.

Flanagan, D. P., & Kaufman, A. S. (2004). *Essentials of WISC-IV assessment.* New York, NY: Wiley.

Flavell, J. H. (2000). Development of children's knowledge about the mental world. *International Journal of Behavioral Development, 24,* 15–23.

Filipek, P. A., Accardo, P. J., Baranek, G. T., et al. (1999). The screening and diagnosis of autism spectrum disorders. *The Journal of Autism and Developmental Disorders, 29,* 439–484.

Gadow, K. D., DeVincett, C. J., Pomeroy, J., & Azizian, A. (2004). Psychiatric symptoms in preschool children with PDD and clinic and comparison samples. *Journal of Autism and Developmental Disabilities, 34,* 379–393.

Ghaziuddin, M., Ghaziuddin, N., & Greden, J. (2002). Depression in persons with autism: Implications for research and clinical care. *Journal of Autism and Developmental Disorders, 32,* 299–306.

Ghaziuddin, M., & Greden, J. (1998). Depression in children with autism/pervasive developmental disorders: A case-control family history study. *Journal of Autism and Developmental Disorders, 28,* 111–115.

Goldberg, E. (2001). *The executive brain: Frontal lobes and the civilized mind.* Oxford: Oxford University Press.

Goldstein, S., Naglieri, J. A., & Ozonoff, S. (2009). *Assessment of autism spectrum disorders.* New York, NY: Guilford Press.

Goodlin-Jones, B. L., & Solomon, M. (2003). *Contributions of psychology.* In S. Ozonoff, S. Rogers, & R. Hendren (Eds.), *Autism spectrum disorders: A research review for practitioner* (pp. 55–85). Arlington, VA: American Psychiatric Publishing.

Grandin, T. (1995). *Thinking in pictures and other reports from my life with autism.* New York, NY: Random House.

Grandin, T. (1996). Brief report: Response to National Institutes of Health Report. *Journal of Autism and Developmental Disorders, 26,* 185–187.

Hall, L. J. (2009). *Autism spectrum disorders. From theory to practice.* Upper Saddle River, NJ: Pearson.

Handleman, J. S., & Delmolino, L. M. (2005). Assessment of children with autism. In D. Zager (Ed.), *Autism spectrum disorders. Identification, education, and treatment* (3rd ed., pp. 269–293). Mahwah, NJ: Lawrence Erlbaum Associates.

Happé, F. (1994) An advanced test of theory of mind: Understanding of story characters' thoughts and feelings by able autistic, mentally handicapped, and normal children and adults. *Journal of Autism and Developmental Disorders, 24,* 129–154.

Happé, F. G. E., & Frith, U. (1996). Theory of mind and social impairment in children with conduct disorder. *British Journal of Developmental Psychology, 14,* 385–398.

Harris, S. L., & Handleman, J. S. (2000). Age and IQ at intake as predictors of placement for young children with autism: A four- to six-year follow-up. *Journal of Autism and Developmental Disorders, 30,* 137–142.

Hermann, B. P., Seidenberg, M., & Bell, B. (2000). Psychiatric co-morbidity in chronic epilepsy: Identification, consequences, and treatment of major depression. *Epilepsia, 41,* 31–41.

Hoover, J. J., & Patton, J. R. (2008). The role of special educator in a multitiered instructional system. *Intervention in School and Clinic, 43*(4), 195–202.

Howlin, P. (1997) *Autism: Preparing for adulthood.* London, UK: Routledge.

Individuals with Disabilities Education Improvement Act of 2004, Pub. L. No. 108-446, 118 Stat. 2647 (2004). Retrieved from http://frwebgate.access.gpo.gov/cgi-bin/getdoc.cgi?dbname=108_cong_public_laws&docid=f:publ446.108.pdf.

Johnson, C. P., & Myers, S. M. (2007). Identification and evaluation of children with autism spectrum disorders. *Pediatrics, 120,* 1183–1215.

Joseph, R. M., Tager-Flusberg, H., & Lord, C. (2002). Cognitive profiles and social-communicative functioning in children with autism spectrum disorder. *The Journal of Child Psychology and Psychiatry, 43,* 807–821.

Kleinman, J. M., Robins, D. L., Ventola, P. E., Verbalis, A., Barton, M., Hodgson, S., . . . Fein, D. (2008). The Modified Checklist for

Autism in Toddlers: A follow-up study investigating the early detection of autism spectrum disorders. *Journal of Autism and Developmental Disorders, 38,* 827–839.

Klin, A., Volkmar, F. R., Sparrow, S. S., Cicchetti, D. V., & Rourke, B. P. (1995). Validity and neuropsychological characterization of Asperger syndrome: Convergence with non-verbal learning disabilities syndrome. *Journal of Child Psychology and Psychiatry, 36,* 1127–1140.

Leong, H. M., & Carter, M. (2008). Research on the efficacy of sensory integration therapy: Past, present, and future. *Australasian Journal of Special Education, 32,* 83–99.

Leyfer, O. T., Folstein, S. E., Bacalman, S., Davis, N. O., Dinh, E., Morgan, J., Tager-Flusberg, H., & Lainhart, J. E. (2006). Comorbid psychiatric disorders in children with autism: Interview development and rates of disorders. *Journal of Developmental Disorders, 36,* 849–861.

Lincoln, A. J., Courchesne, E., Kilman, B. A., Elmasian, R., & Allen, M. (1988). A study of intellectual abilities in high-functioning people with autism. *Journal of Autism and Developmental Disabilities, 18,* 505–524.

Lincoln, A. J. Searcy, Y. M., Jones, W., & Lord, C. (2007). Social interaction behaviors discriminate young children with autism and Williams syndrome. *Journal of the American Academy of Child and Adolescent Psychiatry, 46,* 323–331.

Lord, C., & Corsello, C. (2005). Diagnostic instruments in autism spectrum disorders. In F. Volkmar, R. Paul, A. Klin, & D. Cohen (Eds.), *Handbook of autism and pervasive developmental disorders* (pp. 730–771). New York, NY: Wiley.

Lord, C., & Risi, S. (2000). Diagnosis of autism spectrum disorders in young children. In A. Wetherby & B. Prizant (Eds.), *Autism spectrum disorders: A transactional developmental perspective* (pp. 167–190). Baltimore, MD: Brookes.

Lord, C., Rutter, M., DiLavore, P., & Risi, S. (1999). *Autism Diagnostic Observation Schedule (ADOS).* Los Angeles, CA: Western Psychological Services.

Luyster, R., Gotham, K., Guthrie, W., Coffing, M., Petrak, R., Pierce, K.,. . . . Lord, C. (2009). The Autism Diagnostic Observation Schedule-Toddler Module: A new module of a standardized diagnostic measure for autism spectrum disorders. *Journal of Autism and Developmental Disorders, 39,* 1305–1320.

Mandell, D. S., Maytali, M. N., & Zubritsky, C. D. (2005). Factors associated with age of diagnosis among children with autism spectrum disorder. *Pediatrics, 116,* 1480–1486.

Markova, J. A. (2004). Coping with social stigma: People with intellectual disabilities moving from institutions and family homes. *Journal of Intellectual Disability Research, 48,* 719–729.

Mayes, S. D., & Calhoun, S. L. (2008). WISC-IV and WIAT-II profiles in children with high functioning autism. *Journal of Autism and Developmental Disabilities, 38,* 428–439.

Merrell, K. W. (1999). *Behavioral, social, and emotional assessment of children and adolescents.* Mahwah, NJ: Erlbaum.

Mullen, E. M. (1995). *Mullen Scales of Early Learning, AGS edition.* Circle Pines, MN: American Guidance Service.

National Research Council. (2001). *Educating children with autism.* Committee on Educational Interventions for Children with Autism. Division of Behavioral and Social Sciences and Education. Washington, DC: National Academy of Press.

Oosterling, I. J., Swinkels, S. H., Jan van der Gaag, R., Visser, J.C., Dietz, C., & Buitelaar, J. K. (2009). Comparative analysis of three screening instruments for autism spectrum disorder in toddlers at high risk. *Journal of Autism and Developmental Disorders, 39,* 897–909.

Ozonoff, S. (1995). Reliability and validity of the Wisconsin card sorting test in studies of autism. *Neuropsychology, 9,* 491–500.

Parham, L. D., & Ecker, C. (2002). Evaluation of sensory processing.

Plauché Johnson, C., Myers, S. M., & The Council on Children with Disabilities. (2007). Identification and evaluation of children with autism spectrum disorders. *Pediatrics, 120,* 1183–1215.

Premack, D., & Woodruff, G. (1978). Does the chimpanzee have a 'theory of mind'? *Behavioral and Brain Sciences, 4,* 515–526.

Reynolds, C. R., & Kamphaus, R. W. (Eds.). (2003). *Handbook of psychological and educational assessment of children: Personality, behaviors, and context* (2nd ed.). New York, NY: The Guilford Press.

Reynolds, C. R., & Kamphaus, R. W. (2009). *Behavior assessment system for children,* second edition. Circle Pines, MN: American Guidance Service.

Rice, C. (2007, February 9). Prevalence of autism spectrum disorders—Autism and Developmental Disabilities Monitoring Network, 14 Sites, United States, 2002. *MMWR Surveillance Summaries, 56,* 12–28.

Rice, C. (2009, October 8 & 9). *Autism diagnostic observation schedule. Clinical ADOS Workshop,* Atlanta, GA.

Robbins, D. L. (2008). Screening for autism spectrum disorders in primary care settings. *Autism, 12,* 537–556.

Robbins, D. L., Fein, D., Barton, M. L., & Green, J. A. (2001). The Modified Checklist for Autism in Toddlers: An initial study investigating the early detection of autism and pervasive developmental disorders. *Journal of Autism and Developmental Disorders, 31,* 131–144.

Rutter, M., Le Couteur, A., & Lord, C. (2003). *Autism diagnostic interview-revised (ADI-R).* Los Angeles, CA: Western Psychological Services.

Rutter, M., Bailey, A., & Lord, C. (2003). *Social communication questionnaire.* Los Angeles, CA: Western Psychological Services.

Santrock, J. W. (2008). *Children* (10th ed.). New York, NY: McGraw-Hill.

Sattler, J. M. (2008). *Assessment of children: Cognitive foundations* (5th ed.). San Diego, CA: Jerome M. Sattler Publisher.

Schopler, E., Lansing, M. D., Reichler, R., & Marcus, L. M (2005). *Psychoeducational profile* (3rd ed.): TEACCH individualized psychoeducational assessment for children with autism spectrum disorders. Austin, TX: Pro-Ed.

Schopler, E., Reichler, R. J., DeVellis, R. F., & Daly, K. (1980). Toward objective classification of childhood autism: Childhood Autism Rating Scale (CARS). *Journal of Autism and Developmental Disorders, 10,* 91–103.

Schopler, E., Reichler, R. J., & Renner, B. R. (1988). *The Childhood Autism Rating Scale (CARS).* Los Angeles, CA: Western Psychological Services.

Scott, J., Clark, C., & Brady, M. (2000). *Students with autism. Characteristics and special programming for special educators.* Belmont, CA: Thomas Wadsworth.

Shaffer, D., Fisher, P., & Lucas, C. (2004). *The Diagnostic Interview Schedule for Children (DISC). Comprehensive handbook of psychological assessment, vol. 2: Personality assessment* (pp. 256–270). Hoboken, NJ: Wiley.

Shriver, M. D., Allen, K. D., & Matthews, J. R. (1999). Effective assessment of the shared and unique characteristics of children with autism. *School Psychology Review, 28,* 538–558.

Sparrow, S. S., Balla, D. A., & Cicchetti, D. V. (2005). *Vineland Adaptive Behavior Scales II.* Circle Pines, MN: AGS.

Stephenson, J., & Carter, M. (2009). The use of weighted vests with children with autism spectrum disorders and other disabilities. *Journal of Autism and Developmental Disorders, 39,* 105–114.

Stone, W. L., McMahon, C. R., & Henderson, L. M. (2008). Two-Year-Olds (STAT) for children under 24 months. *Autism, 12,* 557–573.

Thomas, A., & Grimes, J. (2002). *Best practices in school psychology* (4th ed.). Washington, DC: NASP.

Turnbull, A., Turnbull, R., & Wehmeyer, M. L. (2007). *Exceptional lives. Special education in today's schools* (5th ed.). Upper Saddle River, NJ: Merrill/Prentice Hall.

VanDerHeyden, A. M., & Snyder, P. (2006). Integrating frameworks from early childhood intervention and school psychology to accelerate growth for all young children. *School Psychology Review, 35,* 519–534.

Watling, R. L., Deitz, J., & White, O. (2003). Comparison of sensory profile scores of young children with and without autism spectrum disorders. In C. B. Royee, (Ed.), *Pediatric issues in occupational therapy* (pp. 130–139). Bethesda, MD: AOTA Press.

Wechsler, D. (2003). *Wechsler Intelligence Scale for Children–Fourth Edition.* San Antonio, TX: Harcourt Assessment.

Wechsler, D. (2009). *Wechsler Individual Achievement Test–Third Edition.* San Antonio, TX: Harcourt Assessment.

Western Psychological Services. (2010). *Training/ CE.* Retrieved from //portal.wpspublish. com/portal/page?_pageid=53,82860&_ dad=portal&_schema=PORTAL.

Wetherby, A. M., Brosnan-Maddox, S., Peace, V., & Newton, L. (2008). Validation of the Infant-Toddler Checklist as a broadband screener for autism spectrum disorders from 9 to 24 months of age. *Autism, 12,* 487–511.

Wimmer, H., & Perner, J. (1983). Beliefs about beliefs: Representation and constraining function of wrong beliefs in young children's understanding of deception. *Cognition, 13,* 103–128.

Woodcock, R. W., McGrew, K. S., & Mather, N. (2001). *Woodcock Johnson Tests of Achievement, Third Edition.* Rolling Meadows, IL: Riverside Publishing.

Zwaigenbaum, L., Bryson, S., Rogers, T., Roberts, W., Brian, J., & Szatmari, P. (2005). Behavioral manifestations of autism in the first year of life. *International Journal of Developmental Neuroscience, 23,* 143–152.

Zwaigenbaum, L., Bryson, S., Lord, C., Rogers, S., Carter, A., Carver, L., . . . Yirmiya, N. (2009). Clinical assessment and management of toddlers with suspected autism spectrum disorder: Insights from studies of high-risk infants. *Pediatrics, 123,* 1383–1391.

CHAPTER 6

EARLY INTERVENTION AND TRANSITIONING TO ELEMENTARY SCHOOL

In this chapter, you will learn about:

- The importance of early intervention for children with ASD.
- Parents' perceptions of early intervention supports.
- Providing family-centered services.
- The individualized family support plan (IFSP) and transitioning to the individualized education plan (IEP).
- Components of the IEP.
- Successful programs for young children with ASD: TEACCH, the Denver Model, and the Monarch Program.

THE IMPORTANCE OF EARLY INTERVENTION

Early identification and intervention is necessary to ensure optimal outcomes for all children with special needs (Bruder, 2010), including children with Autism Spectrum Disorders (ASD; National Research Council, 2001). Early intervention for children with ASD is associated with a greater likelihood of independence (Howlin, 2005) and overall gains in skills (Corsello, 2005). Early intervention services are defined in many ways. The research literature in early intervention generally considers supports for children 8 years and younger (Bruder, 2010). The federal law defines early intervention services under sections B and C under the Individuals with Disability Education Act (IDEA). Early intervention services are available for children with disabilities ages 0 to 3 under Part C of IDEA (2004). This part of special education legislation specifically addresses the need for family-centered services as the basis for supporting a child's learning (Bruder, 2010). Part B of IDEA covers preschool services (ages 3–5).

The Need for Early Diagnosis

Early diagnosis of ASD allows for early intervention and a better prognosis.

Children with ASD benefit from accurate diagnosis and intensive early intervention addressing language and communication (Chakrabarti & Fombonne, 2001), social development (Dawson & Zanoli, 2003; Dawson et al., 2004), and behavior (Anderson & Romanczyk, 1999). Although the average age of diagnosis of ASD is between 3 to 4 years of age (Mandel et al., 2005; Zwaigenbaum et al., 2009), ASD can be reliably diagnosed as young as 15 to 18 months (National Research Council, 2001; Zwaigenbaum et al., 2005). Unfortunately, diagnosis is often delayed until children are school age (Giarelli et al., 2010; Mandell, Maytali, & Zubritsky, 2005). In fact, many parents report that professionals dismissed their early concerns about their child's development. Thus, in such instances it isn't until the child attends formal schooling that concerns about development and learning are finally addressed. Such experiences are associated with delayed intervention and skepticism about collaborating with professionals in the future (Howlin & Asgharian, 1999). Furthermore, children from non-English-speaking caregivers or minority ethnicity are less likely to have access to early intervention services (Clements, Barfield, Kotelchuck, & Wilber, 2008). Likewise, both children living in rural communities and from families living in poverty are likely to receive later diagnoses and later intervention supports (Mandell et al., 2005).

Although early intervention can significantly improve communication, social skills, self-help skills, academic skills, and behavior, early intervention does not appear to *cure* ASD (Howlin, 2003). Furthermore, there is limited research regarding the optimal intensity of intervention in early intervention. From her review of the literature describing early intervention and autism, Howlin concluded that high-quality early intervention programs offered 15 to 20 hours per week result in optimal effectiveness. There are variable outcomes for all interventions depending on many factors, including intervention design, intensity, and characteristics of the child (Wolery & Garfinkle, 2002). However, two aspects of early interventions with the greatest empirical support include intensity of program and age at which intervention begins (Corsello, 2005).

Early Detection of ASD

Table 6.1   Early Signs of ASD

The following characteristics are useful in distinguishing infants (ages 12–18 months) with ASD from infants with other impairments:

- Atypical visual tracking skills
- Prolonged fixation on objects
- Lack of joint attention and social orienting
- Atypical motor mannerisms
- Delays in motor development
- Atypical development of play skills (such as lack of limited toy play, repetition of motor movements during play, lack of imitation during play)
- Reduced affect, failure to orient to name, lack of social smiles
- Delays in language development

Source: From Zwaigenbaum et al., (2009). Clinical Assessment and Management of Toddlers with Suspected Autism Spectrum Disorder: Insights from Studies of High-Risk Infants. *Pediatrics, 123,* 1383-1391.

PARENT PERCEPTIONS OF EARLY INTERVENTION SERVICES

Meeting the Needs of Families That Have Young Children With ASD

Parents and service providers work closely together to provide early intervention support to children with disabilities. Are we doing enough to meet the needs of families with young children? To investigate this question, Raspa and colleagues (2010) surveyed parents of 2,849 families of children with disabilities enrolled in early intervention programs (under Part C of IDEA) in Illinois and Texas using the Family Outcome Survey. Parents reported that early intervention services helped them better understand their child's development,

The needs of families with young children must be considered when planning intervention services.

needs, and progress. In addition, parents believed that early intervention helped their children to learn, practice new skills, and gain access to medical care and child care. However, parents noted that early intervention services were *less* helpful in connecting them to community supports and helping them learn about services available to their child. Positive outcomes were mediated by ethnicity and income, with Caucasian parents and parents with higher incomes providing the most favorable ratings.

Helping Parents Cope With the Initial Diagnosis

As discussed in Chapter 4, each family has unique characteristics that impact beliefs about child rearing, interpretation of disability, and efforts to collaborate with professionals. In addition, the child's age at diagnosis, severity of the disorder, and supports impact the parent experience of learning of their child's ASD diagnosis. Furthermore, developing a trusting relationship with educational professionals impacts the extent to which parents engage in a collaborative process with school personnel (Stoner & Angell, 2006).

Many parents of children with ASD report early efforts to communicate their concerns about their young child's development were minimized. Consequently, most children with ASD are not diagnosed until age 2 to 3, depending on the severity of the disorder. Parents often experience relief upon finally having their suspicions confirmed by a diagnosis. However, this relief is coupled with the complexity of confirmation that something is "wrong" with their child. Thus, parents begin a process of dealing with a recognized "label" that their child has a disability. Often this experience is associated with anxiety as well as anger at having not had the support they needed earlier (Bailey, 2008). In fact, parents learning of their child's diagnosis of a disability often go through a complicated mourning process reflecting the loss of a preconceived ideal of who their child is and will become, while simultaneously becoming increasingly involved in supporting their child (O'Brien & Daggett, 2006).

The concept of "ambiguous loss" (Boss, 1999) describes another aspect of coming to terms with the ASD diagnosis. Ambiguous loss refers to the fact that in most cases, the *cause* of ASD is unclear and there is no *cure* for the disorder. Furthermore, little is known about a young child's long-term prognosis (Chawarska, 2007; Lord et al., 2006). This mourning process may include stages of shock and denial, anger, anxiety and depression, and ultimately an acceptance of their child and increased clarity regarding their role as advocate and parent (Irvin, Kennell, & Kalus, 1982; Kearney & Griffin, 2001). However, there is no clear time line for when a parent resolves each stage of grief. In fact, "resolution" of grief may be an unrealistic expectation because many parents experience "chronic grief" in which they learn to manage their grief yet never completely stop the grieving process (Lindgren, Hainsworth, & Eakes, 1992; Olshansky, 1962).

Table 6.2 Tips for Helping Parents Cope With the Initial Diagnosis of ASD

- Assure parents that they did not *cause* their child's autism. Their efforts to obtain a diagnosis will result in the ability to access services for their child.
- It is normal to have ambivalent emotions. Many parents both feel relieved that there is a label to describe their child's difficulties, yet sad and anxious about their child's future. Parents often feel both sad about the loss of their dreams for their child, yet hopeful about finding experiences that help their child reach his or her potential.
- Knowledge is power! They may not have the time or energy to investigate all resources, but others can help them with this. Teachers, psychologists, and parents can provide important information about local resources, family support opportunities, local, state, and federal laws that govern available resources. Offer to set up opportunities for parents to observe different educational options for their child and to talk with other parents who have children in those programs.
- Clearly communicate results of the assessment of the child's current functioning. It is important that parents understand their child's areas of strengths as well as the areas of weakness. This is critical to collaborating with educators to establish learning goals with the IEP.
- In addition to helping the parents understand the next step, often determining eligibility for special education services, the parents also may need to know what *they* can do to help their child at home. Bailey (2008) suggests that foremost parents receive guidance with providing a safe environment for their child and addressing challenging behaviors. Furthermore, parents should be encouraged to carve out time to give unconditional love to their child and not feel as if they constantly have to act as a therapist.

For additional information, visit the Family Caregiver Alliance website at http://www.caregiver.org/caregiver/jsp/content_node.jsp?nodeid=2185.

The interview below demonstrates the emotionally intense process experienced by a mother as she pursues a diagnosis for her son with ASD. Consider how the relationship with her son's current teacher has helped empower her to collaborate to create an optimal learning environment for her son.

CHAPTER REFLECTION: Interview With Michelle and Agatha

Author.

Michelle is the mother of Clark, a child with ASD. She also assists with the Early Longitudinal Risk Investigation (ELRI), a longitudinal study investigating the interplay between genetic susceptibility and environmental factors associated with ASD (for more information www.earlistudy. org).

The Initial Diagnosis

It is very hard. First of all it's sort of a denial. Initially Clark was diagnosed with PDD-NOS [Pervasive Developmental Disorder-Not Otherwise Specified] and to me that wasn't autism. It took me a long time to kind of come to terms with that. Then it's *why* did this happen and *why didn't I see it.*

I was very surprised when Clark was diagnosed. He seemed "typical." It wasn't until he started preschool as a 3-year-old that people began to talk about red flags. And his teachers began to talk about "we see red flags." And it was very frustrating because I didn't know what that meant. The message that I took as a parent, and I don't think is was necessarily intended, was that, in short, that Clark was a bad boy and your parenting skills are subpar.

At first you feel shell-shocked from all the sources of information. I realized that I have this much time, this much energy, and this much money. I have a job, [and] I have another child.

The Parent–Teacher Relationship

Clark has an excellent teacher. She is a beautiful fit with Clark. When he went into kindergarten, I wrote a letter to the vice principal describing Clark. I didn't mention his diagnosis. Then I get a call from his teacher who wanted to have a conversation. That to me said she wasn't going, "Oh, no, why is this child in my class?"

Throughout the year, she e-mails or calls me to share something funny. I feel like we're working as a team. She doesn't assume that I have all the ideas or answers and I don't assume that she does.

Teachers should understand that whatever the frustrations they are feeling during those work hours, parents get the child *the whole rest of the day*. Always assume that parents are doing their best!

Reflections and Advice From Clark's Kindergarten Teacher, Agatha

My degree is in generic special education. I teach in an inclusion class. I have been a kindergarten teacher and also a bilingual ESL [English as a second language] teacher. For all of these jobs, I consider my job to be a process. That is significant in assisting the children I work with. As I work with a child like Clark, I remember that every child and every parent is different. I must assess the child and go on individual needs.

Working with Michelle was easy. At first it is hard for parents to say, "My child is on the spectrum." We have lots of communication. I let her know even the minutest thing that has happened, using very kind and positive words. I genuinely make an effort to remember that I am the adult, and I am working with a child. The parents are under a lot of stress. You know the old saying, "You catch more flies with honey than vinegar." Be kind to parents. It is difficult for them. They are sending their best and most precious possessions to us. They need kindness and support. They need us. Find out what is best for them, but don't lay down like a doormat to be walked over either. I try to let parents know that I love many things about their child like his laugh, or the way he delights in science. I want parents to know I think their child is special. Michelle is really supportive, and the whole team really listens.

I operate from my most generous mode. I learned this from the Center for Cognitive Coaching (to learn more about Cognitive Coaching, visit http://www.cognitivecoaching.com). Advice for teachers: try to create a *positive climate*. If a child has a behavioral problem, deal with it and let it go! Follow-through with the consequences, but don't keep bringing it up. Be positive and move on. You don't want to take a bad experience you have had with a child into the team meeting, it creates a negative feeling for the entire team. Learn to let go of struggles. When teachers complain about a

(Continued)

(Continued)

child, those negative feelings follow him like a cloud. The teacher should talk with the proper people and deal with the behavior, but not complain. A positive climate impacts the team and the entire child.

© Agatha Rodriguez.

THE FAMILY-CENTERED APPROACH

Describing a Family-Centered Approach to Early Intervention

The family-centered approach is the cornerstone of early intervention efforts (Dunst, 2002). However, the transition from a deficit-centered (focusing on the child's disability) to a family-centered approach has been a slower process in educational planning for school-aged children in the public school system (Scott, Clark, & Brady, 2000; Stoner et al., 2005). In a family-centered approach, the strengths and priorities of the family are equally important as the recommendations provided by professionals (Bruder, 2000). The child is considered within the context of both the school and the family.

A family-centered approach is important for many reasons. From a legal perspective, this approach is in line with the tenets of IDEA (2004), which mandates family participation in planning and decision making. From a family-systems perspective, the child with ASD is a part of a dynamic family system. Information from the family is essential to understand the needs, interpret behaviors, and set goals for the child.

The Individualized Family Service Plan

Young children spend much time with their family. Because young children are so dependent upon their caregivers for meeting virtually every need, the family must be part of effective early intervention planning. Family-centered

Figure 6.1 The Family-Centered Approach

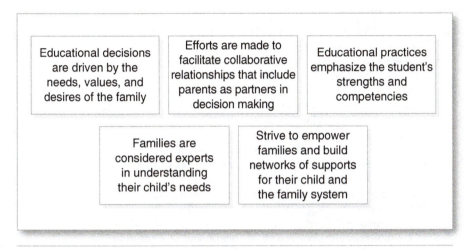

| Educational decisions are driven by the needs, values, and desires of the family | Efforts are made to facilitate collaborative relationships that include parents as partners in decision making | Educational practices emphasize the student's strengths and competencies |

| Families are considered experts in understanding their child's needs | Strive to empower families and build networks of supports for their child and the family system |

Source: Adapted from Dunst, Johanson, Trivette, and Hamby (1991).

practices create partnerships between families and professionals (Dunlap & Fox, 2007), build upon family strengths, and assess family outcomes (Raspa et al., 2010). Unfortunately, many early intervention programs adopt a family-training rather than family support approach (Kohler, 1999; Wolery & Garfinkle, 2002). Family-centered practices are particularly important for families with children on the autism spectrum because of the pervasive nature of the deficits and the significant stress that such needs often place upon the family system.

Furthermore, acknowledgment of the central role of families is particularly important considering the historical belief that poor parenting caused autism.

The recognition of the key role that families play in both identification and early intervention is reflected in Part C of IDEA (2004), in which an Individualized Family Service Plan (IFSP) is created based on family and child needs (Brown, 2003; IDEA). In addition, the IFSP includes ongoing assessment of the family's priorities, expectations, goals, concerns, and their measurement of progress as well as the child's developmental level (IDEA). These services are required to be in a natural environment and one in which same-age *neurotypical* (nondisabled) peers are present (IDEA). IFSP address target skills within the context of family routines and daily activities (Jung, 2007).

Table 6.3   Key Components of the Individualized Family Service Plan

- Assessment of the child's current levels of physical, cognitive, communication, social or emotional, and adaptive development.
- Statement of the family's resources, priorities, and concerns relating to enhancing the development of the child.
- Statement of the measurable results or outcomes to be achieved.
- Statement of specific early intervention services necessary to meet the unique needs of the child, including the frequency, intensity, and method of delivering services.
- Description of the natural environments in which early intervention services will be provided, including justification if services will not be provided in a natural environment.
- Projected dates for initiation of services and anticipated length, duration, and frequency of services.
- Identification of the service coordinator from the profession most closely relevant to the child's or family's needs who will be responsible for the implementation of the plan and coordination with other agencies and persons.
- Steps to be taken in the transition of the child to preschool or other appropriate services.

EFFECTIVE PROGRAMS FOR YOUNG CHILDREN WITH ASD

Components of Effective Early Intervention Programs

Educational interventions for young children with ASD should use evidence-based practices.

The educational plan must be individualized for each child with ASD. Thus, the selection of interventions are dependent upon many factors, including the age of the child, individual goals, level of impairment, behavioral difficulties, communication skills, and family needs and concerns (Schreibman, 2000). However, careful consideration of the following factors (Table 6.4) is associated with the most successful outcomes in meeting the needs with a child on the autism spectrum.

Table 6.4 Factors Associated With Positive Outcomes in Meeting the Needs of Children With ASD

- *Intensity*—Intervention delivered several hours daily and across settings (i.e., instructional time, recess, home).
- *Opportunities to generalize and maintain skills*—This is often best done when skills are learned in natural environments that would normally facilitate or maintain particular skills (i.e., selecting a food choice during a family meal).
- *Structured teaching with reinforcement*—Breaking down tasks into component steps (task analysis) and directly teaching specific skills. Repeated practice followed by reinforcement of success is part of many empirically supported behavioral interventions (Chapter 7). This is critical for children with ASD because they often do not learn through observation or inference. Furthermore, many children with ASD appear less motivated to learn academic skills than their typically developing peers. Teaching can also be structured through use of routines, schedules, and physical organization of the classroom.
- *Modification of environment to promote communication, learning, and reduce stress*—Understanding a child's sensory needs is important in establishing a classroom environment that is comfortable and conducive to learning. Modifications of the classroom environment can promote safety, communication, comfort, and enhance learning.
- *Opportunities for interaction with typically developing same-age peers*—The degree to which a child with ASD can tolerate inclusive opportunities varies. Some children need a more predictable and calm setting. However, even those children may benefit from opportunities to observe and interact with their peers during in play and social experiences. Friendship training can help children learn to interact with their peers with ASD in a manner that is engaging rather than overwhelming (discussed in Chapter 10).

Examples of Effective Early Intervention Programs

There are many different programs designed to address the core deficits and learning needs of children with ASD. Comparing the effectiveness of these programs can be a daunting task for several reasons. One reason is the diverse range of abilities and deficits among children on the autism spectrum (Kasari, 2002). Second, there is often considerable overlap between programs described in the literature (Corsello, 2005). In addition, research investigating the effectiveness of early intervention programs often fails to address family characteristics and family outcomes (Wolery & Garfinkle, 2002). Furthermore, studies of early intervention program effectiveness rarely use random assignment or matching of children to different programs or control groups. Thus, the experimental design used to evaluate early intervention programs for children with autism generally lacks experimental rigor (Kasari). Despite these limitations, available research suggests several notable programs that appear to contribute to positive outcomes for children with ASD.

Chapters 8, 9, and 10 further discuss criteria for choosing intervention practices that are evidence based for teaching individuals with ASD. The Council for Exceptional Children (CEC) Division for Research and the National Autism Center (NAC) provide evaluative information about a wide range of interventions. Choosing evidence-based early intervention practices also takes into account family preference and values and student input when possible. Furthermore, issues such as capacity of the school to provide services (i.e., do teachers need additional training, support staff?), sustainability (i.e., a consultant sets up an Applied Behavior Analysis [ABA] program but is not available to continue implementation after the contract runs out), and school climate/organizational issues (i.e., is there administrational support for systemwide inclusion to generalize skills across naturalistic settings?).

TEACCH

In the 1960s, Eric Schopler pioneered efforts to work with very young children with ASD. His program, Treatment and Education of Autistic and Communication-Handicapped Children (TEACCH), blends behavioral components firmly rooted in ABA with cognitive components, integrated alongside a multitiered education program designed to empower parents and teachers to create environments that allow children with autism to grow and develop throughout the life span.

TEACCH was inspired by Schopler's doctoral dissertation for treating autism (Mesibov, Shea, & Schopler, 2007). Although Schopler originally based his research on the predominant psychoanalytical theories of the day, he soon championed the unpopular stance at that time that autism was caused by something other than poor parenting (Mesibov, 1994). In fact, Schopler and his mentor, Robert Reichler, realized that parents were excellent cotherapists and teachers. Consequently, TEACCH challenged the social policy at the time that blamed parents (primarily mothers) for causing autism in their child through negligent parenting practices (Schopler, 1995).

Consequently, Schopler and Reichler developed a complex support network for children with autism, starting with very young children, including intense parent support and ongoing training, incorporating teacher training and support, and following the child to coordinate lifelong community-based services (Mesibov, 1994). This program was revolutionary at the time and became the

Figure 6.2   Dimensions to Evaluate in Establishing Best Practice for Autism
Interventions

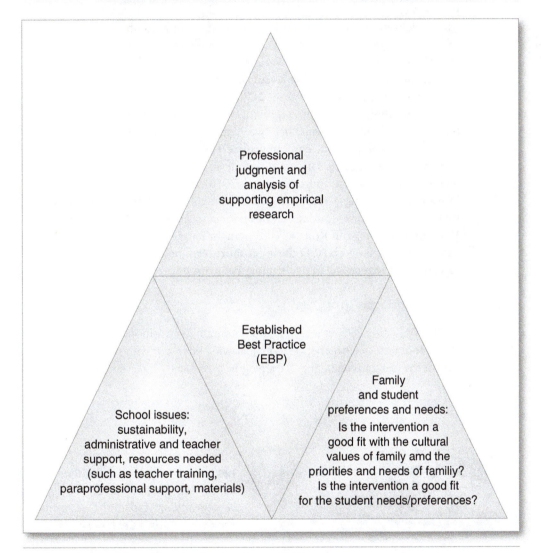

Professional
judgment and
analysis of
supporting empirical
research

Established
Best Practice
(EBP)

School issues:
sustainability,
administrative and teacher
support, resources needed
(such as teacher training,
paraprofessional support, materials)

Family
and student
preferences and needs:
Is the intervention a
good fit with the cultural
values of family amd the
priorities and needs of familiy?
Is the intervention a good fit
for the student needs/preferences?

Based on information from the National Autism Center (2011).

first program to be adopted by a state as an intervention program for autism
in the state of North Carolina. In fact, in 1971 Leo Kanner, who first documented autism as a distinct disorder, testified on behalf of Project TEACCH for
the North Carolina Legislator (Schopler, 1987).

Early Start Denver Model

The Early Start Denver Model (or Denver Model) is another intervention program championing early intervention and parent involvement. The Denver Model delivers an individualized curriculum using a combination of instructional techniques based on behavioral, developmental, and relationship theories and can be presented in a variety of settings, including preschool group instruction, individual therapy sessions, and one-on-one intervention (Rogers, Hall, Osaki, Reaven, & Herbison, 2000).

By integrating developmental, relationship-based, and components of ABA, the Early Start Denver Model has two main goals: (1) to address skill building and (2) to develop social communicative skills. Teaching strategies integrate play, building pragmatic language, and developing skills within the context of relationships. Dawson and colleagues (2010) investigated the efficacy of the Denver Model using a randomized and controlled design with toddlers, and found improvements in adaptive behavior and cognitive skills. Furthermore, Vismara, Colombi, and Rogers (2009) taught parents to implement the Denver Model to children with ASD during a short-term home intervention, resulting in significant reductions in challenging behaviors.

The Monarch program

The Monarch program is an inclusion program to transition children to elementary school inclusive experiences. The following interview with the program manager of the program highlights the strengths of this early intervention approach.

CHAPTER REFLECTION: The Monarch Program

Interview with Sheila Wagner, M.Ed., program manager of the Monarch School-Age program at Emory University, and an Assistant Director at the Emory Autism Center in Atlanta.

What is the Monarch program?

It has been in existence since 1993, focusing on education for children with ASD. The inclusion project is the largest piece. School systems commit to a 2-year involvement with our center to look at programming for students with ASD. We use both a bottom-up and a top-down approach. The bottom-up approach involves consulting with and training teachers. We help set up individualized teaching strategies and data collection.

At the same time, we implement a top-down approach in which we work with special education directors, principals, the board, and the superintendent. We try to design what the school system needs. I work with administration to understand global issues for sustainability. Working to implement inclusion both top down and bottom up, we meet in the middle and get changes made.

Are parents involved in this program?

Parents are a huge factor in this. I am always meeting with parents. I make sure if parents don't have a support group, we set one up. We also establish periodic meetings between parents and teachers. These treatment team meetings are in addition to the IEP meeting to address things as they come up. I consider inclusion more than just being included in school. Inclusion is being included in the community and the world, so family is very important.

How do you deal with challenging behaviors?

We implement incidental teaching in which we build upon a child's interest in the natural environment with the use of positive behavioral reinforcements and FBA. I am most concerned with teaching the replacement skills (teaching behaviors they don't have). We use a very positive behavior support system. Individual behavior plans supplement the classroom behavior management system.

Are there certain aspects of the classroom environment that seem to work best?

We use a lot of visual support systems, but we put them in the context of the natural setting.

How do you address social skill development?

The focus of all of what we do is to generalize appropriate skills across settings, not just on the child with ASD, but for the entire class. We do a lot of peer programming in which we get the peers on board for inclusion. They are the models we need, and all kids need to work and play alongside people with other abilities.

For more information about Ms. Wagner's approach to inclusion, refer to her book *Inclusive Programming for Elementary Students With Autism*.

TRANSITIONING FROM EARLY INTERVENTION
TO SPECIAL EDUCATION SERVICES

After the stress associated with receiving an initial diagnosis of ASD, parents report that the transition from early intervention services to entry in the public school system rates highly as a stressful event in parenting a child with ASD. Parents of young children with ASD have needs that often require coordination of different services and providers (Kohler, 1999). In many cases, parents are responsible for coordinating and monitoring, which often results in a lack of coordinated services and poor communication among service providers. These problems sometimes negatively impacted the services their child received.

Once a child transitions to public school, the Individualized Education Plan (IEP) replaces the IFSP. The IEP, which describes educational goals for the school-aged child ages 3 to 21, is different than the IFSP primarily in regard to the focus on the child within the context of the *educational setting* rather than the child within the context of the *family*. Consequently, this transition proves to be stressful for many parents (Stoner et al., 2005).

Under IDEA Part C (guiding the IFSP), the parent's rights were extensive. In fact, their rights are almost equal to the child's rights (Brown, 2003). As an integral part of the IFSP team, they were able to determine the goals and outcomes that they would like for their child. However, once the child enters the public school system, a more child-focused approach guides planning. Thus, while the IFSP relied on a partnership emphasizing the family's perceptions about their child's goals and intervention strategies (Stoner et al., 2005), the IEP emphasizes the child's needs within the context of school and independence with more deference to the perceptions of professionals (Stoner et al.). Children and parents are thrust into a new environment, with a new staff, laws, and vocabulary that is often overwhelming (Stoner et al.).

Common frustrations about the transition from the IFSP to the IEP include poor communication and interactions with families (Stoner et al., 2005), inadequate delivery of services (Lake & Billingsly, 2000), and focus on academic instruction with less support for other domains such as social development (Klin, Chawarska, & Volkmar, 2008). Parents report frustration with the reduced interaction and communication with professionals, often fostering friction between school and parents (Stoner et al.). Adding to the conflict is the parent's perception that the education professional and school doesn't see their child "as an individual with their own strengths and abilities" (Lake & Billingsly, p. 244), only seeing the child's deficiencies (Lake & Billingsly). Furthermore, parents report that educational professionals seem unwilling to meet their child's needs without being forced (Stoner et al.). It's important to keep in mind that parent's often had to fight for a diagnosis so when their child enters school and there is difficulty obtaining services for their child, parents begin to distrust the professionals (Stoner et al.).

Professionals can help ease the transition from the IFSP to the IEP by trying to meet the parent's need for communication (Stoner et al., 2005). Children with pervasive communication disorders are unable to tell their parents about what happened in schools, progress or problems, so they rely on the educational professional to inform about their child (Stoner et al.). Before the child and service was in the home, now in the new environment, parents feel disconnected. Frequent and open communication can help build trust between the parents and the school (Stoner et al.).

THE INDIVIDUALS WITH DISABILITIES EDUCATION ACT: THE SPIRIT OF PARTNERSHIP

Prior to 1975, children with disabilities were often excluded from attending public school or educated in regular classrooms without modifications or accommodations to address their learning differences (U.S. Department of Education, 2010). In large part, today's special education legislation in the United States was propelled forward by efforts of parents and advocates. The result of landmark class-action lawsuits and case law prompted the federal legislation, Public Law 94-142, the Education for All Handicapped Children Act. This legislation was largely brought into existence by the efforts of parents inspired by the civil rights movement and the subsequent antidiscrimination legislation (Hurwitz, 2008). P/L 94-142 was renamed the Individuals with Disabilities Education Act.

Turnbull and Cilley (1999) describe the IDEA legislation as "the classic 'carrot and stick' approach: federal funds are available only if the SEAs [state educational agencies] and LEA [local educational agencies] agree to comply with IDEA" (p. 1). Thus, schools systems are compelled by law to follow IDEA to receive federal funding.

Autism was not listed as a separate category of disability in IDEA until 1990. Prior to that time, a child with ASD might have received services through the category "Other Health Impaired" or another category of special education if they met the eligibility criteria. Today, children with autism, Asperger's Syndrome, and PDD-NOS are likely to meet eligibility criteria for services under the Autism category of IDEA.

> **CHAPTER REFLECTION: Definition of Autism From the Individuals with Disabilities Education Act (IDEA)**
>
> Autism means a developmental disability significantly affecting verbal and nonverbal communication and social interaction, generally evident before age 3, that adversely affects a child's educational performance. Other characteristics often associated with autism are engagement in repetitive activities and stereotyped movements, resistance to environmental change or change in daily routines, and unusual responses to sensory experiences. Autism does not apply if a child's educational performance is adversely affected primarily because the child has an emotional disturbance, as defined in paragraph (c)(4) of this section.
>
> From the U.S. Department of Education (1999).

The most current reauthorization of IDEA occurred in 2004 (The Individuals with Disabilities Education Improvement Act of 2004). Part B of IDEA addresses educational services for children ages 3 to 21; and Part C addresses educational services for young children, ages 0–3 (Turnbull, Turnbull, Erwin, & Soodak, 2006).

The 2004 reauthorization aligned IDEA with the No Child Left Behind Act (No Child Left Behind [NCLB], 2002), which increased support for early intervention, promoted empirically validated instructional practices (Hurwitz, 2008), and emphasized access to general curriculum (West & Whitby, 2008). In addition, the 2004 reauthorization requires the selection of interventions that have empirical validation supporting their use with a particular population (Turnbull, Stowe, & Huerta, 2006). Furthermore, with each reauthorization IDEA has included parents more fully into the decision making process. Over time, the role of parents has transitioned from consent giver for services to that of partner for decision making. Despite noteworthy changes over the years, six core principles have guided this legislation from its inception to the current version. For states and local public educational agencies to receive federal funding, they must adhere to these core principles (Turnbull et al., 2013).

Increasing numbers of children are being identified with ASD and deemed eligible for special education services. Furthermore, inclusion is increasingly recognized as the most appropriate setting for many children with ASD. Thus, most general education teachers are likely to have a child with ASD in their class at some time. Unfortunately, although the IEP is the blueprint for providing an appropriate and individualized education, general education teachers often report a lack of understanding about and discomfort with the IEP process (Heward, 2009). General education teachers must understand the IEP process and their role in serving on the IEP team and implementing educational decisions documented on the IEP. If the child receives some services within the regular education classroom, it is often the case that the general education teacher is invited to attend the IEP meeting. All teachers working with the child need to share information about the child's current functioning, help formulate educational goals, and help evaluate those goals. In addition, a representative from the grade of the child's typically developing peers must be present to share information about the general curriculum with the parents during the IEP meeting.

The IEP is an individualized plan that formally documents educational goals and objectives, which services will be provided, how and when special education services and related services (such as speech language or occupational therapy) will be implemented, and how goals will be measured. An IEP must be conducted at least annually, but may occur more frequently if parents or teachers request additional meetings.

An IEP for a child with ASD should minimally address the following:

- A description of the child's present level of functioning. For a child with ASD, this should include academic and functional skills, including social skills, language skills and overall communication, and behaviors that impede learning. Depending on the child's overall ability level, this description might also include other functional behaviors, such as independent daily living skills.

- A statement about the extent to which having ASD impacts the child's ability to access the general education curriculum. When the 2004 reauthorization of IDEA became aligned with the NCLB legislation, schools were directed to include children with disabilities within the systemwide testing (which evaluates mastery of general education goals) to the greatest extent possible. Thus, there is a push to begin the goal-setting process considering general education curriculum goals. When necessary, these goals may need to be modified to meet the needs and level of functioning of the student. In some cases, the general education goals are inappropriate for the child and must be replaced with individualized goals. Some children with ASD can access the general education curriculum with appropriate supports such as visual aids (such as daily schedules or work stations with visual prompt) or the use of an alternative communication system. Other individuals, particularly those with intellectual disabilities, may have an IEP that primarily focuses on mastering functional skills that allow them to achieve independence and self-determination.

• Where the child will receive educational instruction (i.e., within the regular education classroom, resource special education classroom for a portion of the day, etc.). To the greatest extent possible, IDEA emphasizes that children should be educated with their nondisabled same-age peers. In addition, the IEP explains the extent to which the child will not participate with his or her nondisabled peers. Opportunities for inclusion and participation with a child's typically developing peers facilitate the development of age-appropriate social skills and behaviors for children with ASD.

• Measurable annual goals. An educational goal must be written in such a way that behaviors or content mastered can be clearly measured. These goals include both academic and functional goals (such as goals that address independent living, social skill development, and communication).

• A description of *how* goals will be measured and how frequently. For instance, goals may be measured by comparing test scores throughout the year. Goals may also be measured by teacher documentation of observed behaviors.

• A description of special education, related services, academic modifications, special interventions, and supplementary aids the child will be getting to support their learning needs. It is important that the teacher understand what these services are and who is in charge of implementing them. Remember, the IEP is a legal document. Thus, you may be accountable for implementing specific modifications and/or interventions. You may need to request additional training or assistance to competently implement certain interventions. Not knowing that a particular modification or intervention was on the IEP or not knowing how to implement are not acceptable excuses for failing to implement something documented on the IEP.

• Other considerations documented on the IEP include whether the child is able to participate in schoolwide testing and transition plans for students 16 or older (considers aspects of life after high school such as vocational training, higher education, employment, and independent living goals).

CREATING A SUPPORTIVE ACADEMIC ENVIRONMENT FOR CHILDREN WITH ASD

Children with ASD have a wide range of academic strengths and weaknesses. For instance, a child may be able to read and write, yet demonstrate expressive and receptive language skills significantly below their same-age peers. Thus, academic goals must be based on ongoing assessment of current functioning.

However, the following general considerations are often helpful for children with autism.

• Incorporate a classroom environment based on principles of Universal Design. Universal Design involves structuring the environment to encourage access to learning without barriers. Access to learning includes providing multiple ways of meeting a learning objective. Universal Design provides students with multiple methods of instruction, opportunities for engagement, and methods of expressing knowledge. For instance, a classroom literacy lesson might include oral instructions, a chart to help remember key points, and an activity involving drawing to illustrate key ideas. Students may provide oral responses, point to correct answers on the chart or underline the correct answer, or create their own picture to represent what they have learned. Children with ASD often have more limited modalities for communication. Providing several options that include a nonverbal means of expressing knowledge can help to build on strengths.

• Focus on teaching skills that are valued by both family and school. Consider which aspects of independent functioning are currently most important for both functioning at school and valued by parents. For instance, both family and school may agree on teaching a unit addressing independent behavior and meals. However, parents may be more interested that their child can sit at the table and eat dinner using utensils, and less interested in their child being able to set the table. Shared decision making is particularly important for individuals with ASD because they will often not generalize skills across settings without opportunities to practice those skills across different settings. Thus, skills that the family values and fits in with the daily routines of their home and community are likely to be practiced and reinforced.

• Implement a strong communication system for providing open channels of communication with parents from the start. This is particularly important when working with children who have limited or impaired communication skills.

• Incorporate structured and systematic teaching. Children with ASD benefit from an organized and systematic presentation of instruction. The use of work systems is a good example of this type of teaching. Work Systems utilize a visual presentation that communicates how much work needs to be done, when the work is completed, and what to do next. Students are given only the materials they need to complete a project. For instance, if they need to count and paste paper apples on a chart to correspond with the number 10, they are only given 10 apples. Times or visual cues promote independence by reminding the student when they have completed a task. The physical arrangement of tasks, such as placing materials required for each step in a row from left to right, can promote independence. A poster with choices of reinforcers (i.e., pictures of computer for computer time, pictures of snack, picture of couch for free reading time), positioned at the end of the task activities serve as a reminder that the task has been completed.

• Incorporate visual aids into instruction and daily routines, such as picture schedules, calendars, and worksheets. Use visual prompts and reminders to help establish a classroom with predictability and consistent routines. Include visual instructions (such as a chart, pictures, a sample or model, an outline or cutout of how something should like, or written instructions if appropriate) to accompany oral instructions. Visual prompt and cues, provide predictability and routine, take into account a child's sensory needs and potential for over-stimulation, and often reduce anxiety associated with feeling overwhelmed.

• Consider the degree to which technology may be integrated into the class-room to enhance clarity and increase communication. Assistive technology is discussed in Chapter 9, "The Development of Communication Skills."

• Consider the degree to which the student may participate in statewide assessment, or need alternative assessments. The goal is to have students with ASD represented in statewide testing results, yet use assessments that adequately reflect a child's learning. Modifications may include additional time for testing to reduce anxiety, writing the letter rather than coloring in a bubble to indicate one's answer, the use of adaptive technology.

• Integrate positive behavioral supports into educational planning. Positive behavioral supports set children up for success by preventing conditions (antecedents) that are likely to trigger challenging behaviors that interfere with learning. For instance, a child may have a temper tantrum when the daily schedule changes because the change is unexpected and confusing. Providing visual supports, such as an up-to-date daily schedule posted on their desk at the beginning of each day and cues for transition, may help prevent such problems. Another example may be using a social story (discussed in Chapter 10) to help a child understand what is going to happen during the day and how they may deal with those changes.

• Provide inclusion experiences and experiences for social communication development with peers. Children with ASD benefit from opportunities to observe, model, and receive feedback from same-age typically developing peers. Chapter 10 discusses the range of social communication difficulties children with ASD may experience, including difficulty predicting and interpreting the behavior of others and atypical sensory processing. In addition, unusual repetitive and stereotypic behavior may interfere with social interactions. Structured inclusive opportunities for children with ASD to spend time with typically developing children in a familiar environment can reduce anxiety and provide positive social experiences. Likewise, typically developing children benefit from learning how to promote positive social interactions with children different from themselves, empowering them to support others and promote tolerance and empathy.

TEACHING TIPS

• Remember that the transition from an IFSP to an IEP (special education services through a public elementary school) is often perceived as less supportive by families. Help parents with this transition by setting up a strong communication system such as a daily notebook that goes home with the child (even if it is just a checklist with a few comments), and inviting parents to send back comments/information.

• Early intervention is most effective when it is delivered with intensity and across settings. Thus, teachers serving a child with ASD should work as a team to ensure that IEP goals are being addressed as consistently across settings as possible. For instance, providing consistent classroom procedures such as the use of daily schedules posted on the child's desk, cues for beginning or ending assignments, and prompts for structuring task completion are likely to reduce anxiety and provide familiar supports for academic success. In addition, teacher should work with parents to integrate the skills within settings outside the school. The home is often the best setting to support the generalization and maintenance of skills in a natural environment. Provide parents with concrete examples of how they may set up opportunities for students to practice new skills at home and within the community.

SUMMARY

Early intervention is critical in helping children with ASD meet their potential. Early diagnosis is key to identifying children in need of early intervention supports. Early interventions are most effective when parents and professionals work together because each family has a unique way of supporting their child with ASD. The family-centered approach draws attention to the strengths and priorities of the family in addition to the child's progress.

The IFSP recognizes the role of family in IDEA by assessing the child's current levels of development, identifying the family's needs, and stating the outcomes that are to be achieved. Important factors in working with children in ASD include intensity, opportunities to generalize and maintain skills, structured teaching with reinforcement, modification, and opportunities to interact with typically developing peers.

TEACCH is an example of an effective early intervention program that empowers parents and teachers to creates learning environments that support communication and learning for young children with ASD. Likewise, the Early Start Denver Model is an early intervention program that involves parents in addressing academic skill building and the development of social communication skills.

Transitioning from an IFSP to an IEP can be a stressful step for families. The stress typically stems from poor communication and interactions with families and can eased by allowing open communication with professionals and families. The IEP can be used to create a supportive academic environment that incorporate a classroom environment based on principles of Universal Design and focuses on teaching skills that are valued by both family and school; includes a strong a strong communication system between school and family; incorporates structured and systematic teaching; incorporate visual aids into instruction and daily routines; and provides inclusive experiences and appropriate behavioral supports.

DISCUSSION AND REFLECTION QUESTIONS

1. What are the components of an IFSP and how do they reflect family-centered practices?

2. Which factors are likely to contribute to a positive experience for families obtaining early intervention services for their child? Describe factors likely to contribute to negative experiences and confusion.

3. Describe how Agatha, Clark's kindergarten teacher, works toward developing a positive relationship with parents.

4. How would you prepare for an IEP meeting for a child in your class? Consider your role in the IEP meeting, information that you would need to bring to the meeting, and the process of goal setting. Write down any questions you have about the IEP process and your role as a teacher collaborating with the team.

5. What are the components of strong early intervention programs, and what are some examples of such programs?

RECOMMENDED FURTHER READINGS AND INTERNET SOURCES

Further Readings

Simpson, R. (2005). *Autism spectrum disorders: Interventions and treatments for children and youth*. Thousand Oaks, CA: Corwin.

Wagner, S. (1999). *Inclusive programming for elementary students with autism*. Arlington, TX: Future Horizons.

Internet Sources

Autism Speaks website: Kit for helping parents deal with the first 100 days after the diagnosis. http://www.autismspeaks.org/community/family_services/100_day_kit.php

CDC website: Learn the signs. Act early. http://www.cdc.gov/ncbddd/actearly/index.html

Families for Early Autism Treatment website: http://www.feat.org

Information about IDEA at the U.S. Department of Education's website: http://www2 .ed.gov/about/offices/list/osers/osep/index .html.

Zero to Three: National Center for Infants, Toddlers & Families. http://www.zerotothree.org

Universal Design for Learning and Autism Spectrum Disorders: http://www.suite101.com/content/universal-design-for-learning-and-autism-spectrum-disorders-a235483#ixzz 1D0dRpIAG

REFERENCES

Anderson, S. R., & Romanczyk, R. G. (1999). Early intervention for young children with autism: Continuum-based behavioral models. *The Journal of the Association for Persons With Severe Handicaps, 24,* 162–173.

Bailey, K. (2008). Supporting families. In K. Chawarska, A. Klin, & F. R. Volkmar (Eds.), *Autism spectrum disorders in infants and toddlers: Diagnosis and treatment* (pp. 300–326). New York, NY: Guilford Press.

Baker-Ericzen, M. J., Brookeman-Frazee, L., & Stahmer, A. (2005). Stress levels and adaptability in parents of toddlers with and without autism spectrum disorders. *Research and Practice for Persons with Severe Disabilities, 30,* 194–204.

Boss, P. (1999). *Ambiguous loss: Learning to live with unresolved grief*. Cambridge, MA: Harvard University Press.

Brown, S. E. (2003). Advocacy for young children under IDEA: What does it mean for early childhood educators? *Infants and Young Children, 16*(3), 227–237.

Bruder, M. B. (2010). Early childhood intervention: A promise to children and families for their future. *Exceptional Children, 76,* 339–355.

Chakrabarti, S., & Fombonne, E. (2001). Pervasive developmental disorders in preschool children. *Journal of the American Medical Association, 285,* 3093–3099.

Chawarska, K. (2007). *Longitudinal study of syndrome expression: ASD from the second to the fourth year*. Paper presented at the Society for Child Development Conference, Boston, MA.

Clements, K. M., Barfield, W. D., Kotelchuck, M., & Wilber, N. (2008). Maternal socioeconomic and race/ethnic characteristics associated with early intervention participation. *Maternal Child Health Journal, 12,* 708–717.

Corsello, C. M. (2005). Early intervention in autism. *Infants & Young Children, 18,* 74–85.

Dawson, G., Rogers, S., Munson, J., Smith, M., Winter, J., Greenson, J., Donaldson, A., & Varley, J. (2010). Randomized, controlled trial of an intervention for toddlers with autism: The Early Start Denver Model. *Pediatrics, 125,* 17–23.

Dawson, G., Toth, K., Abbot, R., Osterling, J., Munson, J., Estes, A., & Liaw, J. (2004). Early social attention impairments in autism: Social orienting, joint attention, and attention to distress. *Developmental Psychology, 40,* 271–283.

Dawson, G., & Zanolli, K. (2003). Early intervention and brain plasticity in autism. In M. Rutter (Ed.), *Autism: Neural bases and treatment possibilities.* London: Novartis.

Dunlap, G., & Fox, L. (2007). Parent-professional partnerships: A valuable context for addressing challenging behaviors. *International Journal of Disability, Development, and Education, 54,* 273–285.

Dunst, C. J. (2002). Family-centered practices: Birth through high school. *The Journal of Special Education, 36,* 141–149.

Dunst, C. J., Johanson, C., Trivette, C. M., & Hamby, D. (1991). Family-oriented early intervention policies and practices: Family-centered or not? *Exceptional Children, 58,* 115–126.

Giarelli, E., Wiggins, L.D., Rice, C.E., Levy, S. E., Kirby, R. S., Pinto-Martin J. A., & Mandell, D. S. (2010). Sex differences in the evaluation and diagnosis of autism spectrum disorders among children. *Disability and Health Journal, 3,* 107–116.

Heward, W. L. (2009). *Exceptional children: An introduction to special education* (9th ed.). Upper Saddle River, NJ: Prentice Hall.

Howlin, P. (2005). Outcomes in autism spectrum disorders. In F. R. Volkmar, R. Paul, A. Klin, & D. J. Cohen (Eds.) *Handbook of autism and pervasive developmental disorders* (3rd ed., Vol. 1, pp. 201–222). Hoboken, NJ: Wiley.

Howlin, P. (2003). Can early interventions alter the course of autism? *Novartis Foundation Symposium, 251,* 250–259.

Howlin P., & Asgharian, A. (1999). The diagnosis of autism and Asperger syndrome: Findings from a survey of 770 families. *Developmental Medicine and Child Neurology, 41,* 834–839.

Hurwitz, K. A. (2008). A review of special education law. *Pediatric Neurology, 39,* 147–154.

Individuals with Disabilities Act (IDEA), P.L. 108-446 § Sec. 631-644, 118 Stat. 2744 (2004).

Irvin, N., Kennell, J., & Kalus, M. (1982). Caring for the parents of an infant with a congenital malformation. In M. Klaus & J. Kennell (Eds.), *Parent-infant bonding* (2nd ed., pp. 227–258). St. Louis, MO: Mosby.

Jung, L. A. (2007). Writing individualized family service plan strategies that fit into the routine. *Young Exceptional Children, 10,* 2–9.

Kasari, C. (2002). Assessing change in early intervention programs for children with autism. *Journal of Autism and Developmental Disorders, 32,* 447–461.

Kearney, P. M., & Griffin, T. (2001). Between joy and sorrow: Being a parent of a child with a developmental disability. *Journal of Advanced Nursing, 34,* 582–592.

Kohler, F. W. (1999). Examining the services received by young children with autism and their families: A survey of parent responses. *Focus on Autism and Developmental Disabilities, 14,* 150–158.

Lake, J. F., & Billingsly, B. S. (2000). An analysis of factors that contribute to parent-school conflict in special education. *Remedial and Special Education, 21,* 240–251.

Lindgren, C. L., Burke, M. L., Hainsworth, M. A., & Eakes, G. G. (1992). Chronic sorrow: A lifespan concept. *Scholarly Inquiry for*

Nursing Practice: An International Journal, 6, 27–40.

Lord, C., Risi, S., DiLavore, P. S., Shulman, C., Thurm, A., & Pickels, A. (2006). Autism from 2-9 years of age. *Archives of General Psychiatry, 63,* 694–701.

Mandell, D. S., Maytali, M. N., & Zubritsky, C. D. (2005). Factors associated with age of diagnosis among children with autism spectrum disorder. *Pediatrics, 116,* 1480–1486.

National Autism Center. (2011). *Evidence-based practices and autism in the schools.* Randolph, MA: Author.

Mesibov, G. B., Shea, V., & Schopler, E. (2007). *Overview: The TEACCH approach to autism spectrum disorder.* New York, NY: Springer-Verlag.

National Research Council. (2001). *Educating children with autism.* Committee on Educational Interventions for Children with Autism. Division of Behavioral and Social Sciences and Education. Washington, DC: National Academy Press.

No Child Left Behind (NCLB) Act of 2001, Pub. L. No. 107-110, § 115, Stat. 1425 (2002).

O'Brien, M., & Daggett, J. A. (2006). *Beyond the autism diagnosis. A professional's guide to helping families.* Baltimore, MD: Paul Brookes.

Olshansky, S. (1962). Chronic sorrow: A response to having a mentally defective child. *Social Casework, 43*(4), 190–193.

Raspa, M., Bailey, D. B., Olmstead, M., Nelson, R., Robinson, N., Simpson, M. E., Guillen, C., & Houts, R. (2010). Measuring family outcomes in early intervention: Findings from a large-scale assessment. *Exceptional Children, 76,* 496–510.

Rogers, S. J., Hall, T., Osaki, D., Reaven, J., & Herbison, J. (2000). The Denver Model: A comprehensive, integrated educational approach to young children with autism and their families. In J. S. Handleman & S. L. Harris (Eds.), *Preschool education programs for children with autism* (2nd ed., pp. 95–133). Austin, TX: Pro-Ed.

Schreibman, L. (2000). Intensive behavioral/psychoeducational treatments for autism: Research needs and future directions. *Journal of Autism and Developmental Disorders, 30,* 373–378.

Schopler, E. (1987). Specific and nonspecific treatment factors in the effectiveness of a treatment system. *American Psychologist, 42,* 379–383.

Schopler, E. (1995). Introduction: Convergence of parent and professional perspectives. In E. Schopler (Ed.), *Parent survival manual. A guide to crisis resolution in autism and related developmental disorders* (pp. 3–20). New York, NY: Plenum Press.

Scott, J., Clark, C., & Brady, M. (2000). *Students with autism: Characteristics and instructional programming.* San Diego, CA: Singular Publishing.

Stoner, J. B., & Angell, M. E. (2006). Parent perspectives on role engagement: An investigation of parents of children with ASD and their self-reported roles with education professionals. *Focus on Autism and Developmental Disabilities, 21,* 177–189.

Stoner, J. B., Bock, S. J., Thompson, J. R., Angell, M. E., Heyl, B. S., & Crowley, E. P. (2005). Welcome to our world: Parent perceptions of interactions between parents of young children with ASD and education professionals. *Focus on Autism and Other Developmental Disabilities, 20,* 39–51.

Turnbull, R., & Cilley, M. (1999). *Explanations and implications of the 1997 Amendments to IDEA.* Upper Saddle River, NJ: Merrill Prentice Hall.

Turnbull, H. R., Stowe, M. J., & Huerta, M. E. (2006). *Free appropriate public education* (6th rev. ed.). Denver, CO: Love Publishing.

Turnbull, A., Turnbull, R., Erwin, E., & Soodak, L. (2006). *Families, professionals, and exceptionalities: Positive outcomes through partnership and trust* (5th ed.). Upper Saddle River, NJ: Pearson Merrill Prentice Hall.

Turbull, A., Turnbull, R., Wehmeyer, M. L., & Shogren, K. A. (2013). *Exceptional lives. Special education in today's schools* (7th ed.). Upper Saddle, NJ: Pearson.

U.S. Department of Education, *IDEA Regulations: I34 C.F.R. § 300.7 (c)(1)* (1999).

U.S. Department of Education, Office of Special Education and Rehabilitative Services. (2010). *Thirty-five years of progress in educating children with disabilities through IDEA*. Washington, DC: Author.

Vismara L. A., Colombi, C., & Rogers, S. J. (2009). Can one hour per week of therapy lead to lasting changes in young children with autism? *Autism, the International Journal of Research and Practice, 13*, 93–115.

West, J., & Whitby, P. S. (2008). Federal policy and the education of students with disabilities: Progress and the path forward. *Focus on Exceptional Children, 41*(3), 1–16.

Wolery, M., & Garfinkle, A. N. (2002). Measures in intervention research with young children who have autism. *Journal of Autism and Developmental Disorders, 32*, 463–478.

Zwaigenbaum, L., Bryson, S., Lord, C., Rogers, S., Carter, A., Carver, L., . . . Yirmiya, N. (2009). Clinical assessment and management of toddlers with suspected autism spectrum disorder: Insights from studies of high-risk infants. *Pediatrics, 123*, 1383–1391.

SECTION III

Addressing the Needs of Individuals With ASD Within the School Setting and the Greater Community

Chapters 7, 8, 9, 10, and 11 consider research, theory, and application of the development of behavior, language, independent living, and social skills necessary for success at home, school, and within the community. Chapter 7 reviews principles of applied behavior analysis (ABA) in addressing core deficits of ASD and replacing challenging behaviors with adaptive skills.

Chapter 8 considers environmental supports needed to address sensory issues and enhance learning in the classroom. Chapters 9 and 10 focus on core deficits of ASD, social communication. Chapter 9 reviews the development of language in children with typical development and ASD and considers interventions to build communication skills. Likewise, Chapter 10 presents an overview of social development and the range of atypical development often found in children with ASD. Both Chapters 9 and 10 review interventions frequently implemented in public schools to address core deficits of ASD and consider issues associated with evaluating evidence-based practices. Interventions based on principles of ABA are highlighted for addressing both communication skill development in Chapter 9 and social skill development in Chapter 10. Finally, Chapter 11 addresses issues germane to transitioning to adulthood, such as self-determination, place of residence, and employment or postsecondary education.

CHAPTER 7

INTERVENTIONS BASED ON APPLIED BEHAVIOR ANALYSIS AT SCHOOL, HOME, AND WITHIN THE COMMUNITY

In this chapter, you will learn about:

- Theoretical frameworks, operant and classical conditioning, underlying applied behavior analysis (ABA).
- Strengths of interventions and the myths surrounding ABA.
- Coordinating data analysis between home and school.
- Interventions incorporating ABA: discrete trial instruction, incidental teaching, and pivotal response training.
- Targeting challenging behaviors using ABA.

OVERVIEW OF APPLIED BEHAVIOR ANALYSIS

Theoretical Framework

Core deficits in communication, social skills, and behavior, in addition to other difficulties associated with Autism Spectrum Disorder (ASD; described in Chapter 2), often provide obstacles for the child to reach her learning potential. ABA is an intervention that teaches specific skills in a carefully determined sequence of behaviors, generally using reinforcement to increase appropriate behaviors. ABA is used in schools, clinics, homes, residential facilities, and other settings to teach children a variety of preacademic, academic, and other types of skills.

Classical Conditioning

ABA was developed from a branch of the science of behavior known as behaviorism. In 1913, John B. Watson (1878–1958), coined the term "behaviorism" (Schneider & Morris, 1987). Classical conditioning involves reflexes and a stimulus–stimulus pairing process wherein new stimuli can begin to elicit reflexive responses. In one of the most well-known examples of classical conditioning, Ivan Pavlov (1849–1936) conditioned dogs to salivate in the presence of a specific sound wherein the sound was the previously neutral stimulus. Although the origins of classical conditioning are linked to Pavlov and his classical conditioning of nonhuman animal reflexes, Watson used classical conditioning as a way of explaining human behavior.

Skinner was a neobehaviorist who developed the learning theory of operant conditioning that is the basis of many variants of applied behavior analysis today.

Operant Conditioning

Soon after Watson, B. F. Skinner (1904–1990) also began to explain human behavior, but from a different behavioral perspective. Eventually Skinner discovered the basic principles of operant behavior that today are used in the applied behavior analytic treatment of ASD. Skinner extended the analysis of behavior to include environmental consequences, and called behavior shaped by its consequences operant behavior.

CHAPTER REFLECTION: What Is Operant Behavior?

Almost everything we do is operant behavior. Examples include raising your hand in class if you have a question or avoiding someone at the supermarket when you are in a hurry. We do these things because of the effects or consequences of the behavior. Raising your hand in class gets the attention of the teacher; avoiding someone prevents us from spending time talking with them.

Practice Activity: Break down the steps involved in taking notes during a classroom discussion. Determine the behaviors associated with this task that are operant behaviors (result in a change in our environment and a consequence).

The initial applications of operant conditioning to individuals with ASD occurred in the1960s (e.g., DeMyer & Ferster, 1962; Lovaas, Berberich, Perloff, & Schaffer, 1966; Wolf, Risley, & Mees, 1964). Results indicated that different types of immediate consequences could help children with an ASD demonstrate new, more complex, socially appropriate behavior, and could help reduce inappropriate behavior.

Lovaas and the Application of ABA to Children With ASD

Using the principle of chaining simple skills together, Dr. Ivar O. Lovaas created interventions that addressed more complex skills like receptive language. Based on his clinical work and research, Lovaas created training manuals for teachers and caregivers with explicit instruction such as *Teaching Developmentally Disabled Children: The ME Book* (1981) and *Teaching Individuals With Developmental Delays: Basic Intervention Techniques* (2003). Prior to the application of ABA to children with ASD, children with ASD were often institutionalized in a hospital-like setting secluded from their family and typically developing peers.

The success of ABA along with other societal changes, such as the deinstitutionalization movement of the 1970s and federal legislation, including the Education for All Handicapped Children Act of 1975, which mandated that all children receive a free and appropriate public education in public schools, created a climate of investing in all children for optimal growth and quality of life.

ABA interventions should involve parents and teachers and take place within the child's natural environments in an intensive manner over time.

Lovaas' (1981) clinical work using ABA to teach children with ASD led to several key considerations that are fundamental to successful ABA programs today:

1. Educational interventions must take place within the *child's natural environment*. Children with ASD will not automatically generalize skills learned in hospital or clinical settings to school settings.

2. *Parents and teachers* should be critical members of planning and administering the educational intervention of children with autism. Although working with a behavioral specialist is helpful, ultimately parents and teachers must be involved in planning, administering, and evaluating the effectiveness of interventions.

3. The intervention must be *intensive and take place over time*. The most effective ABA interventions are those that involve frequent teaching and take place over a significant period of time.

STRENGTHS OF INTERVENTIONS BASED ON ABA

Empirical Validation

Navigating through the array of treatment options can be overwhelming and confusing to both parents and educators. The Internet can be a helpful tool, but it is filled with testimonials of popular new interventions that lack scientific support. Parents of children with ASD, desperate to help their child, are particularly susceptible to interventions that have not been subjected to rigorous scientific investigation yet are presented as a cure (Jacobson, Foxx, & Mulick, 2005).

ABA therapy is tailored to address individual needs and can address a variety of skills. Here a 3-year-old child is learning to say "fork" when presented with the object.

Validation through empirical support is a defining dimension of ABA (Baer, Wolf, & Risley, 1968; National Research Council, 2001). Objective data-based decisions drive applied behavior analytic interventions so that effectiveness can be assessed. In fact, the evaluation of the effectiveness of an individualized intervention is a defining feature of ABA. Thus, ABA meets the criteria of an empirically validated intervention stipulated in the federal legislation of both the No Child Left Behind Act and the Individuals with Disabilities Education Act.

Interventions Tailored to Address Individual Needs

Children with ASD have a wide range of intellectual abilities, cognitive strengths and weaknesses, behavioral concerns. Since ASD is a heterogeneous disorder, what may be effective for one person's symptoms may not be effective in treating another person's symptoms. Therefore, interventions must be tailored for each individual and evaluated objectively to determine the level of effectiveness for a particular individual.

ABA focuses on objectively and reliably assessing and evaluating the various way individuals interact with their environment (see Baer et al., 1968). ABA is meant to be practical and applied. As you will see below, the ABA methods of assessment can optimize the likelihood that a particular intervention will be effective. Interventions can be implemented with one child with an ASD or with multiple individuals in the child's environment such as with siblings (e.g., Strain & Danko, 1995) and/or parents (e.g., Koegel, Symon, & Koegel, 2002).

Flexibility and Generalizations of Interventions

ABA interventions can address basic skills, such as pointing to a picture to indicate choice of a classroom activity. In addition, an intervention can also target more complex skills, such as how to interact with peers during recess. More complex skills are broken down into very small steps so that the child experiences success, yet masters challenging skills.

Furthermore, flexible research designs assist with practical evaluation. For example, a teacher might use different procedure on alternate days to determine the most effective procedure for that child. ABA involves multiple levels of flexibility in each assessment, intervention, and evaluation.

In addition, flexibility can lead to increased generalization of skills. Overall, flexibility allows families to access a variety of different ABA treatment options to help implement the most ecologically valid approach to treatment. In other words, an ABA intervention effective at school might need to be modified to help the child generalize the skill to the home environment. Thus, a child who is able to respond to her name in the classroom can learn to respond to her name in her home, on the playground, and at a friend's house. Dempsey and Foreman (2001) summarized it best by stating that "properly designed and implemented ABA programs contain most if not all of the components of treatment approaches found to be most successful in supporting individuals with autism" (p. 110).

CRITICISMS AND MYTHS SURROUNDING ABA

ABA isn't without criticisms, including the incredible investment of resources required for training, implementation, and data collection, and the early use of aversive punishment (such as mild electric shock) in working with children. It should be noted that the use of aversive punishments to treat autism was later abandoned in virtually all clinical settings. Furthermore, there was the ultimate attack on behaviorism itself, "What about the mind?" Behaviorism focuses on observable behavior and interventions such as ABA are criticized for failing to address more complex issues about thought, reasoning, and perception. Additional controversy involves scientific debate about the methodological rigor of studies investigating the effectiveness of ABA as a treatment for ASD (for more on this topic the reader is referred to Morris [2009]).

CHAPTER REFLECTION: Putting Things Into Perspective

It is sometimes the case that we are tempted to embrace ABA as the *best* or *most appropriate* intervention for *all* students with ASD given the amount of empirical support and longevity of ABA as an effective educational intervention. However, is important to note that ABA is often used effectively in conjunction with other types of interventions used in the school system. Furthermore, ABA is not a *cure* for ASD, but an effective approach to teaching meaningful skills to promote independence and individual goals established by parents, teachers, students with ASD, and others who are part of the educational team.

Myth of the Robotic Child

Many misconceptions about the implementation of ABA interventions seem to stem from a "one size fits all" perspective and a genuine lack of understanding about the complexities of ABA-based programming. Examples include arguments that ABA-based interventions are too rigid, strict, and/or that it turns children into "robots." For instance, ABA-based programming has been criticized for being rote and mechanistic (Leaf, Taubman, & McEachin, 2008) and overly clinical and inhumane (Dempsey & Foreman, 2001).

In reality, ABA-based programs are only as rigid and strict or as natural as are needed for an individual child to learn. The ultimate goal of ABA-based treatment is for children with ASD to be able to learn from their natural environment, without the need for specialized therapy. However, structured teaching, mastery learning involving repeated opportunities for learning, and reinforcement for demonstrating the target behavior are hallmarks of this approach.

Competent behavior analysts consider the least restrictive environment that will effectively support the development of new appropriate behavior. Environments and skill acquisition programs that facilitate appropriate behavior are different for each child. One size does not fit all. One child may initially need to be placed in a distraction-free room to begin to learn while another child may be able to learn in a more complex classroom or community setting. Ongoing analysis of the environment and generalization opportunities that lead to natural child responding, supported by natural consequences, is a focal point of each intervention.

CHAPTER REFLECTION: Confronting Misconceptions of ABA

One of the myths surrounding ABA is that these interventions turn children into robotic learners and stamp out individuality. Two popular books about ABA, one written by a clinician and researcher, and another written by a parent of a child with ASD, address this misconception. In both cases, ABA is described as an intervention that helped bring out the child's individuality by helping them develop skills to fully participate in their own learning.

- In his first ABA manual, *The ME Book* (1981), Ivar O. Lovaas dedicates

the book to the child with autism, explaining:

As a result of following the program presented in this book, the child does become more of a person, an individual, more of a "me." So, we adopted the subtitle The Me Book *(Preface, ix).*

- Likewise, Catherine Maurice (1993) describes the impact of ABA therapy on her child with autism in her book *Let Me Hear Your Voice, A Family's Triumph Over Autism.*

(Continued)

All along, I had worried that we were re-creating her, forcing her into a mold of appropriate behavior and learned language. . . . That worry was gone now. . . . We had not, could not have, "remade" her. She was too much herself now, too joyfully full of her own life, her own thoughts and desires and creativity and intelligence. (p. 196)

Question: Do you think it is possible to effectively stamp out a child's personality and individuality through an educational intervention? Consider how including parents in goal setting and data collection might help them better understand ABA and address such concerns.

Myth of the Reinforcement as a Bribe That Does Not Provide Authentic Learning

Another myth is that the reinforcers often used in ABA-based programming, such as small snacks or stickers, are unnecessary and fail to produce "real" learning experiences (Kohn, 1993). This myth is associated with a basic misunderstanding of how people learn from consequences in their environments on a daily basis. ABA is based on the premise that behavior occurs for a reason and has a function.

Reinforcers refer to reinforcing consequences. If a consequence is reinforcing, it increases the future probability that the behavior that came before the consequence will be repeated again sometime in the future. If children with ASD were learning from their natural environment, they would not need specialized treatment. Unlike typically developing children, children with ASD often have a history of failing to learn from the natural environment. Therefore, the environment needs to be altered. Making consequences, including reinforcers, more salient is typically a necessary part of altering the environment to support appropriate child behavior.

However, one size does not fit all. Children with an ASD who can learn from natural social reinforcers such as social interactions and infrequent teacher or parental praise may not need salient reinforcing consequences or primary reinforcers (e.g., food) to learn. However, because social deficits are a core characteristic of ASD, many children initially respond best to primary reinforcers (such as food treats) and need social reinforcers to be conditioned (associated with primary reinforers) throughout treatment.

ABA-based treatment also includes a technology for systematically thinning the schedule of reinforcement as the child continues to learn and engage in more appropriate behavior. Thus, the child will gradually need less and less of the reinforcement to engage in the desired behavior. Ultimately, the goal is for the child to respond in the natural school and home environments without the need for salient reinforcers on a rich schedule.

Myth of the Use of Aversive Punishment to Teach Behaviors

Another misconception is that ABA interventions rely on aversive punishment, such as shocks, to teach children target behaviors. As noted above, ABA interventions primarily utilize reinforcements (or a desired reward given to a child immediately following a target behavior). However, in the history of ABA aversive punishments have been used to decrease or extinguish undesirable behaviors. From a behavioral perspective, punishment is something given following a behavior to *decrease* that behavior. Aversive punishments typically involve pain such as spanking or shocks, while other punishment may involve taking away a desired toy or limiting attention given to child following an undesirable behavior.

Aversive punishment, such as mild shocks, has been used effectively to treat the most severe instances in which children appear to lack pain sensitivity and engage in self-injurious behaviors, such as poking their eyes and banging their heads to the point of severe injury (i.e., Linscheid, Iwata, Ricketts, Williams, & Griffin, 1990).

However, because of ethical concerns about the use of such techniques have led to the virtual extinction of the use of aversive punishment in ABA programs. The one exception is at the controversial Judge Rotenberg Educational Center in Canton, Massachusetts (http://ww.judgerc.org). The goal of this private residential treatment center is to teach children and adolescents with severe behavioral problems without the use of psychotropic drugs. Recently, this center has been the subject of media attention. The "Chapter Reflection: Use of Punishment in the Public Schools" box discusses the increasingly restricted use of aversive punishment, such as restraints and seclusion, within public schools.

> ### CHAPTER REFLECTION: Use of Punishment in the Public Schools
>
> Parents should be assured that aversive punishments are not routinely associated with ABA interventions and are not used in public schools. In fact, increasingly schools are restricted from even using restraint or seclusion as punishments to decrease undesirable behavior. The Keeping All Students Safe Act (HR 4247) was approved by the House of Representatives on March 3, 2010. This bill was designed to protect children from harmful restraints and seclusions in the school setting (http://www.wrightslaw.com/info/abuse.index.htm). Instead, schools are encouraged to develop *positive behavioral supports*, which incorporate many principles of ABA such as identifying target behavior, identifying replacement behaviors, decisions based on frequent data collection, and generalize skills to a variety of settings (for more information about positive behavioral support, refer to http://www.pbis.org).

SUCCESSFUL IMPLEMENTATION OF ABA INTERVENTIONS

Intensity and Duration Key to Success

Behavioral treatment involving operant conditioning procedures are effective in significantly improving the functioning of children with ASD (Anderson & Romanczyk, 1999; New York State Department of Health, 1999; Smith, Groen, & Wynn, 2000). Many research studies provide evidence of the effectiveness of ABA-based treatment programs for individuals with an ASD (e.g., Lovaas, 1987; McEachin, Smith, & Lovaas, 1993; Sallows & Graupner, 2005).

In particular, ABA interventions are appropriate and effective in early education programs. Early intensive behavior therapy (EIBT) has been shown to be the most effective for children who initiate treatment before the age of 4 (Harris & Handleman, 2001). However, evidence suggests ABA-based programming is effective for individuals of all ages. For instance, Eikeseth, Smith, Jahr, and Eldevik (2002, 2007) found that children entering school-based intensive behavioral treatment at age 7 significantly benefited.

The principles and procedures of ABA can help increase appropriate behaviors and decrease inappropriate behaviors for children with an ASD. Yet, to achieve broad improvements in functioning, such as significant improvements in achievement and adaptive functioning, it is typically necessary for children with ASD to be engaged in intensive treatment over the course of several years.

Research suggests that less intensive ABA-based programs, while still beneficial, do not produce as substantial improvements in functioning as more intense programs. The National Research Council (2001) recommends that children with ASD be engaged in planned, developmentally appropriate, individualized educational activities for a *minimum* of 25 hours per week 12 months per year.

Generalizing Skills to Settings Outside the School Setting

Many children with an ASD have challenges consistently demonstrating what they learn across multiple environments and settings. For example, a child may have learned to spontaneously ask for juice in the school lunchroom, yet does not spontaneously request juice at home. Generalization is a behavioral phenomenon. Evaluating and promoting generalization is a key element of effective ABA programs. Stimulus generalization occurs when a behavior is learned in one setting, and then is demonstrated, without further training, by the same individual, in a different setting. If, in the juice example, the child learned to spontaneously request juice in the lunchroom and then without further training requested it at home, this would be an example of stimulus generalization.

Training peers, parents, and other caregivers helps promote generalization (e.g., Lovaas, Koegel, Simmons, & Long, 1973) as does combining strategies (e.g., Kashinath, Woods, & Goldstein, 2006). In summary, there are many ways to facilitate generalization of skills for children with an ASD from one setting to another. Without careful consideration and implementation of these techniques, the behavior of many children with autism would not likely generalize across different settings.

Limitations and Challenges to Implementing ABA Interventions

Even though ABA interventions are meant to be practical and flexible, there are challenges to implementation.

- *Limited Providers Trained to Implement ABA.* Perhaps the greatest limitation is the lack of competent providers to address the need of services. Consequently, many families and schools struggle to secure and maintain optimally effective ABA services. Limited resources for ABA training and support is particularly problematic in rural areas. Advanced degree programs in behavior analysis and special education are becoming more available. Yet there are still a number of problems that need to be solved on the state and national level to meet the demand.

- *Inadequate Training of ABA Therapist.* ABA programs need to be supervised by well-trained individuals with specific practical experience and training in ABA. Care must be taken that individuals who market themselves as behavioral consultants and specialists actually have the credentials and training to effectively implement ABA-based programming for children with ASD (e.g., Green, 1996; Maurice, 2001). As a parent or teacher it can be difficult to determine whether a person has the skills needed to design an effective curriculum and behavior support plan (see the Chapter Reflection box "Who Is Qualified to Develop and Implement ABA Interventions?").
- *Effective ABA Interventions Require Significant Resources.* ABA is both cost and time intensive. With schools and parents pushed to their financial limits, it can be difficult to acquire resources needed to effectively implement an intensive ABA program. Home-based programs can be costly, ranging upward from $60,000 per year (Schreibman, 2005).

Recently, some state and insurance funding have become available for children with an ASD; however, many families struggle to access or continue home-based services because of cost. Advocates in many states are pushing for state legislation that requires insurance carriers to cover expenses of empirically validated interventions for ASD, including ABA (see http://www.asha.org/public/coverage/autism.htm).

There are also other more personal costs associated with treatment implementation such as elevated levels of stress and personal and marital strain. For example, intensive home-based interventions involve creating a 24-hour-a-day consistent therapeutic environment. In such cases, parents are faced with the challenging task of continuing to implement interventions after school and often during weekends.

CHAPTER REFLECTION: Who Is Qualified to Develop and Implement ABA Interventions?

There are questions parents and educators can ask to establish whether a professional is qualified to work with a child with ASD.

- Inquire whether the therapist is a Board Certified Behavior Analyst (BCBA). If they are a BCBA, then they should have at least a master's degree, have taken coursework in behavior analytic techniques, and also have several hundred hours of supervised clinical experience.

- Ask about professional and clinical experience. The Association for Behavior Analysis International Autism Special Interest Group has a very helpful set of guidelines parents and teachers can use to determine if a professional is qualified to work with children with autism on their website (http://www.autismpppsig.org).
- Ask for references. You will be investing a great deal of effort, time, and financial resources into the ABA intervention. Investigate how satisfied others have been with this service provider.

Coordinating Data Analysis: The Home–School Connection

It is critical for the family and school to develop procedures for frequent opportunities to share data collected, revisit goals, and evaluate data over time. Shared data collection and analysis is important for objective identification and evaluation of interventions. Accurate and reliable data help guide treatment decisions whereas inaccurate data can ultimately slow progress or even harm a child with an ASD. Data can also facilitate communication.

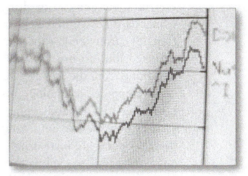

Collected data should include frequency, rate, duration, and latency of target behaviors.

Data are typically collected in terms of:

(a)   frequency—how *often* a behavior occurs in a *specific time period,*

(b)   rate—how *often* a behavior occurs *per unit of time* (i.e., rate per hour),

(c)   duration—how *long* the behavior occurs, and/or

(d)   latency—how much time it takes for the behavior to occur after a stimulus is presented.

Rate is particularly important to calculate when data collection periods vary from day to day, as is often the case when working with children with an ASD. For example, if you are collecting data on the frequency of child vocalizations in a session, it is important that all sessions are the same length. If all sessions are not (for instance, some are half an hour and some are 1hour), then rate should be calculated to make a direct comparison across sessions.

Despite the benefits of data collection and analysis, if not conducted properly, data collection and analysis can become overwhelming and nonfunctional. Data collection may become tedious, time consuming, and disruptive. Creating functional data collection systems provide more user-friendly and accurate data collection that is perceived as useful.

Examples of functional data collection systems that help promote communication across the home and classroom include daily report cards, checklists, and photographs.

Functional data collection also requires a time commitment dedicated to analyzing data and revising interventions as needed. Therefore, designing user-friendly ways to distribute results from data analysis is a challenging yet necessary task. Results can be distributed in short coordination meetings or via a whiteboard posted in the classroom or other posted systems that give a "snapshot" of current child expectations. Essentially, if there are stacks of data being collected, but no time to analyze or share the results, the child is not likely benefiting from the data.

As computer technology progresses, data collection systems have become more user friendly and sophisticated. In fact, many electronic data collection systems now include automatic data analysis (Kahng & Iwata, 1998). In fact, these products are increasingly available and being rapidly refined. Thus, it is an exciting time to explore the many opportunities available to make monitoring and evaluating ABA-based programs easier.

TYPES OF ABA PROGRAMS

Discrete Trial Instruction

Discrete trial instruction (DTI) is the foundation of all ABA-based programming. The approach is built around educational trials always containing three elements:

- a prompt from the teacher
- a response by the child
- a consequence delivered by the teacher

Teaching using DTI involves presenting the child with a series of opportunities (discrete trials) to make a response and then delivering consequences for each response. All ABA-based early intervention models share in common the use of DTI as the primary method of teaching. DTI is flexible and dynamic, and has been used to teach a wide variety of both simple and complex skills to children with an ASD (e.g., Jones, Feeley, & Takacs, 2007; Lund, 2009; Newman, Needelman, Reinecke, & Robek, 2002; Taubman et al., 2001). Furthermore, DTI is often the initial intervention for young children with ASD, especially when they have limited language skill or interest in social interactions or do not appear motivated by mastering a task, such as putting together a simple puzzle (Burggraff & Anderson, 2011).

To start a discrete trial, the teacher delivers a prompt to the child. A prompt is anything that offers additional support to the child during the intervention. For instance, a prompt starts simple (e.g., "Touch 'cat'"), and as skills become more complex, so too do the prompts (e.g., "Tell me your favorite color"). In early programming the prompt stays the same each time (e.g., "Hi" while waving). In later programming the prompt becomes more varied to more closely resemble the natural environment (e.g., "Hi," "How's it going?", and "Hey there" with a variety of hand gestures).

After the prompt is delivered, the child makes a response. Sometimes the teacher may need to further prompt the child to help them respond initially (e.g., guiding their hand to point to the answer), but as soon as possible such prompts should be faded out.

The last component of a trial is the consequence delivered following the response. This is important since the consequences of behavior drive how often it occurs. The success of ABA programming depends on the identification and use of effective consequences; most importantly positive reinforcers. In DTI, every response is followed by a consequence of some kind. If correct, the teacher delivers a small positive reinforcer such as brief access to a toy. If incorrect, the teacher delivers corrective feedback of some kind. Corrective feedback can be as simple as saying, "Try again" and prompting the child respond correctly, or "That's not it" following the response.

Incidental Teaching

Incidental teaching is a type of DTI that takes advantage of a child's interests to guide instruction. First described by Betty Hart and Todd Risley (Hart & Risley, 1980), it is a way to integrate teaching trials into a child's daily life. It is well suited to teaching a child to make requests (e.g., Cowan & Allen, 2007; Haring, Neetz, Lovinger, Peck, & Semmel, 1987) and respond in social situations (e.g., Charlop-Christy & Carpenter, 2000; McGee, Almeida, Sulzer-Azaroff, & Feldman, 1992; Mirenda & Iacono, 1988). For example, suppose a child sees his mother open a cabinet holding a favorite snack. He runs to her and points.

Ordinarily she would give him the snack, but this time she uses incidental teaching. Instead of giving him the snack, she asks, "Tell me what you want" (prompt). If he says, "Crackers" (response), then his mother praises him and gives him the crackers (consequence). Notice how all three elements of DTI are present. Skillful users of incidental teaching "plant" situations into a child's environment that set the occasion for them to make desired responses. For example, keeping preferred games and toys visible but out of reach makes it more likely that a child will approach you to get to them, setting the occasion to practice making a request. Because the desired outcomes are identified by the child, you know the consequence you deliver is likely to be a positive reinforcer. Also, because incidental teaching occurs in the child's natural environment and is initiated by the child, it is more likely the skills practiced will generalize.

Pivotal Response Teaching

An example of a type of ABA programming that utilizes DTI in many forms, including incidental teaching, is pivotal response teaching (PRT). Developed by Robert and Lynn Koegal (Koegel, Koegel, Harrower, & Carter, 1999), the approach focuses on teaching children important skills (pivotal responses) that will exponentially improve their ability to learn and interact with others. An example of a pivotal response is generalized imitation. Once a child with ASD develops the ability to observe another person and mimic their behavior, teaching becomes easier and learning occurs more rapidly. Another example of a pivotal response is learning to walk. When a child walks, they have access to many more activities and reinforcers than they had before.

Programs That Blend ABA With Other Models of Interventions

A comprehensive ABA-based educational plan targets all the needs of a child with an ASD. Doing so means working closely with professionals such as speech, physical, and occupational therapists, pediatricians, and other members of the treatment team to identify deficits and goals. Successful intervention requires that everyone on the team work together to achieve the best outcomes. Incorporating other treatment approaches into an ABA-based program should be done carefully, and you should ensure everyone is on the same page regarding goals and measures of educational success. Your challenge will be to design a program that incorporates the experience, expertise, and specialized knowledge of all of the professionals in a way that maintains data collection and the focus on DTI-based instruction that makes ABA-based interventions so effective. The most important thing is to agree that success for any intervention is ultimately dependent on meeting goals identified by the entire team as important and necessary.

USING ABA TO TARGET CHALLENGING BEHAVIORS

Many children with an ASD exhibit problem behaviors, ranging from distracting (spinning, stacking objects) to life-threatening (self-injurious behavior, aggression). ABA-based interventions have been successful at identifying the *causes* of problem behaviors and developing ways to *reduce or eliminate* them.

Functional Behavioral Assessment to Understand Behavior

One of the most important techniques developed by behavior analysts is functional behavioral assessment (FBA). Although there are several different ways an FBA can be conducted (e.g., Iwata & Dozier, 2008; Kahng & Iwata, 1999; LaRue et al., 2010; O'Reilly et al., 2010; Tarbox et al., 2009), they all share in common a focus on determining why a problem behavior is occurring.

You cannot effectively reduce or eliminate problem behaviors without knowing what is causing them. If you know what consequence is maintaining a behavior or what environmental events make a behavior more likely to occur, you can much more effectively design an intervention to treat the problem behavior.

1. Understanding the function of behaviors

All FBA methodologies share an important assumption: *that behavior occurs for a reason.* We call the reason a behavior occurs its *function.* Thus, if a child learns to ask his mother for a snack, we would say the function of his request was to get a snack. Thus, the snack functions to maintain the child's requesting behavior. The same relationship is found with problem behaviors. Recall that behaviors occur more often when they are reinforced. Thus, when a child with an ASD continues to display problem behavior, we assume the behavior is serving a purpose and we attempt to determine that purpose (function). We want to identify both what occurs before the behavior (antecedents) and what follows the behavior (consequences). Once we can reliably predict when a behavior will occur and when it will not occur, we have completed an FBA.

2. Identifying antecedents triggering challenging behaviors

Antecedents are events that occur prior to a behavior that make the behavior more or less likely to occur. For example, before someone can answer a question a question must be asked. Being asked a question is an antecedent because when it occurs, the behavior of answering is more likely. The prompt delivered at the beginning of an instructional trial in DTI is also an example of an antecedent. One goal of an FBA is to identify equivalent antecedents for the problem behavior you are trying to reduce. The most common ways to identify antecedents are to conduct interviews with people familiar with the child and to conduct observations of the child in the environment in which the problem behavior is occurring.

Common antecedents that predict increases in problem behavior for children with ASD include demands (telling the child to clean their room), unexpected changes in routines (Dad taking the child to school instead of Mom), being ignored by teachers or parents (the child is pointing at something and the parent does not notice), or being denied something they want (a favorite toy is visible but out of reach). Common antecedents that predict an absence of problem behavior include the absence of demands (the child always chooses what to do), a predictable daily routine, regular attention from preferred people, and unrestricted access to preferred items and activities. It is important to remember, however, that every child is different, as is each behavior, so you cannot assume that one of these will be an antecedent for the child with whom you are working.

3. Identifying environmental factors that maintain challenging behaviors

Consequences are events that follow behaviors and make them either more or less likely to occur. For example, a common consequence of smiling and greeting someone in the hallway is a smile and a greeting in return. Such a consequence is likely to make you smile and greet people more often. If, however, a particular person always ignores your greeting, then you will likely greet that particular person less often because you do not receive a reply. Just as with antecedents, the consequences of problem behavior are targets for identification in an FBA. Iwata and colleagues have identified the four most common consequences of problem behavior for people with disabilities as attention from parents and staff, escape from demands, access to preferred items or activities, and automatic, internal, sensory reinforcement (Hanley, Iwata, & McCord, 2003; Iwata et al., 1994; Iwata, Vollmer, Zarcone, & Rodgers, 1993).

Like antecedents, likely consequences are often identified through interviews and direct observations. In addition, since correctly identifying consequences maintaining behaviors plays a vital role in correctly identifying treatments likely to be effective, it is common to conduct a manipulation of the consequences in the environment to determine if rates of problem behavior are affected. This sort of manipulation is called a functional analysis because it involves analyzing the effects of the consequences identified in the FBA by presenting and removing them to see what happens to the rate of problem behavior.

CHAPTER REFLECTION: Three Case Studies on Addressing Challenging Behavior

Billy is a 5-year-old boy with an ASD who often becomes upset at the grocery store. He usually walks next to his mother while she shops, and he will sometimes try to grab items from the shelves when she isn't looking. If she takes the items away or tries to make him put them back he will scream and cry. He usually throws the item at his mother rather than put it back on the shelf. His mother has learned that she can only refuse him one to two items at most if she is going to be able to finish her shopping.

Sally is a 7-year-old girl with an ASD in an integrated first-grade classroom. She is generally pleasant with her teachers and does all of her work with little prompting. The other kids in the class, however, are terrified of her. She regularly hits, kicks, and shoves the other students during free play times, especially when they are playing with her favorite toys. The teacher has begun putting Sally's favorite toys into a special bin for her and asking the other students not to touch them if Sally looks upset.

Demarcus is a 6-year-old boy with an ASD in a half-day kindergarten classroom. His teacher is worried that he will not be able to move on to first grade because he refuses to do most of the assignments she gives him. He is generally compliant during play and circle times, but gets upset easily when the class is asked to complete worksheets and puzzles alone. If the teacher tries to make Demarcus finish a worksheet, even if she is sitting and helping him, he will begin to cry and whine. If she continues to sit with him, he will tear up the worksheet and throw the pieces on the floor. Once he has gotten that angry, his

(Continued)

(Continued)

teacher usually has to let him sit alone in the play area and cool down for at least 30 minutes before he will try again.

Questions: Billy, Sally, and Demarcus are each engaging in behavior that is disruptive and potentially dangerous.

1. Which behaviors are causing the children problems?

2. Which two children seem most alike?

3. Why do you think the children are engaging in the behavior?

Most people would say Billy and Demarcus are the most similar because they are both throwing tantrums that involve screaming and throwing things. However, the results of a FBA would suggest that even though both Billy and Demarcus engage in tantrums, they do so for *different reasons*. Notice that when Billy tantrums, his mother will usually buy him the food he wants at the grocery store. His tantrums lead to a *clear consequence—access to foods that he likes*. Conversely, Demarcus tantrums when his teacher asks him to complete a worksheet. Demarcus' tantrums lead to the removal of the worksheets—*an escape from a task he doesn't want to do*.

Although Sally is hitting her peers and Billy is throwing a tantrum, they both receive something they desire when engaging in challenging behaviors. So Billy and Sally are the *most similar in behavioral function*, even though they engage in different forms of problem behavior. This is an important distinction to understand. ABA-based interventions group behaviors according to *function* (why they occur) rather than *form* (what they look like) (Iwata et al., 1993).

Grouping behaviors by function affects how treatments are selected and delivered because it negates the idea that one form of behavior or another (e.g., aggression) can be treated in a universal way. There is not one treatment program that is most effective for aggression and another that is most effective for self-injury. Instead, treatments to reduce problem behavior must identify why it is happening and develop an intervention targeted at changing the environmental circumstances leading to the problem behavior.

We're now going to turn to a discussion of some of the more common procedures to reduce problem behavior, and how they have been applied to address challenging behaviors displayed by children with ASD.

4. Replacing challenging behaviors with acceptable behaviors

One of the most important and useful techniques to reduce problem behavior is to teach the child a more appropriate way to access things they have been getting by engaging in problem behavior. Whether it is to escape demands or gain access to preferred items, problem behaviors have worked for the child in getting what they want. For example, a teacher might only provide a preferred toy to calm a child down after a tantrum, and never let them have it at other times. As the child learns the only way to get the toy is to tantrum, the child tantrums more often. An easy way to eliminate the tantrums is to teach her to do something else to get the toy instead of throw a tantrum (e.g., completing a worksheet to earn a token she can trade for time with the toy). Table 7.1 offers

Table 7.1   Examples of Alternative Behaviors to Teach Using Case Studies

Replacement Behaviors		
Antecedent	*Behavior*	*Consequence*
Billy Problem Behavior		
Sees food/toy he wants	Tantrum	Mother buys him the toy
Billy Replacement Behavior		
Sees food/toy he wants	Points to item and says, "Can I have that please?"	Mother buys him the toy
Sally Problem Behavior		
Sees other child playing with favorite toys	Hit/Kick/Shove child	Teacher tells other children not to play with toy
Sally Replacement Behavior		
Sees other child playing with favorite toys	Asks child with toy "Can I play with that toy?"	Teacher asks other children to share toy with her
Demarcus Problem Behavior		
Teacher asks him to complete worksheet	Tantrum	Teacher lets him take break to calm down
Billy Replacement Behavior		
Teacher asks him to complete worksheet	Asks teacher, "Can I wait 5 minutes to start this worksheet?"	Teacher lets him take break before starting sheet

examples of potential alternative behaviors for the children described earlier. Notice how the alternative behaviors lead to the same consequences as the problem behaviors.

An ABA-based intervention does not stop with teaching the alternative behavior. ABA interventions incorporate additional programming (such as demand fading described below) to increase the amount of time Demarcus spends working on his school work. In fact, Demarcus is already getting a break by tantruming. By teaching him to request a break, you are offering him an acceptable way of making choices and indicating preference.

This replacement behavior has two very important advantages over tantrums. First, it is less disruptive and dangerous. Second, it shows Demarcus that he can have influence and control over his life and choices in a way that is more socially appropriate than tantrums. Replacement behaviors offer a wonderful opportunity to begin teaching social skills and how to make choices—two skills children with an ASD struggle with.

Modifying the Environment to Meet Immediate Needs

Children with an ASD who have not had their basic needs met engage in more problem behavior than children who are well rested, fed, and comfortable. Sometimes all it takes to improve problem behavior is to change the child's schedule or environment. For example, if you notice a child only becomes noncompliant when he hasn't eaten in a few hours, you could arrange a snack every 2 hours during the day. For Billy, giving him a snack immediately before going to the grocery store may reduce his acting out to get foods.

CHAPTER REFLECTION: Example of Modifying Environment to Meet Immediate Needs

Meeting immediate needs can involve *removing* things from the environment. For example, 7-year-old Sam was distracted by the sound of fluorescent lights and would act out to escape rooms with fluorescent lights. When Sam was allowed to complete his work in a room that was lit by lamps, his disruptive behavior disappeared.

In Sam's case, it was unlikely that he could avoid working in rooms with fluorescent lighting for his entire life, so he needed to learn how to deal with being in a distracting room. For instance, we began reinforcing him for spending more and more time in rooms lit by fluorescent light. Once he could sit in the room without disruption, we began asking him to complete more and more work while there. Within a semester, Sam was spending the majority of his day in classrooms with fluorescent lighting. A procedure to teach a child to cope with academic demands is called demand fading (e.g., Piazza, Moes, & Fisher, 1996).

Teaching Coping Skills

Both Demarcus' and Sam's stories demonstrate the need for another type of intervention for reducing problem behaviors—teaching children *how to cope* with things they find stressful or unpleasant. Teaching coping skills is most often used to reduce behaviors that have been maintained by escape from either demands or aversive situations.

Demand fading involves gradually increasing the amount of work required from a child who had previously engaged in problem behaviors to escape academic tasks. In Demarcus' case, demand fading would involve initially asking him to complete one problem before his break request was honored, then two, then four, until he is doing the entire worksheet to earn a break.

Dealing with severe problem behaviors is difficult and often help is needed to provide safe and effective interventions to address challenging behaviors. Intervening to reduce behaviors such as aggression, self-injury, and elopement should be undertaken with the guidance and supervision of someone trained in the use of appropriate behavioral assessment and intervention procedures. These interventions should only be implemented after an FBA is conducted and within the context of a behavior support plan that also includes the teaching of appropriate alternative behaviors as described above.

Targeting Aggression

Children who are aggressive pose a risk to the safety of everyone in your classroom. Unfortunately, aggression is a highly effective behavior for a child with an ASD. It causes a reaction from everyone in the area, and often leads to escape, access to things, and attention. Thus, interventions to reduce aggression need to address all of the maintaining consequences for the individual child.

One of the most effective ways to eliminate aggression is to use a procedure called *extinction*. Extinction involves not allowing the consequences that maintain a behavior to follow that behavior (Cooper, Heron, & Heward, 2007). A review by Iwata and colleagues suggests that extinction is the most important feature of many of the most effective behavior-analytic procedures, and it has been used to reduce the aggression and other problem behaviors of a wide variety of children with an ASD (Iwata, Pace, Cowdery, & Miltenberger, 1994).

CHAPTER REFLECTION: Using Extinction to Reduce Aggression

Sally has learned that hitting another child will allow her to gain access to the toys she wants. Thus, using extinction involves not allowing Sally to have the toy when she is aggressive. Whenever Sally hits a peer, the teacher takes the toy back from Sally and gives it to the peer. If extinction is used consistently, Sally learns that aggression no longer gets her the toy she wants.

Sometimes when using extinction, the *behavior will get worse before it gets better!* This is called an extinction burst (e.g., Lerman, Iwata, & Wallace, 1999), and explains why extinguishing behaviors can be such a difficult task. Imagine that you just tried to open a door and found it locked. What do you do? You may try the doorknob a few times, shake the door, and knock before walking away. That is an extinction burst. A behavior (turning a knob) that had previously led to an expected consequence (getting into a room) no longer led to that consequence, and so you try several more times before giving up.

It is possible to reduce and often entirely eliminate the occurrence of extinction bursts by teaching an appropriate alternative behavior at the same time extinction is being used (e.g., Lerman & Iwata, 1995). By offering the child another way to get what they want, they don't have to keep trying more intense levels of the aggressive behavior.

Targeting Self-Injurious Behaviors

Self-injurious behavior (SIB) is scary. Few things upset teachers and parents more than seeing a child with ASD hurt themselves, and SIB can make even veteran teachers feel helpless. Nevertheless, SIB is behavior, and there are a number of procedures that can be used to reduce its occurrence.

One procedure is a form of extinction called response blocking (e.g., Cannella, O'Reilly, & Lancioni, 2006; MacDonald, Wilder, & Dempsey, 2002; McCord, Thomson, & Iwata, 2001). A common consequence maintaining SIB for children with ASD is the sensory feedback the child receives as a result of the behavior. Response blocking involves not allowing the child to complete the self-injurious behavior, thus removing the consequence. For example, a child who engages in hand biting may wear a thick glove over their hands, which blocks them from feeling the bites.

Another procedure is called differential reinforcement of other behavior (DRO). DRO has been used with a variety of children with disabilities including ASD (e.g., Charlop-Christy & Haymes, 1996; Johnson, Johnson, & Sahl, 1994; Machalicek, O'Reilly, Beretvas, Sigafoos, & Lancioni, 2007; Wong, Floyd, Innocent, & Woolsey, 1991). DRO involves providing a child with reinforcement for the absence of SIB. For example, if a child regularly engages in SIB roughly every 20 minutes, then the teacher would initially give the child a small reinforcer every time the child went 10 minutes without engaging in SIB. The short interval ensures the child will be successful and earn the reinforcer most of the time. Once the child regularly earns the reinforcer (and thus rarely engages in the SIB), then the interval would be increased (from 10–15 to 20–30 minutes) until the SIB is not occurring.

Targeting Escape Behaviors (Running Away)

Another frightening and dangerous behavior exhibited by some children with ASD is running away from adults (elopement). Elopement can be as minor as a child who runs across the room and as major as a child who runs out of the building. When intervening to reduce elopement, you need to determine if the child is running *to* something or *from* something.

CHAPTER REFLECTION: Examples of Elopement

Running to Something: Reward for Mark

Mark runs from the classroom several times a day. Every time he goes *to the fish pond* at the front of the school. Mark is running *to* something. When a child is running *to* something, whatever they run to is likely a reinforcer, something they desire that increases the behavior (running). Consequently, an effective way to reduce elopement is to offer a way to earn the

(Continued)

(Continued)

Running From Something: Escape for Mary

Mary only elopes when asked to attend a general education math class with a "substitute" paraprofessional (when her paraprofessional is out for the day). When a child is running *from* something, several potential solutions exist. First, the child could be taught to request a break from the environment they do not enjoy. For example, Mary is taught to ask if she may bring her work from the math class to her special education teacher's room on the days that her regular paraprofessional could not attend the class with her. Second, the environment could be changed to remove what is upsetting the child. Finally, the child can be taught to tolerate the situation. In many cases, you could do all three of those things.

reinforcer for engaging in an alternative behavior. For example, Mark was allowed to visit the fish pond at the end of each period during which he stayed in class. He got to visit the fish pond more often and with less trouble than when he had to elope to get there.

INTEGRATING ABA INTERVENTIONS INTO THE FAMILY–SCHOOL INTERVENTION PLAN

A comprehensive ABA-based curriculum grounded in DTI should be the foundation of any intervention plan for a child with an ASD. Because the quality of instruction has been associated with the quality of outcomes, it is important that both the teachers and the parents are comfortable with how ABA-based programming is implemented. Ideally, a behavior analyst will be a member of the team who can act as a consultant and supervisor. However, sometimes it is necessary for the teachers or the parents to take on the supervisory role.

After defining the nature of the working relationship and designing the initial educational and behavioral support plans, a routine should be established to ensure the intervention plan is monitored and revised as needed. Regular monitoring and evaluation of all academic and behavioral goals is a hallmark of effective ABA-based programs, and the more frequently you look at the child's progress, the more responsive your teaching and programming will be. Parents should receive regular updates about both academic and behavioral goals. Establishing open and frequent channels of communication between home and school is essential to clearly understand how a child is functioning across settings. For instance, a daily or weekly progress note is an easy and effective way to maintain communication between home and school. In addition, the team should meet regularly (e.g., once a semester) to evaluate the child's progress.

TEACHING TIPS

- When implementing an ABA-based intervention, intervention decisions are largely made based on data trends. Thus, teachers using ABA need to be sure they understand their role in regular and ongoing data collection. Data are typically collected in terms of frequency of a behavior, rate at which a behavior occurs per unit of time, the duration of a behavior, and how much time it takes for a target behavior to occur after a stimulus is presented (latency).

- Use a reinforcer inventory to determine the activities (such as jumping on a trampoline, playing chase, computer time) and objects (such as food treats, stamps, stars) that the child finds most motivating. This may be completed by the child, a caregiver, and/or the teacher. Not all children are reinforced (willing to repeat a behavior to obtain the reward) by candy or stickers. In fact, some children with ASD may find a "reward" aversive (for instance, they may dislike the feeling of a sticker on their clothing), and avoid repeating a desired behavior to avoid the "reward."

- Teachers implementing ABA should be appropriately trained. If you feel as if you do not have the skills needed to implement an ABA intervention written in a child's individualized education plan, you must make this clear to the appropriate school administrator (this may be a special education supervisor and/or the school principal). It is both ethical and professional to work within your boundaries of competence. Often teachers will work under the supervision of an ABA consultant or a skilled special education teacher to implement aspects of the ABA intervention and collect data.

SUMMARY

ABA is a powerful tool for creating interventions that are tailored to meet individual needs and offer flexibility to address a multitude of issues in a variety of settings. Although there are several myths surrounding ABA, research supports the use of ABA as a valid and practical intervention to address many learning and behavioral difficulties. For ABA interventions to be effective, they must be sufficiently intense, occur over time, and provide opportunities to generalize skills across settings. It can be difficult to adhere to the demands of ABA intervention, particularly in light of limited resources. Parents are an integral part of successful ABA interventions. Interventions should incorporate a plan for communicating between home and school. There are many different types of ABA programs, including the traditional DTI, using a child's interest to guide instruction with incidental teaching, and PRT. There are also programs that blend ABA with other models of intervention. ABA is particularly effective in addressing challenging behaviors. FBAs are useful tools for understanding the antecedent (trigger) and the consequence that maintains a behavior. An FBA can be used to create ABA interventions that address challenging behaviors such as aggression, self-injurious behaviors, and escape behaviors (elopement).

DISCUSSION AND REFLECTION QUESTIONS

1. How would you respond to a parent's concern about using ABA with their child given the myths and controversies surrounding these interventions?

2. Describe strategies for coordinating information between school and home while implementing an ABA intervention for a child with ASD.

3. Describe the key issues associated with successful implementation of ABA interventions.

4. Describe three different types of interventions based on principles of ABA.

5. Determine the antecedent (behavioral trigger) and the consequence for the three case studies of challenging behavior for Billy, Sally, and Demarcus.

RECOMMENDED FURTHER READINGS AND INTERNET SOURCES

Further Readings

Alberto, P., & Troutman, A. C. (2008). *Applied behavior analysis for teachers* (8th ed.). Toronto, Canada: Prentice Hall.

Iwata, B. A., & Worsdell, A. S. (2005). Implications of functional analysis methodology for the design of intervention programs. *Exceptionality, 13*(1), 25–34.

Lovaas, O. I. (1981). *Teaching developmentally disabled children: The ME book*. Baltimore, MD: University Park Press.

Lovaas, O.I. (2003). *Teaching individuals with developmental delays: Basic intervention techniques*. Austin, TX: Pro-ED.

Machalicek, W., O'Reilly, M. F., Beretvas, N., Sigafoos, J., & Lancioni, G. E. (2007). A review of interventions to reduce challenging behavior in school settings for students with autism spectrum disorders. *Research in Autism Spectrum Disorders, 1*(3), 229–246.

Maurice, C. (1993). *Let me hear your voice: A family's triumphs over autism*. New York, NY: Random House.

Internet Sources

Lovaas Institute for Early Intervention: http://www.lovaas.com

The Behavior Analysis Certification Board: http://www.bacb.com

Association for Behavior Analysis International Autism Special Interest Group. Parent Professional Partnership: http://www.autism pppsig.org

Association for Behavior Analysis International: http://www.abainternational.org

REFERENCES

Anderson, S. R., & Romanczyk, R. G. (1999). Early intervention for young children with autism: Continuum-based behavioral models. *Journal of the Association for Persons With Severe Handicaps, 24*, 162–173.

Baer, D. M., Wolf, M. M., & Risley T. R. (1968). Some current dimensions of applied behavior analysis. *Journal of Applied Behavior Analysis, 1*, 91–97.

Burggraff, B., & Anderson, C. A. (2011). Discrete trial intervention for children with limited social and language skills and intellectual delays. In T. Thompson (Ed.), *Individualized autism intervention for young children. Blending discrete trial & naturalistic strategies* (pp. 73–95). Baltimore, MD: Paul Brookes Publishing.

Cannella, H. I., O'Reilly, M. F., & Lancioni, G. E. (2006). Treatment of hand mouthing in individuals with severe to profound developmental disabilities: A review of the literature. *Research in Developmental Disabilities, 27*(5), 529–544.

Charlop-Christy, M. H., & Carpenter, M. H. (2000). Modified incidental teaching sessions: A procedure for parents to increase spontaneous speech in their children with autism. *Journal of Positive Behavior Interventions, 2*(2), 98–112.

Cooper, J. O., Heron, T. E., & Heward, W. (2007). *Applied behavior analysis* (2nd ed.). Upper Saddle River, NJ: Pearson.

Cowan, R. J., & Allen, K. D. (2007). Using naturalistic procedures to enhance learning in individuals with autism: A focus on generalized teaching within the school setting. *Autism Spectrum Disorders, 44*(7), 701–715.

Dempsey, I., & Foreman, P. (2001). A review of educational approaches for individuals with autism. *International Journal of Disability, Development and Education, 48*, 103–116.

DeMyer, M. K., & Ferster, C. B. (1962). Teaching new social behavior to schizophrenic children. *Journal of the American Academy of Child Psychiatry, 1*, 443–461.

Eikeseth, S., Smith, T., Jahr, E., & Eldevik, S. (2002). Intensive behavioral treatment at school for 4-to-7 year old children with autism—A 1-year comparison controlled study. *Behavior Modification, 26*, 49–68.

Eikeseth, S., Smith, T., Jahr, E., & Eldevik, S. (2007). Outcome for children with autism who began intensive behavioral treatment between ages 4 and 7: A comparison controlled study. *Behavior Modification, 31*, 264–278.

Green, G. (1996). Evaluating claims about treatments for autism. In C. Maurice, G. Gree, & S.C. Luce (Eds.), *Behavioral interventions for young children with autism: A manual for parents and profesionals* (pp. 1915–1928). Austin, TX, US: Pro-Ed.

Hanley, G. P., Iwata, B. A., & McCord, B. E. (2003). Functional analysis of problem behavior: A review. *Journal of Applied Behavior Analysis, 36*(2), 147–185.

Haring, T. G., Neetz, J. A., Lovinger, L., Peck, C., & Semmel, M. I. (1987). Effects of four modified incidental teaching procedures to create opportunities for communication. *Journal of the Association for Persons With Severe Handicaps, 12*(3), 218–226.

Harris, S. L., & Handleman, J. S. (2001). Age and IQ at intake as predictors of placement for young children with autism: A four-to six-year follow-up. *Journal of Autism and Developmental Disorders, 30*, 137–142.

Hart, B., & Risley, T. R. (1980). In vivo language intervention: Unanticipated general effects. *Journal of Applied Behavior Analysis, 13*(3), 407–432.

Iwata, B. A., Dorsey, M. F., Slifer, K. J., Bauman, K. E., & Richman, G. S. (1994). Toward a functional analysis of self-injury. *Journal of Applied Behavior Analysis, 27*, 197–209.

Iwata, B. A., & Dozier, C. L. (2008). Clinical application of functional analysis methodology. *Behavior Analysis in Practice, 1*(1), 3–9.

Iwata, B. A., Pace, G. M., Cowdery, G. E., & Miltenberger, R. G. (1994). What makes extinction work: An analysis of procedural form and function. *Journal of Applied Behavior Analysis, 27*(1), 131–144.

Iwata, B. A., Vollmer, T. R., Zarcone, J. R., & Rodgers, T. A. (1993). Treatment classification and selection based on behavioral function. In R. Van Houten & S. Axelrod (Eds.), *Behavior analysis and treatment. Applied clinical psychology* (pp. 101–125). New York, NY: Plenum Press.

Jacobson, J. W., Foxx, R. M., & Mulick, J. A. (2005). *Controversial therapies for developmental disabilities: Fad, fashion, and science in professional practice.* Mahwah, NJ: Lawrence Erlbaum Associates.

Johnson, K., Johnson, C. R., & Sahl, R. A. (1994). Behavioral and naltrexone treatment of self-injurious behavior. *Journal of Developmental and Physical Disabilities, 6*(2), 193–202.

Jones, E. A., Feeley, K. M., & Takacs, J. (2007). Teaching spontaneous responses to young children with autism. *Journal of Applied Behavior Analysis, 40*(3), 565–570.

Kahng, S.W., & Iwata, B. A. (1998). Computerized systems for collecting real-time observational data. *Journal of Applied Behavior Analysis, 31*, 253–261.

Kahng, S. W., & Iwata, B. A. (1999). Correspondence between outcomes of brief and extended functional analyses. *Journal of Applied Behavior Analysis, 32*(2), 149–159.

Kashinath, S., Woods, J., & Goldstein, H. (2006). Enhancing generalized teaching strategy use in daily routines by parents of children with autism. *Journal of Speech, Language, and Hearing Research, 49*, 466–485.

Koegel, L. K., Koegel, R. L., Harrower, J. K., & Carter, C. M. (1999). Pivotal response intervention I: Overview of approach. *Journal of the Association for Persons With Severe Handicaps, 24*(3), 174–185.

Koegel, R. L., Symon, J. B., & Koegel, L. K. (2002). Parent education for families of children with autism living in geographically distant areas. *Journal of Positive Behavior Interventions, 4*, 88–103.

Kohn, A. (1993). Rewards verses learning: A response to Paul Chance. *Phi Delta Kappan. 74*, 783–787.

LaRue, R. H., Lenard, K., Weiss, M. J., Bamond, M., Palmieri, M., & Kelley, M. E. (2010). Comparison of traditional and trial-based methodologies for conducting functional analyses. *Research in Developmental Disabilities, 31*(2), 480–487.

Leaf, R., Taubman, M., & McEachin, J. (2008). *Sense and nonsense in the behavioral treatment of autism: It has to be said.* New York, NY: DRL Books.

Lerman, D. C., & Iwata, B. A. (1995). Prevalence of the extinction burst and its attenuation during treatment. *Journal of Applied Behavior Analysis, 28*(1), 93–94.

Lerman, D. C., Iwata, B. A., & Wallace, M. D. (1999). Side effects of extinction: Prevalence of bursting and aggression during the treatment of self-injurious behavior. *Journal of Applied Behavior Analysis, 32*(1), 1–8.

Linscheid, T. R., Iwata, B. A., Ricketts, R. W., Williams, D. E., & Griffin, J. C. (1990). Clinical evaluation of the Self-Injurious Behavior Inhibiting System (SIBIS). *Journal of Applied Behavior Analysis, 23*, 53–78.

Lovaas, O. I. (1981). *Teaching developmentally disabled children: The me book.* Baltimore, MD: University Park Press.

Lovaas, O. I. (1987). Behavioral treatment and normal educational and intellectual functioning in young autistic children. *Journal of Consulting and Clinical Psychology, 55,* 3–9.

Lovaas, O. I., Berberich, J. P., Perloff, B. F., & Schaffer, B. (1966). Acquisition of imitative speech in schizophrenic children. *Science, 151*, 705–707.

Lovaas, O. I., Koegel, R., Simmons, J. Q., & Long, J. S. (1973). Some generalization and follow-up measures on autistic children in behavior therapy. *Journal of Applied Behavior Analysis, 6*, 131–166.

Lund, S. K. (2009). Discrete trial instruction in early intensive behavioral intervention. In E. Boutot (Ed.), *Autism encyclopedia: The complete guide to autism spectrum disorders* (pp. 2201–2207). Waco, TX: Prufrock Press.

MacDonald, J. E., Wilder, D. A., & Dempsey, C. (2002). Brief functional analysis and treatment of eye poking. *Behavioral Interventions, 17*(4), 261–270.

Machalicek, W., O'Reilly, M. F., Beretvas, N., Sigafoos, J., & Lancioni, G. E. (2007). A review of interventions to reduce challenging behavior in school settings for students with autism spectrum disorders. *Research in Autism Spectrum Disorders, 1*(3), 229–246.

Maurice, C. (1993). *Let me hear your voice: A family's triumph over autism.* New York, NY: Ballantine Books.

Maurice, C. (2001). Autism advocacy or trench warfare? In C. Maurice, G. Green, & R. M. Foxx (Eds.), *Making a difference: Behavioral intervention for autism* (pp. 2001–2009). Austin, TX: Pro-Ed.

McCord, B. E., Thomson, R. J., & Iwata, B. A. (2001). Functional analysis and treatment of self-injury associated with transitions. *Journal of Applied Behavior Analysis, 34*(2), 195–210.

McEachin, J. J., Smith, T., & Lovaas, O.I. (1993). Long-term outcome for children with autism who received early intensive behavioral treatment. *American Journal on Mental Retardation, 97*, 359–372.

McGee, G. G., Almeida, M. C., Sulzer-Azaroff, B., & Feldman, R. S. (1992). Promoting reciprocal interactions via peer incidental teaching. *Journal of Applied Behavior Analysis, 25*(1), 117–126.

Mirenda, P., & Iacono, T. (1988). Strategies for promoting augmentative and alternative communication in natural contexts with students with autism. *Focus on Autistic Behavior, 3*(4), 16.

Morris, E. K. (2009). A case study in the misrepresentation of applied behavior analysis in autism: The Gernsbacher lectures. *The Behavior Analyst, 32*, 205–240.

National Research Council. (2001). *Educating children with autism.* Committee on Educational Interventions for Children with Autism, Division of Behavioral and Social Sciences and Education. Washington, DC: National Academy Press.

New York State Department of Health Early Intervention Program. (1999). *Clinical practice guideline: The guideline technical report, autism/pervasive developmental disorders, assessment and intervention for young children* [Publication #4217]. Albany, NY: Health Education Services.

Newman, B., Needelman, M., Reinecke, D. R., & Robek, A. (2002). The effect of providing choices on skill acquisition and competing behavior of children with autism during discrete trial instruction. *Behavioral Interventions, 17*(1), 31–41.

O'Reilly, M., Rispoli, M., Davis, T., Machalicek, W., Lang, R., Sigafoos, J., et al. (2010). Functional analysis of challenging behavior in children with autism spectrum disorders: A summary of 10 cases. *Research in Autism Spectrum Disorders, 4*(1), 1–10.

Piazza, C. C., Moes, D. R., & Fisher, W. W. (1996). Differential reinforcement of alternative behavior and demand fading in the treating fading in the treatment of escape-maintained destructive behavior. *Journal of Applied Behavior Analysis, 29*(4), 569–572.

Sallows, G. O., & Graupner, T. D. (2005). Intensive behavioral treatment for children with autism: Four-year outcome and predictors. *American Journal on Mental Retardation, 110*, 417–438.

Schneider, S. M., & Morris, E. K. (1987). A history of the term radical behaviorism: From Watson to Skinner. *The Behavior Analyst, 10*, 27–39.

Schreibman, L. (2005). *The science and fiction of autism*. Cambridge, MA: Harvard University Press.

Smith, T., Groen, A. D., & Wynn, J. W. (2000). Randomized trial of intensive early intervention for children with pervasive developmental disorder. *American Journal on Mental Retardation, 105*, 269–285.

Strain, P. S., & Danko, C. D. (1995). Caregivers' encouragement of positive interaction between preschoolers with autism and their siblings. *Journal of Emotional and Behavioral Disorders, 3*, 2–12.

Tarbox, J., Wilke, A. E., Najdowski, A. C., Findel-Pyles, R. S., Balasanyan, S., Caveney, A. C., et al. (2009). Comparing indirect, descriptive, and experimental functional assessments of challenging behavior in children with autism. *Journal of Developmental and Physical Disabilities, 21*(6), 493–514.

Taubman, M., Brierley, S., Wishner, J., Baker, D., McEachin, J., & Leaf, R. B. (2001). The effectiveness of a group discrete trial instructional approach for preschoolers with developmental disabilities. *Research in Developmental Disabilities, 22*(3), 205–219.

Wolf, M., Risley, T., & Mees, H. (1964). Application of operant conditioning procedures to the behavior problems of an autistic child. *Behavior Research Therapy, 1*, 305–312.

Wong, S. E., Floyd, J., Innocent, A. J., & Woolsey, J. E. (1991). Applying a DRO schedule and compliance training to reduce aggressive and self-injurious behavior in an autistic man: A case report. *Journal of Behavior Therapy and Experimental Psychiatry, 22*(4), 299–304.

CHAPTER 8

ENVIRONMENTAL SUPPORTS

Classroom Supports Promoting Academic Success for Children With ASD

The ecology of a classroom has an effect on every area of functioning for students, particularly those with an Autism Spectrum Disorder. John Dewey (1944) said, "We never educate directly, but indirectly by means of the environment" (as cited in Fisher, McLeod, & Hoover, 2003, p. 4). A classroom has a life and culture of its own this culture can have a direct effect on student development and student progress, especially for those with an Autism Spectrum Disorder.

ADDRESSING DIAGNOSTIC CRITERIA

The skills needed to communicate and socially interact can impact the ability of a student who has been diagnosed with autism to independently function in the school setting. Based on the definition by the Autism Society of America (Autism Society of America, n.d.), autism is a developmental disability that typically appears during the first 3 years of life and is the result of a neurological disorder that affects the normal functioning of the brain, impacting development in the areas of social interaction and communication skills. The Centers for Disease Control and Prevention (CDC, 2011) defines autism spectrum disorders (ASDs) as a group of developmental disabilities that can cause significant social, communication and behavioral challenges. The *Diagnostic and Statistical Manual of Mental Disorders, Fourth Edition, Text Revision (DSM-IV-TR)*

Cindy Golden, Ph.D.

(American Psychiatric Association [APA], 2000) states that the criteria for an *autistic disorder* include qualitative impairments in both social interaction and communication along with restricted repetitive and stereotypical patterns of behavior, interests, and activities. In addition, compared with most neurotypical students (i.e., typical functioning students), students with autism do not typically present with the ability to appropriately interpret basic sensory stimuli. This inability to interpret their surroundings, compounded by the difficulty with verbal and nonverbal communication, lends itself toward the student becoming less able to function at an independent level in school and community settings.

The criteria used in the diagnosis of an ASD are also instrumental in outlining the educational needs of those students. Autism is described as a spectrum disorder, meaning that it presents itself with a variety of different behaviors and at different levels. Those with autism have similar characteristics, such as deficits in social interaction and communication along with differences in the interaction of their sensory system to the environment but each one is different in the level in which specific behaviors are presented (Autism Society of America, n.d.).

ADDRESSING INDIVIDUAL NEED

According to the diagnostic criteria of an ASD, there are two dramatic differences in functioning: *communication* and *social interaction* (APA, 2000). These differences lead educators to the need for differentiation of instruction so that each students needs are met. Because it is a spectrum disorder, students demonstrate a wide range of ability in these areas. In the area of communication, some students may be nonverbal with no viable mode of communication while others are hyperlexic and hyperverbal (Marcus, Flagler, & Robinson, 2001) with well-developed reading fluency, spelling, and verbal expression skills. Because of these differences, the accommodations needed to meet the needs of these students are also on a spectrum. Accommodations for a nonverbal or low verbal student could include the use of sign language, picture symbols used to represent objects and concepts or the use of a voice output communication aid (VOCA). Others who present as hyperlexic and have the ability to read, spell, and speak fluently while struggling with reading comprehension and receptive language and may require graphic organizers, social narratives, visual reminders or other higher level supports (Aspen & Austin, 2003; Dawson & Osterling, 1997; Dettmer, Simpson, Myles, & Ganz, 2000; Gray & Garand, 1993; Koegel, 2000).

Deficits or differences in social interaction are also characteristic of students with ASD. Some students may express the desire to have friends and interact with others but not have appropriate behaviors to use when interacting with same-age peers (Marcus et al., 2001). These students may also not understand the intricacies of reading nonverbal social cues, may have interests that are consistent with a much younger child, or may have restricted interests on which they spend an inordinate amount of time, which causes them to appear eccentric. Others students on the autism spectrum may withdraw from social contact and may act aloof as if they do not hear or see others around them (Marcus et al.). These students may also have behaviors that are quite significant, such as self-injurious behaviors, self-stimulating behaviors, and aggressive behaviors. The accommodations and educational interventions required for each of these groups of students are varied and may range from structured program based on prolific amounts of data to less intrusive, self-management strategies (Heflin & Simpson, 1998; Quill, 1997; Schilling & Schwartz, 2004; Schopler & Mesibov, 1994; Smith-Myles & Schapman, 2004).

The spectrum nature of autism is demonstrated in the significant range of behavioral characteristics. Even though there are commonalities, the differences are quite varied. Each child must be comprehensively assessed to determine the uniqueness of his or her learning, communicative, social interactive and behavioral profile to create an educational plan that will meet each child's specific needs.

TYPES OF EDUCATIONAL SETTINGS

The educational setting in which a student with autism can be educated is dependent upon their specific needs. As with all students with disabilities, the students are educated in the least restrictive environment (LRE) necessary. Within the special education environment, there are several different types of environments that may be considered as options for students on the spectrum, and the description of those options is as follows:

- Special education services all day in a separate classroom or school setting: This type of setting may be necessary for students who are not able to function in another environment because of the significance of their behaviors.

- Special education service for one or two segments a day in a separate classroom: This environment may be required by students who are able to function adequately in a regular education setting for most of the school day but because of academic, social, behavior, or communication needs, may require a few smaller, pull-out segments with a special education teacher.

- Coteaching environment in which a special education teacher provides support to the student in a regular classroom: This support may be an effective option for a student who could function in a regular education classroom but would require an extra level of supervision and assistance by an additional teacher within that setting.

- Collaborative support: Collaborative support within a regular education classroom may be provided to the student by a special education teacher or paraprofessional who comes into the regular education setting for only part of a class time period.

- Consultative support: This type of support may be appropriate for students who can be included in a regular classroom all day but need to be monitored by a special education teacher and trained in how to provide support to students with autism.

- Accommodations and differentiation techniques provided to the student by the regular education teacher within a regular education setting: Some students on the spectrum may have the ability to function in a regular classroom with only simple accommodations and differentiated instruction techniques that could be provided by the regular education teacher. Other students may be able to function in a regular education setting with assistance from a paraprofessional who works in the regular education classroom.

- Regular classroom with no accommodations: Some students with autism may have developed the coping mechanisms that would allow for full inclusion without accommodations in a regular classroom setting.

EVIDENCED-BASED PRACTICES FOR SUPPORTING CHILDREN WITH ASD IN THE CLASSROOM

The term *evidenced-based practice* as used in the special education arena can be defined as educational interventions and strategies whose efficacy is based on a substantial number of rigorous scientific research studies. The outcomes of these research studies support the effectiveness of the practices (APA, 2006; No Child Left Behind, 2002).

In terms of educational practices specifically used for students with autism, the field is inundated with teaching tools, techniques, and strategies focused on the remediation of the social and communication deficits characteristic of the disorder. To determine the most appropriate interventions to use in the classroom setting based on the characteristic needs of the student with autism, the National Autism Center (NAC; 2009) produced a report that examined the interventions currently used in education. The NAC states that the development of children with autism can be significantly enhanced by the delivery of carefully planned and data-driven instruction that targets the characteristic nature of autism in specific areas such as communication, social skills, play, cognition, and independence.

The National Standards Report, produced by the NAC (2009) provides a guide to the most current evidence-based interventions to help with decision-making as to their effectiveness. The report (2009) divides the treatment methods into those that are *established*, *emerging*, and *unestablished* as based on evidenced-based research. This document defines *established* practices as those in which "sufficient evidence is available to confidently determine that a treatment produces beneficial treatment effects for individuals on the autism spectrum. That is, these treatments are established as effective" (NAC, p. 32). It outlines 11 of the established best practice interventions used to enhance the performance of students with autism. Among those considered to be *established* and empirically based are 11 interventions discussed below.

Antecedent Package

- The Antecedent Package involves the manipulation and modification of events that occur prior to a behavior that requires intervention (Bainbridge & Myles, 1999; Carr & Kemp, 1989; Dunlap & Koegel, 1980; Kennedy, 1994; Schilling & Schwartz, 2004).
    - These interventions may include cuing/prompting/fading procedures; environmental enrichment; modification to presentation of tasks; errorless learning; priming; noncontingent reinforcement; seating; errorless compliance; thematic activities; positive behavior supports/motivational operations; and incorporating special interests.

Behavioral Package

- The Behavioral Package includes interventions that focus on decreasing inappropriate behavior and increasing the use of more appropriate replacement behaviors (Apple, Bilingsley, & Schwartz, 2005; Charlop, Kurtz, & Casey, 1990; Koegel, Schreibman, Britten, & Laitinen, 1979; Maione & Mirenda, 2006).

- These interventions may include discrete trial training; mand training; generalization training; token economy; shaping; reinforcement; task analysis; chaining; functional communication training; and a combination of behavioral procedures such as redirection, choice, overcorrection, reinforcement, schedules, and modeling.

Comprehensive Behavioral Treatment for Young Children

- This intervention is typically referred to as an applied behavior analysis (ABA) or early intervention program (Lovaas, 1987; Reed, Osbourne, & Corness, 2007; Sallows & Gaupner, 2005).
  - These interventions are typically used for children less than 8 years of age and may include applied behavior analytic procedures such as discrete trial training and incidental teaching.

Joint Attention Intervention

- Joint Attention interventions involve teaching the specific subskills needed to learn the skill of maintaining joint attention with others and may involve pointing to shared objects or activities (Jones, Carr, & Feeley, 2006; Martins & Harris, 2006; Whalen & Schreibman, 2003).
  - These interventions may include teaching techniques such as pointing to or showing objects and focuses on getting students to respond to the actions of other people.

Modeling

- Interventions using modeling are dependent upon adult or peer demonstration of a target behavior. This should result in an imitation of the target behavior by the student with autism (Apple et al., 2005; Blew, Schwartz, & Luce, 1985; Buggey, 2005; Buggey, Toombs, Gardener, & Cervetti, 1999; Charlop, Schreibman, & Tryon, 1983; Krantz & McClannahan, 1998; Murzynski & Bourret, 2007; Nikopoulou & Keenan, 2007).
  - These interventions may include a student watching a live or video modeling performance that depicts a peer demonstrating a desired behavior or task.

Naturalistic Teaching Strategies

- Naturalistic teaching strategies involve interacting with the child, following his or her lead in a natural setting such as a play area or playground (Lifter, Ellis, Cannon, & Anderson, 2005; Sigafoos et al., 2006; Yoder & Stone, 2006).
    - These interventions may include the creation of a stimulating environment; encouraging conversation; modeling how to play; reinforcement; and providing choices.

Peer Training Package

- This package of strategies involves having the students with autism interact with students without disabilities who have undergone training (Lee, Odom, & Loftin, 2007; Odom & Watts, 1991; Tsao & Odom, 2006).
    - These interventions may include peer mediation/initiation and friends groups.

Pivotal Response Treatment

- Pivotal Response Treatment involves teaching the "pivotal" behaviors required in communication, such as motivation, responsiveness, and engagement. This is typically used in a natural setting and involves parental involvement (Koegel, Carter, & Koegel, 2003; Pierce & Schreibman, 1995; Vismara & Lyons, 2007).
    - This intervention that uses a behavioral approach to gain attention, give choices, take turns, encourage, and extend conversation and model social behavior.

Schedules

- The NAC (2009) refers to the use of a visually supported, task analyzed, or serial list of activities or steps required to complete a specific task as a schedule. These schedules make use of pictures, words, or a photograph to communicate a task's the requirements (Bryan & Gast, 2000; Hall, McClannahan, & Krantz, 1995; Hume & Odom, 2007; Krantz,

MacDuff, & McClannahan, 1993; O'Reilly, Sigafoos, Lancioni, Edrisinha, & Andrews, 2005).

  ○ These schedules may include those used for a large group in a classroom, an individual student, or to depict individual steps to a task.

Self-Management

- Strategies integrating self-management skills assist students in becoming monitors of their own behavior. They promote independence by having the students record the frequency of behaviors using a self-management system (Apple et al., 2005; Koegel, Koegel, Hurley, & Frea, 1992; Newman & Ten Eyck, 2005; Reinecke, Newman, & Meinberg, 1999).

  ○ These interventions may include setting one's own goals, checklists, wrist counters, and token systems.

Story-Based Intervention Package

- Story-Based Intervention Package uses a written narrative of an event. It involves a story that explains to the student the types of behaviors that will be required in the event and the types of things that will take place (Bledsoe, Myles, & Simpson, 2003; Bock, 2007; Hagiwara & Myles, 1999; Scattone, Wilczynski, Edwards, & Rabian, 2002).

  ○ This intervention package most typically includes social narratives or social stories.

When choosing the types of interventions and strategies for students with autism, it is imperative that evidence-based treatments be used.

CREATING A SUPPORTIVE ENVIRONMENT FOR CHILDREN WITH ASD

Today's educators are given the important task of developing programs that will meet the needs of students on the autism spectrum. In doing so, they not only look at the specific areas of need based on the diagnostic criteria for the disability, but they also review empirically based best practice, choosing interventions based on research. Teachers already implement educational learning interventions to teach basic subject matter, such as reading, math, and writing skills. But for students on the spectrum, there are additional areas of structure and support (Schopler & Mesibov, 1994), recommended to meet student needs. The additional classroom structure and support supplement the already implemented best practice teaching strategies and help to create an environment that evens the playing field for students so they are able to access the same basic types of teaching and learning strategies used with other students. The four additional areas of support are as follows:

- Environmental Supports
- Communication Supports
- Social Interaction Supports
- Sensory Supports

These areas of support are steeped in research and follow the needs outlined by the definition of autism, and each is described in the section below.

Addressing Environmental Needs

CHAPTER REFLECTION: Temple Grandin and Environmental Needs in the Classroom

"Some autistic people are bothered by visual distractions and fluorescent lights. They can see the flicker of the 60-cycle electricity. To avoid this problem, place the child's desk near the window or try to avoid using fluorescent lights. . . . The flickering of fluorescent lights can also be reduced by putting a lamp with an old-fashioned incandescent lightbulb next to the child's desk."

From Grandin (2002).

Research basis

Planning and providing for educational interventions needed by students with autism typically begins with providing structure to the setting and creating a climate that is organized and controlled. According to Fullan (1993), "Beyond better pedagogy, the teacher of the future must actively improve the conditions for learning in his or her immediate environments" (p. 10). This control and structure of the classroom is vitally important to meeting the diverse needs of students on the spectrum.

According to an early study by Schopler and Mesibov (1994), a structured teaching environment for students with autism begins by creating a clear and minimally distracting physical setting. A structured teaching environment can be described as one that is organized and makes use of visual supports or pictures to symbolize abstract concepts in the environment, enabling the students to better understand and predict what is required of them in the setting. This structure helps to maximize the student's ability to independently function in the environment while minimizing the need for adult prompts or assistance (Schopler, Mesibov, & Hearsey, 1995). The use of a structure that relies heavily on visual cues also plays a part in creating an environment that is conducive to promoting independent functioning of students with special needs (Dawson et al., 1995, as cited in Dawson & Osterling, 1997).

In the late 1980s and early 1990s, research by Dalrymple (1989, 1995) indicated a need for structure in educational environments used by students with autism. Because these students are required to organize conflicting stimuli and confusing information, it is important that the information be presented in formats that they can understand and use (Dalrymple, 1989). Dalrymple's research (1989, 1995) suggests that subjects with autism required four types of environmental supports in the classroom. These include the following:

- Sequencing supports for structuring time
- Visual procedural supports for activities
- Visual supports for environmental organization
- Visual supports to assist with interactions between others

In the 1990s, Eric Schopler focused his approach on environmental structure for tasks in his development of the Treatment and Education of Autistic and Related Communication-Handicapped Children, or TEACCH, method. The TEACCH method (Mesibov, Shea, & Schopler, 2005) makes use of different types of tasks placed in shoebox-type workboxes. This structure helped to create structured activities that clarified the *where, how, when,* and *how long* of the tasks. The method employed the use of structure, task analysis, and visual organization to create an environment the students could maneuver independently (Ferrante, Panerai, & Zingale, 2002).

In 2000, Dettmer, Smith, Myles, and Gantz continued to investigate the impact structured work systems that included the use of visual supports had on independent task completion ability of students on the spectrum. Structured work systems were described as task-analyzed work tasks that were divided into discrete steps and could be taught in sequential order using the organization of materials and the application of visual supports. The research conclusions indicated the use of a structured method of organizing work tasks in the classroom shortened the time between verbal instructions given by the staff members and independent compliance behavior exhibited by the student, which maximized the time spent on-task in the classroom. The implementation of this visually supported system also reduced the frequency and level of adult prompting of tasks. Dettmer and colleagues (2000) stated that the implementation of an organized work system enhanced with visual supports appeared to have a positive impact on a student's ability to complete classroom tasks in an educational classroom setting.

Organized work systems, environmental structure, and visual supports are all important interventions appropriate for students with autism. These support the students by creating an academic environment that is predictable with a method of communication to help alleviate frustration and promote independence.

Link to the NAC's standards report

In determining appropriate interventions to use in the environmental setup of a classroom for students with ASD, it is important that educators review those grounded in research. Of the 11 established interventions outlined by the National Standards Report (2009), several of these can be effective in the organization of the classroom environment.

The interventions contained within the *Antecedent Package* (Bainbridge & Myles,1999; Carr & Kemp, 1989; Dunlap & Koegel, 1980; Kennedy, 1994; Schilling & Schwartz, 2004) involve the manipulation of the antecedent, which can be the environment, in order to create a setting that is conducive to student learning and one that accommodates for the needs of the students with autism. This manipulation may involve such things as creating a room arrangement that is predictable to the students, including separate work areas with visuals that trigger a nonverbal understanding of the behavioral expectations of that area. These areas of the environment may include the following: work area, leisure area, group area, and reading area.

The *Naturalistic Teaching Strategies* (Lifter et al., 2005; Sigafoos et al., 2006; Yoder & Stone, 2006) listed by the NAC (2009) as established interventions can be implemented within the classroom by including an area to teach and practice appropriate leisure skills. In a younger age setting, this may be a play area with dolls, cars, trains, and a place for housekeeping. In an older classroom, leisure skills may be taught in an area with a table with puzzles, board games, or a couch with books and a place to listen to music. Even though these strategies may be implemented differently in a preschool versus a high school classroom, they are an important part of the environmental structure of both developmental age groupings

The *Self-Management* strategies (Apple et al., 2005; Koegel et al., 1992; Newman & Ten Eyck, 2005; Reinecke et al., 1999) outlined in the NAC report (2009) also play an instrumental role in teaching students to monitor their own behavior, learn self-advocacy skills, and to become independent and self-sufficient participants of the school environment. Educators can implement some of the strategies within the environment arrangement and organizational structure. The classroom arrangement should be one where materials are organized and labeled in a format that promotes easy access by the students. Baskets of crayons, pencils, and paper should be accessible so that when students realize they need a certain material to complete a task, they can retrieve the material themselves and are not reliant on others for assistance. Materials should be clearly labeled by using both words and visual symbols to support the communication differences of the students.

An environment that includes self-management strategies should also include a place to calm down or cool off when frustrated. This area could be arranged by placing a beanbag in the corner of a room, using a small tent to crawl in within a younger classroom environment or a chair placed in a location that is separated from the main activity of the classroom. As part of the self-management plan, the student may choose to use the area to escape the sensory stimulation that may be impacting their ability to remain calm. Always structure the space as much as is necessary for independent maneuvering by the students.

The organization and structure of a classroom should be built around the *Schedule* (Bryan & Gast, 2000; Hall, McClannahan, & Krantz, 1995; Hume & Odom, 2007; Krantz, MacDuff, & McClannahan, 1993; O'Reilly et al., 2005). These schedules are used for the organization and global sequence of daily activities and the more discrete sequence of steps to a task. This assists in making the abstract nature of time more concrete and breaks down larger types of tasks into smaller sequential steps. Schedules should utilize the use of both words and visual symbols or pictures to represent the activity to enhance understanding of the tasks. These can be implemented as large daily group schedules that indicate which class or activity comes next or as individual work task schedules which indicates the next step of a task.

When developing a classroom schedule for students with autism, it is important that the schedule include time for inclusive interaction with nondisabled peers. These activities implement the strategies outlined in the *Peer Training Package* (Lee et al., 2007; Odom & Watts, 1991; Tsao & Odom, 2006) of the NAC Standards Report (2009). Peer training activities that are included on the schedule may be as structured as participation in a formal peer group or friendship group that focuses on the development of social skills or as unstructured as time spent eating lunch with a peer who is knowledgeable about prompting interaction and working with a student on the spectrum.

Examples of classroom structure

In structuring an environment for students with autism, educators must create a setting that is predictable and visually based. This includes the physical arrangement of the furniture in the classroom, the schedule around which it is built and the visuals that support the environment making it appear less abstract and more easily understood by those with language deficits. Here are several examples of the types of supports that may be used in any type of setting to create a more structured environment:

1. To *encourage independent functioning and self-management skills*, the classroom environment must be organized and clutter free. Visual clutter must be kept to a minimum; common objects should be kept in a common place using bins and storage units; areas and objects should be labeled for easy retrieval by both the staff and the students; and a predictable traffic flow and floor plan for the classroom should be implemented (see Picture 8.1).

The picture shows a classroom area where group learning will take place. The crates hold student materials pertinent to the student's individual educational plan. All areas of the wall are clearly labeled and each board is backed in solid color fabrics that minimize visual clutter. Everything posted has a purpose and nothing is used for decoration only. Materials are housed in clear shoeboxes on the shelves and labeled by word and picture symbol. Every object in the classroom has a "home" to create a predictable space that is easily used by students.

Create an environment with a predictable structure; one where each area of the room has an explicit purpose and is supported with visuals.

2. Design the classroom setting so that there are *clear boundaries* between areas of the room.

This can be completed with the use of floor rugs in solid colors, placement of furniture to create boundaries or using masking tape to indicate clear margins for personal space.

The student's day should be predictable because it is built around a classroom schedule. The schedule should be easily understood by the students and interactive, displaying pictorial representations of the different activities.

This furniture arrangement creates a space that is less distracting to a student who becomes visually overstimulated by other students.

3.   The classroom organization and structure is based on its schedule. The schedule, whether a large one to be used for a group or an individual one to be used for one student, is important in building a sense of independence in the students. Students begin to develop the ability to maneuver through the school day from activity to activity without the need for constant adult prompting. It also assist in helping the students predict what is coming next within the school day. The schedule should be simple and make use of visual supports (see Picture 8.2).

Picture 8.2 shows a well-developed schedule for a classroom of younger students with more severe autism. The font used on the schedule is easily read and the analog clock indicates the time of the activity. This clock also reinforces an understanding of time, which is an important functional skill. Included is a picture symbol representing each activity of the day. The schedule uses a pocket chart for ease in modifying if necessary.

4.   Use color coding for easy organization of student materials. Color coding materials in the classroom will help to further *simplify the environment* so that students can become independent in obtaining and returning materials they need and use. If the student is not able to read her name that labels her materials, she may be able to match a color that has been assigned to them. Try coding the student's school supply cubby, backpack hook, books, and classroom materials for easy retrieval.

5. Some students work better in a location that is designed to *block out distracting stimuli* from the classroom (see Picture 8.3). If the teacher is using specific teaching techniques for the particular student (i.e., discrete trial training), it is important to have all of the required materials within reach. These materials may include data sheets, flash cards, pencils, and a timer and can easily be stored in the student's area.

Picture 8.3 shows how a separate cubby can be made with small tables and teacher-made wooden partitions. Hooks placed on the partition are wonderful places to hang clipboards for data sheets.

The workbox tasks are presented in a way that is structured and easily understood by the student who requires a more concrete lesson. This structure is appropriate for teaching several different types of basic skills.

6. The TEACCH (Mesibov et al., 2005) method of organizing work tasks, shown in Picture 8.4, is used in many types of special educational settings. This method has also been called the "workbox method." It is a way of presenting several different types of tasks in shoeboxes and provides a more structured way of teaching tasks to students.

There are several advantages to this type of workbox presentation:

- All required materials for the task are contained and easily accessible.
- There is a defined beginning and ending to the task.
- Several types of tasks can be taught using this format: basic skills, functional skills, and vocational skills.
- This is a great way to maintain the skills introduced and mastered in discrete trial sessions.

The *goal for the organization and structure of a classroom* is to create an environment with the amount of structure necessary for the students to be able to independently maneuver the space, performing all required daily activities and tasks with as few adult-driven prompts as possible. There are behaviors and difficulties that may arise if the student is not able to interact with the environment. The students may become confused as to the expectations of the space. Several of these behaviors are noted in Table 8.1.

Table 8.1   Behaviors or Difficulties That May Be Triggered by an Unstructured Environment

Student may:

- Over-rely on adult prompting in order to follow a classroom routine.
- Keep an unorganized work space.
- Be unable to find papers or classroom materials (i.e., paper, pencil/pen, homework, etc.).
- Be unable to complete assignments on time.
- Have little awareness of time.
- Demonstrate inappropriate behaviors (i.e., tantrums and aggression).
- Demonstrate an inability to transition from one task to another or one environment to another.
- Not understand which materials are required for a task.
- Display global sense of being unorganized and ill prepared.
- Demonstrate the inability to independently maneuver the classroom and school setting.
- Demonstrate difficulty with task completion without constant reminders/ prompts.
- Demonstrate difficulty with following multistep directions.
- Have difficulty with time management.
- Have difficulty in managing long-term assignments.
- Be unable to independently follow the sequence of a task.
- Demonstrate boundary/personal space issues.

Addressing Communication Needs

CHAPTER REFLECTION: Temple Grandin and Communication Needs in the Classroom

"I think in pictures....I translate both spoken and written words into full-color movies...which run like a VCR tape in my head. When somebody speaks to me, his words are instantly translated into pictures. Language-based thinkers often find this phenomenon difficult to understand, but in my job as an equipment designer for the livestock industry, visual thinking is a tremendous advantage."

From Grandin (2006).

Research basis

The National Research Council (2001) indicates an estimate of one third to one half of those with autism do not possess functional speech and language skills. A deficit in the area of communication is one of the initial markers that assist professionals in making a diagnosis of autism in young children. These deficits continue to impact the child's life as they mature to school age. "Language and communication are major areas of concern for children with autism" (Marckel, Neef, & Ferreri, 2006, p. 109), and, for a student to adequately function in the classroom, he must have some mode of communication.

The use of visual supports or pictures that represent concepts or activities is one of the most widely used interventions to accommodate for communication deficits in the classroom. Kathleen Quill (1997) wrote extensively on the use of visual supports with subjects with autism. Her seminal research indicated that subjects with autism tend to be visual learners and function well with routine (Quill). Her rationale for the use of visual supports was based on research in several areas. Quill found that children with autism had a stronger ability to encode visual-spatial information than to encode and process auditory information. This strength seemed to be influenced by the fixed aspect of the pictorial symbol versus the fleeting aspect of the auditory word. Quill also described the struggle a child with autism may have with attending to an auditory sequence of linguistic events and how the memory skills of a child with autism seem to be impacted by the disability. Based on this information, it appeared to Quill that a student's memory for visually cued information is stronger than the ability to recall auditory information, leading to the need for more visually supported instruction.

In 2000, Kogel stated that practitioners appeared to be making progress in helping to remediate many of the characteristic communication weaknesses in students with autism with the use of visual supports. Ogletree, Oren, and Fisher (2007) described the most effective communication-related practices for individuals with ASD as a group of evidence-based intervention techniques that include prompting, modeling, visual structure, and visual supports. In 2003, Aspen and Austin (2003) report the "addition of visuals to support language may even promote growth in the areas of both receptive and expressive language" (p. 11). The authors continued, stating that photos and picture symbols are among the recommended types of visual supports designed to enhance a subject's communication ability. In 2006, Pries also suggested the use of visual supports in the form of picture symbols was found to be effective for the generalization and maintenance of verbal commands and basic communication for students with autism. In the interview below, Kimberly McGuiness discussed her work contracting with a public school system to create individualized visual schedules.

CHAPTER REFLECTION: Interview With Kimberly McGuiness, Mother of Julia and Consultant to Floyd County Public Schools for Creating Individualized Visual Schedules

I have a 23-year-old deaf autistic daughter. I have been creating visuals for 20 years based on her needs and have been managing her business of disability for 23 years. I've volunteered at her schools supporting speech-language pathologists and teachers, which led to crafting together a parent packet with visuals for parents to use in the home and helping to bridge the communication gap between home and school.

Visual schedules are used in the classroom to help students transition from one task to another. They are used for group activities, daily activities, engaging students during the morning meeting to start their day, discussing an event, sequencing events, and to redirect behaviors in a more positive manner.

If the schedule is student specific, I ask the teacher if there needs to be a second copy to send home to the parents. I've created many visuals for parents to utilize in their homes with children. One of my goals is to share with parents the importance of them becoming part of their child's team. It takes a team effort so I strive to educate parents to be aware of the tools and strategies available.

Ms. McGuiness invites readers to visit her blog for additional information about visual schedules and supporting students who have both ASD and sensory impairments. http://projectjuliasworld.blogspot.com.

Link to the NAC's standards report

In designing a classroom that meets the communication needs of students on the autism spectrum, educators should be aware of the empirical basis for each intervention. Several of the strategies listed by the National

Standards Report (NAC, 2009) as established by research, can be put into place to assist in the remediation and accommodation of communication differences.

One of the most widely used group of strategies are those in the *Story-Based Intervention Package* (Bledsoe et al., 2003; Bock, 2007; Hagiwara & Myles, 1999; Scattone et al., 2002). Once the physical environment has been organized, the classroom staff can further structure the space by posting social narratives or social stories (Gray & Garrand, 1993) in the different areas of the classroom to prompt the student to the types of behavioral expectations that are required for that area of the classroom. These help to further clarify the abstract nature of the environment.

The *Schedules* (Bryan & Gast, 2000; Hall, McClannahan, & Krantz, 1995; Hume & Odom, 2007; Krantz, MacDuff, & McClannahan, 1993; O'Reilly et al., 2005) used in the classroom can also be used to support the student's communication needs. If created with visual supports (i.e., picture symbols representing activities of the day or steps to a task) schedules used in a classroom help to structure the setting so that the students understand the flow of the school day. This lessens the impact that deficits in communication can cause due to the constant barrage of oral language/instructions typical of a classroom.

The strategies from the *Joint Attention Intervention* (Jones et al., 2006; Martins & Harris, 2006; Whalen & Schreibman, 2003) area can be integrated into the communication supports of the classroom to enhance students' verbal and nonverbal communication as it relates to social ability. Technology has become an integral part of enhancing these skills with the use of interactive white boards used with groups of students on the spectrum. Teachers using interactive tablets (i.e., iPad) and projection systems with applications specific to teaching specific curriculum topics can help gain the joint attention of several students at one time. This can include the use of video modeling tools to enhance communication in social skill development (Apple et al., 2005; Blew et al., 1985; Buggey, 2005; Buggey et al., 1999; Charlop, Schreibman, & Tryon, 1983; Krantz & McClannahan, 1998; Murzynski & Bourret, 2007; Nikopoulou & Keenan, 2007). Students gathered around a table watching a video of another same-age child modeling appropriate social skills is a wonderful way to encourage joint attention while teaching appropriate social communication skills.

To build lifelong functional skills, teachers should continually enhance and support the students' ability to communicate their wants and needs. One method is the use of *Pivotal Response Treatment* (Koegel et al., 2003; Pierce & Schreibman, 1995; Vismara & Lyons, 2007) techniques, reinforcing communication with objects and activities that are motivating to the student. The use of *mand*, or request training, which falls in the *Behavioral Package* (Apple et al., 2005; Charlop et al., 1990; Koegel et al., 1979; Maione & Mirenda, 2006) is another way to support communication in the classroom. For example, a teacher can provide the student with a picture symbol card of "water" or a preferred object and prompt the student to use the picture card to request the object or activity before accessing it. This type of communication technique follows an organized format that lessens the prompt levels based on behavioral data. If the student is not able to request the object or activity independently, then prompt at the level that is required (i.e., hand over hand), lessening the prompt levels (i.e., to pointing to the picture card) as they are ready.

Examples of communication supports

(All symbols created with Mayer-Johnson's Boardmaker software; http://www.mayer-johnson.com/boardmaker-software)

There are several practical ways in which visual supports can be used to accommodate students with communication differences. Here are a few:

1. Students must have the ability to *communicate their wants and needs*. For the student who is low verbal or nonverbal, create an area in the room to display visual supports that depict both objects and activities he or she may want or need throughout the school day. These may include bathroom, water, break, help, and so on. These visual supports should be located near the student's desk or in a location that is accessible throughout the school day to encourage their use.

This communication strip provides a way for the student who struggles with verbal expression to communicate their wants and needs.

2. As students progress, it is important to encourage them to begin forming simple sentence requests instead of relying of one-word responses. Picture 8.6 shows an example of one way students can request something they want or need. This visual support uses a combination of picture symbols and words and is written in a grammatically correct simple sentence.

Prior to accessing the bathroom or water fountain, the student will request using this visual support by choosing the correct picture to place in the square. This will then be given to one of the teaching staff indicating a communicative request. The staff member will then read the sentence aloud to the student and grant the request, reinforcing the use of the visual support for communication.

3. Some nonverbal students will develop oral language and some will not. The students who do not learn to use verbal communication should develop an alternate form of communication, and one option is sign language. It is important that those working with very young nonverbal students not settle on one alternate form of communication but pair the use of sign with picture symbols and oral language prior to the students settling in on the use of one method. Teachers will need to become careful observers as most beginning sign language will initially present as approximations. It may be difficult to determine that the young child is actually forming a sign. It is also extremely important that some method of communication be introduced very early in a child's life. This will help to minimize behavioral issues whose function is communication.

4. In *developing your classroom expectations,* it is important that you use simple language to enhance student understanding of the expectation. Instead saying "Do not take things that are not yours," turn this request around to make a simple positive request that states what you want the student to do. Using simple vocabulary, state the request in two to three words. Enlarge each one as a *super symbol* (see Picture 8.7), adding a visual to further explain the expectation.

Enlarge a simply stated behavior expectation that includes a visual symbol to create a tool for teaching appropriate social skills to a group of students.

The *goal for the use of communication techniques* and structure within a classroom is to create an environment that provides the student with a way to communicate their wants and needs, and to further learning. If a communication plan is not developed and implemented in the classroom, students may begin to exhibit inappropriate types of behavior in their pursuit for a mode of communication. These may include the following:

Table 8.2   Behaviors or Difficulties That May Be Triggered by Communication Difficulties

Student may:

- Demonstrate inability to complete tasks independently.
- Demonstrate the inability to understand oral or written instructions.
- Demonstrate the inability to be independent in the classroom and follow typical routines.
- Demonstrate the inability to have typical interpersonal relationships with adults or peers.
- Display frustration or anger.
- Display sadness or crying.
- Appear confused.
- Exhibit selective mutism or refusal to speak.
- Display inappropriate behaviors (i.e., tantrums, throwing objects, yelling, saying "no").
- Demonstrate self-stimulating behavior.
- Refuse to comply with directives.
- Act aloof or as if they cannot hear.
- Refuse to begin tasks.
- Refuse to participate with a group.
- Self-isolate or withdraw.
- Watch classroom activities from afar or watching others in order to complete tasks.
- Demonstrate self-injurious behaviors.
- Demonstrate physical aggression toward others.
- Rely on adult prompting to complete tasks independently.
- Rely on adult prompting to follow a classroom routine.

Addressing Social Interaction Needs

CHAPTER REFLECTION: Temple Grandin and Visual Strengths

"I didn't have a concrete visual corollary for the abstraction known as 'getting along with people'.... The door jammed while I was washing the inside panes [of a bay window].... In order to get out without shattering the door, I had to ease it back very carefully. It struck me that relationships operate the same way."

From Grandin (2006).

Research basis

The area of Social Interaction is one of the deficit characteristics key to making a diagnosis of an ASD. The ability to use appropriate social skills involves the ability to comprehend verbal directives, to understand the social environment, to generalize previously learned skills, and to know which of the learned skills to use in which situation (Bryan & Gast, 2000; Ganz et al., 2008). The abstract fleeting nature of the oral language required in social interaction lends itself to interventions involving the use of concrete visual supports.

Pries' (2006) research stated that the use of visual supports serve as a trigger to recall or maintain previously learned skills, which is crucial to maneuvering the social environment. The use of these visually supported interventions have been seen as effective in helping subjects attend to relevant information in their environment, attain and maintain joint attention (Yoder & Stone, 2006), generalize and maintain learning skills (Pries), organize tasks (Mesibov et al., 2005), and predict and make sense of their environment (Heflin & Simpson, 1998).

In the 1990s, Carol Gray continued the development of a strategy to be used for students with autism that began with the priming technique used by the Koegels (2000) in the 1970s. *Social Stories* (Gray & Garand, 1993) were created as a visual technique for teaching children with autism how to read the intricacies of the social environment. This technique used a four-word to six-word sentence to describe a social interaction (Thiemann & Goldstein, 2001), often including pictorial representations of the ideas presented in narrative form. This technique was intended to visually demonstrate social situations and provide support to students who struggle in comprehending the quick exchange of information which typically occurs in a verbal conversation. These techniques turn an abstract social situation into a concrete representation that allows time for reflection in choosing the appropriate social response.

Link to the NAC's National Standards Report

It is important that educators become familiar with several types of empirically based interventions to develop a plan that will enhance a student's ability to socially interact with peers and adults specific to his or her needs. These strategies should be based in behavioral data such as those included in the *Behavioral Package* (Apple et al., 2005; Charlop et al., 1990; Koegel et al., 1979; Maione & Mirenda, 2006) of strategies. Shaping of behavior by modeling and using reinforcement and redirection are key strategies many educators use. Many teachers also use redirection strategies with students who may interact inappropriately. This simple redirection will serve as a prompt to help guide the students in making a more appropriate choice in behaviors.

The interventions included in the *Comprehensive Behavioral Treatment for Young Children* or ABA are also an important part of the structure for a social skills–based classroom (Lovaas, 1987; Reed et al., 2007; Sallows & Gaupner, 2005). These strategies include discrete trial training (DTT) and incidental teaching. Discrete trial training (Lovaas, 1987) is a structured teaching technique involving the practice and mastery of small steps to a task. Each small step is mastered prior to moving to the next step. Incidental teaching, or teaching a task within another more motivating task, like play (McGee & Daly, 2007), is also an appropriate strategy to use for teaching social skills. Incidental teaching in a natural environment is one way to assist students in the generalization of learned social skills taught in a more structured lesson. These *Natural Teaching Strategies* involve taking advantage of the social setting the students are immersed in to teach an appropriate way to interact. Saying "thank you" or "good morning" when meeting someone coming down the school hallway is one good example (Lifter et al., 2005; Sigafoos et al., 2006; Yoder & Stone, 2006).

Many teachers use group board games as the activity through which they will use a variety of different teaching interventions to teach several types skills (i.e., social interaction, communication, and basic academic/prereadiness skills). There will be several different types of skills required of students as they play board games. Students with autism who playing board games with other students at a table will be required to use joint attention to interact appropriately. *Joint Attention Intervention* strategies (Jones et al., 2006; Martins & Harris, 2006; Whalen & Schreibman, 2003) can be used by the teacher to enhance a groupwide focus on the same activity. Teachers will use a variety of prompting techniques such as gesturing, verbal directives, and picture symbols to remind and redirect student to jointly attend to and focus on the activity.

Using the same board game activity, teachers and classroom staff members can also use *Modeling* strategies (Apple et al., 2005; Blew et al., 1985; Buggey, 2005; Buggey et al., 1999; Charlop et al., 1983; Krantz & McClannahan, 1998; Murzynski & Bourret, 2007; Nikopoulou & Keenan, 2007) to provide a real-life example of how to appropriately interact with others. Taking turns, praising the winner of a game, being a good loser, and calling peers by their names could be modeled by the staff within the classroom or by a nondisabled peer who joins the group as part of *Peer Training* (Lee et al., 2007; Odom & Watts, 1991; Tsao & Odom, 2006).

Social narratives and social stories (Gray & Garrand, 1993) are widely used as a way to make an abstract skill, such as social interaction, become more concrete. These interventions are considered to be established strategies and are included in the *Story-Based Intervention Package* (Bledsoe et al., 2003; Bock, 2007; Hagiwara & Myles, 1999; Scattone et al., 2002). A great time to use these strategies is during a formal social skills lesson. This could be scheduled during group time in the morning or after lunch during a slower part of the day. Creating these social stories and using an interactive whiteboard to project them onto a big screen provides a way to encourage joint attention while teaching these skills.

Examples of social interaction supports in the classroom

Characteristic to the nature of autism, students on the spectrum have deficits in the development of interpersonal relationship skills. Dependent upon their level of functioning, they will require accommodations in the social arena. The following are examples of accommodations that could be used in any type of educational setting.

1. Even the simplest tasks can be problematic to students on the spectrum. The unstructured task of eating in the lunchroom and knowing how to interact with others while eating is difficult. One way to visually support the expectations of this unstructured setting is to create a placemat (Picture 8.8) using a large sheet of construction paper, placing a visual supported sequence of events creating a more structured lunchroom experience. The steps could include the following: *stand in line, get lunch, sit down, eat lunch, wipe face, talk to friends, throw away trash, go back to class.*

This teacher-created placemat enhances social skills by providing visual reminders of the behaviors that are appropriate to a school cafeteria.

If the student has an issue with eating food from other student's plates, the staff member may prompt the student to eat the food that is on "the blue." The staff may also need to touch the picture symbols to remind the student to "talk to your friend" or "drink" or "throw away trash." This prompting should lessen as the student moves toward more appropriate social behavior in the cafeteria.

2. Video modeling can be used to teach age-appropriate social skills to students on the spectrum. There are several social skills videos sets available to teachers, such as *Model Me Kids,* or the teacher may wish to create her own using neurotypical peers from the school. The students with autism may also want to participate in the videotaping of what appropriate behavior looks like.

This poster provides a visual support that will assist students in understanding what happens to their body when they feel angry or frustrated.

Regardless of whether the students are functioning with more significant needs or at the higher-functioning end of the spectrum, it is vital that teachers set aside time to teach social skills on a consistent basis. After teaching the skill, use a naturalistic setting to practice and teach generalization of the skill. These skills can include behaviors such as *greeting people, hallway behavior, receiving a compliment, apologizing when you are wrong,* or *taking turns.*

3. To deal with emotions and feelings in the classroom, the student should be taught to label his or her feelings and appropriate ways in which to express them. For example, when a student feels happy, he should know that he can smile or laugh and if he feels scared, he can tell an adult. There are some feelings students may have that are more serious in nature, if acted upon inappropriately. If a student recognizes he is angry, instead of resorting to physical or verbal aggression, the student needs to learn a replacement behavior.

The poster shown in Photo 8.9 is one way in which a visual support can be used to teach the skill of recognizing emotions prior to acting on the emotion. It remains posted so that the teacher can refer to it when the student begins to show signs of anger.

This may require that the teacher prompt the student by coming over to the poster and modeling for the student how to recognize they are angry. This should be taught before the student is actually exhibiting these behaviors so that they can attend to and focus on learning the skill. After recognizing they are angry, it is necessary that there be visuals indicating the next step, such as: "When I'm angry I can ask for a break." This will begin to teach the students self-management skills.

4. When students are able to access an inclusive setting, it is important that they have access to visual supports reminding them of the social behaviors they are to exhibit (i.e., walk in the hallway, ask for help, etc.). Even though students may be academically prepared for an inclusive setting, they may still struggle with knowing what to do when situations arise in a social setting. Create for the student a list of "rules" from the hidden curriculum (Smith-Myles & Schapman, 2004). These are "rules" the student will need to remember in each class (i.e., Ms. Smith's class – Do not chew gum, Sit up front, Bring textbook, Raise hand

to speak). Place a copy of these inside the student's notebook for that particular class. Each inclusive classroom may have a different set of rules, dependent upon the personality of the teacher.

The ability to socially interact with others using appropriate skills is vital to becoming an independent adult. A difference in the ability to appropriately interact in a social setting is also part of the initial diagnosis of an ASD. These skills are not typically learned through simply observing the behavior of others but must be taught directly. When students have a difficult time with social interaction, behavioral issues may occur, and Table 8.3 outlines some of the issues that may occur.

Table 8.3 Behaviors or Difficulties That May Be Triggered by Social Interaction Difficulties

Student may:

- Be unable to make or keep friends.
- Demonstrate inability to enter, exit, or carry on an appropriate conversation with same-age peers or adults.
- Feel more comfortable in spending time with younger children or adults.
- Exhibit social awkwardness.
- Have difficulty with transition to new environments.
- Demonstrate inability in knowing what is age appropriate in terms of dress, topics, of conversation, etc.
- Withdraw or self-isolate.
- Exhibit inappropriate behaviors in social settings (i.e., tantrums, physical aggression, verbal aggression).
- Blurt out inappropriate things to both peers or adults.
- Have issues with personal space (i.e., standing too close or touching peers or adults).
- Exhibit depression or sadness.
- Exhibit fears.
- Feel frustration or anger.
- Exhibit self-injurious behaviors.
- Exhibit attention-seeking behaviors (doing things to call attention to himself or herself).
- Play with objects or in activities that is more typical of much younger children.
- Not take care of personal hygiene.
- Not dress in a manner that is socially appropriate for his or her age.
- Not use appropriate manners or acting in a way that is atypical for his or her age group.

Addressing Sensory Needs

CHAPTER REFLECTION: Temple Grandin Addressing Sensory Needs

"One of my sensory problems was hearing sensitivity, where certain loud noises, such as a school bell, hurt my ears. . . . I was also very touch sensitive; scratchy petticoats felt like sandpaper ripping off my skin. There is no way a child is going to function in a classroom if his or her underwear feels like it is full of sandpaper."

From Autism-Help.org (1996).

Research basis

First-person anecdotal information (i.e., Autism-Help.org, 1996; Grandin, 1995) suggests that people with ASD often experience distress associated with sensory experiences that are well tolerated by others. Furthermore, research suggests that many children with ASD experience higher rates of sensory difficulties than their typically developing peers (Watling, Deitz, & White, 2003). Children with ASD may demonstrate both hypersensitivities (i.e., overly sensitive to certain sounds, type of physical contact, or textures) and hyposensitivities (i.e., seems not to notice people in the room, high tolerance for pain; Johnson & Myers, 2007). Because these differences in processing sensory stimuli may play a role in the level of engagement and the behavior of students in an educational setting, educators must select interventions that accommodate for these differences.

Sensory integration therapy is designed to help the child organize sensory stimuli by exposure to increased and reduced levels of sensory stimuli; however, the effectiveness of sensory integration therapy is not well documented (Baranek, 2002; Bundy, Shia, Qi, & Miller, 2007; Dawson & Watling, 2000; Leong & Carter, 2008; National Research Council, 2001; Stephenson & Carter, 2009).Conversely, stronger research literature supports the use of behavioral interventions, such as sensory extinction and replacement techniques, to address some types of sensory difficulties. For instance, Devlin, Leader, and Healy (2009) found that a behavioral intervention based on a functional behavior analysis was more effective in reducing self-injurious behavior than sensory integration therapy.

It is important to note that many individuals with ASD report finding sensory interventions helpful. Likewise, parents and teachers report a reduction in challenging behaviors following interventions based on sensory integration techniques (such as weighted vests and brushing). Thus, much work is needed in this area to better understand the contributions of sensory integration therapy to reducing sensory difficulties. Regardless of the interventions used to address sensory difficulties, the experience of unusual sensory perceptions appears to be a significant problem for many individuals with ASD

Link to national standards

Even though sensory supports in the classroom differ greatly based on age and developmental level of the students, they all hold a common focus: to arouse or calm the sensory systems of a student in order to engage them in learning.

Educators can manipulate aspects of the classroom environment to enhance learning and engagement. These types of interventions or strategies are considered part of the *Antecedent Package* (Bainbridge & Myles, 1999; Carr & Kemp, 1989; Dunlap & Koegel, 1980; Kennedy, 1994; Schilling & Schwartz, 2004). This manipulation of the sensory environment may include such things as lowering the lights, the use of incandescent rather than fluorescent lighting, playing soft music to mask unwanted noise, the use of noise-reducing headphones, and clearing the environment of visual clutter.

The practice of including different types of sensory breaks or activities within the classroom schedule is also important. Interventions and strategies from the *Schedule* (Bryan & Gast, 2000; Hall, McClannahan, & Krantz, 1995; Hume & Odom, 2007; Krantz, MacDuff, & McClannahan, 1993; O'Reilly et al., 2005) area of the National Standards Report (NAC, 2009) indicates that the advantage of using structured schedule, which could include the inclusion of sensory activities to be used at predetermined times. These breaks used noncontingent upon student behavior are important in providing for the sensory needs of students with autism. Sensory breaks are used by most adults, as they get up and take a walk during a long work session, take a coffee break to rejuvenate the mind, and stretching to increase blood flow to the brain. The same types of activities are necessary in classrooms. A properly developed schedule will proactively meet the needs of the student prior to behavioral issues ensuing because of inadequate sensory stimulation.

There are several types of sensory activities that can be used within *Naturalistic Teaching* (Lifter et al., 2005; Sigafoos et al., 2006; Yoder & Stone, 2006) environments. These may include swinging on the playground swings, walking around the track, running an errand to the front office of the school while carrying a heavy object (i.e., stack of books), or wearing an iPod to listen to music.

Self-Management (Apple et al., 2005; Koegel et al., 1992; Newman & Ten Eyck, 2005; Reinecke et al., 1999) sensory strategies should be encouraged as they lend themselves to the student generalizing the skills to other situations in the community. In learning self-management skills, students with autism will learn how to monitor and plan ways of meeting their own sensory needs. Contrived activities, with materials that are not easily accessible and can be only used in a certain settings, are less likely to enhance the self-management of sensory needs. Naturally occurring strategies that focus on meeting these same needs will assist the student in moving to an independent functioning level.

Examples of sensory supports in the classroom

Swings can be an important part of a sensory plan for a child by helping provide vestibular input.

Regulating sensory input for students with autism is vital to their overall educational plan. Accommodations and interventions can be put into place in any type of setting. The following provides a few ideas of interventions that can be used for sensory awareness and regulation.

1. Swings and mini trampolines are wonderful sensory items to have in a classroom or a sensory room. The vestibular input from these activities is calming to do many students with autism. This swing can be removed from a hook in the ceiling when not being used by the student.

It is important that the teacher use the swing activity with input from the student's occupational therapist, who specializes in sensory activities.

2. Create a list of sensory activities that can be used by a student in any setting. The following items/activities can easily be used by a regular education teacher in a more inclusive environment:

- Use headphones to block sound or listen to soft music
- Providing access to lotion for massaging on hands/arms
- Use a weighted lap blanket

- Running errands carrying heavy objects (i.e., books)
- Allowing standing up/walking/pacing around the room
- Watching fish in an aquarium
- Weighted pencils/raised lined paper

This list can be used on a choice board for the students. The students may choose one of the activities during the "sensory time." The activities may also be used as an antecedent to time of frustration (i.e., before a stressful task, prior to getting on the bus in the afternoon, if the student begins to display behaviors indicating frustration or anger). This proactive approach to redirecting the intense feelings is one way of implementing the *Antecedent Package of* strategies.

3. This ball chair, as seen in Picture 8.11, is a great sensory item for students who tend to be more active while sitting in a regular desk chair. It requires that the students concentrate on sitting so that they do not become complacent and sedentary. Research (Schilling & Schwartz, 2004) indicates a positive effect on engagement and arousal. The chairs provide the students a way to "both actively move and maintain an optimal arousal level" (p. 424).

4. Foods can be also be used as a sensory activity. Crunchy snacks, sour mints, cold beverages, lollipops, or chewing gum can easily be used to stimulate sense of taste and the oral motor system. This can be used as an arousal activity as students need more sensory input.

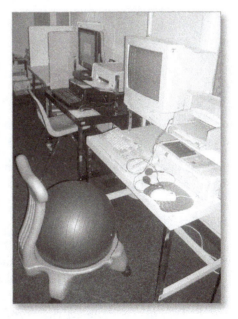

One of the most important things to remember about the use of sensory activities in the classroom is that they should not be used as reinforcement activities but should be available noncontingent upon behavior. Some students may need scheduled sensory breaks that are scattered throughout the school day. If sensory needs are not planned for and met, students may seek the same input in other ways (Case-Smith & Bryan, 1999; Jung et al., 2006; Linderman, & Stewart, 1999). Sometimes the manner in which the student chooses to seek input or calm their sensory systems is not appropriate and may cause difficulties within the school setting. Table 8.4 provides examples of these types of behaviors.

As part of a student's sensory plan, ball chairs can assist in enhancing engagement in the classroom.

Table 8.4   Behaviors or Difficulties That May Be Triggered by Sensory Difficulties

Student may:

- Demonstrate over- or under-arousal.
- Have limited eye contact or use peripheral vision during social interactions.
- Show an aversion to change or novelty.
- Display atypical sensory exploration (such as licking or sniffing nonfood objects).
- Show sensory aversions (such as smells, fabric textures, food textures, certain sounds).
- Have a heightened desire for sensory stimuli.
- Show unusual posture.
- Have issues with personal space.
- Display inappropriate behaviors (i.e., tantrums, physical aggression toward people, physical aggression toward objects, or screaming).
- Walk on toes.
- Spin around in room.
- Tip in chair or wanting to spin in a chair.
- Bump into objects and gets scrapes/bruises frequently.
- Display self-injurious behaviors.
- Show a fear of touching new objects (i.e., play dough, glue, bubbles, etc.).
- Place hands over ears.
- Have anxiety.
- Many aspects of the classroom environment can impact learning and overall functioning of children with ASD.

TEACHING TIPS

- Maximize your students' independence by providing environmental supports that promote understanding and help students predict what is coming next. Visual supports can help students understand the structuring of time, steps needed to complete an activity, and interpreting social interactions.

- Create a learning environment that is predictable and visually based. Physical arrangements of classroom furniture that provide clear boundaries between areas of the room create a learning environment that is predictable and visually based. In addition, labeling classroom materials stored in functionally meaningful locations and a predictable traffic flow of classroom activities provide a supportive learning environment.

- Organized work systems, such as workbox tasks, provide a structured way of teaching the steps needed to complete a task. These workbox tasks provide access to all necessary materials, have a clear beginning and end, and can introduce and maintain skill many types of skills.

• Provide a classroom area designed to block out distracting stimuli. This may include a cubby or a small table with wood partitions.

SUMMARY

Classroom environments can address individual needs of students with ASD in many ways. These supports may include the physical structures of the classroom, communication supports, social interaction supports, and sensory supports. Classrooms supports are enhanced when they include visual information. The TEACCH method includes classroom organization strategies providing structure, task analysis, and visual organization to create a classroom environment that enhances independence. The National Standards Report (2009) reviews 11 established interventions for teaching children with ASD that can be effective in creating a supportive classroom learning environment. Organization and structure of a classroom should be built around a schedule. This schedule should be individualized for each student depending on their level of functioning, communication strengths, and goals. The physical layout of the classroom should include clear boundaries that help students understand daily routines and promote independence. The use of actual objects, photos, picture symbols, and words provide visual supports that promote communication. These can be displayed on the wall of an appropriate part of the room or on a strip by the student's desk. In addition, posting social narratives or social stories in appropriate areas of the classroom communicates behavioral expectations and provides predictability. The classroom environment can also address sensory needs. Swings and mini trampolines provide vestibular input and may be calming to students with ASD. A specific area of the classroom may be devoted to sensory choices such as using lotion, blowing bubbles, playing with clay, sitting in a beanbag chair, or watching fish in an aquarium. Other areas may be provided that block out sensory stimuli. For instance, a classroom may have a section of the room with a cubby and headphones. Sensory needs may trigger challenging behaviors if opportunities to meet those needs in an inappropriate manner are not available.

DISCUSSION AND REFLECTION QUESTIONS

1. What is meant by *evidence-based practice?*

2. Name three of the established interventions as indicated by the *National Standards Report.*

3. How might you use environmental supports to provide a safe environment, a comfortable learning setting, and a structured learning experience?

4. What types of communication supports might be used in the classroom to accommodate for communication differences of a student with autism?

5. How might the social deficits of a teenage student with autism begin to affect their emotional health?

6. Describe creative ways in which a teacher could accommodate for the sensory needs of a student with autism while continuing to meet the need of neurotypical peers in an inclusive environment.

RECOMMENDED FURTHER READINGS AND INTERNET SOURCES

Further Readings

Attwood, T. (1997). *Asperger's syndrome—A guide for parents and professionals.* Philadelphia, PA: Jessica Kingsley Publishers.

Dunn, B. K., & Curtis, M. (2003). *The incredible 5-point scale.* Shawnee Mission, KS: Autism Asperger Publishing.

Golden, C. (2012). *The special educator's toolkit.* Baltimore, MD: Paul H. Brookes.

Hodgdon, L. (1996). *Visual strategies for improving communication volume 1: Practical supports for school and home.* Troy, MI: Quirk Roberts Publishing.

Maurice, C., Green, G., & Luce, S. C. (1996). *Behavioral intervention for young children with autism: A manual for parents and professionals.* Austin, TX: Pro-Ed.

McClannahan, L., & Krantz, P. (1999). *Activity schedules for children with autism.* Bethesda, MD: Woodbine House.

Quill, K. A. (1995). *Teaching children with autism: Strategies to enhance communication and socialization.* New York, NY: Delmar Publishers.

Quill, K. A. (2002). *Do-watch-listen-say: Social and communication intervention for children with autism.* Baltimore, MD: Paul H. Brookes.

Internet Sources

Washington State Department of Education. (2009). *Autism guidebook for Washington state: A guide for both parents and professionals on autism.* Retrieved from http://here.doh.wa.gov/materials/autism-guidebook/13_AutismGd_E10L.pdf.

Sensory Processing Disorder Foundation website provides information about SPD, how it is diagnosed, and treatments. http://www.spdnetwork.org/about-sensory-processing-disorder.html

Special Needs Resource Magazine website provides good information and resources for teachers of students with autism and other developmental disabilities. http://www.snrmag.com

Treatment and Education of Autistic and Communication Related Handicapped Children (TEACCH). http://teacch.com

REFERENCES

American Psychiatric Association. (2000). *Diagnostic and statistical manual of mental disorders* (4th ed., Text Rev.). Washington, DC: Author.

American Psychological Association. (2006). *APA presidential task force on evidence based practice.* Washington, DC: Author.

Apple, A. L., Billingsley, F., & Schwartz, I. S. (2005). Effects of video modeling alone and with self-management on compliment giving behaviors of children with high-functioning ASD. *Journal of Positive Behavior Interventions, 7*(1), 33–46.

Aspen, A., & Austin, M. (2003). How to visualize success in the treatment of autism. *CSHA Magazine, 33*(2), 10–12.

Autism-Help.org. (1996). *Interview with Dr. Temple Grandin.* Retrieved from http://www.autism-help.org/story-temple-grandin-autism.htm.

Autism Society of America. (n.d.). *About autism.* Retrieved from http://www.autism-society.org/about-autism.

Bainbridge, N., & Myles, B. S. (1999). The use of priming to introduce toilet training to a child with autism. *Focus on Autism and Other Developmental Disabilities, 14*(2), 106–109.

Baranek, G. T. (2002). Efficacy of sensory and motor interventions for children with autism. *Journal of Autism and Developmental Disorders, 32,* 397–422.

Bledsoe, R., Myles, B. S., & Simpson, R. L. (2003). Use of a social story intervention to improve mealtime skills of an adolescent with Asperger syndrome. *Autism: The International Journal of Research and Practice, 7*(3), 289–295.

Blew, P. A., Schwartz, I. S., & Luce, S. C. (1985). Teaching functional community skills to autistic children using nonhandicapped peer tutors. *Journal of Applied Behavior Analysis, 18*(4), 337–342.

Bock, M. A. (2007). The impact of social-behavioral learning strategy training on the social interaction skills of four students with Asperger syndrome. *Focus on Autism and Other Developmental Disabilities, 22*(2), 88–95.

Bryan, L., & Gast, D. (2000). Teaching on-task and on-schedule behaviors to high-functioning children with autism via picture-activity schedules. *Journal of Autism and Developmental Disorders, 30*(6), 553–567.

Buggey, T. (2005). Video self-modeling applications with students with autism spectrum disorders in a small private school. *Focus on Autism and Other Developmental Disabilities, 20,* 52–63.

Buggey, T., Toombs, K., Gardener, P., & Cervetti, M. (1999). Training responding behaviors in students in autism: Using video-taped self-modeling. *Journal of Positive Behavior Interventions, 1*(4), 205–214.

Bundy, A. C., Shia, S., Qi, L., & Miller, L. J. (2007). How does sensory processing dysfunction affect play? *American Journal of Occupational Therapy, 61,* 201–208.

Carr, E. G., & Kemp, D. C. (1989). Functional equivalence of autistic leading and communicative pointing: Analysis and treatment. *Journal of Autism and Developmental Disorders, 19*(4), 561–578.

Case-Smith, J., & Bryan, T. (1999). The effects of occupational therapy with sensory integration emphasis on preschool-age children with autism. *The American Journal of Occupational Therapy, 53*(5), 489–497.

Centers for Disease Control and Prevention. (2011). *Autism spectrum disorders.* Retrieved from http://www.cdc.gov/ncbddd/autism/facts.html.

Charlop, M. H., Kurtz, P. F., & Casey, F. G. (1990). Using aberrant behaviors as reinforcers for autistic children. *Journal of Applied Behavior Analysis, 23*(2), 163–181.

Charlop, M. H., Schreibman, L., & Tryon, A. S. (1983). Learning through observation: The effects of peer modeling on acquisition and generalization in autistic children. *Journal of Abnormal Child Psychology, 11*(3), 355–366.

Dalrymple, N. J. (1989). *Functional programming for people with autism: Learning to be independent and responsible.* Bloomington The Institute for the Study of Developmental Disabilities, Indiana Resource Center for Autism.

Dalrymple, N. J. (1995). Environmental supports to develop flexibility and independence. In K. A. Quill (Ed.), *Teaching children with autism: Strategies to enhance communication and socialization* (pp. 243–264). New York, NY: Delmar Publishers.

Dawson, G., & Osterling, J. (1997). Early intervention in autism: Effectiveness and common elements of current approaches. In M. J. Guralnick (Ed.), *The effectiveness of early intervention* (pp. 307–326). Baltimore, MD: Paul H. Brookes.

Dawson, W., & Watling, R. (2000). Interventions to facilitate auditory, visual, and motor integration in autism: A review of the evidence. *Journal of Autism and Developmental Disorders, 30,* 415–421.

Dettmer, S., Simpson, R., Myles, B. S., & Ganz, J. B. (2000). The use of visual supports to facilitate transitions of students with autism. *Focus on Autism and Other Developmental Disabilities, 15*(3), 163–169.

Devlin, S., Leader, G., & Healy, O. (2009). Comparison of behavioral intervention and sensory-integration therapy in the treatment of self-injurious behaviour. *Research in Autism Spectrum Disorders,* 223–231.

Dewey, J. (1944). *Democracy and education.* New York, NY: The Free Press.

Dunlap, G., & Koegel, R. L. (1980). Motivating autistic children through stimulus variation. *Journal of Applied Behavior Analysis, 13*(4), 619–627.

Ferrante, L., Panerai, A., & Zingale, M. (2002). Benefits of the Treatment and Education of Autistic and Communication Handicapped Children (TEACCH) programme as compared with a non-specific approach. *Journal of Intellectual Disability Research, 46*(4), 318–327.

Fisher, J., McLeod, J., & Hoover, G. (2003). *The key elements of classroom management: Managing time and space, student behavior, and instructional strategies.* Alexandria, VA: ASCD.

Fullan, M. (March, 1993). Why teachers must become change agents. *Educational Leadership, 50*(6).

Grandin, T. (2002). *Teaching tips for children and adults with autism.* Retrieved from http://www.iidc.indiana.edu/index.php?pageId=601.

Grandin, T. (2006). *Thinking in pictures: Chapter 1. Autism and visual thought.* Retrieved from http://www.grandin.com/inc/visual.thinking.html.

Gray, C., & Garand, J. (1993). Social stories: Improving responses of students with autism with inaccurate social information. *Focus on Autism and Other Developmental Disabilities, 8*(1), 1–10.

Hagiwara, T., & Myles, B. S. (1999). A multimedia social story intervention: Teaching skills to children with autism. *Focus on Autism and Other Developmental Disabilities, 14*(2), 82–95.

Hall, L. J., McClannahan, L. E., & Krantz, P. J. (1995). Promoting independence in integrated classrooms by teaching aides to use activity schedules and decreased prompts. *Education and Training in Mental Retardation and Developmental Disabilities, 30,* 208–217.

Heflin, J., & Simpson, R. (1998). Interventions for children and youth with autism: Prudent choices in a world of exaggerated claims and empty promises: Part 11: Legal policy analysis and recommendations for selecting interventions and treatments. *Focus on Autism and Other Developmental Disabilities, 13*(4), 212–220.

Hume, K., & Odom, S. (2007). Effects of an individual work system on the independent functioning of subjects with autism. *Journal of Autism and Developmental Disorders, 37,* 1166–1180.

Johnson, C. P., & Myers, S. M. (2007). Identification and evaluation of children with autism spectrum disorders. *Pediatrics*, 120(5), 1183–1215.

Jones, E. A., Carr, E. G., & Feeley, K. M. (2006). Multiple effects of joint attention intervention for children with autism. *Behavioral Modification*, 30(6), 782–834.

Jung, K., Lee, H., Lee, Y., Cheong, S., Choi, M., Suh, D., . . . Lee, J.-H. (2006). The application of a sensory integration treatment based on virtual reality-tangible interaction for children with autistic spectrum disorder. *Psychology Journal*, 4(2), 149–159.

Kennedy, C. H. (1994). Manipulating antecedents conditions to alter the stimulus control of problem behavior. *Journal of Applied Behavior Analysis*, 27(1), 161–170.

Koegel, L. K. (2000). Interventions to facilitate communication in autism. *Journal of Autism and Developmental Disorders*, 30(5), 383–391.

Koegel, L., Carter, C., & Koegel, R. (2003). Teaching children with autism self-initiations as a pivotal response. *Topics in Language Disorders*, 23, 134–145.

Koegel, L. K., Koegel, R. L., Hurley, C., & Frea, W. D. (1992). Improving social skills and disruptive behavior in children with autism through self-management. *Journal of Applied Behavior Analysis*, 25(2), 341–353.

Koegel, R. L., Schreibman, L., Britten, K., & Laitinin, R. (1979). The effects of schedule of reinforcement on stimulus overselectivity in autistic children. *Journal of Autism and Developmental Disorders*, 9(4), 383–396.

Krantz, P. J., MacDuff, M. T., & McClannahan, L. E. (1993). Programming participation in family activities for children with autism: Parents' use of photographic activity schedules. *Journal of Applied Behavior Analysis*, 26(1), 137–138.

Krantz, P. J., & McClannahan, L. E. (1998). Social interaction skills for children with autism: A script-fading procedure for beginning readers. *Journal of Applied Behavior Analysis*, 31(2), 191–202.

Lee, S., Odom, S. L., & Loftin, R. (2007). Social engagement with peers and stereotypic behavior of children with autism. *Journal of Positive Behavior Interventions*, 9(2), 67–79.

Leong, H. M., & Carter, M. (2008). Research on the efficacy of sensory integration therapy: Past, present and future. *Australasian Journal of Special Education*, 32, 83–99.

Lifter, K., Ellis, J., Cannon, B., & Anderson, S. R. (2005). Developmental specificity in targeting and teaching play activities to children with pervasive developmental disorders. *Journal of Early Intervention*, 27(4), 247–267.

Linderman, T. M., & Stewart, K. B. (1999). Sensory integrative-based occupational therapy and functional outcomes in young children with pervasive developmental disorders: A single-subject study. *The American Journal of Occupational Therapy*, 53(2), 207–213.

Lovaas, O. (1987). Behavioral treatment and normal educational and intellectual functioning in young autistic children. *Journal of Consulting and Clinical Psychology*, 55(1), 3–9.

Maione, L., & Mirenda, P. (2006). Effects of video modeling and video feedback on peer-directed social language skills of a child with autism. *Journal of Positive Behavior Interventions*, 8(2), 106–118.

Marckel, J., Neef, N., & Ferreri, S. (2006). A preliminary analysis of teaching improvisation with the Picture Exchange Communication System to children with autism. *Journal of Applied Behavioral Analysis*, 39, 109–115.

Marcus, L. M., Flagler, S., & Robinson, S. (2001). Assessment of children with autism. In R. J. Simeonsson & S. L. Rosenthal (Eds.), *Psychological and developmental assessment: Children with disabilities and chronic conditions* (pp. 267–291). New York, NY: Guilford Press.

Martins, M. P., & Harris, S. L. (2006). Teaching children with autism to respond to joint attention initiations. *Child & Family Behavior Therapy*, 28(1), 51–68.

McGee, G. G., & Daly, T. (2007). Incidental teaching of age-appropriate social phrases to children with autism. *Research and Practice for Persons With Severe Disabilities*, 32, 112–123.

Mesibov, G. B., Shea, V., & Schopler, E. (2005). *"The Culture of Autism" from the TEACCH approach to autism spectrum disorders* (pp. 19–32). New York, NY: Kluwer Academic/Plenum Publishers.

Murzynski, N. T., & Bourret, J. C. (2007). Combining video modeling and least-to-most prompting for establishing a response chain. *Behavioral Interventions, 22*, 147–152.

National Autism Center. (2009). *National Standards Report.* Retrieved from http://www.nationalautismcenter.org.

National Research Council. (2001). *Educating children with autism.* Washington, DC: National Academies Press.

Newman, B., & Ten Eyck, P. (2005). Self-management of initiations by students diagnosed with autism. *Analysis of Verbal Behavior, 21,* 117–122.

Nikopoulou, C. K., & Keenan, M. (2007). Using video modeling to teach complex social sequences to children with autism. *Journal of Autism and Developmental Disorders, 37*(4), 678–693.

No Child Left Behind (NCLB) Act of 2001, Pub. L. No. 107-110, § 115, Stat. 1425 (2002).

Odom, S. L., & Watt, E. (1991). Reducing teachers prompts in peer-mediated interventions for young children with autism. *Journal of Special Education, 25*(10), 26–43.

Ogletree, B. T., Oren, T., & Fischer, M. A. (2007). Examining effective intervention practices for communication impairment in autism spectrum disorder. *Exceptionality, 15*(4), 233–247.

O'Reilly, M., Sigafoos, J., Lancioni, G., Edrisinha, C., & Andrews, A. (2005). The examination of the effects of a classroom activity schedule on levels of self-injury and engagement for a child with severe autism. *Journal of Autism and Developmental Disorders, 35*(3), 305–311.

Pierce, K., & Schreibman, L. (1995). Increasing complex social behaviors in children with autism: Effects of peer-implemented pivotal response training. *Journal of Applied Behavior Analysis, 28*(3), 285–295.

Pries, J. (2006). The effect of picture communication symbols on the verbal comprehension of commands by young children with autism. *Focus on Autism and Other Developmental Disabilities, 21*(4), 194–210.

Quill, K. A. (1997). Instructional considerations for young children with autism: The rationale for visually cued instruction. *Journal of Autism and Developmental Disorders, 27,* 697–714.

Reed, P., Osbourne, L. A., & Corness, M. (2007). The real-world effectiveness of early teaching interventions for children with autism spectrum disorder. *Exceptional Children, 73*(4), 417–433.

Reinecke, D. R., Newman, B., & Meinberg, D. L. (1999). Self-management of sharing in three pre-schoolers with autism. *Education and Training in Mental Retardation and Developmental Disabilities, 34*(3), 312–317.

Sallows, G. O., & Gaupner, T. D. (2005). Intensive behavioral treatment for children with autism: Four year outcome and predictors. *American Journal of Mental Retardation: AJMR, 110*(6), 417–438.

Scattone, D., Wilczynski, S. M., Edwards, R. P., & Rabian, B. (2002). Decreasing disruptive behaviors of children with autism using social stories. *Journal of Autism and Developmental Disorders, 32*(6), 535–543.

Schilling D. L., & Schwartz, I. S. (2004). Alternative seating for young children with autism spectrum disorder: Effects on classroom behavior. *Journal of Autism and Developmental Disorders 34,* 423–432.

Schopler, E., & Mesibov, G. (Eds.). (1994). *Behavioral issues in autism.* New York, NY: Plenum Press.

Schopler, E., Mesibov, G., & Hearsey, K. (1995). Structured teaching in the TEACCH system. In E. Schopler & G. Mesibov (Eds.), Learning and cognition in autism (pp. 243–268). New York, NY: Plenum Press.

Sigafoos, J., O'Reilly, M., Ma, C., Edrisinha, C., Cannella, H., & Lancioni, G. E. (2006). Effects of embedded instruction versus discrete-trial training on self-injury, correct responding, and mood in a child with autism. *Journal of Intellectual and Developmental Disabilities, 31*(4), 196–203.

Smith-Myles, B., & Schapman, A. (2004). Making sense of the hidden curriculum. *Autism News, 1*(3), 16–18.

Stephenson, J., & Carter, M. (2009). The use of weighted vests with children with autism spectrum disorders and other disabilities. *Journal of Autism and Developmental Disorders, 39*, 105–114.

Thiemann, K. S., & Goldstein, H. (2001). Social stories, written text cues and video feedback: Effects of social communication of children with autism. *Journal of Applied Behavior Analysis, 34*(4), 425–446.

Tsao, L., & Odom, S. L. (2006). Sibling-mediated social interaction intervention for young children with autism. *Topics in Early Children Special Education, 26*(2), 106–123.

Vismara, L. A., & Lyons, G. L. (2007). Using perseverative interests to elicit joint attention behaviors in young children with autism: Theoretical and clinical implications for understanding motivation. *Journal of Positive Behavior Interventions, 9*(4), 214–228.

Watling, R. L., Deitz, J., & White, O. (2003). Comparison of sensory profile scores of young children with and without autism spectrum disorders. In C. B. Royee (Ed.), *Pediatric issues in occupational therapy* (pp. 130–139). Bethesda, MD: AOTA Press.

Whalen, C., & Schreibman, L. (2003). Joint attention training for children with autism using behavior modification procedures. *Journal of Child Psychology and Psychiatry and Allied Disciplines, 44*(3), 456–468.

Yoder, P., & Stone, W. (2006). Randomized comparison of two communication interventions for preschoolers with autism spectrum disorders. *Journal of Counseling and Clinical Psychology, 74*(3), 426–435.

CHAPTER 9

THE DEVELOPMENT OF COMMUNICATION SKILLS

> **In this chapter, you will learn about:**
>
> - Social communication as a core deficit.
> - Language and communication developmental milestones.
> - Atypical language development in children with Autism Spectrum Disorder (ASD).
> - Assessing communication skills.
> - Choosing evidence-based interventions for building communication skills.
> - Strategies that promote language skills based on Applied Behavior Analysis (ABA).
> - Social Communication Emotional Regulation Transactional Supports (SCERTS).
> - Augmentative and alternative communication systems.

THE IMPORTANCE OF SOCIAL COMMUNICATION

Defining Social Communication as a Core Deficit in ASD

Both communication and socialization are core deficits of autism (American Psychiatric Association [APA], 2000; National Research Council, 2001). In fact, the proposed revisions to the *Diagnostic and Statistical Manual of Mental Disorders* (*DSM,* 5th edition) combine social and communication deficits to include a core deficit in social communication (APA, 2010) as a diagnostic feature of autism spectrum disorder. Currently, the APA (2010) describes these as *significant deficits* in:

- both verbal (language) and nonverbal communication (body language, gestures, facial expressions) used for social interaction
- social reciprocity (such as the give-and-take of turn taking in conversation)
- establishing and maintaining peer relationships

However, the severity and types of deficits vary greatly across the autism spectrum. Furthermore, severity of deficits is considered in light of skills typically demonstrated by children of the same chronological age.

Social Communication and Language

Social communication promotes interactions that allow for the development of relationships. In addition, social communication promotes learning, independence, and quality of life. In fact, many effective educational strategies and interventions are based on theories of learning that describe how learning occurs through interactions with others (i.e., Bandura, 1977; Skinner, 1954; Vygotsky, 1978). Increasing social communication skills is a priority when planning interventions for individuals with ASD.

There are many forms of communication. Language is a type of communication that involves the use of symbols to represent objects, concepts, and ideas. The use of language also involves structure and rules. Mastering language promotes social communication because it provides more complex and precise tools for individuals to express themselves and relate to others.

The ability to communicate with language allows for independence and a higher quality of life. Scheuermann and Webber (2002) describe the relationship between language and independence.

- Language allows individuals to convey their preferences. Being able to communicate your desires and needs is critical to living independently.
- Without the means to express oneself, individuals without language often demonstrate a low motivation to respond to their environment. They may not recognize a link between how their own actions can influence their environment.
- Without language, individuals may resort to inappropriate behaviors to have their needs met such as screaming, aggressive behaviors, and self-injurious behaviors. Engaging in such behaviors may result in even greater limitations and less opportunities to interact with others.

DEVELOPMENTAL MILESTONES IN TYPICALLY DEVELOPING CHILDREN

Understanding the trajectory of development in typically developing children can help set goals and understand current functioning of children with atypical development. ASD is a pervasive developmental disorder in which the development of social skills, communication skills, and behaviors/interests are atypical. For some children, *atypical development* means functioning significantly below their same-age peers across skill domains. For other children with ASD, *atypical* development may reflect skill development out of sequence (i.e., a child may be writing words but not speaking). Another type of atypical development in children with ASD is regression or loss of skills. Between 15% to 40% of children with ASD experience language loss at about 15 to 30 months of age (Lord, Shulman, & DilVore, 2004; Simkin, Charman, Chandler, Loucas, & Baird, 2009; Tuchman & Rapin, 1997). Deficits in other cognitive skills, such as the inability to use symbols and difficulty understanding the relationship between cause and effect, are often associated with language deficits (Scheuermann & Webber, 2002).

In addition, many children with ASD demonstrate low motivation to communicate beyond meeting their needs. Issues related to social communication, such as the desire to communicate with others, must be considered when planning language interventions.

Development of Receptive Language

Receptive language, understanding language, tends to develop at a faster pace than expressive language, the ability to express one's thoughts with language (Bruce & Hansson, 2008). For instance, infants just a few days old can discriminate between phonemes present in the language spoken by their mother and another language (Mehler et al., 1988). At 1 month, infants can distinguish between phonemes (the simplest unit of sound) such as /p/ and /b/ (Hoff, 2005). In fact, babies appear to be neurologically primed to attend to and learn to comprehend spoken language. Infants begin to demonstrate an understanding of words at about 6 months of age (Trawick-Smith, 2010). Although infants tend to learn nouns first, what they learn is dependent upon their culture. Babies not only learn to understand the language in which they are raised, but the objects that are valued and are available, parenting style, and customs for using language influence the types of words babies learn (Trawick-Smith).

Receptive Language in Children With ASD

Retrospective studies (generally based on home videos or parent interviews) indicate that receptive language is often impaired in very young children with ASD. For instance, eye gaze of infants later diagnosed with ASD is often different from typically developing infants. Infants with ASD are more likely to stare at specific objects and appear more focused on parts of objects rather than an integrated whole (Boucher & Lewis, 1972). In addition, typically developing infants tend to spend a lot of time looking at faces, particularly eye-to-eye gaze (Morton & Johnson, 1991; Symons, Hains, & Muir, 1998). However, infants later diagnosed with ASD demonstrate an atypical processing of faces (Sasson, 2006) and appear more interested in geometric patterns than faces (Pierce, Conant, Hazin, & Desmond, 2010).

Around 6 months of age, infants begin to engage in joint attention, in which they share in the attention of an object or event with someone. Frequent interactions involving joint attention and protodeclarative pointing (using index finger to identify something of interest) are typically achieved by 18 months of age (Liebal, Carpenter, & Tomasello, 2010). Failure to engage in these behaviors by 18 months is considered an early indication of ASD. Screening tools used in early childhood, such as the Checklist for Autism in Toddlers (CHAT; Baron-Cohen, Allen, & Gillberg, 1992; Baron-Cohen et al., 1996), specifically ask questions related to the development of these skills.

Development of Expressive Language

Babies produce sounds from birth. In fact, there are several different types of infant cries (i.e., pain, hunger, tired), and parents are generally able to differentiate between them. Other sounds include cooing (approximately 1 to 2 months, gurgling sounds indicating pleasure) and babbling (middle of first year, repetitive consonant-vowel combinations such as da-da-da). Toward the end of the first year (8–12 months), infants begin communicating both with preverbal gestures, such as intentional pointing, waving, and nodding "yes" or "no," and words (Berk, 2010). By 2 years of age, toddlers are putting two words together to create short sentences, sometimes described as "telegraphic" speech (i.e., "go outside").

Two types of errors are a normal part of language development for toddlers as they begin to develop words. One error is overextension, the tendency to overgeneralize and use a word to refer to many different things. For instance, a toddler may say "doggie" to describe a dog, cat, and horse. Underextension (or overrestriction) involves limiting a word to refer to only one particular person, place, or thing. For example "blanky" may only represent a particular baby blanket the child sleeps with; and no other blanket can be called "blanky."

The National Institute of Deafness and Other Communication Disorders (NIDCD) organized a working group of experts to create benchmarks for defining expressive language acquisition in young children with ASD. This working group described five key phases in expressive language acquisition (Tager-Flusberg et al., 2009) important for early screening, intervention, and assessing developmental progress summarized below.

Table 9.1 Five Key Phases of Expressive Language Acquisition

1. Preverbal communication, such as babbling and gestures (6–12 months)
2. First words—Spontaneous words to communicate. May include labeling objects, requesting something, or commenting (12–18 months)
3. Word combinations—Creatively combine words to communicate (18–30 months)
4. Communicates using sentences (30–48 months)
5. Use of complex language, including varied vocabulary grammar and range of topics (by end of preschool, 5 years)

Detailed objective benchmark criteria for evaluating expressive language acquisition in children with ASD can be found in Tager-Flusberg et al. (2009).

Expressive Language in Children With ASD

Overall, children with ASD exhibit a wide range of expressive language difficulties. Some parents of children with ASD report that their child did not demonstrate expressive language milestones. Concerned about delays in babbling and speaking first words, parents may ask their pediatrician to evaluate their child's hearing. In addition, some parents of children with ASD report expected development of language skills followed by a significant loss of skills around 18 months to 2 years of age. Research indicates that 15% to 40% of children with autism experienced autistic regression, in which language and social skills are lost around age 2 (Lord, Shulman, & Dilavore, 2004; Luyster et al., 2005).

Conversely, some children with ASD do not have early delays or regression of language skills, and vocabulary development may actually be an area of relative strength. Expressive language skills at age 5 are a predictor of later functioning

(Gillberg & Steffenburg, 1987) and play a significant role in determining school placement and educational planning (Venter, Lord, & Schopler, 1992).

Thrum and colleagues (2007) conducted a study investigating predictors of language acquisition in preschoolers with ASD. Overall, emerging receptive and expressive language skills at ages 2 and 3 were predictive of expressive and receptive language skills at age 5. More specifically, responding to joint attention (such as perceiving communicative intent of others and orienting to social stimuli) and verbal imitation skills at ages 2 and 3 were predictive of expressive language skills at age 5. Impaired skills in joint attention, the use of gesture or gaze to share attention of an object or event with someone, is one of the earliest observable characteristics of ASD (Charman, 1998).

Echolalia

Many children with ASD demonstrate echolalia, or the repetition of words, phrases, or segments of speech (Bryson,1996; Lord & Paul, 1997). In fact, the majority of children with ASD who learn to speak go through a phase of echolalic speech (National Research Council, 2001; Wetherby, Yonclas, & Bryan, 1989).

Although echolalia is often present in typically developing young children, it decreases with age. In fact, echolalia may represent a stage in language acquisition for both children with ASD and typically developing children. The occurrence of echolalia indicates that the child is trying to process language and may even serve a communicative function. However, many children with ASD continue to exhibit echolalia into their school-age years and beyond. The prolonged use of echolalia highlights an important characteristic about children with ASD. Children with ASD not only demonstrate deficits in communication skills, but they also appear to *learn* language in a different manner than their peers. For instance, children with ASD appear to utilize a "gestalt" (or big picture) approach to learning language. A gestalt approach involves memorizing large chunks of language without fully understanding underlying rules of how language breaks down into its components.

Immediate echolalia is the repetition of all or part of an utterance that has just been spoken. Generally, immediate echolalia matches the speaker in tone, pitch, and intonation. Delayed echolalia is the repetition of all or part of an utterance after a delay. This delay may be an hour or even several days. Sometimes the echolalia is mitigated, or changed in some way. For instance, the child may be told to wash her hands before dinner. She may use the phrase "wash hands" to indicate that she is hungry or ready for a meal. When used functionally (to communicate), echolalia may be a type of overextension error (Siegel, 1996) in which a word or phrase is used to represent words, thoughts, or concepts other than the original meaning of the word.

Today it is recognized that certain phrases or memorized segments of speech repeated by individuals with ASD represent requests, concerns, or things different from the word's actual meaning. Understanding how a child uses echolalia can provide valuable information for planning appropriate educational interventions that support the development of language skills.

Table 9.2 provides examples of how immediate echolalia may serve communicative or "interactive" functions. The term "interactive" is used to describe communication directed toward another person.

Table 9.2 Examples of Communicative or "Interactive" Functions of Immediate Echolalia

- *Turn-taking function,* allowing for the participation in a conversation. For instance, in response to "Johnny, tell us about your day," an individual with autism might respond, "Tell us about your day," allowing for participation in the conversation.
- *Declarative function,* allows for naming/labeling objects, people, and events. For instance, the teacher says, "This is our daily calendar." The child with autism touches the calendar and repeats, "This is our daily calendar."
- *Affirmation,* used to answer questions or make requests. For instance, when asked, "Would you like a cookie?", the child with autism responds, "Would you like a cookie?", and reaches for a cookie.

Source: Prizant and Duchan (1981); Vicker (2009).

Immediate echolalia does not always appear to have an interactive function. For instance, some children with autism exhibit echolalia when afraid, upset, or experiencing a high arousal state; others appear to use echolalia to help process new spoken information or as a means of self-regulation (Prizant & Duchan, 1981).

Using an analysis of videotaped language segments conducted in a natural setting with familiar people, Prizant and Rydell (1984) found that delayed echolalia also has different functions, many of them communicative. Although individuals with autism may repeat a word, phrase, or segment of speech that does not appear contextually relevant, the delayed echolalia may allow them to participate in a turn-taking scenario (such as conversation), request something, protest something they do not want or like, provide labels, or even provide direction for certain actions to take place (such as going to lunch or turning off the light). Delayed echolalia may also help an individual with autism follow through on a task, label items without the intent to communicate, rehearse, or may be a type of repetitive stereotypic behavior. The Chapter Reflection box presents a case of a child communicating using delayed echolalia.

CHAPTER REFLECTION: Delayed Echolalia: Thomas the Train Video Script

During a meeting about 6-year-old Marcus, a boy with autism, his mother relayed this story. Marcus loved to watch his Thomas the Train DVDs. His mother often put on Marcus' favorite Thomas the Train DVD while preparing meals at home. One day at a school meeting, his teacher noted that Marcus sometimes recited the same dialogue about Thomas the Train right before lunch, especially if lunch is a little later than usual. She remarked, "It sounds like he is acting out something from a Thomas the Train video, but it has nothing to do with lunch time. It is the same script every time." Marcus' mother suspected that Marcus was using the Thomas the Train script to communicate that he was ready for lunch because he had associated the DVD with waiting for mealtime. In fact, the video script that Marcus recited before lunch was from the DVD he often chose to view while his mother prepared dinner.

From the personal files of Michelle Haney, Ph.D. (2010).

COMPONENTS OF LANGUAGE AND ASD

There are many ways to communicate. Individuals may use gestures, facial expressions, and sounds. The way in which individuals communicate is called form. Language is a type of communication that is based on a system of symbols with rules, including phonology, morphology, syntax, semantics, and pragmatics (Santrock, 2008). Table 9.3 displays the components of a language system.

Table 9.3 Components of a Language System

- **Phonology**—Pronunciation and articulation of the sounds in words. Phonemes are the individual sounds in language. For instance, the word "cat" has three phonemes: c/a/t. Verbal children with ASD often have good articulation. However, an aspect of phonology, *prosody,* is often impaired in individuals with ASD. Prosody includes the rhythm, stress, and intonation of speech (Wilkinson, 1998).
- **Morphology**—A morpheme is the smallest unit of meaning. Children with autism and high-functioning cognitive skills often have good vocabularies because they can memorize the word meaning. However, they demonstrate more difficulty with organizing their speech and using the appropriate vocabulary word given a particular social context (pragmatics, discussed below).
- **Syntax**—The rules of how language is put together. Children with autism often display unusual syntax. For instance, many children with autism have difficulty with the personal pronoun such as "I," "me," "you," tenses, and plurals. Often children with autism reverse pronouns (i.e., request a cookie by saying, "You want a cookie"). Pronoun reversal may be associated with core deficits in *theory of mind,* understanding that others have different perspectives and can develop different theories about the world.
- **Semantics**—The content of language, including the use of vocabulary to express meaning. Children with autism often use *idiosyncratic,* or unusual words or word patterns.
- **Pragmatics**—The social convention of language. Using verbal and nonverbal (i.e., eye gaze, body posture, gestures) language appropriately given a particular social situation. For instance, the degree of formality (such as greeting someone with a title or their first name or the use of slang) reflects an understanding of what is socially appropriate given the circumstance. Even children with autism who have strong cognitive skills demonstrate difficulties with pragmatics. The social implications for these difficulties can be considerable.

Vocabulary

Most babies speak their first word by 13 months. By 18 months, babies can speak about 50 words. Around 18 months, babies demonstrate a burst of vocabulary growth resulting in approximately 200 words by age 2 (Santrock, 2008).

Some children with ASD, especially those with strong cognitive skills, demonstrate vocabulary development appropriate or even advanced for their age. However, many children with ASD demonstrate atypical vocabulary development (Landa & Garrett-Mayer, 2006). Vocabulary development is enhanced by exposure to stimulating language experiences the child's environment (Hart & Risely, 1995). However, children with ASD are less likely to engage in communication interchanges and may actively avoid such interactions, leading to reduced opportunities to build and refine vocabulary (Koegel, 2000).

Pragmatic Language Skills

Children with ASD often have difficulty understanding the social rules of language.

Individuals with ASD may have strong vocabulary, expressive language, and receptive language skills, yet still experience significant deficits with social communication. Weaknesses in pragmatic language frequently underlie such difficulties (Koegel, 2003). Pragmatic language involves the use of context and connecting relevant information to interpret one's social world (Loukusa et al., 2006).

Examples of pragmatic language include understanding complexities of social communication, such as understanding why a joke is funny (play on words); irony; why certain phrases or gestures are appropriate in some settings, but not others; how to determine whether an individual really means what they are saying based on body language, tone, volume, and choice of words; which topics are appropriate in which settings. Thus, individuals with ASD tend to interpret language literally and fail to understand the intended meaning behind many nonverbal behaviors such as gestures and facial expressions (Adams, 2002; Philofsky, Fidler, & Hepburn, 2007; Tager-Flusberg, Paul, & Lord, 2005). Furthermore, individuals with ASD often demonstrate difficulties with expressive pragmatics, including failing to use appropriate facial expressions, body language, intonation or prosody, using made-up words (neologisms) or idiosyncratic language (odd choice of words) as well as difficulty using repair strategies during conversational breakdowns (Philofsky, Fidler, & Hepburn, 2007). Koegel (2003) describes four general areas of pragmatic skills described in Table 9.4.

Table 9.4 Four Areas of Pragmatic Skills

- **Paralinguistic features**—Use of intonation and prosody. For instance, speaking with a rising intonation at the end of a sentence or phrase indicates a question. Individuals with ASD who speak in monotone with no inflection or change in intonation may fail to communicate intent (such as interest) and fail to sustain interest of the communication partner.
- **Nonverbal features (Extralinguistic)**—Posture, hand movements gestures, and facial expressions provide linguistic support for verbal communication. Failure to use appropriate nonverbal features or to interpret nonverbal features correctly can impair social communication.

- **Linguistic intent**—Linguistic intent involves using language (or utterances) to request, state, or comment, and regulate behavior. In addition, linguistic intent taps into "theory of mind" in which an individual infers the knowledge available to their social communication partner. However, individuals with ASD demonstrate deficits on theory of mind tasks (Baron-Cohen, 1995; Baron-Cohen, Leslie, & Frith, 1985). In addition, individuals with ASD often do not pay sufficient attention to their communicative partner during the communication interchange, and/or may not have adequate language skills to fully express their linguistic intent.
- **Social competence**—Social competence is demonstrated when the speaker uses appropriate skills during communication interactions. These include both nonverbal (i.e., appropriate distance between speaker and communication partner, eye contact when speaking) and verbal (i.e., topic selection, maintaining conversation, turn taking, initiating discourse, providing feedback to speaker, use of social conventions such as saying "please," using appropriate vocabulary for the social context, etc.).

Source: Koegel, L.K., (2003). Communication and Language Intervention. In R.L. Koegel & L.K. Koegel. (Eds.), *Teaching Children with Autism.* *Strategies for Initiating Positive Interactions and Improving Learning* (pp. 17-32). Baltimore, MD: Paul H. Brookes Publishing Co., Inc. Adapted by permission.

The following case example illustrates some of the pragmatic skill difficulties frequently demonstrated by individuals with high-functioning ASD.

Kelly is a fourth-grade girl with autism. She scores on tests of expressive vocabulary at the fifth-grade level and has good articulation skills. Kelly wants to be included with her peers and attempts to interact with them. However, she is virtually ignored during social opportunities during the school day. In structured group activities at school, she monopolizes the conversation and fails to interpret the facial expressions, tone of voice, or body language of her group members who become frustrated when trying to work as a group with her. Kelly becomes confused when group members use figurative language such as the idiom "that's the way we roll" to describe why a decision was made. If the group changes direction and decides to try a new approach, she becomes upset and sits alone at her desk. She does not know how to rejoin a conversation once the conversation has been interrupted.

Although Kelly's social communication strategies are generally effective when she works one-on-one with her teacher or at home with her parents, she has difficulty working in a group setting or making friends. She does not understand the social rules of language.

- Kelly has impaired reciprocal language. She does not follow conversational rules, such as giving others a chance to respond to her ideas, staying on topic, and directing the conversation in a natural way (Scheuermann & Webber, 2002).
- Kelly does not *accurately interpret the social messages embedded in language* that are not necessarily part of the vocabulary. For instance, she fails to interpret the tone, facial expressions, or body language of her peers indicating frustration and displeasure.
- Kelly does not understand *figurative language*, using language to create ideas beyond the actual meaning of the words. For instance, she would interpret "It's raining cats and dogs" literally as cats and dogs are pouring down from the sky.
- Kelly is not skilled at *conversational repairs* once there has been an interruption or the communication partner clearly loses interest. For instance, Kelly is likely to continue with her topic even if there is an interruption in the conversation or the conversation partner starts to walk away.

Because Kelly interprets her attempts to socially communicate with others as failure, she often gives up and misses out on social learning opportunities. Over time, many children like Kelly acquire *learned helplessness,* where they learn that their actions fail to procure changes in their environment (such as making friends). Thus, they stop trying and often experience depression.

Although Kelly has some cognitive and language strengths, her difficulties with pragmatic language interfere with opportunities to learn from her peers, strengthen social communication skills, and develop relationships with her classmates. Children with ASD not only have difficulty with the social nature of language, but also with many other skills related to social development including play, perspective taking, self-regulation, and peer relations.

Individuals like Kelly may also need help understanding the *hidden curriculum* necessary for social success. Most children learn the rules and protocol for social behavior within a context (such as school) through observation and inference. However, individuals with ASD often fail to pick up these implicit social rules. The penalty for failing to follow the hidden curriculum can be severe. Individuals with ASD may end up getting in trouble with teachers, offending their peers, being the target of bullying and exclusion, or hurting their peers when they fail to understand these rules (Myles & Smith, 2001). Teachers may need to elicit help of a socially competent and mature peer to develop an appropriate list of the hidden curriculum to explicitly teach to a student with ASD. Explicit (Direct) instruction in the hidden rules, the use of social stories, role-playing activities, and social autopsies (a process of identifying social mistake, determining the impact of that

Table 9.5   Examples of the Hidden Curriculum for an Adolescent

- Some words are OK to say to some people but not others. For example, you would not say, "Hey, girlfriend" to your teacher, but you might to a girl friend. You might be teased if you refer to your mother as "mommy" or use other pet names when talking about family members to peers.
- You should not share personal stories about your family with peers who are not close friends.
- You should not touch private body parts when in a public place where others can see you.
- If you have personal hygiene needs (such as having digestive problems, needing a feminine hygiene product), you should whisper this quietly to the teacher so others cannot hear you if possible.
- There are some clues you can look for to determine whether people are really your friend or just pretending to be your friend. For instance, if a peer is asking you to do something you are not sure is allowed or right, they might be trying to trick or tease you. Friends do not take your things, eat your lunch, or ask you to pay them to be their friend.

mistake, and developing a plan to avoid the mistake the future) are effective ways of teaching the hidden curriculum (Myles & Simpson, 2001).

The following chapter, Chapter 10, "Social Development in Children With ASD," discusses interventions that support the development of pragmatic skills such as social language stories, video modeling, peer-mediated interventions, and relationship-developmental-based interventions. The development of pragmatic skills is supported by teaching activities taking place within the individual's natural environment, social language opportunities involving areas of interest, explicit feedback about verbal and nonverbal communication that may involve modeling, and reinforcement (Atwood, 1998, 2008; Ingersoll et al., 2005). Atwood (1998) suggests the following strategies (Table 9.6) to support the development of social pragmatics for individuals with high-functioning ASD.

Table 9.6   Strategies to Support the Development of Social Pragmatics

- Teach appropriate comments for beginning conversations.
- Teach how to admit when one does not know the answer or does not understand.
- Teach cues for replying, interrupting, or changing the topic of conversation.
- Help individuals understand metaphors and figurative language to avoid incorrect literal interpretations.

From Atwood (1998).

Nonverbal Communication

In addition to difficulties with verbal language, many children with ASD have deficits in nonverbal communication. These difficulties impact both their expression of their desires and feelings as well as their ability to read nonverbal communication of others. Deficits in nonverbal communication skills impair social development and peer relationships. For instance, individuals with ASD may not realize they are grimacing or clenching their arms tightly to their chests. Thus, they may be unaware that their body language signifies to others feelings of anger or frustration. Other examples of difficulties with nonverbal communication include violations of body space, unusual appearance (such as dress, hairstyle), atypical eye contact, and unusual gestures.

ASSESSING COMMUNICATION SKILLS

A comprehensive assessment of communication is critical prior to determining communication goals and intervention strategies. Most students will have a formal assessment of communication skills during the psychoeducational evaluation required for eligibility for special education services under the Individuals with Disabilities Education Improvement Act (IDEA) of 2004. Teachers, parents, the school psychologist, and the speech-language pathologist (SLP) often collaborate in the assessment of communication skills. It is important that at least some of the evaluation take place within the child's natural setting, such as home, school, or within the community, in order to best understand skills needed to support the development of functional skills. A comprehensive assessment of communication will include both standardized and informal assessments, such as observations and interviews of teachers and caretakers (Wetherby, 2006). Although standardized assessments offer age and developmental norms that may aid in goal setting, they are likely to rely on elicited or prompted communication rather than spontaneous communication. Furthermore, standardized assessment tools are especially problematic in assessing nonverbal communication and communication of children with severe ASD (National Research Council, 2001).

Interactive Sampling

Interactive sampling is the most common method of assessing social communication skills (Wetherby, 2006), and is a useful method for collecting data about social communication of young children or those with low verbal skills (Buzolich, 2009). Interactive sampling involves collecting data about communication behavior within interactive settings (Buzolich). The Communication Sampling and Analysis (CSA; Buzolich, Russell, Lunger-Bergh, & McCloskey, 2011; http://csa.acts-at.com/csa-info.html) is an example of an objective clinical assessment tool designed to collect data (nonverbal and verbal behavior) about social communication occurring in natural settings (Buzolich).

In addition to evaluating the content of communication, an assessment of social communication skills for a child with ASD should include at least three key aspects of communication: frequency, form, and function (Drew, Baird, Taylor, Milne, & Charman, 2006).

- Frequency of communication—Involves an analysis of how often communication occurs. This is often accomplished using language sample across different settings with different communication partners.

- Form or communication style—Such as pointing, gestures, exchanging pictures, repeating phrases, speaking in sentences, use of technology, sign language, use of tone, and so on. Considers *how* the child attempts to communicate. Children with ASD may have fewer communication styles than their typically developing peers (Koegel, 2003).

- Function or use of language—One aspect of language function is the communicative intent, such as to request, refuse or protest, ask a question, provide information, self-regulation or social engagement (Landa, 2005). For very young children or individuals with low-functioning ASD, joint attention or eye gaze may be assessed to determine communicative intent (Landa). A second aspect of language function is presupposition, which is one's understanding of the information available to a communication partner (Landa). Thus, presupposition involves a degree of perspective taking (or theory of mind) in that it involves inferring what the communication partner knows (Paul, 2007). A third aspect of language function is discourse management, which involve skills such as staying on topic, conversational turn taking, and repairing conversational breakdowns (Landa). Understanding the function of communication is helpful in determining the communicative intent of challenging behaviors. In most cases, any behavior is an attempt to communicate. When the message is not understood by a communicative partner, the individual may engage in challenging behaviors such as temper tantrums, aggression, or self-injurious behaviors (Goldstein, 2002; Koegel, 2001). In fact, the majority of challenging behaviors function as communication (Iwata et al., 1994).

Assessment of the degree of spontaneity of communication is also important because isolated speech does not support the development of functional communication (Diehl, 2003). An assessment should consider whether the child initiates communication or if communication is primarily prompted by others. Other aspects of communication that should be assessed to develop functional and developmentally appropriate goals include the ability to use and understand symbols and play skills (National Research Council, 2001).

The Speech-Language Pathologist

While the teacher and school psychologist may provide information about aspects of communication skills, the SLP conducts a more formal and comprehensive evaluation. For instance, the SLP will often provide a detailed analysis of the individual's language (such as use of nouns, verbs, pragmatic language, mean length of utterance, echolalia, and proper use of pronouns).

The American Speech-Language Hearing Association's (ASHA) Ad Hoc Committee on Autism Spectrum Disorders created a position statement describing the roles and responsibilities of Speech-Language Pathologists in assessment and treatment of individuals with ASD (ASHA, 2006). The position statement asserts that the SLP plays a critical role as part of a multidisciplinary team in screening, diagnosis, identifying goals, selecting interventions, and ongoing assessment for individuals with ASD. Furthermore, the position statement states that assessments of children with ASD should address spontaneous communication in functional activities, reciprocal communication, and both verbal and nonverbal means of communication across social partners and settings.

Examples of Standardized Tests for Assessment of Communication Functioning for Individuals With ASD

- Autism Diagnostic Observation Schedule (ADOS; Lord et al., 2001). The ADOS measures social communication for ages 14 months to adult and is an interactive semistructured instrument for assessing social communication with strong psychometric properties. A unique feature involves the presentation of high-interest activities (such as play or having a snack) that provide a context for social communication.
- Communication and Symbolic Behavior Scales Developmental Profile (CSBS DP; Wetherby & Prizant, 2001). A norm-referenced tool to assess

communication in young children or individuals with low-functioning ASD. Assesses language predictors, including eye gaze, gestures, communication, sounds, words, understanding, and object use/play.

- Social Responsiveness Scale (SRS: Constantino & Gruber, 2005). Completed by teachers or caregivers for individuals ages 4 through 18. Addresses social awareness, social cognition, social communication, and social motivation.

- The Test of Pragmatic Language-Second Edition (TOPL-2): Phelps-Terasaki & Phelps-Gunn, 1992) is administered by an SLP and evaluates social communication in context for individuals ages 6 through 18. The TOPL-2 addresses six subcomponents of pragmatic language, including the physical setting, audience, topic, purpose of speech, visual-gestural cues, and use of abstract language.

- Social Language Development Test (Bowers, Huisingh, & LoGuidice, 2008) can be administered by an SLP or a psychologist with training in language disorders. The Social Language Development Test provides visual stimuli and prompts individuals to make inferences and answer questions about social interactions such as negotiation and what other people may be thinking. In addition, there is a subtest that asks individuals to generate multiple interpretations from a single picture. There is an elementary and an adolescent version.

A thorough discussion of assessment tools for evaluating communication skills in individuals with ASD is not possible within the scope of this chapter. Recommendations for more specific assessment tools and standardized tests include *Assessment of Social Communication Skills in Preschoolers* (Landa, 2005) and *Handbook of Autism and Pervasive Developmental Disorders: Volume 2: Assessment, Interventions, and Policy* (Volkmar, Rhea, Klin, & Cohen, 2007).

BUILDING SOCIAL COMMUNICATION SKILLS

Choosing Evidence-Based Interventions

As noted in earlier chapters (i.e., 6 and 8), public schools require the use of practices that are evidence-based. Evidence-based practices, as outlined by organizations such as the Council for Exceptional Children (CEC) Division for Research and the National Autism Center (2009, 2011), are believed to result in the best

Evidence-based interventions based on a thorough assessment of communication skills are most effective when implemented at school, in the community, and within the child's home environment.

outcomes for individuals with ASD. An established intervention using evidence-based practices has strong empirical support for treatment validity; emerging interventions use practices with some limited support; and unestablished practices have virtually no empirical support. Choice of intervention should also take into consideration other factors, particularly family preference and values and student input when possible (NAC, 2011). Furthermore, issues such as capacity of the school to provide services (i.e., do teachers need additional training, support staff?), sustainability (i.e., a consultant sets up an ABA program but is not available to continue implementation after the contract runs out), and school climate/organizational issues (i.e., is there administrational support for systemwide inclusion to generalize skills across naturalistic settings?) (NAC, 2011).

Likewise, Simpson's (2005) analysis of interventions and treatments for children and youth with ASD reviews the research literature, considering

- the appropriateness of the intervention in terms of the child's age, ability, and developmental level,
- reported benefits and outcomes associated with the intervention, specifically noting research in which the interventions were used with individuals with ASD,
- assessment of potential risks associated with implementing the intervention or treatment,
- the financial commitment associated with an intervention, and
- and the methods (if any) that have been used to evaluate the effectiveness of an intervention or treatment.

Based on these considerations, Simpson assigns a rating to each intervention: *scientifically based* ("those that have significant and convincing empirical efficacy and support" (p. 9), *a promising practice* (has limited supporting information), *a practice for which there is limited supporting information* (not necessarily without merit, but information lacking to make a decision about the intervention based on scientific methodology), and *not recommended* ("interventions and treatments that have been shown to lack efficacy and that may have the potential to do harm" (p. 9).

Readers are referred to the Council for Exceptional Children (CEC) Division for Research, the National Autism Center (2009, 2011), and Simpson (2005) for a more detailed analysis of the extent to which interventions addressing communication skills utilize evidence-based practices.

Speech-Language Therapy

Children and adolescents meeting eligibility criteria for ASD should be eligible for SLP services, given the core deficits in communication (ASHA, 2006). The SLP collaborates with families, support personnel (such as paraprofessionals, bus drivers, cafeteria workers), and other professionals supporting the individual with ASD. In addition, the SLP may also work with the child's peers to provide a supportive environment that maximizes communication opportunities and the development of functional skills.

SLPS utilize evidence-based practices that are individually designed to achieve communication goals that promote social communication. In addition to addressing social communication skills, speech-language therapy may also include interventions that address speech difficulties such as qualities of prosody, fluency, or voice that impair communication. Speech therapy should be generalized across settings and with multiple communication partners to promote flexibility and functional communication skills (Diehl, 2003).

The American Speech-Language-Hearing Association (ASHA; 2005) has created a set of clinical practice guidelines to support the selection of evidence-based practices in speech-language therapy. These practice guidelines can be found at http://www.asha.org/members/ebp/compendium. Furthermore, there is a specific map for considering practices for individuals with ASD, including speech, language, and hearing.

Strategies That Promote Communication Skills Based on Applied Behavior Analysis

Many evidence-based practices for teaching skills to individuals with ASD utilize Applied Behavioral Analysis (ABA), which is based on the principles of operant conditioning. ABA can be used to systematically modify and evaluate the development of language and other communication skills. There are a variety of strategies based on principles of ABA that have been proven effective for teaching language and other communication skills. These include the traditional discrete trial training, pivotal response training, which incorporates principles of ABA in a more naturalistic setting, and more contemporary approaches that integrate ABA with developmental oriented interventions. ABA interventions are described in more depth in Chapter 7.

Discrete trial training

Discrete trial training (DTT) is among the earliest interventions for teaching communication skills to children with autism (National Research Council, 2001). DTT involves breaking down a skill into smaller parts and teaching that component until mastered (Lovass, 1977, 2003). These trials can take place in any environment and are extremely versatile. In fact, because the teaching trials are scripted, it is easy for more than one teacher to implement the intervention and data collection. DTT can be used to teach a wide range of communication skills, from basic gestures to more complex verbal responses. Initially, discrete trials may involve very short teaching trials. As attention and motivation increase, the length of the teaching trials can increase.

During DTT, an adult initiates teaching by providing a prompt (the antecedent). If the child's behavior following the prompt is correct, she receives a reward (reinforcement). If the child provides an incorrect response, an error correction procedure is used. For instance, this may involve the teacher taking the child's hand and placing it on the correct object. Ultimately, the correct response is shaped through very structured teaching sessions. The use of tangible rewards that are reinforcing to the child serves to increase both motivation and attention in children. This is important because children with ASD, particularly those with more severe ASD, often have problems with motivation and attention that impeded learning. Benefits of DTT are the breakdown of more complex tasks into simpler steps, versatility for teaching many types of behaviors, and reducing challenging behaviors (Simpson, 2005). DTT is described by Simpson (2005) as a *scientifically based practice* and meets the criteria of the NAC as an *established treatment* based on empirically supported practices.

A criticism of DTT is that skills learned through the trials may not generalize well to more natural settings and the child may be overly reliant on adult prompts (Hall, 2009; Simpson, 2005). These concerns may be due the child's reliance on a specific teaching prompt to initiate the behavior. Overall, DTT provides an effective tool for teaching children with ASD discriminative skills.

Furthermore, DTT provided the framework for the development of intervention strategies that teach more sophisticated language skills generalizing across settings (Goldstein, 2002).

Pivotal response training

Previously called Natural Language Paradigm, Pivotal Response Training (PRT) is an intervention based on ABA created to address some of the criticisms of DTT. PRT promotes greater generalizing of skills to a natural setting and tends to require fewer teaching trials (Koegel & Koegel, 2006). This training approach also uses systematic teaching but focuses on the child's interests within the child's natural environment. In addition, natural reinforcers are used that are associated with what the child is trying to communicate (National Research Council, 2001).

The term *pivotal* refers to behaviors selected because a change alters and improves other behaviors. Because gains in the pivotal behaviors result in many important skill gains, these are sometimes called "collateral gains" (Simpson, 2005).

Similar to other applied behavioral analysis strategies, PRT uses a discrete trial format, with clear starts and stops (Koegel, Koegel, & Carter, 1999). Both motivation and learning to respond to multiple cues are considered pivotal to learning new skills.

In addition to low motivation to engage in learning tasks, children with ASD often demonstrate stimulus overselectivity. Stimulus overselectivity refers to difficulty using relevant cues available in their learning environment (Schreibman, 1988). PRT helps children identify and utilize multiple cues to support learning. For instance, a child with ASD may focus on the picture of a cup, but not associate it with the word "cup." PRT encompasses reinforcing attempts and using natural consequences, allowing the child to make choices and following the child's lead (Koegel et al., 1989). PRT was initially designed to increase language skills by incorporating choice making and turn taking into instruction. The NAC considers PRT an *established treatment*. Likewise, Simpson describes PRT as a *scientifically based practice*.

Social Communication Emotional Regulation Transactional Supports

Social Communication Emotional Regulation Transactional Supports (SCERTS), developed by Prizant and colleagues (2006), addresses the development of social communication skills such as joint attention, symbolic behavior, sharing emotions, and expressing emotions. To teach such complex skills, this intervention not only teaches communication skills, but also teaches children emotional self-regulation. In addition, the intervention embeds a variety of other supports (called "transactional supports") that include supports for family, learning and social development, and professionals implementing interventions (Prizant, Wetherby, Rubin, & Laurent, 2003). Thus, SCERTS provides a framework for individualizing an intervention that addresses social communication needs as well as emotional supports in a family- and child-centered manner.

SCERTS is described as an "emerging" rather than an "established" intervention by organizations such as the National Research Council (2001) and the National Autism Center's National Standards Project (2009). A literature review conducted by the textbook author revealed few empirical studies evaluating the effectiveness of SCERTS. However, SCERTS appears popular with parents and educators based on the inclusion of SCERTS in private and public schools, workshops and books devoted to training material for SCERTS, and first-person testimony.

SCERTS has many appealing characteristics, including an integration of several long-standing and empirically supported interventions for ASD such as ABA and visual communication supports. SCERTS also embraces a child- and family-centered approach that highlights the importance of emotionality in communication and learning. Unlike more established interventions, SCERTS does not provide a scripted intervention, but rather a framework for designing an intervention.

A SCERTS program addresses social communication through goals that enhance joint attention and symbolic behavior. Initial goals involve helping the child build skills to enhance their ability to participate as a social partner in a reciprocal relationship. Symbolic behaviors may be facilitated by promoting increasingly complex and interactive play skills, preverbal skills, and verbal skills. Developing several modalities for communicating (i.e., gestures, pictures, verbal) is a priority to increase communication competence (Prizant et al., 2002). Addressing these social competence goals is done within the child's natural environment.

For instance, Prizant and colleagues (2002) describe a case in which a scavenger hunt, one of the child's favorite games, was used to develop social communication skills. The therapist hid the child's favorite Pooh characters under the table, behind the door, etc. Within the context of this familiar game, the child would be asked, "Where did you look? What did you do?" The child increased his use of social/shared gaze and responded to "WH" questions within the context of a meaningful, familiar, and enjoyable play activity. Furthermore, visual prompts including "stop signs" were interspersed within the room where the hunt took place. These cues helped the child learn to pay attention to the symbols and learn the meaning of a meaningful symbol, stop signs.

A SCERTS program also addresses emotional self-regulation and mutual regulation. These goals may include:

- Identifying one's feelings with pictures, numbers, or words (Prizant et al., 2002)
- Learning to seek support from others when needed (Prizant et al., 2003)
- Learning to use sensory-motor strategies to increase or lower one's arousal such as jumping on trampoline or use of calming transition objects like squishy ball (Prizant et al., 2003)
- Learning to use socially appropriate gestures for requesting and protesting

A strength of the SCERTS model is the intentional consideration of the types of transactional supports that best supports a child within his/her natural setting. Planning for transactional supports includes an analysis of interpersonal support and potential barriers to successful social interactions. In addition, transactional supports may include creating interaction opportunities with peers using environmental supports to promote success (such as visual supports, motivating activities, and selection of peers likely to provide good models), and the use of educational supports that promote communication. Family support may involve providing information, skills through training and observational opportunities, and emotional support such as addressing parental stress, helping families prioritize, and assisting parents in setting reasonable expectations (Prizant et al., 2003). For additional information about implementing the SCERTS model, refer to *The SCERTS Model: Volume I Assessment; Volume II Program Planning and Intervention* (Prizant, Wetherby, Rubin, Laurent, & Rydell, 2006).

Augmentative and Alternative Communication Systems

Some individuals with ASD have limited or no functional speech. Likewise, many individuals with ASD experience severe difficulties processing and understanding verbal language. Alternative and Augmentative Communication (AAC) refers to types of communication supports to help individuals with ASD communicate, such as visual symbols (such as pictures, objects, or

Many options exist to support the development of communication using augmentative and alternative communication systems.

words), sign language, and specialized computers that provide a voice corresponding with visual icons. IDEA requires that every individualized educational plan considers whether assistive technology is necessary to support educational goals, such as communication. To determine a child's needs, the school may conduct an assessment to determine if and what types of AAC are necessary. Table 9.7 lists factors recommended by Scheuermann and Webber (2002) to be considered when planning AAC supports for children with ASD.

Visual communication systems aid communication by pairing verbal speech with visual information (Drager, 2009). Depending on the level of symbolic representation best understood by the child, a sequence of objects (such as milk carton to represent lunch), pictures, or words can be used to support communication. Drager notes that in addition to building on visual strengths of the child, these types of interventions also arise from natural interactions and model verbal language.

Table 9.7   Factors to Be Considered When Planning Supports for Children With ASD

- Motivation (for instance, is the child motivated to interact with machines or pictures? How easy is it to prompt responses?)
- Vocabulary skills (Does the system allow flexibility for specific vocabulary and function? Does it allow for the development of expanded language?)
- Environmental needs (i.e., Does it need to be portable?)
- Extent to which the communicative responses will be understood by those in the child's life, such as peers, teachers, and family members

Picture exchange communication system

Developed for the Delaware Autistic Program by Frost and Bondy (1994, 2002), the Picture Exchange Communication System (PECS) supports the development of functional communication. Children are taught to exchange pictures, photographs, or three-dimensional figures of objects to communicate choices, interests, and needs. Social interactions are embedded in this communicative approach, as children learn to initiate communication with someone in order to exchange their picture for a desired object, activity, and so on (as depicted on the card). However, there is limited empirical support for the use of PECS with overall communication development in a social context (Ganz & Simpson, 2004; Sulzer-Azaroff et al., 2009; Tincani & Devis, 2010; Tincani, Crozier, & Alazett, 2006). PECS is designed to teach children to initiate communication and can be faded over time (Heflin & Alaimo, 2007).

Children learn to exchange images such as these to communicate their needs, preferences, desires, and interests.

In the PECS program, adults assist the child with a prompt cuing the child to select and hand the adult a card representing a requested picture. This program can be adjusted to develop more complex language skills by arranging pictures into sentences and expanding expressive speech by commenting on the environments around them (Bondy & Frost, 2001). Often this program is used initially to promote intentional communication and gradually faded and replaced by other types of communication (Heflin & Alaimo, 2007). Research supports the use of PECS as an effective intervention for young children (preschool and elementary) across settings (Howlin, Gordon, Pasco, Wade, & Charman, 2007; Yoder & Stone, 2006). However, there is a growing body of research demonstrating the effectiveness of PECS with older children (Charlop-Christy, Carpenter, Le, LeBlanc, & Kellet, 2002) and adults (Chambers & Rehfeldt, 2003; Rehfeldt & Root, 2005).

PECS is a flexible program that can be adjusted to accommodate individual interests, needs, skill levels, and goals in a natural setting. This system does not require spoken language, motor movements or direct eye contact, which makes communication a more comfortable experience for those who experience discomfort with such forms of nonverbal communication. In addition, PECS facilitates spontaneous communication by initiating conversation without prompting. This helps improve the quality of life by reducing the possibility of becoming prompt dependent and providing the student with strategies for initiating functional communication. Furthermore, PECS has shown to accelerate the imitation of simple sounds that leads to the emergence of spoken language and facilitating social interactions (Bondy & Frost, 1995; Cummings & Williams, 2000; Tincani, 2004). In fact, individuals who reach the final stage of PECS (stage IV) often develop spontaneous language (Flippin, Reszka, & Watson, 2010).

Simpson (1995) describes PECS as a *promising practice*. Likewise, based on their meta-analysis of research on the use of PECS from 1994 to 2009, Flippin, Reszka, and Watson (2010) concluded that PECS was a "promising, although not yet established, evidence-based practice for promoting communication in children with autism" (p. 189). The meta-analysis revealed that characteristics of children with ASD most likely to benefit from PECS include limited joint attention, an interest in exploring objects, and limited motor imitation.

CHAPTER REFLECTION: TEACCH: Embedding Visual Supports to Enhance Communication and Independence

Visual supports to enhance social communication and independence are embedded in several programs, including TEACCH. TEACCH, discussed in Chapter 6 as an example of an early intervention program, is a perceptual-cognitive intervention that promotes independence, self-reliance, and social interaction for individuals with ASD across the life span. For instance, in addition to application in the school setting, the TEACCH program can be used to promote independence and social communication at work sites, vocational training, and in the home. Key components of a TEACCH program involve providing visual supports in the environment to organize tasks, provide work systems that promote task completion, create context-relevant schedules, and an overall environment that supports independence and appropriate behavior. TEACCH provides individualized structured teaching with visually cued instruction to promote skills underlying social communication, such as joint attention and receptive language. More information about the teach program can be found at http://teacch.com/about-us-1/what-is-teacch.

Speech-generating devises

Other forms of augmented or alternative communication technology may include speech-generating devices (SGD) that provide an understandable message. These devices typically have preset phrases that are frequently used in typical conversation. By having a device that can store multiple phrases and thousands of words, it is easier to communicate more effectively. Although a common concern is that the use of a SGD might impede the development of verbal language, research indicates that using an SGD to communicate supports language development by providing a model for verbal language and increasing social communication opportunities (Romski et al., 2010). Teachers working with students using SGD must receive ongoing training in using the device and working with parents to promote generalizability across settings. Additional considerations when working with a student using a SGD are listed in Table 9.8.

Table 9.8   Tips for Teaching Children Using a Speech-Generating
                Device

* Establish technical support and ongoing funding resources.
* Frequently revise and reevaluate symbols and language appropriate for the target environments. Include parents in establishing symbols and language options that promote social communication and address motivating aspects of the individual's environment (i.e., use of swing, television, access to a desirable toy, a particular snack).
* Provide opportunities to use the SGD across settings (including classrooms, lunch, recess, bus or other transitions, home, and community events).
* Train multiple communication partners (such as parents, peers, and siblings) in how to respond to SGD. For instance, explain what types of questions or comments the individual can make using their SGD and demonstrate how the language will sound.

Source: Franzone, E., & Collet-Klingenberg, L. (2008). Overview of speech generating devices for children and youth with autism spectrum disorders. Madison, WI: The National Professional Development Center on Autism Spectrum Disorders, Waisman Center, University of Wisconsin.

DynaVox is an example of a popular manufacturer of SGD that aid people in the home, classroom, and community. DynaVox offers assessment tools and personal sales reps that are able to evaluate the areas of deficit and help equip the individual with the device that is most suitable for them. The company offers

Sign language may be an effective form of communication because many individuals with ASD have visual learning strengths. From Wikimedia Commons.

online classes to provide the individual support to learn how to use the device. Collaboration with parents, teachers, speech-language pathologists, and support representatives is an important factor to assisting the child to communicate effectively (DynaVox, 2010).

Sign language

Research has shown that teaching a child with ASD sign language can make it easier to communicate with others and increase the likelihood of developing verbal skills (National Research Council, 2001; Tincani, 2004). Sign language may be an effective form of communication because many individuals with ASD have a strength for processing visual information, signs and gestures are easier to prompt than verbal utterances, and signs offer a more concrete means of communication (Goldstein, 2002). The decision to use sign language should take into account the student's fine motor control and ability to imitate. In particular, total communication instruction, which involves both sign language and verbal language instruction, appears most promising for individuals with ASD (Goldstein). Many individuals with developmental disabilities have been taught to successfully to use sign language and initiate conversations (Tincani).

TEACHING TIPS

• Conduct an analysis of the child's interests and reinforcement preferences. To heighten motivation for communication, embed communication opportunities within high-interest activities, and reward with highly reinforcing consequences.

• Ongoing assessment of interventions is essential. Frequent assessments may result in revising intervention intensity, intervention strategies, or even taking another look at prioritizing goals.

- Family preferences and priorities should be integrated into goal planning and delivery of services. Cultural sensitivity and awareness are paramount to developing meaningful goals that promote functional communication skills within a natural setting, including home, the community, and the classroom.

- Be sure to communicate frequently with family about the development of communication skills outside of school. During discussions with the family, try to find out about upcoming or recent high-interest activities that can be built upon in the classroom. For instance, an upcoming visit from a beloved relative may be a topic to explore in play, informal conversation, and academic classroom activities.

- Evaluate how the child's environment can support communication opportunities. Consult with the child's SLP for ideas about creating classroom environments that support communication development.

DISCUSSION AND REFLECTION QUESTIONS

1. What is social communication and what are some of the core deficits in this area associated with ASD?

2. How is the development of expressive language skills often different for children with ASD?

3. What are some of the difficulties children with ASD often experience with pragmatic language?

4. Outline the components of communication that should be included in an assessment of communication functioning for a child with ASD.

5. What is PECS and how can it be used to promote communication and language development in children with ASD? Discuss to what extent PECS blends components of ABA into the model.

6. Describe several alternative and augmentative systems for increasing communication in children with ASD.

SUMMARY

Both verbal and nonverbal communication skills, particularly those supporting communication, are core deficits of ASD. Understanding the trajectory of development in receptive and expressive language, vocabulary, pragmatic language, and nonverbal communication in typically developing children can help set communication goals for children with atypical development. Many children with ASD exhibit echolalia, which has implications for how children with ASD learn language and interventions to support language development. A comprehensive assessment of communication skills, including an assessment of frequency, form, and function of communication, is important for developing goals and choosing appropriate interventions. Guidelines are available for evaluating the extent to which interventions utilize evidence-based practices. Interventions based on ABA, such as DTT and PRT, are effective for strengthening communication skills. Augmentative and alternative communication systems, such as PECS, speech-generated language, and sign language, can break down language barriers for children with no or very poor language skills.

RECOMMENDED FURTHER READINGS AND INTERNET SOURCES

Further Readings

Beukelman, D. R., & Mirenda, P. (2005). *Augentative and alternative communication: Supporting children and adults with complex communication needs* (3rd ed.). Baltimore, MD: Paul H. Brookes.

Koegel, R. L., & Koegel, L. K. (2006). *Pivotal response treatment for autism. communication, social, and academic development.* Baltimore, MD: Paul H. Brookes.

National Autism Center. (2011). *Evidence-based practices and autism in the schools.* Randolph, MA: Author.

Schlosser, R., & Wendt, O. (2008). Effects of augmentative and alternative communication intervention on speech production in children with autism: A systematic review. *American Journal of Speech-Language Pathology, 17,* 212–230.

Snodgrass, C. S. (2004). *Super silly sayings that are over your head: A children's illustrated book of idioms.* Higganum, CT: Starfish Specialty Press.

Internet Sources

American Speech-Hearing Association. http://www.asha.org

Applied Behavioral Analysis. http://www.abainternational.org

The Center for AAC and Autism. http://www.aacandautism.com/why-aac

Dynavox. http://www.dynavoxtech.com/autism-awareness/

Picture Exchange Communication System—USA. http://www.pecsusa.com/

The TAM (Technology and Media) division of the Council for Exceptional Children. http://www.tamcec.org/

United States Society for Augmentative and Alternative Communication. http://www.ussaac.org

REFERENCES

Adams, C. (2002). Practitioner review: The assessment of language pragmatics. *Journal of Child Psychology and Psychiatry, and Allied Disciplines, 43,* 973–987.

American Psychiatric Association (2010). *American Psychiatric Association DSM-5 Development: A 05 Autism Spectrum Disorder.* Retrieved from http://www.dsm5.org/

ProposedRevisions/Pages/proposedrevision. aspx?rid=94.

American Psychiatric Association. (2000). *Diagnostic and statistical manual of mental disorders* (Revised 4th ed., Text Rev.). Washington, DC: Author.

American Speech-Language-Hearing Association. (2006). *Roles and responsibilities of speech-language pathologists in diagnosis, assessment, and treatment of autism spectrum disorders across the life span: Position statement.* Retrieved from http://www.asha.org/docs/html/ps2006-00105.html

Atwood, T. (1998). *Asperger's syndrome. A guide for parents and professionals.* London, UK: Jessica Kingsley Publications.

Atwood, T. (2008). The complete guide to Asperger's syndrome. London, UK: Jessica Kingsley Publications.

Bandura, A. (1977). *Social learning theory.* New York, NY: General Learning Press.

Baron-Cohen, S. (1995). *Mindblindness: An essay on autism and theory of mind.* Cambridge, MA: MIT Press.

Baron-Cohen, S., Allen, J., & Gillberg, C. (1992). Can autism be detected at 18 months? The needle, the haystack, and the CHAT. *British Journal of Psychiatry, 61,* 839–843.

Baron-Cohen, S., Cox, A., Baird, G., Swettenham, J., Nightingale, N., Morgan, K., . . . Charman, T. (1996). Psychological markers in the detection of autism in infancy in a large population. *British Journal of Psychiatry, 168,* 58–63.

Baron-Cohen, S., Leslie, L. M., & Frith, U. (1985). Does the autistic child have a theory of mind? *Cognition, 21,* 37–46.

Berk, L. (2010). *Exploring lifespan development* (2nd ed.). Boston, MA: Allyn & Bacon.

Bondy, A., & Frost, L. (1995). Educational approached in preschool: Behavior techniques in a public school setting. In E. Schopler & G. Mesibov (Eds.), *Learning and cognition in autism* (pp. 311–333). New York, NY: Plenum.

Bondy, A., & Frost, L. (2001). The Picture Exchange Communication System. *Behavior Modification, 25,* 725–744.

Boucher, J., & Lewis, V. (1992). Unfamiliar face recognition in relatively able autistic children. *Journal of Child Psychology and Psychiatry, 33,* 843–859.

Bowers, L., Huisingh, R., & LoGiudice, C. (2008). *The social language development test.* East Moline, IL: Linguisystems.

Bryson S. (1996). Brief report: Epidemiology of autism. *Journal of Autism and Developmental Disorders, 26,* 165–168.

Bruce, B., & Hansson, K. (2008). Early communication skills: Important in screening for language impairment and neuropsychiatric disorders. *Current Pediatric Reviews, 4,* 53–57.

Buzolich, M. J. (2009). Communication sampling and analysis. *Perspectives on Augmentative and Alternative Communication, 18,* 88–95.

Buzolich, M. J., Russell, D. B., Lunger-Bergh, J., & Burns-McCloskey, D. *CSA communication and sampling analysis.* Retrieved from http://csa.acts-at.com/csa-info.html.

Chambers, M., & Rehfeldt, R. (2003). Assessing the acquisition and generalization of two main forms with adults with severe developmental disabilities. *Research in Developmental Disabilities, 24,* 265–280.

Charlop-Christy, M. H., Carpenter, M., Le, L., LeBlanc, L. A., & Kellet, K. (2002). Using the Picture Exchange Communication System (PECS) with children with autism: Assessment of PECS acquisition, speech, social-communicative behavior, and problem behavior. *Journal of Applied Behavior Analysis, 35,* 213–231.

Charman, T. (1998). Specifying the nature and course of the joint attention impairment in autism in the preschool years: Implications for diagnosis and intervention. *Autism, 2,* 61–29.

Constantino, J. N., & Gruber, C. P. (2005). *Social Responsiveness Scale (SRS).* Los Angeles, CA: Western Psychological Services.

Diehl, S. F. (2003). The SLP'S role in collaborative assessment and intervention for children with ASD. *Topics in Language Disorders, 23,* 95–115.

Drager, K. D. R. (2009). Aided modeling interventions for children with autism spectrum disorders who require AAC. *Perspectives on Augmentative and Alternative Communication, 18,* 114–120.

Drew, A., Baird, G., Taylor, E., Milne, E., & Charman, T. (2007). The Social Communication Assessment for Toddlers with Autism (SCATA): An instrument to measure the frequency, form, and function of communication in toddlers with autism spectrum disorder. *Journal of Autism and Developmental Disorders, 37,* 648–666.

Flippin, M., Reszka, S., & Watson, L. R. (2010). Effectiveness of the Picture Exchange Communication System (PECS) on communication and speech for children with autism spectrum disorders: A meta-analysis. *American Journal of Speech-Language Pathology, 19,* 178–195.

Franzone, E., & Collet-Klingenberg, L. (2008). *Overview of speech generating devices for children and youth with autism spectrum disorders.* Madison, WI: The National Professional Development Center on Autism Spectrum Disorders, Waisman Center, University of Wisconsin.

Frost, L., & Bondy, A. (1994). *PECS: The Picture Exchange Communication System training manual.* Cherry Hill, NJ: Pyramid Educational Consultants.

Frost, L., & Bondy, A. (2002). *PECS: The Picture Exchange Communication System training manual* (2nd ed.). Cherry Hill, NJ: Pyramid Educational Consultants.

Ganz, J. B., & Simpson, R. L. (2004). Effects on communicative requesting and speech development of the Picture Exchange Communication System in children with characteristics of autism. *Journal of Autism and Developmental Disorders, 34,* 395–409.

Gillberg, C., & Steffenburg, S. (1987). Outcome and prognostic factors in infantile autism and similar conditions: A population-based study of 46 cases followed through puberty. *Journal of Autism and Developmental Disorders, 17,* 273–287.

Goldstein, H. (2002). Communication intervention for children with autism: A review of treatment efficacy. *Journal of Autism and Developmental Disorders, 32,* 373–396.

Hall, L. J. (2009). *Autism spectrum disorders: From theory to practice.* Upper Saddle River, NJ: Pearson.

Heflin, L. J., & Alaimo, D. F. (2007). *Students with autism spectrum disorder.* Upper Saddle River, NJ: Pearson.

Hoff, E. (2005). *Language development.* Belmont, CA: Wadsworth.

Howlin, P., Gordon, R. K., Pasco, G., Wade, A., & Charman, T. (2007). The effectiveness of Picture Exchange Communication System (PECS) training for teachers of children with autism: A pragmatic, group randomized controlled trial. *Journal of Child Psychology and Psychiatry, 48*(5), 473–481.

Ingersoll, B., Dvortcsak, A., Whalen, C., & Sikora, D. (2005). The effects of a developmental, social-pragmatic language intervention on rate of expressive language production in young children with autistic spectrum disorders. *Focus on Autism and Other Developmental Disabilities, 20,* 213–222.

Iwata, B. A., Pace, G. M., Dorsey, M. F., Zarcone, J. R., Vollmer, T. R., Smith, R. G., . . . Willis, K. D., (1994). The functions of self-injurious behavior: An experimental-epidemiological analysis. *Journal of Applied Behavior Analysis, 27,* 215–240.

Koegel, L. K. (2000). Interventions to facilitate communication in autism. *Journal of Autism and Developmental Disorders, 30,* 383–391.

Koegel, L. K. (2003). Communication and language intervention. In R. L. Koegel & L. K. Koegel (Eds.), *Teaching children with autism. strategies for initiating positive interactions and improving learning* (pp. 17–32). Baltimore, MD: Paul H. Brookes.

Koegel, R. L., Koegel, L. K., & Carter, C. M. (1999). Pivotal teaching interactions for children with autism. *School Psychology Review, (28),* 185–191.

Koegel, R. L., Schreibman, L., Good, A., Cerniglia, L., Murphey, C., & Koegel, L. K.

(1989). *How to teach pivotal behaviors to children with autism: A training manual.* Santa Barbara, CA: University of California, Santa Barbara.

Koegel, R. L., & Koegel, L. K. (2006). *Pivotal response treatment for autism. Communication, social, and academic development.* Baltimore, MD: Paul H. Brookes.

Landa, R. J. (2005). Assessment of social communication skills in preschoolers. *Mental Retardation and Developmental Disorders, 11,* 247–252.

Landa, R., & Garrett-Mayer, E. (2006). Development in infants with autism spectrum disorders: A prospective study. *Journal of Child Psychology and Psychiatry, 47,* 629–638.

Liebal, K., Carpenter, M., & Tomasello, M. (2010). Infants' use of shared experience in declarative pointing. *Infancy, 15,* 545–556.

Lord, C., & Paul, R. (1997). Language and communication in autism. In D. Cohen & F. R. Volkmar, *Handbook of autism and pervasive developmental disorders* (2nd ed., pp. 195–225). New York, NY: Wiley.

Lord, C., Shulman, C., & DiLavore, P. (2004). Regression and word loss in autistic spectrum disorders. *Journal of Child Psychology and Psychiatry, 45,* 936–955.

Loukusa, S., Leinonen, E., Kuusikko, S., Jussila, K., Mattila, M., Ryder, N., Ebeling, H., & Moilanen, I. (2006). Use of context in pragmatic language comprehension by children with Asperger syndrome or high-functioning autism. *Journal of Autism and Developmental Disorders, 37,* 1049–1059.

Luyster, R., Richler, J., Risi, S., Hsu, W. L., Dawson, G., Bernier, R., . . . Lord, C. (2005). Early regression in social communication in autism spectrum disorder: A CPEA study. *Developmental Neuropsychology, 27,* 311–336.

Mehler, J., Jusczyk, P., Lambertz, G., Halsted, N., Bertoncini, J., & Amiel-Tison, C. (1988). A precursor of language acquisition in young infants. *Cognition, 29,* 143–178.

Morton, J., & Johnson, M. H. (1991). CONSPEC and CONLERN: A two-process theory of infant face recognition. *Psychological Review, 2,* 164–181.

Myles, B., & Simpson, R. L. (2001). Understanding the hidden curriculum: An essential social skill for children and youth with Asperger syndrome. *Intervention in School and Clinic, 36,* 279–286.

National Autism Center. (2009). *National Standards Report.* Randolph, MA: Author.

National Autism Center. (2011). *Evidence based practices and autism in the schools.* Randolph, MA: Author.

National Research Council. (2001). *Educating children with autism.* Washington, DC: The National Academies Press.

Paul, R. (2007). Assessing communication in autism spectrum disorders. In F. R. Volkmar, R. Paul, A. Klin, & D. Cohen (Eds.), *Handbook of autism and pervasive developmental disorders: Volume 2: Assessment, interventions, and policy* (3rd ed.). Hoboken, NJ: John Wiley and Sons.

Phelps-Terasaki, D., & Phelps-Gunn, T. (1992). *Test of pragmatic language, second edition (TOPL-2).* Torrance, CA: Western Psychological Services.

Philofsky, A., Fidler, D., & Hepburn, S. (2007). Pragmatic language profiles of school-age children with autism spectrum disorders and Williams syndrome. *American Journal of Speech-Language Pathology, 16,* 368–380.

Pierce, K., Conant, D., Hazin, R., Stoner, R., & Desmond, J. (2010). Preference for geometric patterns early in life as a risk factor for autism. *Archives of General Psychiatry, 10,* 131–138.

Prizant, B. M., & Duchan, J. F. (1981). The functions of immediate echolalia in autistic children. *Journal of Speech and Hearing Disorders, 46,* 241–249.

Prizant, B. M., & Rydell, P. J. (1984). Analysis of functions of delayed echolalia in autistic children. *Journal of Speech and Hearing Research, 27,* 183–192.

Prizant, B. M., Wetherby, A. M., Rubin, E., & Laurent, A. C. (2003). The SCERTS model: A transactional, family-centered approach to enhancing communication and socioemotional abilities of children with autism spectrum disorder. *Infants and Young Children, 16,* 296–316.

Prizant, B. M., Wetherby, A. M., Rubin, E., Laurent, A. C., & Rydell, P. (2002). The SCERTS model: Enhancing communication and socioemotional abilities in children with autism spectrum disorder. *Jenison Autism Journal, Winter Issue,* 2–32.

Rehfeldt, R., & Root, S. (2005). Establishing derived requesting skills in adults with severe developmental disabilities. *Journal of Applied Behavior Analysis, 38,* 101–105.

Romski, M., Sevcik, R. A., Adamson, L. B., Cheslock, M., Smith, A., Barker, R. M., & Bakeman, R. (2010). Randomized comparison of augmented and nonaugmented language interventions for toddlers with developmental delays and their parents. *Journal of Speech, Language, and Hearing Research, 53,* 350–364.

Santrock, J. W. (2008). *Children* (10th ed.). New York, NY: McGraw-Hill Higher Education.

Sasson, N. J. (2006). The development of face processing in autism. *Journal of Autism and Developmental Disorders, 36,* 381–394.

Scheuermann, B., & Webber, J. (2002). *Autism. Teaching does make a difference.* Belmont, CA: Wadsworth.

Schreibman, L. (1988). *Autism.* Newbury Park, CA: Sage.

Siegel, B. (1996). *The world of the autistic child: Understanding and treating autistic spectrum disorders.* Oxford, UK: Oxford University Press.

Simkin, A., Charman, T., Chandler, S., Loucas, T., & Baird, G. (2009). Loss of language in early development of autism and specific language impairment. *Journal of Child Psychology and Psychiatry, 50,* 843–852.

Simpson, R. L. (2005). *Autism spectrum disorders: Interventions and treatments for children and youth.* Thousand Oaks, CA: Corwin.

Skinner, B. F. (1954). The science of learning and the art of teaching. *Harvard Educational Review, 24*(2), 86–97.

Sulzer-Azaroff, B., Hoffman, A., Horton, C., Bondy, A., & Frost, L. (2009). The Picture Exchange Communication System (PECS): What do the data say? *Focus on Autism, 24,* 89–103.

Symons, L. A., Hains, S. M. J., & Muir, D. W. (1998). Look at me: Five-month-old infants' sensitivity to very small deviations in eyegaze during social interactions. *Infant Behavior & Development, 21,* 531–536.

Tager-Flusberg, H., Paul, R., & Lord, C. (2005). Language and communication in autism. In F. Volkmar, R. Paul, & A. Klin (Eds.), *Handbook on autism and pervasive developmental disorders* (3rd ed., pp. 335–364). New York, NY: Wiley.

Tager-Flusberg, H., Rogers, S., Cooper, J., Lana, R., Lord, C., Paul, R., . . . Wetherby, A. (2009). Defining spoken language benchmarks and selecting measures of expressive language development for young children with autism spectrum disorders. *Journal of Speech, Language, and Hearing Research, 52,* 643–652.

Thrum, A., Lord, C., Lee, L., & Newschaffer C. (2007). Predictors of language acquisition in preschool children with autism spectrum disorder. *Journal of Autism and Developmental Disorders, 37,* 1721–1734.

Tincani, M. (2004). Comparing the picture exchange communication system and sign language training for children with autism. *Focus on Autism and Other Developmental Disabilities, 12,* 152–163.

Tincani, M., & Devis, K. (2010). Quantitative synthesis and component analysis of single-participant studies on the Picture Exchange Communication System (Online First). *Remediation and Special Education,* 1–13.

Tincani, M., Crozier, S., & Alazett, S. (2006). The Picture Exchange Communication System: Effects on manding and speech development for school-aged children with autism. *Education & Training in Developmental Disabilities, 41,* 177–184.

Trawick-Smith, J. (2010). *Early childhood development [a multicultural perspective]* (5th ed.). Upper Saddle River, NJ: Merrill.

Tuchman, R. F., & Rapin, I. (1997). Regression in pervasive developmental disorders: Seizures and epileptiform electroencephalogram correlates. *Pediatrics, 99,* 560–566.

Venter, A., Lord, C., & Schopler, E. (1992). A follow-up of high-functioning autistic children. *Journal of Child Psychology and Psychiatry, 33,* 489–507.

Vicker, B. (2009). *Functional categories of immediate echolalia.* Bloomington, IN: Indiana Resource Center Autism.

Vygotsky, L. S. (1978). *Mind in society.* Cambridge, MA: Harvard University Press.

Weiss, M. J., & Harris, S. L. (2001). *Reaching out, joining in. Teaching social skills to young children with autism.* Bethesda, MD: Woodbine House.

Wetherby, A. M. (2006). Understanding and measuring social communication in children with autism spectrum disorder. In T. Charman & W. Stone (Eds.), S*ocial and communication development in autism spectrum disorders: Early identification, diagnosis, and intervention* (pp. 3–34). New York, NY: Guilford Press.

Wetherby, A. M., & Prizant, B. M. (2001). *Communication and Symbolic Behavior Scales Developmental Profile (CSBS DP).* Baltimore, MD: Paul H. Brookes.

Wetherby, A. D., Yonclas, D., & Bryan, A. (1989). Communicative profiles of handicapped preschool children: Implications for early identification. *Journal of Speech and Hearing Disorders, 54,* 148–158.

Wilkinson, K. M. (1998). Profiles of language and communication skills in autism. *Mental Retardation and Developmental Disabilities Research Reviews, 4,* 73–79.

Yoder, P., & Stone, W. L. (2006). Randomized comparison of two communication interventions for preschoolers with autism spectrum disorders. *Journal of Consulting and Clinical Psychology, 74*(3), 426–435.

CHAPTER 10

SOCIAL DEVELOPMENT IN CHILDREN WITH ASD

In this chapter, you will learn about:

- Core deficits of socialization.
- Foundation skills for developing peer relationships.
- Assessment and identification of target social skills goals.
- Determining evidence-based practices.
- Interventions for supporting social skill development, including Applied Behavior Analysis, story-based interventions, video modeling and video self-modeling, relationship- and developmental-based interventions, and peer-mediated interventions.

CORE DEFICITS OF SOCIALIZATION ASSOCIATED WITH ASD

Although individuals with Autism Spectrum Disorder (ASD) demonstrate a wide range of functioning, socialization is a core deficit across the spectrum. Both the proposed *Diagnostic and Statistical Manual of Mental Disorders, Fifth Edition (DSM-V)* definition of ASD (American Psychiatric Association, 2011) and the *DSM-IV-TR* (American Psychiatric Association, 2000) criteria for autism describe social deficits in verbal and nonverbal communication, social reciprocity, and the development of age appropriate peer relationships.

Both skill acquisition deficits (absence of a skill) and performance deficits (difficulties performing a particular skill) contribute to the core social deficits of ASD (Bellini, 2006). Understanding the development of social skills in typically developing children helps teachers identify specific skill or performance deficits to target for children with ASD.

Most typically developing children are motivated to interact with their peers. Although there are individual differences in traits, such as extraversion and shyness, children are usually interested in socially engaging with other children. Furthermore, typically developing children learn how to interact with other children through both nonverbal and verbal feedback they receive from them. In addition, observation, imitation, and creative play allow children to refine skills, such as initiating social interactions, social-emotional reciprocity, and self-regulation. Typically developing children enjoy increasingly more complex peer relationships that change with growth in cognitive skills and social competence. In the following sections, we consider these core deficits and the specific skills associated with the development of peer relationships.

Motivation to Interact With Others

The motivation to interact with others is a prerequisite for developing age-appropriate social skills. However, some children with ASD, although not all, appear uninterested in interacting with others. They do not seem motivated to interact with peers, family members, or others. In fact, some of these children may seem to find social interactions stressful and aversive. Other children with ASD may be more comfortable interacting with adults rather than other children. Pivotal response training has been used to increase motivation to play with peers through offering choices and focusing on the child's preferred activities (Lavie & Sturmey, 2002; Pierce & Schreibman, 1995; Terpstra, Higgins, & Pierce, 2002).

Many children with ASD *are* interested in interacting with peers. In fact, many children with ASD (particularly those with high-functioning ASD) desire to have friends and to be included in social activities, but have difficulty with a range of skills associated with successful social interactions (Atwood, 1998; Bauminger, Solomon, Aviezer, Heung, Brown, & Rogers, 2008). Skill deficits in reading nonverbal cues of others, interpreting and using pragmatic language (the social aspect of language), initiating peer interactions, navigating the complexity of a social peer group, and maintaining social interactions are examples of difficulties often associated with social skill deficits in children with high-functioning ASD. Unfortunately, as these children approach middle school they are prone to suffering from anxiety and depression associated with their failure to establish a peer social support group (Vickerstaff, Heriot, Wong, Lopes, & Dossetor, 2007).

Impairments in Nonverbal Communication

Body language and facial expressions communicate a great deal of information. Nonverbal behaviors may include facial expressions, eye contact and eye gaze, body posture, and gestures. In addition to difficulties interpreting the nonverbal social cues of others, children with ASD may not realize the messages they are sending with their own body language. For example, they may not realize that they are perceived by others as feeling angry because of a facial grimace, disinterested because they fail to make eye contact, or aggressive because they are perceived as invading another's personal space. Some of these difficulties may be related to sensory issues. For instance, a child may experience physical discomfort when making eye contact.

Failure to Develop Age-Appropriate Peer Relationships

Impairments in nonverbal communication are often associated with rejection or neglect from peers. Being rejected or overlooked may cause children and teens with ASD to feel depressed and lonely. Furthermore, social skills deficits result in reduced opportunities to engage with peers in a way that would strengthen their social development. Peer interactions provide important opportunities for learning how to interact with people outside their family. In addition, peers provide support and practice navigating the social complexities of social relationships. Peers also provide feedback about emotional regulation and other behaviors for psychological development.

An early sign of ASD in young children is the failure to engage in *joint attention,* in which the child and caregiver are jointly looking at a specific object or event (Dawson et al., 2004). Difficulty sharing experiences with others early in development may be related to later deficits in the development of social play and perspective taking (Charman, 1997).

Atypical play development is another likely contributing factor to early deficits in developing peer relationships. The development of play and perspective taking is explored in the next section. In addition, idiosyncratic and challenging behaviors (such as insistence of certain routines or age-inappropriate temper tantrums) negatively impact the development of peer relationships.

Social-Emotional Reciprocity

Social-emotional reciprocity, the give-and-take of social interactions, is critical to establishing friendships. Friends listen to one another, try to understand each other's point of view, and display appropriate emotions to demonstrate support and understanding. Such skills are often lacking in children with ASD. Individuals with ASD are less likely to initiate interactions or respond to interactions initiated by typically developing peers. Deficits in social-emotional reciprocity may be related to deficits in joint attention (Charman, 2003), visual fixation (Merin, Young, Ozonoff, & Rogers, 2007), and eye gaze (Klin, Jones, Schultz, Volkmar, & Cohen, 2002).

The discovery of joint attention, one of the earliest types of reciprocal social interactions, has allowed for the diagnosis and study of autism as early as 1 year of age. Joint attention develops between 6 to 12 months and involves the shared attention or experience with another individual, usually a caregiver (Charman, 2003). Recognition of joint attention allows for earlier interventions as well as explorations in new types of interventions to help develop skills such as shared attention. Joint attention appears critical to the development of more complex social interactions and may be a preliminary step to developing Theory of Mind. Theory of Mind (TOM) refers to understand the mental state of someone else and in a sense "engage in a form of mind reading" (Durand, 2005, p. 92). The finding that individuals with autism seem to lack TOM, sometimes called "mindblindness" (Baron-Cohen, 1995), is thought to be a core deficit associated with later difficulties with social development.

Figure 10.1   Core Deficits in Social Communication Skills for Individuals With ASD

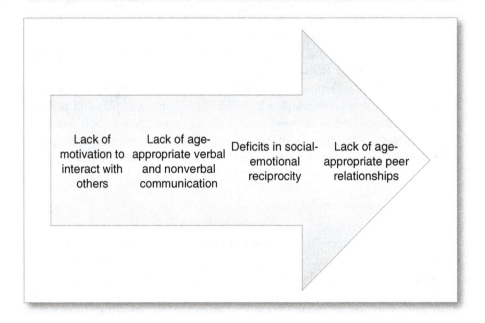

Individual Differences: Atypical Behavior or Deficit?

A *deficit* indicates that the social behavior (or lack of) *impairs* the child's functioning, such as their ability to share ideas and interests, to interact with others appropriately in school, home, and community settings, to engage in age-appropriate leisure activities, or to establish age appropriate peer relationships. It is important to note that individual differences in social functioning (such as shyness and extraversion) are both found within both the *neurotypical* (individuals experiencing normal development for their chronological age) and the ASD populations. There is a wide range of individual differences based on personality, culture, and previous experiences that should be taken into consideration when targeting social interventions. Idiosyncratic behaviors (different from the norm) is consider problematic when it interferes with functioning at school, home, or in other settings.

CHAPTER REFLECTION: Intersection of Culture and Social Interest: The Case of Pooh-San

Children with ASD have a wide range of social skills and social interests. Some children experience greater deficits than others in many areas across the spectrum. Furthermore, individual differences in personality and preferences impact many aspects of social functioning. Culture is another layer that impacts social development.

I once visited the home of a teacher in Okinawa, Japan, who provided respite care for families of her high school students with disabilities. I joined her, a student, and the student's parents for lunch one day at the teacher's home. I was introduced to a teenage girl with a developmental disability holding a Winnie the Pooh stuffed bear named "Pooh-San" (Mr. Pooh). Her teacher smiled and told me that the girl carried it with her wherever she went. I was struck by how many teachers in the United States would likely consider playing with a stuffed bear an *inappropriate* interest for a teenager and would likely discourage the girl from carrying it with her to school or community events. However, in Japan it is not unusual for both girl and boy teens to collect stuffed animals and carry backpacks decorated with brightly colored cartoon animals.

FOUNDATION SKILLS FOR DEVELOPING PEER RELATIONSHIPS

To have friends, children must demonstrate prosocial behaviors, including altruism (offering help to others in need) and empathy (identifying with the mental state of others). Furthermore, children are more likely to have friends when they are able to regulate their own behavior. Children who demonstrate positive behaviors (laughing, smiling), and limited negative behaviors (aggression, sadness, withdrawal) are more likely to have friends (Mayeux & Cillissen, 2003).

Social Cognition and Social Competence

Social cognition refers to the way in which individuals perceive, process, and understand social information (Scourfield, Martin, Lewis, & McGuffin, 1999). Being able to take the perspective of another, understanding how one's own behavior is perceived by others, monitoring one's own emotions and behavior, and understanding social rules that may change from setting to setting reflect social cognition skills.

These social cognition skills are embedded in the development of play and social reciprocity, the give-and-take of social relationships. Social cognitive skills are needed to support the initiation and development of peer relationships. Social competence describes the ability to interact with others in an appropriate manner based on age and context (Iarocci, Yager, & Elfers, 2007). A socially competent person is perceived by others to perform in a socially appropriate manner across settings (Hops, 1983). The development of play skills is fundamental to developing social competence and ultimately friendships. Likewise, social reciprocity is an important component of developing play skills with peer.

The Development of Play and Social Reciprocity

Play is an important aspect of social-emotional and cognitive development. In addition, play provides an important forum for learning about the give-and-take (social reciprocity) of social interactions that lead to relationships. Young children use play to learn about the world, problem solve, and develop relationships. Infants engage in sensory exploration of objects (Santrock, 2008) and gradually move toward play involving social interaction and fantasy during the preschool years. Increasing levels of social play reflect developing cognitive skills, awareness of self, and others (Santrock). Parten (1932) outlined a developmental sequence of social play behaviors in children that is still used today to evaluate aspects of social development described in Table 10.1.

Cognitive skills needed to engage in social play also occur in a predictable stagelike progression in typically developing children. Aspects of cognitive development demonstrated in play are described in Table 10.3. Children with ASD often demonstrate atypical development in these cognitive skills.

Children with ASD may exhibit deficits in play skills at each level, including functional play (Christensen et al., 2010), symbolic (Dawson & Adams, 1984), constructive, and socio-dramatic (Weiss & Harris, 2001). Instead, they may engage in repetitive or stereotypic play, or solitary play focusing on a restricted set of interests. Weaknesses with fine or gross motor skills may further impair the development of play in children with ASD. Occupational and physical therapists can adapt play materials and activities to increase accessibility.

Overall, children with ASD often demonstrate play behavior less advanced than would be expected based on their chronological age. Individuals with more severe characteristics of ASD may primarily engage in sensor-motor play, exploring objects by sniffing, licking, spinning, and touching. Children with ASD may line up toys rather than engage fantasy play (such as using cars to race).

Table 10.1   The Development of Social Play

- *Solitary play*—9 months of age. Infant interacting with an object.
- *Parallel play*—2 years. Playing side-by-side with another child but rarely interacting.
- *Associative play*—3 years. Interacting with another child in some ways, such as sharing toys.
- *Cooperative play*—The preschool years. Play involves working together often with rules or agreed-upon roles (such as the "mother" in playing house), and experimenting with the give-and-take of social relationships.

Source: Parten (1932).

Table 10.2 Play Reflecting Cognitive Skill Development

- Functional play—Interacting with an object in the manner in which it is intended. For instance, putting sand in a bucket.
- Symbolic play—Substituting one object for another during play. For instance, pretending that a brush is a microphone. The ability to use symbols to represent other things is fundamental to the development of language, literacy, mathematics, music, and many other forms of communication, culture, and knowledge.
- Socio-dramatic play—Imaginary play involving role-playing such as playing school. Pretend play, especially when it involves role-playing with others, represents high level of cognitive complexity. Socio-dramatic play allows children to test out different roles, work through difficult experiences, and practice complex emotional interchanges.

From Frost, Wortham, and Reifel (2005).

Some children with ASD appear uninterested in pursuing social play. Their play may appear rigid and unimaginative, such as spinning a top or lining up toys (Wolfberg & Schuler, 1993). Other children with ASD attempt to engage peers in play and join them on the playground, but lack the social skills for success and experience chronic rejection. Over time, they may give up and choose to observe from the sidelines or play alone. Because the development of play is atypical in many children with ASD, assessment of play skills is incorporated into many frequently used instruments to assess autism, including the Modified Checklist for Autism in Toddlers (M-CHAT; Robbins, Fein, Barton, & Green, 2001), Autism Diagnostic Interview-Revised (ADI-R; Rutter, Le Couteur, & Lord, 2003), and the Autism Diagnostic Observation Scale (ADOS; Lord, Rutter, DiLavore, & Risi, 2001).

Developing Peer Relationships and Friendships

Around age 2, children begin to develop peer friendships that include reciprocity and increased time interacting with each other in a friendly manner (Dunn, 2004). During the preschool years (ages 3–5), children regularly engage in shared play and supportive prosocial behaviors with friends (Dunn, 2004). In particular, fantasy play with peers contributes to the development of intimacy

Around age 8, typically developing children experience an increase in self-understanding. They are able to reflect upon their own feelings and describe their emotional states (Flavel, Flavel, & Green, 2001). Also at this time, children demonstrate an increased sense of empathy (Berk, 2010). In addition, children become better at regulating their own behavior and emotions as they compare their own behavior against their peers in pursuit of peer approval (Berk, 2010).

The ability to perspective-take, in which a child considers the feelings, beliefs, and experiences of a peer, increases in predictable stages based on a child's age (Selman, 1975). Deficits in social-emotional reciprocity are, in large part, a weakness in perspective taking. Enhanced social cognitive skills such as self-understanding, self-regulation, and perspective taking contribute to the ability to make friends for typically developing children in middle childhood (elementary to middle school). Selman describes the developmental stages of perspective taking.

Whereas preschool children consider a "friend" an available playmate with good prosocial skills (are nice, willing to play with them, share), school-age children have a more complex understanding of friendships. Around the age of 8, children consider friends to be peers who shared interests who they can trust to respond to their needs and emotions (Berk, 2010). Friendships become increasingly defined by trust. Violations of trust, such as failing to anticipate and respond to need for help or sharing private information with others, negatively impact friendships (Kahn & Turiel, 1988). Consequently, skills involving conflict resolution and compromise develop to manage the growing complexity of friendships (Dunn, 2004).

Children with ASD experience difficulties establishing and maintaining positive peer relationships. Some children with ASD actively avoid or have low motivation to interact with their peers. Furthermore, children with ASD may have far less opportunities to interact with peers and develop friendships. Consequently, children with ASD tend to have fewer friends than their typically developing peers, and are more likely to experience peer rejection and loneliness (Bauminger & Kasari, 2000; Bauminger, et al., 2008; Lasgaard, Nielsen, Eriksen, & Goossens, 2010).

Roeyers (1995) describes the "self-perpetuating" nature of deficits in socialization for children with ASD. Deficits in social skills result in fewer opportunities to engage with peers. Consequently, children with ASD have fewer experiences from which to learn about social interactions that result in positive outcomes. Motivation to engage with peers is further reduced when they are neglected or rejected by their peers because of unusual behaviors or lack of age-appropriate social skills.

Children with ASD often experience difficulties with social cognitive skills that are important for developing positive peer relationships, and ultimately friendships. Table 10.4 describes social cognitive skills important for developing positive peer relationships.

Despite these deficits, individuals with ASD can establish and maintain friendships with peers. Support from teachers and school personnel, peers, and family provide opportunities to learn and practice the foundation skills that contribute to friendships. An evaluation of a child's current social skills and overall social functioning is important to identifying target goals and interventions to support social development (Quill, 2000).

Table 10.3   Social Cognitive Skills Critical for Developing Positive Peer Relationships

- **Taking the perspective of another.** Considering what another person may have experienced, information they have available, and how that might influence their thoughts and behavior. *Children with ASD have difficulty with taking the perspective of another, sometimes called theory of mind or mind-reading.*
- **Establishing reciprocity.** As children get older, the "give-and-take" of relationships becomes increasingly critical to developing friendships. Children desire friends who listen to what they have to say, support them in their efforts, and provide comfort to them when they are distressed. In turn, they expect to provide those emotional supports to their friend. *Children with ASD often engage in conversations that appear one sided. They may appear to talk about and insist on engaging in activities that they consider high interest. Consequently, they may come across as overly self-focused by their peers.*
- **Using verbal and nonverbal pragmatic language.** We communicate a great deal about our current emotional state, our preferences, and attitudes through nonverbal communication (i.e., eye contact, posture, gestures, facial expressions, physical proximity to another). In addition, our verbal language is laden with important clues about the social experience. For instance, tone of voice, choice of words (such as sarcasm or slang), and even the rate with which we speak may convey hidden messages. Although social convention suggests it is impolite to tell someone you are uninterested in a topic or desire to end the social interaction, pragmatic language conveys this information. *Children with ASD often fail to decipher the pragmatic language during a conversation. Failure to understand the "hidden" messages in verbal and nonverbal language negatively impacts opportunities to socialize with others. They often fail to read, or misread, body language and verbal cues embedded in social interactions.*

ASSESSMENT OF SOCIAL FUNCTIONING AND
IDENTIFICATION OF TARGET GOALS

Assessment Tools for Evaluating Social Skills in Children With ASD

Assessment of current social functioning is necessary prior to setting relevant goals and choosing appropriate interventions. When collecting information about a child's level of social functioning, data should be collected from multiple sources, across time, and across settings (Bellini, 2006; Sattler, 2006). It is particularly important to include observations in naturalistic settings (such as observations during class group activities, playground, free time, family interactions, and community activities) in addition to information from teachers, parents, and others working with the child.

Information about functioning in daily settings and routines provides a check of *ecological validity* (measuring real-life functioning). Observations may be informal and descriptive, or structured providing normative standard scores comparing functioning to typically developing peers. Assessments tools that provide normative standard scores (compare scores with typically developing peers) help determine the child's current developmental level of social functioning.

In addition to observations, rating scales are often used to collect information from caregivers and teachers about a child's social skills in comparison to same-age peers. Furthermore, older children with the necessary skills may provide information about their perceived social competence, social strengths/interests, and areas of weaknesses through interviews or self-report questionnaires.

The following instruments are examples of useful tools for evaluating aspects of social functioning of children with ASD.

- Autism Diagnostic Observation Scale (ADOS; Lord, Rutter, DiLavore, & Risi, 2001) is an assessment tool primarily used as part of a comprehensive battery to diagnose ASD. However, it can also be used to identify areas of strengths and weaknesses in social functioning. The ADOS test stimuli creates a social world in which social behavior can be observed (Rice, 2009). There are three modules that can be administered, based on the individual's level of receptive language skills. However, the ADOS is most appropriate for individuals with receptive language skills (understanding language) of at least 18 months. The ADOS sets up scenarios where the child demonstrates play skills and interests, social skills embedded within social interactions, and social communication skills. Data from the ADOS may be helpful in better understanding the reason, or key skill deficit, underlying a social difficulty. For instance, the ADOS is useful in differentiating problems with social reciprocity from social anxiety or noncompliance (Rice).

• Social Communication Questionnaire (SCQ; Rutter, Bailey, & Lord, 2003) is a short questionnaire (40 items), completed by caregivers, to provide information about the child's social communication skills. The Current Form is used to assess current functioning within the past 3 months. Thus, this instrument may be useful for determining current functioning for establishing goals and evaluating the effectiveness of interventions. The instrument is most useful for children above age 4, with a developmental age of at least 2 years. Scores are provided in three social communication domains, including Reciprocal Social Interaction, Communication, and Restricted, Repetitive, and Stereotyped Patterns of Behaviors.

• Autism Social Skills Profile (ASSP; Bellini, 2006) is specifically designed to assist with goal setting and monitoring interventions, rather than diagnosing ASD. The ASSP is a 49-item questionnaire completed by a teacher or caregiver familiar with the daily functioning of the child, and is most appropriate for school ages (6–17). Domain scores include Social Reciprocity, Social Participation/Avoidance, and Detrimental Social Behavior. In addition, an overall score of social functioning is provided.

• Profile of Social Difficulty (POSD; Coucouvanis, 2005) identifies social difficulties of children with ASD in four prosocial behavior areas: Fundamental Skills, Social Initiation Skills, Social Responsiveness Skills, and Getting Along With Others. The POSD is an informal assessment that can be completed by multiple individuals who know the child (including caregivers, teachers, siblings, and even a self-report by the child). Strengths of this tool include the accumulation of information across settings by multiple informants and the opportunity for the individual with ASD to share his or her perceptions about social skills strengths and weaknesses to prioritize the social skills most valued and in need of support. Social skills lessons are available to support the development of target areas identified by the POSD.

• Assessment of Social Communication Skills for Children With Autism (Quill, Bracken, & Fair, 2001) is part of a social skills training curriculum aimed at creating instructional goals and interventions using the DO-WATCH-LISTEN-SAY curriculum (Quill, 2000). Professionals (teachers, psychologists, or other service providers) respond to four assessment checklists. Checklists can be used to create behavioral objectives in the following areas: core skills (nonverbal social interaction, imitation, and organization), social skills (play, group skills, community social skills), and communication skills (basic communication functions, socioemotional skills, and basic conversational skills).

- Social Skills Improvement System (SSIS; Gresham & Elliot, 2008), a revision of the Social Skills Rating Scale (SSRS), includes parent, teacher, and self-report forms. Although not specifically designed for children with ASD, the SSIS is a psychometrically strong and useful tool for comparing social behaviors of children and adolescents (ages 3–18) with ASD to typically developing peers. Standard scores are provided for three scales: Social Skills, Competing Behaviors, and Academic Competence. There is an English and Spanish version for parent and student forms. The *Social Skills Improvement System—Intervention Guide* (Elliot & Gresham, 2008) supports the development of intervention plans based on the results of the SSIS. The intervention plan is based on a multitiered system structured much like response to intervention used in public schools.

Identifying and Prioritizing Social Skill Goals

A comprehensive assessment of social skill functioning is likely to reveal multiple areas of deficits. Thus, parents, teachers, and the student must collaborate to prioritize which social skills goals to address first. A meta-analysis by Bellini, Peters, Benner, and Hoff (2007) revealed that few studies of social skill interventions matched specific skill deficits with intervention strategy. Furthermore, Bellini, Peters, Benner, and Hoff (2007) found few research studies considered the social validity, or social importance, of the intervention.

Participants in educational planning perceive a socially valid goal as relevant and important in addressing social skill deficits (Gresham, 1985). Overall, gaining consensus of all participants in educational planning (including teachers, parents, and the child whenever possible) improves intervention fidelity, or the valid implementation of interventions (Bellini et al., 2007). However, gaining consensus requires communication skills, an openness to understanding multiple perspectives, and the willingness to compromise.

Consider the following case example:

At Mary's individualized education plan (IEP) meeting, her teacher discusses the results of her recent social skills evaluation. Notably, Mary's assessment revealed deficits in initiating peer interactions and a tendency to withdraw from peers. Other areas of weakness included deficits in reciprocal social interactions and a tendency to perseverate on topics associated with plants and botany.

- *Teacher-generated goal:* Her teacher suggests an IEP goal to help Mary work better in cooperative groups and learn to participate more fully in class activities.
- *Parent-generated goal:* Although she would like Mary to be included in classroom activities, it is her mother's opinion that her teacher has provided an academic-focused goal that will not help her in the *real world*. Instead, her mother advocates for a goal for Mary to demonstrate turn-taking skills so she does not monopolize the conversation with her interest in plants.
- *Mary's self-generated goal:* Mary reports that she would like a friend who shares her interest in plants, but fears being teased or harassed. She reports that she wants to initiate interactions with her peers but isn't sure how to do this without experiencing failure.

All three parties recognize that Mary has a weakness with social skills. These difficulties negatively impact her ability to participate in group activities within the classroom, engage in conversation that is reciprocal and perceived as polite (follows social conventions), and develop friendships. Not every goal has to be related to academic grades or statewide testing. Sometimes the most relevant social skills goals indirectly support a child's academic functioning by reducing anxiety and providing emotional support. These are sometimes referred to as collateral skills. Table 10.4 provides tips for creating relevant social goals for children with ASD.

Table 10.4   Creating Relevant Social Goals for Children With ASD

- Choose social skill goals that are specific and have real function in the classroom and other real-life settings. Such goals are considered socially valid and contribute to an effective implementation of the chosen intervention (treatment fidelity).
- Input from *all* members of the educational team should be considered in formulating social skill goals. Often all participants in an educational

planning meeting recognize different aspects of the same underlying social skill deficit. In Mary's case, all participants in educational planning discuss an aspect of interpersonal relationship skills that need to be addressed. It is important to determine if identified concerns are due to skill acquisition deficits (i.e., Does Mary have knowledge about the skills involved in initiating a peer interaction?) or a performance deficit (i.e., Is Mary so anxious and unsure of herself that she is unable to implement the skills needed to initiate a peer interaction?).

- Consider both strengths and deficits. Mary is motivated to establish a friendship. She has identified an interest in making a friend. In addition, both Mary and her mother have identified a potential strength for Mary. Mary is knowledgeable about plants and would like to find a friend who shares her interests.

INTERVENTIONS FOR SUPPORTING SOCIAL SKILL DEVELOPMENT

Determining Evidence-Based Practices

Selecting the most appropriate intervention to address social skills deficits can be a daunting task. Research reviews not only lament the lack of empirical support for many strategies that are used in schools and clinics throughout the country (e.g., Bellini et al., 2007; Vaughn et al., 2003; Wang & Spillane, 2009), but also the lack of operational definitions and guidance for evaluating "evidence-based practice" (Odom et al., 2005; Zhang & Wheeler, 2011).

The Council for Exceptional Children (CEC) Division for Research has a taskforce working toward creating a process for defining, evaluating, and identifying *evidence-based practices*. Several papers written by the taskforce members and a manual for evaluating evidence-based practice can be found on the CEC website (www.cec.sped.org). Furthermore, the National Autism Center (2009) has written a guide for evaluating evidence-based practices of autism in the schools (2009) and a description of research support for available interventions for children with ASD. Interventions are described as established, emerging, or unestablished treatments (discussed in Chapter 8). Table 10.5 highlights factors for choosing social interventions using evidence-based practices.

First, consideration should be given to interventions with empirical support attesting to their validity (effectiveness) to address social skill deficits for children with ASD. Other considerations include the degree to which the child has

Table 10.5 Considering Evidence-Based Practices

- Federal and state legislation require that *evidence-based practices* be implemented in public school settings to address learning goals of children with special needs (i.e., No Child Left Behind Act of 2001; Individuals with Disabilities Education Improvement Act of 2004).
- Identify peer-reviewed research studies of social skill intervention in which participants are sufficiently described with a clear confirmation of a diagnosis of ASD.
- When possible, participants in the study are *randomly assigned* to conditions (i.e., treatment condition and control condition). Random assignment improves the clarity for determining whether positive outcomes are due to the intervention (treatment effects) rather than other factors (such as characteristics of the individuals in the study). However, multiple research methodologies are warranted to address different types of research questions.
- Consider the degree of *treatment fidelity,* or extent to which the treatment was implemented effectively.

From Gersten et al. (2005).

prerequisite skills, such as motivation to interact with others, attention, engagement, imitation, and play skills. When these types of prerequisite skills are lacking, an adult-directed instruction may be most effective (National Research Council, 2001). Adding child-centered strategies and peer involvement may be helpful for practicing skills and learning to generalize skills across settings (National Research Council).

A review of interventions often used to address social skill deficits for children with ASD follows. For a more detailed review of social skills interventions for children with ASD, refer to books by Bellini (2006), Simpson (2005), and Weiss and Harris (2001).

Social Skill Interventions Based on Applied Behavior Analysis

Many social skills interventions incorporate some aspects of Applied Behavior Analysis (ABA). Of all the interventions available to support children with ASD, ABA has the strongest empirical support as an effective intervention method for teaching skills to children with ASD and other developmental disorders (i.e., Eikeseth, 2009; Howard et al., 2005; Lilienfeld, 2005; National Research Council, 2001; Simpson, 2005). These interventions are often adult directed but may include peer teaching and self-monitoring as well.

Using reinforcement to reward approximations of target behaviors, ABA can shape behavior associated with social interactions, such as eye contact, verbally responding to a question, or requesting something desired. Social skill target goals are analyzed into distinct steps that comprise the more complex behaviors. A technique called chaining is used to teach specific skills that together allow a child to engage in a complex social interaction, such as ordering at a restaurant, playing a game, and inviting a peer to play. Prompting is often used to provide support to the child during learning, ensuring success. A technique called error-less learning uses prompts that are gradually faded to provide the child with a learning experience with minimal frustration. For instance, prompts may include physical help from the instructor, a model to imitate, or several items from which to choose. Prompts are gradually faded until the child can correctly perform the skill independently. An overview of ABA is provided in Chapter 7.

Discrete trial instruction (DTI), incidental teaching, and pivotal response training (PRT) are examples of teaching strategies based on principles of ABA that are frequently used to teach social skills to children with ASD. Furthermore, interventions based on ABA tend to have strong empirical support in the research literature.

• DTI. Interventions that include principles of ABA often use DTI. Learning trials are individually developed to address a particular learning goal. During a discrete learning trial, a child is presented with an instruction (such as "Say your name"). After the child responds, correct responses are rewarded and mistakes may be corrected or ignored, depending on the child's program. A reinforcement survey may be used to identify what the child finds rewarding. An example of a reinforcement survey can be found on the Able-differently website (http://www.able-differently.org/otherresources/forms_ho.html). A paired-stimulus preference assessment can be used with nonverbal students to identify preferred objects and activities from a series of paired choices (Mason, Mcgee, Farmer-Dougan, & Risely, 1989). A criticism of DTI is that learning may not generalize well across settings and contexts. Thus, a child who learns to initiate interactions in the classroom may not spontaneously use that skill on the playground.

• Incidental teaching is a type of DTI that increases the generalizability of the learned skill by teaching during daily activities with highly motivating materials (Hart & Risely, 1980). A learning environment is created that motivates the child to engage in target goals. For instance, the child's favorite snack is placed within sight but out of the child's reach. The child is prompted to initiate a request for the snack. The child is rewarded (given the snack) after making the request.

- PRT is another type of DTI and utilizes incidental teaching. However, PRT teaches responses to *multiple cues* increasing the likelihood that the learned skill with be generalized to multiple settings. PRT focuses teaching on key (or pivotal) skills that support the development of more complex skills. Pivotal areas targeted in PRT include responding to multiple cues relevant in a given context, initiation of social interactions, motivating the child to participate in social interactions, and teaching the child independence and self-monitoring (Bellini & Peters, 2011). In addition to teaching pivotal skills for social interactions, PRT often results in increased motivation for interaction (Koegel, O'Dell, & Koegel, 1987).

Strategies That Build on Visual Strengths and Address Need for Predictability

All children have individual interests, strengths, and weaknesses. However, there are certain patterns of strengths and weaknesses more common among the population of individuals with ASD. Notably, individuals with ASD often experience difficulty predicting future events, particularly those involving social interactions. As noted earlier, this difficulty may be associated with deficits in perspective taking and understanding the *hidden* clues in social interactions. Consequently, individuals with ASD often experience anxiety surrounding new experiences, which may translate to avoidance, refusal to participate in an activity, or challenging behaviors.

Social skill interventions that prepare the child for what to expect in a new situation can ameliorate anxiety associated with facing a novel experience. In addition, many individuals with ASD appear to learn best with visual stimuli. The following are examples of interventions that combine a visual presentation (such as videos, pictures, written text) with explicit information about social interactions helpful in teaching social skills.

Story-based interventions

Social stories provide a brief story with specific information about a particular social experience using text, pictures, or both. The complexity of the social story varies depending on the needs of the child. For instance, a story-based intervention about lunchtime may include a series of photographs representing lining up for lunch, walking to the cafeteria, selecting a meal choice, sitting at the table to eat lunch, and lining up to return to the classroom. The story may include single words, sentences, or paragraphs to explain each event.

Rather than photographs, the social story may include more abstract cartoon pictures depicting events, or only text. Often social stories are presented in a booklet designed specifically for an individual child based on their daily routines, needs, and concerns. The main components of a social story, as suggested by Gray (2004) are described in Table 10.6.

Table 10.6 Components of a Social Story

- **Description of the social setting,** such as where it is occurring and what people are doing. This helps create sequential steps for the story. *The cafeteria is in the middle of the school by the front door. This is where I eat lunch at school.*
- **Perspective**—How others feel and respond in the story. *Everyone in the class is hungry and wants to eat lunch. We would all like to be first in line.*
- **Directive information**—Explains appropriate behavior in a given situation. Most of the story sentences should be directive (ratio of one directive sentence for every two to five affirmative, descriptive, or perspective sentence). *I walk to the door when the teacher says to line up for lunch. I walk to lunch with my class in a line.*
- **Affirmative statement** to express a value or opinion shared by the culture or community in which the story takes place. *It is good to speak in quiet voice in the lunchroom.*

Although social stories are widely used in public school settings (Test, Richter, Knight, & Spooner, 2011), research provides mixed reviews for their effectiveness in teaching social skills. Social stories are considered a *promising practice* as opposed to an *established-evidence best practice* (Reynhout & Carter, 2006; Test et al., 2011). These findings are likely due in part to the varied ways in which social stories are created and implemented (Sansoti, Powell-Smith, & Kinciad, 2004). In a meta-analysis of studies of stories, Kokina and Kern (2010) found that social stories may be more useful in helping students reduce inappropriate social behaviors in comparison to teaching them prosocial behaviors. In addition, this meta-analysis revealed that social stories were most effective in teaching single behaviors and when the stories were read just prior to engaging in the target situation.

Cartooning is another visual-based story intervention to help enhance the understanding of social expectation and protocol embedded in social interactions. *Comic strip conversations* (Gray, 1994) use cartooning to teach social skills to children with ASD. This technique may appeal to older children and teens who enjoy comics and graphic novels, popular with teens and young adults.

Another example of cartooning to teach social skills is the *Bubble Dialogue program*. This intervention can be implemented on the computer to assist with role-taking and interpersonal understanding (Jones & Prince, 2001; Rajendran & Mitchell, 2000). The use of computer technology may increase the appeal for some children. A cartoon story maker can be downloaded for free at http://cartoon-story-maker.software.informer.com.

- Video modeling is an intervention using video of a social behavior to model an appropriate social skill. A child imitates a behavior from a video segment demonstrating a particular skill such as initiating social interactions, joining a playgroup, or any skill that has been identified as an area of deficit. This strategy has been receiving increasing attention as an effective practice for teaching a range of social skills to children with ASD. There is a growing body of research demonstrating the effectiveness of video modeling techniques for addressing social skill deficits for children with ASD (e.g., Bellini, Akullian, & Hopf, 2007; Buggey, Hoomes, Sherberger, & Williams, 2011; Nikopoulos & Keenan, 2004; Paterson & Arco, 2007).

Video Self-Modeling (VSM) is a type of video modeling in which the child, the target of the intervention, is filmed exhibiting the prosocial behavior. The video may be edited to demonstrate the child engaging in a sequence of behaviors that clearly demonstrate the social skill goal. Both video modeling and VSM provide explicit demonstrations of target behaviors by playing to the visual learning strength held by many children with ASD. The added advantage of VSM is that the child watches himself or herself performing the desired behavior. Thus, social skill instruction is presented in a more concrete manner using VSM. Bellini and Peters (2008) report that both video modeling and VSM promote skill acquisition that generalizes across social settings and is maintained over time.

Video modeling and VSM are increasingly cost-effective interventions for creating individualized social skill interventions in a public school setting. Buggey and colleagues (2011) describe how technology available in most public schools can be used to create 3-minutes videos in less than 30 minutes using iMovie® and iMovie HD ®. Advantages of video modeling and VSM are outlined in Table 10.7.

Table 10.7 Advantages of Video Modeling and VSM

- *Intervention can be individualized* to address a child's specific social skill goal.
- Intervention takes place in a *naturalistic environment*, increasing the chance that skills will generalize to real life.
- Many children with ASD seem to enjoy watching videos and learning from visually presented stimuli. Furthermore, *children with limited receptive language skills will also benefit* from these interventions.
- *Treatment fidelity is likely to be strong* when using this intervention due to the consistency (watching the same model), and ease of implementation (turning on the DVD).
- Can be *combined with behavior analysis to provide strong data analysis for assessing the effectiveness of the intervention.* Nikopoulos and Keenan (2006) provide an excellent guide for combining behavior analysis with video modeling to teach social skills to children with ASD.

Relationship- and Developmental-Based Interventions

There are different theoretical perspectives that drive interventions for children with ASD. This group of interventions is based on a developmental- and relationship-oriented understanding of learning social skills. A developmental perspective considers an unfolding sequence of skills associated with social functioning. A relationship-oriented perspective focuses on connecting the child with others (particularly caregivers) and developing reciprocal interactions leading to intimacy.

The following interventions incorporate relationship and developmental perspectives that sometimes integrate behavioral strategies for teaching social skills. However, these types of interventions currently lack the empirical support of many of the strategies discussed earlier (Simpson, 2005; Zane, David, & Rosswurm, 2008).

- Developmental, Individual-Difference, Relationship-Based Model (Floor Time) is a play-based intervention in which the caregiver interacts with the child to develop trust, intimacy, and engage in reciprocal interaction. Caregivers learn to carefully observe the child and match their emotions and play as a means of opening a circle of communication (Greenspan, Wieder, & Simons, 1998). Within the context of a warm and sensitive caregiving relationship, the caregiver engages the child by initially following the child's lead, and later extending play to promote the development of more advanced skills. Although much has been written about floor time, there is little empirical research published in peer-reviewed journals (Simpson, 2005).

• Relationship Development Intervention (RDI) is described as a "parent-based, cognitive-developmental approach, in which primary caregivers are trained to provide daily opportunities for successful functioning in increasingly challenging dynamic systems" (Gustein et al., 2007, p. 397). Caregivers receive intensive training workshops followed by regular (often weekly) planning and progress meetings (Gustein et al.). RDI focuses on social skill deficits that are considered critical for social competence such as enjoyment of social interactions, social reciprocity, and repairing conflicts (Gustein & Sheely, 2002).

Currently there exists limited peer-reviewed empirical research demonstrating the effectiveness of RDI. Furthermore, Zane and colleagues (2008) note that core deficits described by RDI are at odds with the diagnostic criteria outlined in the *DSM-IV-TR*.

• SCERTS (Social Communication/Emotional Regulation/Transactional Supports) is described as a family-centered educational approach that systematically identifies the child's needs, determines supports that are meaningful and purposeful, and monitors progress over time (Prizant, Wetherby, Rubin, Laurent, & Rydell, 2006).

Although SCERTS incorporates a variety of different strategies (e.g., ABA, PECS, social stories), the emphasis is on developing spontaneous and functional social communication, helping the child develop self-regulation to manage emotions, and facilitating transactional support to coordinate efforts of caregivers and others supporting the child with ASD. The emphasis on supports for families, including emotional support, information, and skills to support their child (Prizant, Wetherby, Rubin, & Laurent, 2003), is an attractive feature of this model. However, there is a notable lack of empirical support for this intervention model. Additional information about SCERTS is presented in Chapter 9.

Service dogs

Within the autism autobiographical literature (i.e., Temple Grandin) there is anecdotal testimony reporting benefits of individuals with ASD spending time with animals. There is limited empirical support suggesting that individuals with ASD and other disabilities benefit from learning to care for animals, particularly pets (Law & Scott, 1995). Although pet therapy is best described as having limited supporting evidence for practice (Simpson, 2005), individuals with ASD may experience pleasure in having a relationship with a pet and learning to care for their pet. In addition, a pet dog may provide social opportunities by attracting people to ask questions or comment about the dog, and dogs do not require well-developed social or communication skills to form bonds with a human (Grandin, Fine, & Bowers, 2010). Prothmann and colleagues (2009) suggest that children with ASD may benefit from a service dog and/or pet because dogs make their behavioral intentions more easily understood than humans. Thus, they offer social interactions that are predictable and easy to interpret. Dogs may also provide sensory advantages, enjoyed by all children who spend time petting and playing with their pets. "Chapter Reflection; Pet Therapy: Will and Garland" tells a story of a boy with ASD who benefits in many ways from the relationship with his dog.

CHAPTER REFLECTION: Pet Therapy: Will and Garland

Will and Garland are best friends. This is an especially important relationship for Will, because he has difficulty making friends. Garland is a very special friend and dog. He was in a Canine Assistant program but failed the training because he suffers from carsickness. Will's mom decided rather than wait for years to receive a Canine Assistant trained to support a child with ASD, she would take one of the "dropouts." Garland provides Will with companionship and attracts children who are interested in interacting with and learning about Garland. Garland helps Will feel calmer in public settings by staying close to him. Will has gained confidence as he mastered dog-training skills. Will's mother describes their relationship as "a wonderful, priceless gift."

From an interview with Heather Kelly Hughes, Will's mother.

Increasing Social Opportunities

- Peer-mediated interventions (PMI) involve identifying and training peers as mentors to initiate and respond to their peers with ASD (Bellini, 2006). Thus, children with ASD experience real-life experience with peer interactions, often in a natural setting (such as during lunch or recess). They also receive feedback about their social skill and have opportunities to model age-appropriate social

Author.

Will and Garland are the best of friends. For more information about autism service dogs, visit the link for Autism Service Dogs of America at http://autismservicedogsof america.com.

behavior from *experts* of their social culture. Bellini suggests that PMI are most successful when implemented in a structured setting (like an organized play group or social skill group) as well as within a natural setting. Furthermore, PMI are most effective when the child is motivated to interact with peers but lacks necessary social skills for initiating and sustaining peer interactions.

During peer mediation, teachers monitor and facilitate the intervention rather than provide social engagement, providing greater opportunities for the student to interact with same-age peers (Odom & Strain, 1984). PMI may emphasize peer modeling, peers initiating social interactions, peer-monitoring social skills, enhancing peer networking skills, peers tutoring, or group contingencies so that all members of the group must learn to work together for success (Utley, Mortweet, & Greenwood, 1997). Table 10.9 presents guidelines for selecting a peer mentor for PMI.

Table 10.9   Guidelines for Selecting a Peer Mentor for PMI

1. Select only socially competent peers.
2. Select peers who are approximately the same age or grade as the child with ASD.
3. Make sure peer mentors have a neutral or positive history with child with ASD.
4. Choose peers who exhibit age-appropriate play.
5. Select socially responsive peers.
6. Select peers who are likely to follow adult instructions.
7. Ensure peers are willing to participate.

Source: Bellini, S. 2006. Building Social Relationship: A Systematic Approach to Teaching Social Interaction Skills to Children and Adolescents with Autism Spectrum Disorder and Other Social Difficulties. Shawnee Mission, KA: Autism Asperger Publishing Co.

A meta-analysis of 45 peer-mediated interventions for young children with ASD (ages 0–8) indicated that PMI was a highly effective social skills intervention for young children with ASD (Zhang & Wheeler, 2011). Older peers were especially effective models for boys. Other factors associated with the best outcomes were the use of peer modeling, implementation in the home, and collaboration with family, school, and peers. Furthermore, the authors noted that few girls were included in the studies evaluated and girls needed to be intentionally included in future intervention research.

- Circle of Friends is an example of a PMI. Emerging research suggests that Circle of Friends is a promising intervention for children with ASD to build skills such as increasing social initiation, reducing anxiety during social interactions, and increasing social reciprocity (Kalyva & Avramidis, 2005). A circle of friends includes six to eight peer volunteers trained to empathize and understand the needs of the target child with ASD. The peer mentors meet regularly with the adult facilitator to discuss goals and concerns. At least weekly, the circle meets with the target child. This may take place during lunch, class time, or a special group meeting after or before school.

Both the child with ASD and the peers can benefit from PMI. Peers may experience increased levels of empathy and understanding of ASD and feel empowered to help others (Whitaker, Barratt, Joy, Potter, & Thomas, 1998). An interesting benefit of PMI, reported by Owen-DeSchryver, Carr, Cale, and Blakeley-Smith (2011), was the increased social initiation and interest of untrained peers in their classmates with ASD after observing the peer mentors.

TEACHING TIPS

- Build a classroom community that provides opportunities to get to know each other, value the skills and ideas each student brings to the class, and teaches respect for individual differences and styles of interaction. In her book *you're Going to Love This Kid!*, Paula Kluth (2003) discusses strategies for creating such a classroom community through cooperative learning activities, service learning, and social-justice projects that encourage and teach sharing and mutual respect.

- Identify several students in your class who demonstrate good social skills and sensitivity/kindness toward others. Invite them to join a Circle of Friends group. Ask the school counselor or school social worker if they might work with you to create a weekly (or more frequent) opportunity for these students to meet with the children in your class with ASD to engage in social activities, such as playing a game or enjoying a special pizza lunch. Make sure that a teacher or other professional spends some time with the student volunteers to help them understand ASD, answer questions as they arise, and process the experience.

• Prepare students with ASD for new social opportunities to prevent anxiety and increase the chances they will initiate and reciprocate social interactions. For instance, if there is to be a class party, spend some time preparing the child with ASD several days in advance. For instance, the party could be included on their class schedule. In addition, one or more social stories might be created to help students predict the sequence of activities and how they might respond (i.e., first we will finish lunch, then begin a special holiday craft activity, after putting away the materials we will have party snacks such as chips and cupcakes. If the party gets too loud, I can ask my teacher if I could visit the library).

SUMMARY

Social-emotional reciprocity, nonverbal communication, and maintaining peer relationships are deficits for individuals with ASD across the spectrum. These deficits may be in skill acquisition or performance. Deficits in play skills, along with difficulty with perspective taking and pragmatic language, contribute to difficulty establishing and maintaining peer relationships. Assessment of social functioning is the first step to identifying target goals. Interventions should be selected based on identified goals and consideration of evidence-based practice. Many social skill interventions incorporate ABA. Story-based interventions are promising interventions frequently used in the school setting, but lack the degree of empirical support found for ABA. Video modeling and VSM are gaining attention for their effectiveness and empirical support in teaching a range of social skills to children with ASD. RDI are also popular and have many appealing features, yet lack the empirical support of other interventions described. Peer-mediated interventions are promising strategies for supporting children and adolescents with social skills within their school and community settings.

DISCUSSION AND REFLECTION QUESTIONS

1. Describe the core deficits of socialization in ASD.

2. How are the stages of play development related to the development of friendships?

3. Describe the social skills deficits associated with establishing peer relationships often experienced by children with ASD.

4. Henry is a 9-year-old boy with ASD. He has good cognitive skills and attends a third-grade class with his same-age peers. However, Henry is withdrawn and appears

lonely. His mother is concerned he is feeling depressed due to lack of friends. How might you go about evaluating Henry's social skills functioning in order to plan an intervention strategy?

5. Consider the case study of Mary and her IEP goals. Which interventions might be most effective in meeting the IEP goals you identified?

6. Describe several different interventions that might be used to help build skills associated with initiating peer interaction in a social group at school.

RECOMMENDED FURTHER READINGS AND INTERNET SOURCES

Further Readings

Bellini, S. (2006). *Building social relationships: A systematic approach to teaching social interaction skills to children and adolescents with autism spectrum disorders and other social difficulties.* Shawnee Mission, KS: Autism Asperger Publishing.

Howlin, P., Baron-Cohen, S., & Hadwin, J. (1999). *Teaching children with autism to mind-read: A practical guide.* Chichester, UK: John Wiley, & Sons.

Weiss, M. J., & Harris, S. L. (2001). *Reaching out, joining in: Teaching social skills to young children with autism.* Bethesda, MD: Woodbine House.

Internet Sources

Informal assessments and handouts for identifying strengths and building resiliency http://www.able-differently.org/otherresources/forms_ho.html#stories

Writing Social Stories http://www.thegraycenter.org/social-stories/how-to-write-social-stories

Technology and Social Skills http://www.watchmelearn.com/index.shtml http://www.social

skillbuilder.com http://www.modelmekids.com http://www.autismkey.com/top-ipad-apps-for-children-with-autism

Promoting Friendships (Circle of Friends program) http://www.circleoffriendsct.org

Video Self-Modeling http://www.alaskachd.org/products/video_futures/index.html

Autism Service Dogs http://www.4pawsforability.org

REFERENCES

American Psychiatric Association. (2000). *Diagnostic and statistical manual of mental disorders* (4th ed., Text Rev.). Washington, DC: Author.

American Psychiatric Association. (2011). *American Psychiatric Association DSM-5*

development. Retrieved from http://www.dsm5.org/ProposedRevisions/Pages/proposedrevision.aspx?rid=94.

Atwood, T. (1998). *Asperger's syndrome: A guide for parents and professionals.* Philadelphia, PA: Kingsley.

Baron-Cohen, S. (1995). *Mindblindness: An essay on autism and theory of mind*. Cambridge, MA: MIT Press.

Bauminger, N., & Kasari, C. (2001). Loneliness and friendship in high-functioning children with autism. *Child Development, 71*, 447–456.

Bauminger, N., Solomon, M., Aviezer, A., Heung, K., Brown, J., & Rogers, S. J. (2008). Children with autism and their friends: A multidimensional study of friendship in high-functioning autism spectrum disorder. *Journal of Abnormal Child Psychology, 36*, 135–150.

Bauminger, N., Solomon, M., Aviezer, A., Heung, K., Gazit, L., Brown, J., & Rogers, S. (2008). Friendship in high-functioning children with autism spectrum disorder: Mixed and non-mixed dyads. *Journal of Autism and Developmental Disorders, 38*, 1211–1229.

Bellini, S. (2006). *Building social relationships: A systematic approach to teaching social interaction skills to children and adolescents with autism spectrum disorder and other social difficulties*. Shawnee Mission, KS: Autism Asperger Publishing.

Bellini, S., Akullian, J., & Hopf, A. (2007). Increasing social engagement in young children with autism spectrum disorders using video self-modeling. *School Psychology Review, 36*, 80–90.

Bellini, S., Peters, J. K., Benner, L., & Hoff, A. (2007). A meta-analysis of school-based social skills interventions for children with autism spectrum disorders. *Remedial and Special Education, 28*, 153–162.

Bellini, S., & Peters, J. K. (2008). Social skills training for youth with autism spectrum disorders. *Child and Adolescent Psychiatric Clinics of North America, 17*, 857–873.

Berk, L. E. (2010). *Exploring lifespan development* (2nd ed.). Boston, MA: Allyn & Bacon.

Buggey, T., Hoomes, G., Sherberger, M. E., & Williams, S. (2011). Facilitating social initiations of preschoolers with autism spectrum disorders using video self-modeling. *Focus on Autism and Other Developmental Disabilities, 26*, 2–36.

Charman, T. (1997). The relationship between joint attention and pretend play in autism. *Development and Psychopathology, 9*, 1–16.

Charman, T. (2003). Why is joint attention a pivotal skill in autism? *Philosophical Transaction of the Royal Society London, 358*, 315–324.

Christensen, L., Hutman, T., Rozga, A., Young, G. S., Ozonoff, S., Rogers, S. J., . . . Sigman, M. (2010). Play and developmental outcomes in infant siblings of children with autism. *Journal of Autism and Developmental Disorders, 40*, 946–957.

Coucouvanis, J. (2005). *Super skills. A social skills group program for children with Asperger syndrome, high functioning autism, and related challenges*. Shawnee, KS: Autism Asperger Company.

Dawson, G., & Adams, A. (1984). Imitation and social responsiveness in autistic children. *Journal of Abnormal Child Psychology, 12*, 209–225.

Dawson, G., Toth, K., Abbot, R., Osterling, J., Munson, J., Estes, A., & Liaw, J. (2004). Early social attention impairments in autism: Social orienting, joint attention, and attention to distress. *Developmental Psychology, 40*, 271–283.

Dunn, J. (2004). *Children's friendships. The beginnings of intimacy*. Malden, MA: Blackwell.

Durand, V. M. (2005). Past, present, and emerging directions in education. In D. Zager (Ed.), *Autism spectrum disorders: Identification, education, and treatment* (3rd ed.). Mahwah, NJ: Lawrence Erlbaum Associates.

Eikeseth, S. (2009). Outcome of comprehensive psycho-educational interventions for young children with autism. *Research in Developmental Disabilities, 30*, 158–178.

Elliot, S. N., & Gresham, F. M. (2008). *Social skills improvement system-intervention guide*. Bloomington, MN: Pearson Assessments.

Flavel, J. H., Flavel, E. R., & Green, F. L. (2001). Development of children's understanding of connections between thinking and feeling. *Psychological Science, 12*, 430–432.

Frost, J. L., Wortham, S. C., & Reifel, S. (2005). *Play and children* (2nd ed.). Upper Saddle River, NJ: Pearson.

Gersten, R., Fuchs, L., Compton, D., Coyne, M., Greenwood, C., & Innocenti, M. (2005). Quality indicators for group experimental and quasi-experimental research in special education. *Exceptional Children, 71,* 149–164.

Grandin, T., Fine, A. H., & Bowers, C. M. (2010). The use of therapy animals with individuals with autism spectrum disorders. (3rd ed.). In H. F. Aubrey (Ed.), *Handbook on animal assisted therapy: Theoretical foundations and guidelines for practice* (pp. 247–264). London, UK: Academic Press.

Gray, C. (1994). *Comic strip conversations: Colorful, illustrated interactions with students with autism and related disorders.* Jenison, MI: Jenison Public Schools.

Gray, C. (2004). Social Stories ™ 10.0: The new defining criteria and guidelines. *Jenison Autism Journal, 15,* 2–21.

Greenspan, S. I., Wieder, S., & Simons, R. (1998). *The child with special needs: Encouraging intellectual and emotional growth.* Reading, MA: Addison Wesley.

Gresham, F. M., & Elliot, S. N. (2008). *Social skills improvement rating scales.* Bloomington, MN: Pearson Assessments.

Gresham, F. M. (1985). Strategies for enhancing the social outcomes of mainstreaming: A necessary ingredient for success. In C. J. Meisel (Ed.), *Mainstreaming handicapped children: Outcomes, controversies, and new directions.* Hillsdale, NJ: Erlbaum.

Gutstein, S. E., & Shelly, R. K. (2002). *Relationship development intervention with young children: Social and emotional development activities for Asperger syndrome, autism, and PDD and NLD.* London, UK: Jessica Kingsley.

Gutstein, S. E., Burgess, A. F., & Montfort, K. (2007). Evaluation of the relationship development intervention program. *Autism, 11,* 397–411.

Hart, B., & Risley, T. R. (1980). In vivo language intervention: Unanticipated general effects. *Journal of Applied Behavior Analysis, 13,* 407–432.

Hops, H. (1983). Children's social competence and skill: Current research practices and future directions. *Behavior Therapy, 14,* 3–18.

Howard, J. S., Sparkman, C. R., Cohen, H. G., Green, G., & Stanislaw, H. (2005). A comparison of intensive behavior analytic and eclectic treatments for young children with autism. *Research in Developmental Disabilities, 26,* 359–383.

Iarocci, G., Yager, J., & Elfers, T. (2007). What gene-environment interactions can tell us about social competence in typical and atypical populations. *Brain and Cognition, 65,* 112–127.

Individuals with Disabilities Education Improvement Act of 2004, Pub. L. No. 108-446. (2004). Retrieved from http://idea.ed.gov/explore/view/p/%2Croot%2Cstatute%2C.

Jones, A., & Price, E. (2001). Bubble dialogue: Using a computer application to investigate social information processing in children with emotional and behavioural difficulties. In: I. Hutchby & J. Moran-Ellis (Eds.), *Children, technology and culture: The impacts of technologies in children's everyday lives: The future of childhood* (pp. 133–150). London, UK: Falmer Press.

Kahn, P. H., & Turiel, E. (1988). Children's conceptions of trust in the context of social expectations. *Merill-Palmer Quarterly, 34,* 403–419.

Kalyva, E., & Avramidis, E. (2005). Improving communication between children with autism and their peers through the 'circle of friends': A small-scale intervention study. *Journal of Applied Research in Intellectual Disabilities, 18,* 253–261.

Klin, A., Jones, W., Schultz, R., Volkmar, F., & Cohen, D. (2002). Visual fixation patterns during viewing of naturalistic social situations as predictors of social competence in individuals with autism. *Archives of General Psychiatry, 59,* 809–816.

Kluth, P. (2003). *"You're going to love this kid!" Teaching students with autism in the inclusive classroom.* Baltimore, MD: Paul H. Brookes.

Koegel, R. L., O'Dell, M. C., & Koegel, L. K. (1987). A natural language teaching paradigm for nonverbal autistic children. *Journal of Autism and Developmental Disorders, 17,* 187–200.

Kokina, A., & Kern, L. (2010). Social story interventions for students with autism spectrum disorders: A meta-analysis. *Journal of Autism and Developmental Disorders, 40,* 812–826.

Lasgaard, M., Nielsen A., Eriksen, M. E., & Goossens, L. (2010). Loneliness and social support in adolescent boys with autism spectrum disorders. *Journal of Autism and Developmental Disorders, 40,* 218–226.

Lavie, T., & Sturmey, P. (2002). Training staff to conduct a paired-stimulus preference assessment. *Journal of Applied Behavior Analysis, 35,* 209–211.

Law, S., & Scott, S. (1995). Pet care: A vehicle for learning. *Focus on Autistic Behavior, 10,* 17–18.

Lilienfeld, S. O. (2005). Scientifically unsupported and supported interventions for childhood psychopathology: A summary. *Pediatrics, 115,* 761–764.

Lord, C., Rutter, M., DiLavore, P., & Risi, S. (2001). *Autism Diagnostic Observation Schedule (ADOS).* Los Angeles, CA: Western Psychological Services.

Mason, S. A., Mcgee, G. G., Farmer-Dougan, V., & Risely, T. R. (1989). A practical strategy for reinforcer assessment. *Journal of Applied Behavior Analysis, 22,* 171–179.

Mayeux, L., & Cillissen, A. (2003). Development of social problem solving in early childhood: Stability, change, and associations with social competence. *Journal of Genetic Psychology, 164,* 153–173.

Merin, N., Young, G. S., Ozonoff, S., & Rogers, S. J. (2007). Visual fixation patterns during reciprocal social interaction distinguish a subgroup of 6-month-old infants at-risk for autism from comparison infants. *Journal of Autism and Developmental Disorders, 37,* 108–121.

National Autism Center. (2009). *Evidence-based practice and autism in the schools: A guide to providing appropriate interventions to students with autism spectrum disorders.* Randolph, MA: Author.

National Research Council. (2001). *Educating children with autism.* Committee on Educational Interventions for Children with Autism, Division of Behavioral and Social Sciences and Education. Washington, DC: National Academy Press.

Nikopoulos, C. K., & Keenan, M. (2004). Effects of video modeling on social initiations by children with autism. *Journal of Applied Behavior Analysis, 37,* 93–96.

Nikopoulos, C. K., & Keenan, M. (2006). *Video modeling and behaviour analysis: A guide for teaching social skills to children with autism.* London, UK: Jessica Kingsley Publishers.

No Child Left Behind Act of 2001, 20 U.S.C. § 6319 (2008).

Odom, S. L., & Strain, R. S. (1984). Peer-mediated approaches to promoting children's social interaction: A review. *American Journal of Orthopsychiatry, 54,* 544–557.

Odom, S. L., Brantlinger, E., Gersten, R., Horner, R. H., Thompson, B., & Harris, K. R. (2005). Research in special education: Scientific methods and evidence-based practices. *Exceptional Children, 71,* 137–148.

Owen-DeSchryver, J. S., Carr, E. G., Cale, S. I., & Blakeley-Smith, A. (2008). Promoting social interactions between students with autism spectrum disorders and their peers in inclusive school settings. *Focus on Autism and Other Developmental Disabilities, 23,* 15–28.

Parten, M. (1932). Social participation among preschool children. *Journal of Abnormal and Social Psychology, 27,* 243–269.

Paterson, C. R., & Arco, L. (2007). Using video modeling for generalizing toy play in children with autism. *Behavior Modification, 31,* 660–681.

Pierce, K., & Schreibman, L. (1995). Increasing complex social behavior in children with autism: Effects of peer-implemented pivotal response training. *Journal of Applied Behavior Analysis, 28,* 285–295.

Prizant, B. M, Wetherby, A., Rubin, E., & Laurent, A. C. (2003). The SCERTS model: A transactional, family-centered approach to enhancing communication and socio-emotional abilities of children with autism spectrum disorder. *Infants and Young Children, 16*, 296–316.

Prizant, B., Wetherby, A., Rubin, E., Laurent, A., & Rydell, P. (2006). *The SCERTS model: A comprehensive educational approach for children with autism spectrum disorders.* Baltimore, MD: Paul H. Brookes.

Prothmann, A., Ettrich, C., & Prothmann, S. (2009). Preference for and responsiveness to people, dogs, and objects in children with autism. *Anthrozoös, 22*, 161–173.

Quill, K. A. (2000). *Do-Watch-Listen-Say: Social and communication intervention for children with autism.* Baltimore, MA: Paul H. Brookes.

Quill, K. A., Bracken, K. N., & Fair, M. E. (2001). *Do-Watch-Listen-Say: Assessment of social communication skills for children with autism.* Baltimore, MD: Paul H. Brookes.

Rajendran, G., & Mitchell, P. (2000). Computer mediated interaction in Asperger's syndrome: The Bubble Dialogue program. *Computers & Education, 35*,189–207.

Reynhout, G., & Carter, N. (2006). Social stories for children with disabilities. *Journal of Autism and Developmental Disorders, 36*, 445–469.

Rice, C. (2009, October). *Autism Diagnostic Observation Schedule (ADOS).* Presentation at the ADOS Clinical Administration Workshop, Atlanta, GA.

Robbins, D. L., Fein, D., Barton, M. L., & Green, J. A. (2001). The Modified Checklist for Autism in Toddlers: An initial study investigating the early detection of autism and pervasive developmental disorders. *Journal of Autism and Developmental Disorders, 31*, 131–144.

Roeyers, H. (1995). A peer-mediated proximity intervention to facilitate the social interactions of children with a pervasive developmental disorder. *British Journal of Special Education, 22*, 161–164.

Rutter, M., Bailey, A., & Lord, C. (2003). *The Social Communication Questionnaire manual.* Los Angeles, CA: Western Psychological Services.

Rutter, M., Le Couteur, A., & Lord, C., (2003). *Autism Diagnostic Interview-Revised (ADI-R).* Los Angeles, CA: Western Psychological Services.

Rutter, M., Le Couteur, A., & Lord, C. (2008). *Autism Diagnostic Interview-Revised. WPS edition manual.* Los Angeles, CA: Western Psychological Services.

Sansosti, F. J., Powell-Smith, K. A., & Kinciad, D. (2004). A research synthesis of social stories intervention for children with autism spectrum disorders. *Focus on Autism and Other Developmental Disabilities, 19*, 194–204.

Santrock, J. W. (2008). *Children* (10th ed.). New York, NY: McGraw-Hill Higher Education.

Sattler, J. M., & Hogge, R. D. (2006). *Assessment of children: Behavioral, social, and clinical foundations* (5th ed.). Le Mesa, CA: Jerome M. Sattler Publisher.

Scourfield, J., Martin, N., Lewis, G., & McGuffin, P. (1999). Heritability of social cognitive skills in children and adolescents. *British Journal of Psychiatry, 175*, 559–564.

Selman, R. L. (1975). Level of social perspective taking and the development of empathy in children: speculations from a social-cognitive viewpoint. *Journal of Moral Education, 5*, 35–43.

Simpson, R. L. (2005). *Autism spectrum disorders: Interventions and treatments for children and youth.* Thousand Oaks, CA: Corwin.

Terpstra, J. E., Higgins, K., & Pierce, T. (2002). Can I play? Classroom-based interventions for teaching play skills to children with autism. *Focus on Autism & Other Developmental Disabilities, 17*, 119–127.

Test, D.W., Richter, S., Knight, V., & Spooner, F. (2011). A comprehensive review and meta-analysis of the social stories literature. *Focus on Autism and Other Developmental Disabilities, 26*, 49–62.

Utley, C. A., Mortweet, S. L., & Greenwood, C. R. (1997). Peer mediated instruction and interventions. *Focus on Exceptional Children, 29*, 1–23.

Vaughn, S., Kim, A. H., Sloan, C. V. M., Hughes, M. T., Elbaum, B., & Sridhar, D. (2003). Social skills interventions for young children with disabilities. *Remedial and Special Education, 24*, 2–15.

Vickerstaff, S., Heriot, S., Wong, M., Lopes, A., & Dossetor, D. (2007). Intellectual ability, self-perceived social competence, and depressive symptomatology in children with high-functioning autistic spectrum disorders. *Journal of Autism and Developmental Disorders, 37*, 1647–1664.

Wang, P., & Spillane, A. (2009). Evidence-based social skills interventions for children with autism: A meta-analysis. *Education and Training in Developmental Disabilities, 44*, 318–342.

Weiss, M. J., & Harris, S. L. (2001). *Topics in autism: Reaching out, joining in. teaching social skills to young children with autism.* Bethesda, MD: Woodbine House.

Whitaker, P., Barratt, P., Joy, J, Potter, M., & Thomas, G. (1998). Children with autism and peer group support: Using 'circle of friends.' *British Journal of Special Education, 25*, 60–64.

Wolfberg, P. J., & Schuler, A. L. (1993). Integrated playgroups: A model for promoting the social and cognitive dimensions of play in children with autism. *Journal of Autism and Developmental Disorders, 23*, 467–489.

Zhang, J., & Wheeler, J. J. (2011). A meta-analysis of peer-mediated interventions for young children with autism spectrum disorders. *Education and Training in Autism and Developmental Disabilities, 46*, 62–77.

CHAPTER 11

TRANSITIONING TO ADULTHOOD: PROMOTING INDEPENDENCE AND SELF-DETERMINATION

In this chapter, you will learn about:

- ASD and adulthood.
- Self-determination and human rights.
- Transitioning from high school: the transition plan.
- Adults with ASD and residential choices.
- Employment.
- Postsecondary education.
- Leisure, recreation, and integration into the community.

ASD AND ADULTHOOD

ASD is a lifelong developmental disorder with core deficits in language, socialization, and behaviors existing across the life span (Eaves & Ho, 2008; Hendricks & Wehman, 2009; Interagency Autism Coordinating Committee, 2011). Prevalence studies estimate that approximately 1% of children in the United States have ASD, which translates to approximately 730,000 individuals 21 years of age or younger (Centers for Disease Control and Prevention, 2009; Kogan et al., 2009). Although there are no current prevalence studies for adults with ASD (Autism Society of America, 2007), undoubtedly, there will be a very large number of adults with ASD leaving the public schools and accessing community supports. For instance, it is estimated that more than 380,000 people will need adult services by the year 2023 (Davis, 2009). Gerhardt and Lainer (2011) describe the upcoming needs of adolescents and adults with ASD as a "looming crisis of unprecedented magnitude" (p. 37).

Transition planning needs to occur as early as possible.

There is a growing body of research addressing early intervention and the needs of children with ASD. Unfortunately, far less research addresses the life course and best practice for supporting individuals with ASD during adulthood (Eaves & Ho, 2008; Interagency Autism Coordinating Committee, 2011). ASD is a lifelong disorder and needs are likely to change throughout the life span. The goals of least restrictive environment and inclusion are integral to a high quality of life throughout the life span. Given that ASD is a heterogeneous disorder, individuals with ASD have unique needs and may require a wide range of supports throughout their lives (Hendricks & Wehman, 2009).

Intentional and well-coordinated planning and implementation of plans is critical for effective transitioning from educational to community supports. In addition, support for realizing self-determination and the ability to express choice should be part of educational planning. Successful transitioning to adulthood depends upon identifying goals and providing foundational skills to realize those goals for individuals at all ability levels.

SELF-DETERMINATION

Self-Determination Recognized as a Fundamental Human Right

The ability to make choices about one's life is considered a fundamental human right and is formally recognized on a federal and international level. Rights of self-determination for citizens of the United States are documented within the United States Constitution. Furthermore, Public Law 94-142 (IDEA), Section 504 of the Rehabilitation Act, and the Americans with Disabilities Act are examples of federal laws that specifically protect such rights of people with disabilities in the United States (Baker & Tabor, 2006). In 1971, the United Nations adopted the "Declaration of the Rights of Mentally Retarded Persons," affirming that people with intellectual disabilities have the same rights as other people (United Nations General Assembly, 1971).

Self-determination is more than deciding what food to eat or clothes to wear. Rather, it refers to making *meaningful* decisions about your life based on an understanding of yourself and real-world experiences (Wehmeyer & Kelcher, 1996), and without undue influences or interferences (Wehmeyer, 1996). Examples of expressions of self-determination are presented in Table 11.1.

Table 11.1 Examples of Expressing Self-Determination

- Choosing where you would like to live as an adult.
- Choosing with whom you would like to spend your time.
- Choosing what type of job and/or postsecondary education you would like to pursue.
- Choosing recreation and leisure activities you would like to spend time doing.

These examples of self-determination have implications for identifying skills needed to be successful in the community, providing opportunity for learning those skills, and determining other supports necessary to realize these goals. Self-determination goes hand-in-hand with the autism rights movement, which advocates for helping people with autism learn to be successful in community, but embracing choice and individuality (Solomon, 2008).

Facilitating the Development of Self-Determination

In addition to the philosophical and ethical reasons for promoting and supporting self-determination, individuals with ASD demonstrating strong self-determination have better outcomes as adults (Wehmeyer & Schwartz, 1998; Wehmeyer et al., 2010). In fact, self-determination contributes to an overall higher quality of life (Schalock, 1996). However, the development of self-determination does not occur in a vacuum but is facilitated by individuals and policies that provide supports and reduce barriers (Abery & Stancliffe, 1996). Furthermore, research indicates that instruction can be effective in promoting self-determination behaviors (Cobb, Lehmann, Newman-Gonchar, & Morgan, 2009).

Wehmeyer and colleagues (2010) describe areas to target for instruction to promote self-determination in individuals with ASD. Depending on the student's ability level instruction may target goal setting and attainment, choice making, problem solving, self-advocacy, and self-regulation. These components of self-determination are depicted in Figure 11.1 and described further below.

Figure 11.1   Components of Self-Determination

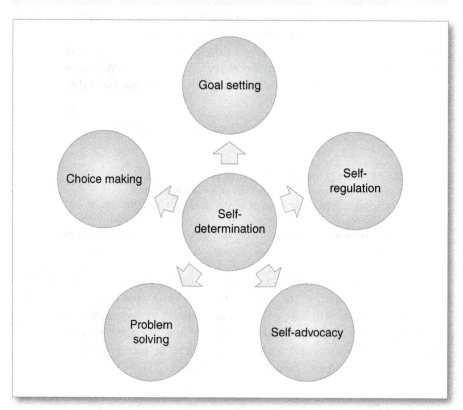

- Goal setting and attainment—Learning to break complex goals into smaller component parts.
- Choice making—Providing opportunities for students to make choices throughout their day using visual prompts when needed.
- Problem solving—Learning how to identify that a problem exists and define what that problem entails, listing potential solutions, and considering what the outcomes may be for proposed solution. Predicting possible outcomes, particularly those involving the reaction of others, is often difficult for individuals with ASD. Social-emotional interventions addressing these skills (discussed in Chapter 10) may be an important component of this instruction. For instance, students can be taught to use social autopsies to analyze social problems, determine who was impacted and

how to correct the error, and develop a plan to prevent the error from occurring again (Simpson, 2005).

- Self-regulation—Learning how to manage one's own behavior involves observing and evaluating oneself, setting target goals, and providing self-reinforcement for achieving those goals. Self-regulation is a type of cognitive behavior modification.
- Self-advocacy—Teaching students to advocate for themselves. Provide examples and models for how they can address situations that they feel are unfair. Provide feedback and reinforcement for successful attempts. Help students to establish their own class schedule, asserting their preferences, and meeting with teachers to address questions or concerns helps develop self-advocacy skills. Self-advocacy skills are dependent upon communication skills. Students with limited expressive language can be taught to self-advocate using augmentative communication systems (Kleinert, Harrison, Fisher, & Kleinert, 2010). Speech/language pathologists can create individualized education plan (IEP) goals that specifically address self-advocacy skills (Kleinert et al., 2010).

Person-Centered Planning

Person-centered planning (PCP) is an approach to determining and setting goals that focuses on the hopes, dreams, and desires of the individual and his or her family (Klim & Turnbull, 2004). PCP is a strategy that can be used to support self-determination during the transition from secondary school to the community. A PCP a team consists of the person with a disability, family members, educators, professionals involved in providing current or future supports, and others that are part of the student's life (e.g., friends, community workers, and neighbors).

An example of PCP is Making Action Plans, or MAPs (Forest & Lusthaus, 1990; University of Kansas, 2002). A facilitator works with the individual with a disability to tell his or her "life story." Next, the individual with a disability identifies short-term and long-term goals and dreams, assisted by a supportive team outlining time lines, resources, and supports available to reach the goals and the steps required to get there. MAPS may be an especially useful PCP tool for individuals with ASD, because each step is visually presented. Thus, the end result is a graphic representation of a plan of action, steps needed for achieving goals, and supports available.

Cultural Issues Related to Self-Determination

Although behaviors associated with self-determination (such as asserting preferences, setting goals, and self-advocacy) are linked to positive outcomes in adulthood, one's understanding of self-determination reflects cultural values. For instance, asserting one's independence, expressing individuality, being future oriented, and fulfilling desires of self versus the needs of a group are culturally laden values (Rueda, Monzo, Shapiro, Gomez, & Blacher, 2005; Zhang, Landmark, Grenwelge, & Montoya, 2010). Thus, families from non-Western and collective cultural orientations may be less familiar, and possibly less comfortable, with the concept of self-determination embraced by public institutions (Smith & Routel, 2010; Zhang et al., 2010).

Furthermore, families from diverse cultural perspectives may have different understandings of what it means to have a disability and the family's role of caring for a family member with a disability (Garcia et al., 2000; Rueda et al., 2005). Language barriers may provide additional barriers to addressing issues of self-determination (Rueda et al.). For instance, Blue-Banning, Turnbull, and Pereira (2002) conducted focus group interviews with Hispanic parents of youth and young adults with developmental disabilities. Focus group results reflected a diversity of goals for their children. Focus group themes included a desire for acceptance by family and community and expectations of their adult child living at home with them until marriage. PCP and other planning strategies that consider the cultural context of the family are likely to support positive outcomes when transitioning from public school (Smith & Routel, 2010). Cultural reciprocity, which involves developing collaborative relationships by respecting and striving to understand differences in perspectives and values, contributes to culturally sensitive services (National Center on Secondary Education and Transition, 2005).

TRANSITIONING FROM HIGH SCHOOL

Research on Evidence-Based Practice

There is limited research on the transition from school to community living and employment for youth with ASD (Hart, Grigal, & Weir, 2010; Hendricks & Wehman, 2009; Seltzer et al., 2004). Furthermore, although evidence-based practices are required in the public school system, there is limited empirical research about interventions that promote successful transitions to community living (Wehman, Smith, & Schall, 2009). Based on a review of available research on transition planning, Hetherington and colleagues (2010) suggest five components including: (1) student involvement, (2) parent and family involvement, (3) personalized relationships between students, educators, and families, (4) a meaningful curriculum driven by individual goals rather than standardized academic goals, and (5) student-oriented outcome-based goals. Overall, Hetherington and colleagues (2010) stress that transition planning needs to occur much earlier, include significantly more involvement of families and the student, and include implementation activities and outcome measures to support reaching transition goals.

Poor transition planning and implementation can result in less support and a reduced quality of life after high school. In fact, support characteristics provided in adulthood are a better predictor quality of life than severity and type of disability (Renty & Roeyers, 2006). To investigate these concerns, Shattuck and colleagues (2011) examined rates of service use as young adults with ASD transitioned from high school. Data collected from a nationally representative sample of parents of young adults with ASD revealed sharp decreases in services following high school. The study found that nearly 40% of young adults with ASD were no longer receiving any services, although they received them in high school through special education. The study also found differences in services by race and socioeconomic status. Adults with ASD who were African American and those living in families earning $25,000 or less were far less likely to receive services.

The Individualized Transition Plan

The Individuals with Disabilities Education Act (IDEA) is an example of federal legislation encouraging the development of self-determination in people with disabilities. IDEA mandates that, to the extent possible, students be encouraged to participate in the planning and decision-making process of the IEP alongside parents and educators. Thus, even in the elementary school years, teachers and parents must show students that they value their choices and preferences. At age 18, a student is said to have reach the "age of majority" and is allowed to make his own decisions, unless appointed a guardian or

It is important that the transition plan considers goals that promote independence.

chosen to share decision making. Students and parents must be informed of this transfer of parental rights to student at least 1 year before the student turns 18. Regardless of the child's age, communication skills, or ability level, her input in making choices about her life should be encouraged and valued.

In 1990, the reauthorization of IDEA included a mandate for providing transition services to students receiving special education services. A *statement of transition service needs* should be included in the student's IEP by age 14. The 2004 reauthorization of IDEA requires that an individualized transition plan (ITP) be written for a student receiving special education services by age 16. However, transition planning, can (and should) occur much earlier.

Integral to the transition plan is identifying the student's preferences for their lives after public school, including employment or further education, leisure and recreation, social/interpersonal, and residential. Based on transition goals established by the student, family, and educators, specific skill sets can be targeted within the IEP to support the successful transition from high school to the community. IDEA requires that, to the extent possible, students be involved in the IEP process, and particularly in the transition planning. In a study of 276 students with disabilities, Williams-Diehm and colleagues (2008) found that active involvement in transition planning was associated with higher levels of self-determination.

Preparing the ITP requires active student involvement, alongside a multidisciplinary team (National Council on Disability, 2000). Optimally, the multidisciplinary team includes the student and his family, educators and professionals associated with the school, and community supports associated with transition goals. However, a study commissioned by the Office for Special Education Programs of the U.S. Department of Education revealed that the majority of ITP meetings lack a representative from external support agencies in the community (Cameto, Levine, & Wagner, 2004). The lack of representation of community supports during transition planning is problematic given the variety of supports often needed for successful transitioning of individuals with ASD into the community (Wolfe, 2005). Table 11.2 describes key features of an ITP.

HOUSING

Lack of Residential Supports

Regardless of an individual's level of impairment, it is important that they have the opportunity to express their preference in future living arrangements. Although individuals with greater needs (e.g., communication, mobility, sensory

Table 11.2 Key Features of an Individualized Transition Plan

- Individualized based on the student's skills, goals, interests, and preferences for life after secondary school.
- Consists of a multidisciplinary team, including the student with a disability, family members, educators, professionals working with the student, and representatives of community supports in areas such as housing, employment, leisure, and recreation. Thus, interagency collaboration (e.g., school personnel, social security administration, department of vocational rehabilitation, and supportive employment agencies) is essential.
- Has outcome-oriented goals oriented to life after high school, not just focused on what can be accomplished while in school. Goals consider planning for vocational training, integrated employment, postsecondary education, recreation and leisure, independent living, and community participation. A *functional vocational evaluation,* an assessment providing information about job or career interests, aptitudes, and skills may be requested to assist with the ITP.
- Transition goals must be reviewed and progress toward meeting goals considered during each IEP meeting after age 16.
- Schools must provide a *summary of performance* when a student transitions from public school, due to exceeding age for public school services (usually after age 22) or graduating, which documents academic achievements and functional performance.
- Other issues to address in ITP to support successful transition may include interpersonal skills needed for success in a job setting, self-advocacy, self-monitoring, and safety skills associated with privacy, communicating needs, and issues related to sexuality. Furthermore, many individuals with ASD have comorbid mental health disorders, particularly depression and anxiety. These difficulties may be exasperated by the stress of transitioning to a new routine. Supports to address mental health should be part of transition plan discussions.

impairments) may require more diverse and intensive supports, level of impairment should not be the determining factor as to where an individual with ASD should live.

The majority of individuals with ASD will require some degree of residential service or support during their lifetime (Gerhardt & Lanier, 2011). While the demand for services of adults with ASD is increasing, the available supports are in limited supply (Autism Society of America, 2007; Gerhardt & Lanier, 2011). Unlike educational services under IDEA, services to adults with ASD are not a federal mandate. For instance, states determine the criteria for eligibility for the Medicaid HCB Waiver program, one of the major funding sources for services for adults with developmental disabilities. Depending on the population and financial resources of the state, there are often long waiting lists for Waiver slots (Autism Society of America, 2007).

The Autism Society of America reported in its position paper *The National Crisis in Adult Services for Individuals With Autism* (2007) that there are approximately 25 agencies in the United States having highly specialized programs for adults with ASD. Furthermore, the report describes poor-quality services overall due to high rates of staff turnover, poor staff training about ASD, and inadequate Medicaid reimbursement rates.

Theoretically, there are many options for individuals with ASD. However, the cost and availability of these options vary widely. Available supports, opportunities for community integration, and number of individuals residing in the residence are the main differences among the choices. However, the types of care available and the quality of that care are not tied to the residential model (Gerhardt, 2009). Issues that may prevent individuals with ASD from living independently include affordability (difficulty finding paid employment, high costs of living as compared with government support or other means of financial support), accessibility (particularly for individuals who use wheelchairs or other mobility devices), and availability of supportive housing due to limited governmental funding (The ARC, 2011).

Residential Options

Living at home with family

Recent studies of adults with ASD living in the United States indicate that as many as 79% (Shattuck, 2011) are currently living with their parents. For some families and individuals with ASD, living in the family home is the preferred residential setting. Individuals with ASD living at home with their parents may be eligible for government funds such as Supplemental Security Income (SSI), Social Security Disability Insurance (SSDI), and Medicaid waivers. However, families need to be proactive in securing these financial supports (National Institute of Mental Health, 2010). Funding may also be available to provide supports for transportation, job training, respite care, and other services. It is essential that future residential preferences be discussed during transition planning, and the transition planning team invite community agencies to facilitate interagency collaboration. Although family living has potential benefits (e.g., living in a familiar environment with loved ones who understand ASD and the individual), caregiver burnout and limited opportunities for socialization and community integration may become problematic. Many caregivers desire to continue having their adult child with ASD live at home, but need more in-home support. Parents are often concerned about the lack of future residential opportunities, and who would care for their adult children with ASD when they are no longer able to do so. Adults with ASD living at home with aging caregivers face an uncertain future without careful planning for transition services.

Supportive group living

Underlying the concept of supportive living is the belief that severity of disability should not prevent individuals from life experiences typical of their nondisabled peers. Thus, with appropriate supports, individuals with ASD (and other disabilities) can choose to live outside their family's home and within the community. People with ASD may benefit from exercising self-determination to choose a residence that allows them to live in a particular setting and follow routines they find most comfortable (Gerhardt & Lanier, 2011). Some parents are surprised at the increased independence of their adult child with ASD after moving into a partially supported living environment; yet, parents may be unsure if the support staff can provide the same level of care that they provided their child (Hitzing, Saverino, Leary, & Sousa, 1995).

Transitioning to a supportive living environment presents many opportunities for increasing skills in socialization, problem solving, and negotiation through experiences. For instance, successful living in a shared household may require planning for and negotiating issues such as furniture arrangements, paying bills, addressing undesirable behaviors, rules about visitors, groceries purchased and meal preparation, household duties like cleaning, and access to television (Muller, 2009).

Supportive living may involve only limited supports with supportive staff visiting periodically to address concerns, offer training, help pay bills, etc. On the other hand, some individuals with ASD may require greater support, sometimes called community living arrangements (CLA), in which support staff provide 24/7 assistance with home and community supports (Autism Society, Greater Philadelphia Chapter, 2009). Both supervised living situations with limited supports and those with more intensive supports differ from traditional group homes, with a greater focus on consumer choice, self-determination, and smaller number of individuals living in the residence.

Other options

Across the country, long-term institutional care is being phased out. Today only the most disabled and medically fragile individuals live their lives in institutions. The goal is for integration of individuals with disabilities into the community to the greatest extent possible. However, there are some interesting larger residential models, such as farmstead programs, that offer unique living experiences with opportunities for personal development, vocational training, independence, and socialization (Gerhardt & Lanier, 2011).

Another option for high-functioning individuals with ASD is fully independent living without supervision. Only a small percentage of adults with ASD live independently. However, with social support, strong transition planning and implementation, and vocational/job preparation, fully independent living is possible for some individuals with ASD.

In addition to the residential models discussed in this chapter, sometimes parents and community leaders collaborate to create unique residential and community supports for adults with developmental disabilities. Consider the following interview (see the Chapter Reflection box "Meeting the Needs of Adults With Developmental Disabilities") with Barbara Monday, one of the founding parent members of DIGS (Develop Independence, Growth, and Security for adults with developmental disabilities in our community).

CHAPTER REFLECTION: Meeting the Needs of Adults With Developmental Disabilities: Develop Independence, Growth, and Security (DIGS) for Adults With Developmental Disabilities in Our Community

Author.

Barbara Monday is a founding parent of DIGS and shares her experiences creating this organization.

DIGS was developed by a group of parents, caregivers, and concerned citizens to address the lack of social, recreational, work opportunities, and residential options for adults with developmental disabilities in our community.

When we first got together, we each wrote a mission statement about what we hoped to accomplish. It was interesting how similar our mission statements were. They *all* involved securing safe long-term housing, recreation, and leisure activities for the adults with developmental disabilities in our community. Our long-term goal was to create a residential option for adults with developmental disabilities that was safe, offered choice and independence, and could be permanent. We didn't want our children in a community-based home that could close and for our children to be transferred from home to home throughout their lives.

Over the years, DIGS has provided adults with developmental disabilities a core group of friends, opportunities to learn new skills and develop leisure skills and interests. Also, the parents have found a support group of friends with whom they can share concerns and ideas. For instance, after a birthday party for her adult son, a mother came over to me crying. She hugged me and thanked me for the opportunity to have a birthday party for her son. She said that she never gave him a party with his peers before, because she didn't think anybody would come. But everyone in DIGS came to this party and had a great time! Children with developmental disabilities are often bussed to schools far from their homes. So parents rarely get to know the parents of their child's classmates.

DIGS has become a bridge to the community. We currently have an adult choir that has weekly rehearsals and performs all over the county. We also have a camera club, dance club, and an art club. Being in the DIGS choir teaches many skills that may serve as a bridge to joining a church choir. For instance, you learn how to behave in a rehearsal, how to stand on the stage and look out toward the audience, and how to sing in public. Our camera club members can learn skills serving as a bridge to joining the local camera club in town. Furthermore, leisure activities can lead to future work opportunities. For instance, we make and sell garden art as a fund-raiser, and learn many useful skills in the process.

One of the best things about DIGS is that these adults have a peer group of friends. They learn how to be a friend and how to engage with friends during community events.

Tom is Barbara's son. He is an adult with a developmental disability and an active member of DIGS.

When asked what he liked most about DIGS, Tom named six to ten friends. Despite expressive language deficits, Tom enthusiastically described where his closest friends worked and other things about them. He mentioned a girlfriend as well. Tom is looking forward to living on his own someday, especially living with his friends!

Visit the DIGS website at http://www.orgsites.com/ga/digs. For additional information about residential options for individuals with ASD, refer to the National Association of Residential Providers for Adults with Autism (NARPAA) at http://www.narpaa.org. In addition, *Autism Advocate* published by the Autism Society, Greater Philadelphia Chapter (2009) devotes an entire issue to residential options for individuals with ASD.

PLANNING FOR EMPLOYMENT

Transition Planning

Adults with ASD across the spectrum have low rates of employment compared with their peers (Eaves & Ho, 2008; Taylor & Seltzer, 2011). In a review of the literature on ASD and employment, Hendricks (2010) reported 50% to 75% of individuals with ASD are unemployed. Furthermore, employed individuals with ASD tend to work fewer hours and earn less in weekly wages than individuals with other types of disabilities (Cimera & Cowan, 2009). There is a need for better transitional planning, including vocational evaluations, internships/shadowing, and teaching skills needed for success such as communication and social skills used in a job setting. Educators with knowledge about state and community vocational supports are better able to assist with planning and implementing the transition plan for young adults with ASD (McDonough & Revell, 2010). Employment has many benefits for all individuals. For instance, in addition to providing financial benefits, employment offers social opportunities, promotes personal dignity that is associated with a high quality of life, and may enhance cognitive skills (Hendricks, 2010).

Vocational rehabilitation is available to some individuals with ASD. However, adults with ASD are often denied services, especially those on the severe end of the spectrum (Lawer et al., 2009). Overall, individuals with ASD are underserved by state and federal vocational rehabilitation programs (Dew & Alan, 2007). It is important that families understand that after age 22, support services are no longer entitlement based (such as IDEA mandates for free and appropriate education). Instead, different laws translate to a new array of eligibility criteria for obtaining services. There is no agency that is charged with serving adults with ASD. Rather, factors such as presence of an intellectual disability, physical or sensory impairments, comorbid mental health conditions, and the economic resources of the community impact the types of services available.

Students with ASD and their families benefit from transition planning guiding by educators who identify key resources that can clarify these processes for families (McDonough & Revell, 2010). Early vocational training is critical for obtaining meaningful employment as an adult (Carter, Austin, & Trainor, 2011). Using data from the National Longitudinal Transition Study-2, Carter and colleagues (2011) found that students with an intellectual disability were almost four times as likely to be employed than individuals with ASD without an intellectual impairment. Furthermore, good communication, independent self-care skills, and parent expectations of employment were predictive of early employment. Parent expectations played a role in early job experiences.

EMPLOYMENT MODELS

Despite similar core deficits, individuals with ASD have a wide range of interests and skills. The level of independence and need for supports varies significantly across the spectrum. Different models for employment and meaningful work experiences should be considered. Work experiences are selected based upon the individual's needs, skills, job availability, and available supports. Other issues such as transportation and mental health concerns are also important considerations.

Competitive employment

Competitive employment refers to engagement in meaningful paid employment with limited supports (Holmes, 2007). Success on the job is greatly enhanced by employers and employees who provide a supportive environment (Hendricks, 2010). This may include tolerance for unusual behaviors (such as stereotypic or repetitive behaviors under stress), a need for routine, and difficulty with pragmatic and abstract language. Thus, it is often important that colleagues of individuals with ASD understand the disorder. To this end, adults with ASD must learn how and when to self-disclose information about ASD.

Workplace modifications may also promote job success. Hillier and colleagues (2007) suggest an environmental assessment addressing noise level, interruptions, crowding, lighting, and space navigation. Flexible employers willing to make environmental accommodations can provide an environment for the individual with ASD to be a productive asset to the organization.

Supportive employment

Many individuals with ASD will require some degree of support while employed. As an alternative to the traditional sheltered group workshops, that generally provided a rote-working task in an environment segregated from the community, supportive employment helps individuals with ASD work within their community. Many individuals with ASD benefit from on-the-job supports, which allow them to participate in meaningful and sometimes paid employment (Lawer et al., 2009). Callahan (1986) identified four characteristics of supported employment:

- Integration—Work with nondisabled coworkers and integrated at work.
- Paid work—Pay commensurate with work performed.
- Individualized services—Job selection, training, and supports individualized based on the needs of the individual.
- Wide variety of ongoing supports—These include transportation, time management, and advocacy.

Sometimes, supports are needed only at the beginning of the job, involving training and helping the individual advocate for accommodations. Other times, more intensive support is needed on a daily basis. A job coach (sometimes referred to as employment specialist or consultant) helps identify a job that fits the individual's interests and skills, provides supports for initial employment, and gradually reduces the coaching role as the individual adjusts to the job setting. A job coach systematically analyzes the tasks needed to perform the job and teaches elements of the task needed for success. Often, applied behavior analysis is used to teach tasks, collect data on performance, and gradually fade prompts and reinforcers (Rusch & Hughes, 1989). Another role of the job coach is to identify and implement natural supports to facilitate integration of the individual with a disability into the work setting (Hagner, Rogan, & Murphy, 1992). For instance, the job coach may work with the supervisor to create a visual and frequent feedback system, identify and train a peer mentor, and help the individual with ASD socialize with colleagues (Gerhardt, 2009). A job coach may slowly scale back in daily contact and check in weekly or monthly. The type and extent of these supports depend on the needs of the individual with ASD.

Other Opportunities for Meaningful Work Experiences

Some individuals with ASD who have more significant impairments may require greater support than what is offered through supported employment. However, despite the level of impairment, all individuals have the right to meaningful work experiences. Access to these experiences may be provided through adult day service programs, which may include sheltered workshops or day activity centers. From their study of post–high school educational and occupational activities of young adults, Taylor and Seltzer (2010) found that over half of the study participants (56%) attended either sheltered workshops or day activity centers. Generally, these work opportunities provide work for groups of individuals with disabilities until the job is complete. In addition, volunteer activities provide individuals with ASD opportunities to contribute to society, to socialize and be included in their community, and to learn new skills.

POSTSECONDARY EDUCATION

Postsecondary education increases the chances that people with ASD will develop skills resulting in meaningful employment and increased opportunities for inclusion in the community (Holmes, 2007; Stodden & Mruzek, 2010). College provides a transition to adulthood marked by enhanced experiences with socialization and independence, fundamental to being a successful adult (Hart, Grigal, & Weir, 2010). Students with all types of disabilities, including intellectual disabilities, may benefit from participating in postsecondary education experiences (Hart et al.).

College provides a transition to adulthood marked by enhanced experiences with socialization and independence, fundamental to being a successful adult.

Legislation Supporting Postsecondary Education for People With Disabilities

Over the years, societal changes have led to increased support for integrating individuals with disabilities into the community at all levels, including education, employment, residential, and other aspects of community life (Stodden & Mruzek, 2010). Legislation and policy changes reflect these views. For instance, current federal legislation, such as No Child Left Behind (NCLB) and IDEA, are more focused on academic preparedness requiring students with ASD and other disabilities to have increased access to the general academic curriculum and inclusion in statewide standardized testing. Furthermore, the American with Disabilities Act (ADA, amended in 2008) requires public institutions to provide reasonable accommodations ensuring equal access in both work and educational settings.

The Higher Education Opportunity Act (HEOA) of 2008 provides further support for people with ASD and other developmental disabilities. In October 2009, a Government Accountability Office (GAO) report was published to address questions about HEOA (U.S. Governmental Accountability Office, 2009). The report cited that 11% of students attending colleges and universities were identified as having a disability and that these numbers were increasing. In the report, the GAO recommended a coordinated approach to supporting people with disabilities in postsecondary schools and providing technical assistance. The report noted that postsecondary schools face challenges in addressing needs of students with disabilities, such as ASD, because they may require specialized knowledge.

Postsecondary Education and ASD

Postsecondary education is associated with a greater likelihood of economic and social independence (Levy & Perry, 2011). Results from the National Longitudinal Transition Study 2 (NLTS2; Wagner, Newman, Cameto, Garza, & Levine, 2005) indicated that approximately 20% of individuals with ASD attend a vocational, business, or technical school; 35% attend a 2-year college; and 1% attend a 4-year college. However, other studies report smaller percentages of individuals with ASD pursuing postsecondary education (Levy & Perry). Parents and teachers are encouraged to discuss the possibility of attending a postsecondary education program early in transition planning.

The following topics are recommended to support transition planning for students considering postsecondary education:

• Investigate community colleges, public 4-year, and private colleges and universities. Invite a school guidance counselor to attend the ITP meeting to share information about local colleges and preparing applications for admission. Consider the pros and cons of different types of postsecondary programs. For instance, a 2-year program may offer more individualized support for students with disabilities. Likewise, though a small private school may not have the resources of a large university, some private schools offer a more personalized approach to supporting students with disabilities. Students with ASD may be eligible for testing accommodations for the ACT and SAT. Students who are not earning an academic diploma may consider taking continuing education courses or auditing college courses.

- Consider vocational postsecondary programs. Vocational programs offer the development of skill sets associated with specific career paths. According to the National Longitudinal Transition Study 2 (NLTS2), only 22% of students with ASD have postsecondary vocational training documented on their ITP (Wagner et al., 2005).

- Teach students to self-disclose and self-advocate. Unlike public high schools, students with disabilities *must* self-identify and advocate for themselves to receive support services. Although this may seem embarrassing to the student, the sooner they self-identify as having ASD the more quickly they will receive supports to help them succeed. One of the first steps is identifying the office of disability services at the postsecondary school. It may be helpful to contact the director and determine if there are other students with ASD and the types of accommodations typically provided. Each postsecondary institution determines if a student is eligible for accommodations. If they are found eligible, the postsecondary institution determines what they consider to be *reasonable* accommodations. This is likely to vary greatly from college to college.

- Often students will need to contact their professor to share information about their learning needs. The director of disability services will provide a letter of accommodations stipulating the accommodations a professor needs to make. These accommodations are not necessarily the same as those on the student's high school IEP. In fact, the college professors will have nothing like an IEP, only a list of basic accommodations. These accommodations will *not* reduce the course workload or change the nature of the assignments. For instance, the student may be given extra time on exams or the opportunity to take them in the office of disability services, have access to adaptive technology, be provided academic support such as a tutor, or be provided with a note taker during class. However, the student is unlikely to be given different tests, different assignments, or extended time for turning in written assignments like term papers or projects. Questions or concerns students have about the course need to be addressed to the professor teaching the class. Approaching a professor can be a daunting task for any student. Students need to be able to describe their preferred learning style. For instance, they may need to explain to the professor that they process auditory information (such as lecture) more slowly than visual information. Thus, they might request copies of the professor's PowerPoint slides if they are not already available, and/or permission to audiotape the course lecture. Tips on how to contact and talk with professors (email letters, checking office hours, etc.) will be helpful.

- *Request a current psychological evaluation before graduating.* Generally, a current psychoeducational evaluation may be requested by the IEP team during the student's last year of high school. Most postsecondary institutions will require formal documentation of ASD (or another disability). For ASD this will be in the form of a psychological evaluation that has been conducted within the past 3 years (U.S. Governmental Accountability Office, 2009). Postsecondary institutions rarely implement or pay for these costly evaluations, and insurance companies are unlikely to reimburse students for a psychological evaluation for the purpose of documenting a disability. Thus, if the evaluation is not done before leaving public high school, the student would be responsible for the cost of the evaluation.

Additional information for teachers supporting students with the transition to postsecondary education can be found in the report *"Transition of Students With Disabilities to Postsecondary Education: A Guide for High School Educators"* available at http://www2.ed.gov/print/about/offices/list/ocr/transitionguide.html.

TEACHING TIPS

- Collaborate with parents, teachers, and the student each year to identify goals after high school. Provide opportunities to visit different job sites, talk with and shadow employees, and build skills needed for employment. Skills that may be associated with a particular job, such as completing paperwork, stacking items on a shelf, or cleaning, can be broken down into discrete steps and written into the IEP. Include professionals that support vocational exploration and conduct vocational assessments to participate in IEP and transition planning meetings.

- Work with parents and the student with ASD to consider residential options after high school. Identify the skills needed to build independence to the fullest extent possible, particularly if living away from one's family home is the goal. Help families identify resources for investigating residential options. School social workers, state representatives from community agencies, or others may need to be invited to transition planning meetings to provide current information about resources and how to obtain them.

- Work with the school counselor to help students with ASD who are interested in pursuing postsecondary education identify and evaluate programs. Include self-advocacy skills into IEP goals to help students transition successfully to educational environments where a special education teacher will not be available to navigate accommodations.

SUMMARY

Unprecedented numbers of young adults with ASD will be transitioning from high school in the near future. However, residential, housing, and community living support services for adults with ASD are limited. Furthermore, there is little research regarding best practices for effectively transitioning individuals from school to the adult life. Self-determination, the fundamental human right to make meaningful decisions about one's life, contributes significantly to overall quality of life. Teachers can teach skills that help students with ASD become actively involved in communicating their preferences, self-advocate, and participate in constructing their educational and transition plans.

The ITP is written by the IEP team in collaboration with relevant community agencies. IDEA requires an ITP by the time a student with an IEP turns 16, but earlier planning is encouraged. The transition plan is important for helping students plan for housing, employment and/or postsecondary education opportunities as they transition from high school.

Although most adults with ASD reside with their families, supportive group living is receiving increasing attention as a living option allowing for greater independence and community integration. However, availability and cost can make supportive living difficult to access. Transition plans are essential for preparing for competitive or supportive employment. Work experiences, such as day activity shelters and sheltered workshops, may be options for individuals with more severe impairments. Increasingly, postsecondary education is an option for individuals with ASD, enhancing vocational opportunities.

DISCUSSION AND REFLECTION QUESTIONS

1. How can teachers help students with ASD develop self-determination? Consider how educators can collaborate with families to recognize cultural differences in the conceptualization of self-determination.

2. Describe components of an ITP and the types of issues that should be addressed. Make a list of agencies in your community that support adults with disabilities who might be invited to transition planning meetings.

3. What are the residential options for adults with ASD, and why do so many adults with ASD live with their families? Consider supports necessary to improve the overall quality of life for adults with ASD living with their families and their families.

4. Describe the models of employments available in the United States for people with ASD.

5. What types of activities are important for preparing a high school student with ASD for future employment or transitioning to postsecondary education?

RECOMMENDED FURTHER READINGS AND INTERNET SOURCES

Autism Society of America: Position Paper on *The National Crisis in Adult Services for Individuals With Autism.* http://support .autism-society.org/site/DocServer/Adult_ Services_vMay2007.pdf?docID=2601.

Transition and Self-Determination

Issue of *Focus on Autism and Other Developmental Disabilities,* 25 (2010, September) devoted to postschool transition.

Leake, D., & Black, R. (2005). *Essential tools: Cultural and linguistic diversity: Implications for transition personnel.* Minneapolis, MN: University of Minnesota, Institute on Community Integration, National Center on Secondary Education and Transition.

Oregon Health and Science University, Center for Self-Determination National Center on Secondary Education and Transition. http:// www.ncset.org

Self-Advocacy Synthesis Project: reviews research on self-advocacy models for students with disabilities. http://sdsp.uncc.edu/

Self-determination resource website for teachers. http://www.selfdeterminationak.org/ resources_for_teachers.html

Wehman, P., Datlow, S., & Schall, C. (2008). *Autism and the transition to adulthood. Success beyond the classroom.* Baltimore, MD: Paul H. Brookes.

Employment

Advancing Futures for Adults With Autism: National consortium seeking to create meaningful futures for adults with autism including homes, jobs, recreation, friends, and supportive communities. www.afaa-us .org

Postsecondary Education

Going to college website funded by a grant from the U.S. Department of Education, Office of Special Education and Rehabilitative Services to help students with disabilities prepare for college. http://www.going-to-college.org/ index.html

Students With Disabilities Preparing for Postsecondary Education: Know Your Rights and Responsibilities—guide from the Office for Civil Rights. http://www.ed.gov/about/offices/ list/ocr/transition.html

Transition of students with disabilities to postsecondary education: A guide for high school educators. http://www2.ed.gov/print/about/ offices/list/ocr/transitionguide.html

Think College: a web site about college options for people with intellectual disabilities. http://www.thinkcollege.net/

Housing/Residential Issues

National Association of Residential Providers for Adults with Autism. http://www.narpaa.org

REFERENCES

Abery, B., & Stancliffe, R. (1996). The ecology of self-determination. In D. J. Sands & M. L. Wehmeyer (Eds.), *Self-determination across the life span: Independence and choice for people with disabilities* (pp. 111–146). Baltimore: Paul H. Brookes.

The ARC. (2011). *Housing for people with disabilities. Public policy.* Retrieved from http://www.thearc.org/page.aspx?pid=2588.

Autism Society, Greater Philadelphia Chapter. (2009). Planning for housing for adults with Autism Spectrum Disorder. *Autism Advocate, 56,* 21–24.

Autism Society of America. (2007, May). *National crisis in adult services for individuals with autism* (Position Paper). Retrieved from http://support.autismsociety.org/site/DocServer/Adult_Services_vMay2007.pdf?docID=2601.

Baker, S., & Tabor, A. (2006). *Human rights committees. Staying on course with services and supports for people with intellectual disabilities.* Homewood, IL: High Tide Press.

Blue-Banning, M., Turnbull, A. P., & Pereira , L. (2002). Group Action Planning as a support strategy for Hispanic families: Parent and professional perspectives. *Mental Retardation, 38,* 262–275.

Callahan, M. (1986). Systematic training strategies for integrated workplaces. In *Accommodating individual abilities in the workplace: Jobs for people with special needs (Draft).* Omaha, NE: The Center on Applied Urban Research.

Cameto, R., Levine, P., & Wagner, M. (2004). *Transition planning for students with disabilities. A Special Topic Report from the National Longitudinal Transition Study-2 (NLTS-2).* Menlo Park, CA: SRI International.

Carter, E. W., Austin, D., & Trainor, A. A. (2011). Factors associated with the early work experiences of adolescents with severe disabilities. *Intellectual and Developmental Disabilities, 49,* 233–247.

Centers for Disease Control and Prevention. (2009). *CDC statement on autism data.* Retrieved from www.cdc.gov/ncbddd/autism/data/html.

Cimera, R. E., & Cowan, R. J. (2009). The costs of services and employment outcomes achieved by adults with autism in the US. *Autism, 13,* 285–302.

Cobb, B., Lehmann, J., Newman-Gonchar, R., & Morgan, A. (2009). Self-determination for students with disabilities: A narrative metasynthesis. *Career Development for Exceptional Individuals, 32,* 108–114.

Davis, L. H. (2009, April). *Still overlooking autistic adults.* Retrieved from http://www.washingtonpost.com/wp-dyn/content/article/2009/04/03/AR2009040303169.html.

Dew, D. W., & Alan, G. M. (Eds.). (2007). *Rehabilitation of individuals with autism spectrum disorders* (Institute on Rehabilitation Issues Monograph No. 32). Washington, DC: The George Washington University, Center for Rehabilitation Counseling Research and Education.

Eaves, L. C., & Ho, H. H. (2008). Young adult outcome of autism spectrum disorder. *Journal of Autism and Developmental Disorders, 38,* 739–747.

Forest, M., & Lusthaus, E. (1990). Everyone belongs with MAPS action planning system. *TEACHING Exceptional Children, 22,* 32–35.

Garcia, S., Perez, A., & Ortiz, A. (2000). Mexican American mothers' beliefs about disabilities: Implications for early childhood interventions. *Remedial and Special Education, 21,* 90–100.

Gerhardt, P. F., & Lanier, I. (2011). Addressing the needs of adolescents and adults with autism: A crisis on the horizon. *Journal of Contemporary Psychotherapy, 41,* 37–45.

Gerhardt, P. F. (2009). *The current state of services for adults with autism.* Arlington, VA: Organization for Autism Research.

Hagner, D., Rogan, P., & Murphy, S. (1992). Facilitating natural supports in the workplace: Strategies for support consultants. *The Journal of Rehabilitation, 58*, 29–34.

Hart, D., Grigal, M., & Weir, C. (2010). Expanding the paradigm: Postsecondary education options for individuals with autism spectrum disorder and intellectual, disabilities. *Focus on Autism and Other Developmental Disabilities, 25*, 134–150.

Hendricks, D. (2010). Employment and adults with autism spectrum disorders: Challenges and strategies for success. *Journal of Vocational Rehabilitation, 32*, 125–134.

Hendricks, D. R., & Wehman, P. (2009). Transition from school to adulthood for youth with Autism Spectrum Disorders: Review and recommendations. *Focus on Autism and Other Developmental Disabilities, 24*, 77–88.

Hetherington, S. A., Durant-Jones, L., Johnson, K., Nolan, K., Smith, E., Taylor-Brown, S., & Tuttle, J. (2010). The lived experiences of adolescents with disabilities and their parents in transition planning. *Focus on Autism and Other Developmental Disabilities, 25*(3), 163–172.

Hillier, A., Campbell, H., Mastriana, K., Izzo, M., Kool-Tucker, A., Cherry, L., & Beversdorf, D. Q. (2007). Two-year evaluation of a vocational support program for adults on the autism spectrum. *Career Development for Exceptional Individuals, 30*, 35–47.

Hitzing, W., Saverino, C., Leary, M., & Sousa, M. E. (1995). *The transition to supported living: Realizing the moment and moving on* (Report of an Evaluation of Supported Living Services). Mission Hills, CA: Jay Nolan Community Services. Retrieved from http://thechp.syr.edu/jncs.pdf.

Holmes, D. W. (2007). When the school bus stops coming. The employment dilemma for adults with autism. *Autism Advocate, 46*, 16–21.

Interagency Autism Coordinating Committee. (2011). *2011 strategic plan for autism spectrum disorder research.* Retrieved from http://iacc.hhs.gov/strategic-plan/2011/index.shtml.

Kleinert, J. O., Harrison, E. M., Fisher, T. L., & Kleinert, H. L. (2010). 'I can' and 'I did'—Self-advocacy for young students with developmental disabilities. *Teaching Exceptional Children, 43*, 16–26.

Klim, K., & Turnbull, A. (2004). Transition to adulthood for students with severe intellectual disabilities: Shifting toward person-family interdependent planning. *Research & Practice for Persons With Severe Disabilities, 29*, 53–57.

Kogan, M. D., Blumberg, S. J., Schieve, L. A., Boyle, C. A., Perrin, J. M., Ghandour, R. M., . . . van Dyck, P. C. (2009). Prevalence of parent-reported diagnosis of autism spectrum disorder among children in the US. *Pediatrics, 124*, 1395–1403.

Levy, A., & Perry, A. (2011).Outcomes in adults and adolescents with autism. A review of the literature. *Research in Autism Spectrum Disorder, 5*, 1271–1282.

McDonough, J. T., & Revell, G. (2010). Accessing employment supports in the adult system for transitioning youth with autism spectrum disorders. *Journal of Vocational Rehabilitation, 32*, 89–100.

Muller, S. (2009). Entering the adult residential service system. Helping parents and advocates adjust to their new role. *Autism Advocate, 56*, 15–16.

National Center on Secondary Education and Transition (NCSET). (2005). *Essential tools. Improving secondary education and transition for youth with disabilities. cultural and linguistic diversity: Implications for transition personnel.* Minneapolis, MN: Author.

National Institute of Mental Health. (2010, December). *Adults with an autism spectrum disorder.* Retrieved from http://www.nimh.nih.gov/health/publications/autism/complete-index.shtml#pub5.

Renty, J., & Roeyers, H. (2005). Quality of life in high-functioning adults with autism spectrum disorder: The predictive value of disability and support characteristics. *Autism, 10*, 511–524.

Rueda, R., Monzo, L., Shapiro, J., Gomez, J., & Blacher, J. (2005). Cultural models of transition: Latina mothers of young adults with developmental disabilities. *Exceptional Children, 71*, 401–414.

Rusch, F. R., & Hughes, C. (1989). Overview of supported employment. *Journal of Applied Behavior Analysis, 22*, 351–363.

Schalock, R. L. (1996). Reconsidering the conceptualization and measurement of quality of life. In R. Schalock (Ed.), *Quality of life: Conceptualization and measurement* (Vol. I, pp. 123–139). Washington, DC: American Association of Mental Retardation.

Seltzer, M. M., Shattuck, P., Abbeduto, L., & Greenberg, J. S. (2004). Trajectory of development in adolescents and adults with autism. *Mental Retardation and Developmental Disabilities Research Reviews, 10*, 234–247.

Shattuck, P. T., Wagner, M., & Narendorf, S., Sterzing, P., & Hensley, M. (2011). Post-high school service use among young adults with an autism spectrum disorder. *Archives of Pediatrics & Adolescent Medicine, 165*, 141–146.

Simpson, R. (2005). *Autism spectrum disorders: Interventions and treatments for children and youth.* Thousand Oaks, CA: Corwin.

Smith, P., & Routel, C. (2010). Transition failure: The cultural bias of self-determination and the journey to adulthood for people with disabilities. *Disability Studies Quarterly, 30*, 175–182.

Solomon, A. (2008, May 25). The autism rights movement. *New York Magazine.* Retrieved from http://nymag.com/news/features/47225.

Stodden, R. A., & Mruzek, D. W. (2010). Expanding the paradigm: Postsecondary education options for individuals with autism and developmental disabilities. *Focus on Autism and Other Developmental Disabilities, 25*, 131–133.

Taylor, J. L., & Seltzer, M. M. (2011). Employment and post-secondary educational activities for young adults with autism spectrum disorders during the transition to adulthood. *Journal of Autism and Developmental Disorders, 41*, 566–574.

United Nations General Assembly. (1971). *United Nations Declaration on the Rights of Mentally Retarded Persons.* General Assembly Resolution 2856 (XXVI).

University of Kansas Circle of Friends Project. (2002). *The MAPS process: Seven questions.* Retrieved from http://www.circleofinclusion.org/english/guidelines/modulesix/a.html.

U.S. Governmental Accountability Office. (2009, October). *Report to the Chairman, Committee on Education and Labor, House of Representatives. Higher education and disability. Education needs a coordinated approach to improve its assistance to schools in supporting students.* Retrieved from http://www.gao.gov/new.items/d1033.pdf.

Wagner, M., Newman, L., Cameto, R., Garza, N., & Levine, P. (2005). *After high school: A first look at the postschool experiences of youth with disabilities. A report from the National Longitudinal Transition Study-2 (NLTS2)* Menlo Park, CA: SRI International. Retrieved from www.nlts2.org/reports/2005_04/nlts2_report_2005_04_complete.pdf.

Wehmeyer, M. L. (1996). Self-determination as an educational outcome: Why is it important to children, youth, and adults with disabilities? In D. J. Sands & M. L. Wehmeyer (Eds.), *Self-determination across the lifespan: Independence and choice for people with disabilities* (pp. 15–34). Baltimore, MD: Paul H. Brookes.

Wehmeyer, M. L., & Kelchner, K. (1996). Perceptions of classroom environment, locus of control, and academic attributions of adolescents with and without cognitive disabilities. *Career Development for Exceptional Individuals, 19*, 15–29.

Wehmeyer, M., & Schwartz, M. (1998). The relationship between self-determination and quality of life for adults with mental retardation. *Education and Training in Mental Retardation and Developmental Disabilities, 33,* 3–12.

Wehmeyer, M. L., Shogren, K. A., Smith, T. E. C., Zager, D., & Simpson, R. (2010). Research-based principles and practices for educating students with autism: Self-determination and social interactions. *Education and Training in Autism and Developmental Disabilities, 45,* 475–486.

Williams-Diehm, K., Wehmeyer, M. L., Palmer, S. B., Soukup, J. H., & Garner, N. W. (2008). Self-determination and student involvement in transition plans: A multivariate analysis. *Journal on Developmental Disabilities, 14,* 27–39.

Wolfe, P. S. (2005). Service delivery. In P. Wehman, P. J. McLaughlin, & T. Wehman (Eds.), *Intellectual and developmental disabilities: Toward full community inclusion* (3rd ed., pp. 60–76). Austin, TX: Pro-Ed.

Zhang, D., Landmark, L., Grenwelge, C., & Montoya, L. (2010). Culturally diverse parents' perspectives on self-determination. *Education and Training in Autism and Developmental Disabilities, 45,* 175–186.

Appendix: Addressing CEC's Standards for Teachers of Individuals with Developmental Disabilities/Autism

The following table identifies chapters addressing the Knowledge and Standards for Teachers as established by the Council for Exceptional Children's Division of Autism and Developmental Disabilities.

Chps Standard 1 Foundations

		Knowledge
2, 4, 5, 6, 7, 8, 9, 10, 11	ICC1K1	Models, theories, philosophies, and research methods that form the basis for special education practice
7	ICC1K2	Laws, policies, and ethical principles regarding behavior management planning and implementation
2, 4, 6	ICC1K3	Relationship of special education to the organization and function of educational agencies
4, 5, 6	ICC1K4	Rights and responsibilities of students, parents, teachers, and other professionals, and schools related to exceptional learning needs
2, 5, 6	ICC1K5	Issues in definition and identification of individuals with exceptional learning needs, including those from culturally and linguistically diverse backgrounds
2, 4, 5, 6, 8	ICC1K6	Issues, assurances and due process rights related to assessment, eligibility, and placement within a continuum of services
1, 4, 6, 11	ICC1K7	Family systems and the role of families in the educational process

1, 4	ICC1K8	Historical points of view and contribution of culturally diverse groups
1, 2, 4	ICC1K9	Impact of the dominant culture on shaping schools and the individuals who study and work in them
6, 11	ICC1K10	Potential impact of differences in values, languages, and customs that can exist between the home and school
2, 5, 6	DDA1. K1	Definitions and issues related to the identification of individuals with developmental disabilities/autism spectrum disorders
2, 6, 8	DDA1. K2	Continuum of placement and services available for individuals with developmental disabilities/ autism spectrum disorders
1	DDA1.K3	Historical foundations and classic studies of developmental disabilities/autism spectrum disorders
2, 3, 7, 8, 9, 10	DDA1.K4	Trends and practices in the field of developmental disabilities/ autism spectrum disorders
7	DDA1.K5	Theories of behavior problems of individuals with developmental disabilities/autism spectrum disorders
8, 9, 10, 11	DDA1.K6	Perspectives held by individuals with developmental disabilities/ autism spectrum disorders
10, 11	DDA1.K7	Concepts of self determination, self-advocacy, community and family support and impact in the lives of individuals with developmental disabilities/autism spectrum disorders
		Skills
4	ICC1S1	Articulate personal philosophy of special education

Chps Standard 2 Development and Characteristics of Learners

		Knowledge
8, 9	ICC2K1	Typical and atypical human growth and development
6, 8, 9	ICC2K2	Educational implications of characteristics of various exceptionalities
4, 5, 6, 9, 10, 11	ICC2K3	Characteristics and effects of the cultural and environmental milieu of the individual with exceptional learning needs and the family

4	ICC2K4	Family systems and the role of families in supporting development
8, 9	ICC2K5	Similarities and differences of individuals with and without exceptional learning needs
2	ICC2K6	Similarities and differences among individuals with exceptional learning needs
3	ICC2K7	Effects of various medications on individuals with exceptional learning needs
3	DDA2.K1	Medical aspects and implications for learning for individuals with developmental disabilities/autism spectrum disorders
2	DDA2.K2	Core and associated characteristics of individuals with developmental disabilities/autism spectrum disorders
2, 3	DDA2.K3	Co-existing conditions and ranges that exist at a higher rate than in the general population
2, 3	DDA2.K4	Sensory challenges of individuals with developmental disabilities/autism spectrum disorders
2, 9	DDA2.K5	Speech, language, and communication of individuals with developmental disabilities/autism spectrum disorders
7, 11	DDA2.K6	Adaptive behavior needs of individuals with developmental disabilities/autism spectrum disorders
		Skills
		None in addition to the Common Core

Chps Standard 3 Individual Learning Differences

		Knowledge
1, 8, 9, 10, 11	ICC3K1	Effects an exceptional condition(s) can have on an individual's life
11	ICC3K2	Impact of learners' academic and social abilities, attitudes, interests, and values on instruction and career development
4, 5, 6, 9, 10, 11	ICC3K3	Variations in beliefs, traditions, and values across and within cultures and their effects on relationships among individuals with exceptional learning needs, family, and schooling

4, 6, 9, 10	ICC3K4	Cultural perspectives influencing the relationships among families, schools, and communities as related to instruction
4	ICC3K5	Differing ways of learning of individuals with exceptional learning needs, including those from culturally diverse backgrounds and strategies for addressing these differences
2	DDA3.K1	Impact of theory of mind, central coherence, and executive function on learning and behavior
3	DDA3.K2	Impact of neurological differences on learning and behavior
7, 8, 10	DDA3.K3	Impact of self-regulation on learning and behavior
		Skills

Chps Standard 4 Instructional Strategies

		Knowledge
6, 8, 9, 11	ICC4K1	Evidence-based practices validated for specific characteristics of learners and settings
6, 7, 8, 9, 10	DDA4K1	Specialized curriculum designed to meet the needs of individuals with developmental disabilities/autism spectrum disorders
		Skills
6, 8, 9, 10	ICC4S1	Use strategies to facilitate integration into various settings
8, 10	ICC4S2	Teach individuals to use self-assessment, problem-solving, and other cognitive strategies to meet their needs
6, 8, 9, 10	ICC4S3	Select, adapt, and use instructional strategies and materials according to characteristics of the individual with exceptional learning needs
6, 7, 8, 9, 10, 11	ICC4S4	Use strategies to facilitate maintenance and generalization of skills across learning environments
8, 10	ICC4S5	Use procedures to increase the individual's self-awareness, self-management, self-control, self-reliance, and self-esteem
6, 8, 9,10, 11	ICC4S6	Use strategies that promote successful transitions for individuals with exceptional learning needs

8	DDA4.S1	Match levels of support to changing needs of the individual
8, 9	DDA4.S2	Implement instructional programs that promote effective communication skills using verbal and augmentative/alternative communication systems for individuals with developmental disabilities/autism spectrum disorders
8, 9	DDA4.S3	Provide specialized instruction for spoken language, reading and writing for individuals with developmental disabilities/ autism spectrum disorders
6, 7, 8, 9, 10	DDA4.S4	Use instructional strategies that fall on a continuum of child-directed to adult-directed in natural and structured context
6, 7, 8, 9, 10	DDA4.S5	Consistently use of proactive strategies and positive behavioral supports
4, 11	DDA4.S6	Involve individuals with developmental disabilities/autism spectrum disorders in the transition planning process
11	DDA4.S7	Plan for transition needs including linkages to supports and agencies focusing on life long needs

Chps Standard 5 Learning Environments/Social Interactions

		Knowledge
6, 8	ICC5K1	Demands of learning environments
7	ICC5K2	Basic classroom management theories and strategies for individuals with exceptional learning needs
7, 8	ICC5K3	Effective management of teaching and learning
4	ICC5K4	Teacher attitudes and behaviors that influence behavior of individuals with exceptional learning needs
2, 10	ICC5K5	Social skills needed for educational and other environments
6, 7, 10	ICC5K6	Strategies for crisis prevention and intervention
4	ICC5K7	Strategies for preparing individuals to live harmoniously and productively in a culturally diverse world
4	ICC5K8	Ways to create learning environments that allow individuals to retain and appreciate their own and each other's respective language and cultural heritage

4	ICC5K9	Ways specific cultures are negatively stereotyped
4	ICC5K10	Strategies used by diverse populations to cope with a legacy of former and continuing racism
		Skills
4 ,6, 10	ICC5S1	Create a safe, equitable, positive, and supportive learning environment in which diversities are valued
10	ICC5S2	Identify realistic expectations for personal and social behavior in various settings
6, 8	ICC5S3	Identify supports needed for integration into various program placements
8, 10	ICC5S4	Design learning environments that encourage active participation in individual and group activities
7, 8	ICC5S5	Modify the learning environment to manage behaviors
5, 6, 7	ICC5S6	Use performance data and information from all stakeholders to make or suggest modifications in learning environments
4, 6	ICC5S7	Establish and maintain rapport with individuals with and without exceptional learning needs
10	ICC5S8	Teach self-advocacy
8, 10	ICC5S9	Create an environment that encourages self-advocacy and increased independence
7, 8	ICC5S10	Use effective and varied behavior management strategies
7	ICC5S11	Use the least intensive behavior management strategy consistent with the needs of the individual with exceptional learning needs
7, 8, 9	ICC5S12	Design and manage daily routines
4, 10	ICC5S13	Organize, develop, and sustain learning environments that support positive intracultural and intercultural experiences
4, 10	ICC5S14	Mediate controversial intercultural issues among students within the learning environment in ways that enhance any culture, group, or person
4	ICC5S15	Structure, direct, and support the activities of paraeducators, volunteers, and tutors

4	ICC5S16	Use universal precautions
6, 7, 9, 10, 11	DDA5.S1	Provide instruction in community-based settings
-	DDA5.S2	Demonstrate transfer, lifting and positioning techniques
8	DDA5.S3	Structure the physical environment to provide optimal learning for individuals with developmental disabilities/autism spectrum disorders
8, 10	DDA5.S4	Provide instruction in self-regulation
10	DDA5.S5	Utilize student strengths to reinforce and maintain social skills

Chps Standard 6 Language

		Knowledge
4, 6, 9, 10	ICC6K1	Effects of cultural and linguistic differences on growth and development
4, 10	ICC6K2	Characteristics of one's own culture and use of language and the ways in which these can differ from other cultures and uses of languages
4	ICC6K3	Ways of behaving and communicating among cultures that can lead to misinterpretation and misunderstanding
8, 9	ICC6K4	Augmentative and assistive communication strategies
		Skills
8, 9	ICC6S1	Use strategies to support and enhance communication skills of individuals with exceptional learning needs
6, 9	ICC6S2	Use communication strategies and resources to facilitate understanding of subject matter for students whose primary language is not the dominant language
9, 10	DDA6.S1	Provide pragmatic language instruction that facilitates social skills
9, 10	DDA6.S2	Provide individuals with developmental disabilities/autism spectrum disorders strategies to avoid and repair miscommunications

Chps Standard 7 Instructional Planning

		Knowledge
6, 8, 9, 10	ICC7K1	Theories and research that form the basis of curriculum development and instructional practice
8, 9, 10	ICC7K2	Scope and sequences of general and special curricula
6, 8, 9, 10	ICC7K3	National, state or provincial, and local curricula standards
7, 8, 9	ICC7K4	Technology for planning and managing the teaching and learning environment
4	ICC7K5	Roles and responsibilities of the paraeducator related to instruction, intervention, and direct service
11	DDA7.K1	Evidence-based career/vocational transition programs for individuals with developmental disabilities/autism spectrum disorders
		Skills
8, 9, 10	ICC7S1	Identify and prioritize areas of the general curriculum and accommodations for individuals with exceptional learning needs
4, 5, 6, 9, 10	ICC7S2	Develop and implement comprehensive, longitudinal individualized programs in collaboration with team members
4, 5, 6, 9, 10, 11	ICC7S3	Involve the individual and family in setting instructional goals and monitoring progress
7	ICC7S4	Use functional assessments to develop intervention plans
7, 9	ICC7S5	Use task analysis
9, 10	ICC7S6	Sequence, implement, and evaluate individualized learning objectives
8, 9, 10	ICC7S7	Integrate affective, social, and life skills with academic curricula
4, 6	ICC7S8	Develop and select instructional content, resources, and strategies that respond to cultural, linguistic, and gender differences
8, 9	ICC7S9	Incorporate and implement instructional and assistive technology into the educational program

-	ICC7S10	Prepare lesson plans
8, 9, 10	ICC7S11	Prepare and organize materials to implement daily lesson plans
8	ICC7S12	Use instructional time effectively
7, 9, 10	ICC7S13	Make responsive adjustments to instruction based on continual observations
10	ICC7S14	Prepare individuals to exhibit self-enhancing behavior in response to societal attitudes and actions
6, 7, 9, 10	ICC7S15	Evaluate and modify instructional practices in response to ongoing assessment data
7, 8, 9, 10, 11	DDA7.S1	Plan instruction for independent functional life skills and adaptive behavior
6, 7, 8, 9, 10, 11	DDA7.S2	Plan and implement instruction and related services for individuals with developmental disabilities/autism spectrum disorders that is both age-appropriate and ability-appropriate
8, 9	DDA7.S3	Use specialized instruction to enhance social participation across environments
7, 9, 10	DDA7.S4	Plan systematic instruction based on learner characteristics, interests, and ongoing assessment

Chps Standard 8 Assessment

		Knowledge
5, 6		Basic terminology used in assessment
5, 6		Legal provisions and ethical principles regarding assessment of individuals
2, 5, 6		Screening, prereferral, referral, and classification procedures
5, 9, 10		Use and limitations of assessment instruments
5		National, state or provincial, and local accommodations and modifications
5		Specialized terminology used in the assessment of individuals with developmental disabilities/autism spectrum disorders

5, 7		Assessments of environmental conditions that promote maximum performance of individuals with developmental disabilities/autism spectrum disorders
5, 9, 10		Components of assessment for the core areas for individuals with developmental disabilities/autism spectrum disorders
5		Individual strengths, skills and learning styles
		Skills
4, 5, 6, 9, 10	ICC8S1	Gather relevant background information
5	ICC8S2	Administer nonbiased formal and informal assessments
5	ICC8S3	Use technology to conduct assessments
5	ICC8S4	Develop or modify individualized assessment strategies
5, 9	ICC8S5	Interpret information from formal and informal assessments
5, 6	ICC8S6	Use assessment information in making eligibility, program, and placement decisions for individuals with exceptional learning needs, including those from culturally and/or linguistically diverse backgrounds
5, 6	ICC8S7	Report assessment results to all stakeholders using effective communication skills
5, 6, 7, 9, 10	ICC8S8	Evaluate instruction and monitor progress of individuals with exceptional learning needs
5, 6, 9, 10	ICC8S9	Create and maintain records
5, 9, 10	DDA8.S1	Select, adapt and use assessment tools and methods to accommodate the abilities and needs of individuals with developmental disabilities/autism spectrum disorders
7, 9	DDA8.S2	Develop strategies for monitoring and analyzing challenging behavior and its communicative intent
7	DDA8.S3	Conduct functional behavior assessments that lead to development of behavior support plans

Chps Standard 9 Professional And Ethical Practice

		Knowledge
2, 3, 4	ICC9K1	Personal cultural biases and differences that affect one's teaching
4	ICC9K2	Importance of the teacher serving as a model for individuals with exceptional learning needs
2, 4	ICC9K3	Continuum of lifelong professional development
6, 9, 10	ICC9K4	Methods to remain current regarding research-validated practice
		Skills
6, 8, 9, 10	ICC9S1	Practice within the CEC Code of Ethics and other standards of the profession
4, 5, 6, 8, 9, 10	ICC9S2	Uphold high standards of competence and integrity and exercise sound judgment in the practice of the professional
4, 5, 6	ICC9S3	Act ethically in advocating for appropriate services
4, 5, 6	ICC9S4	Conduct professional activities in compliance with applicable laws and policies
4	ICC9S5	Demonstrate commitment to developing the highest education and quality-of-life potential of individuals with exceptional learning needs
4	ICC9S6	Demonstrate sensitivity for the culture, language, religion, gender, disability, socioeconomic status, and sexual orientation of individuals
4	ICC9S7	Practice within one's skill limits and obtain assistance as needed
4, 6	ICC9S8	Use verbal, nonverbal, and written language effectively
4	ICC9S9	Conduct self-evaluation of instruction
2, 3, 4	ICC9S10	Access information on exceptionalities
1, 2, 4	ICC9S11	Reflect on one's practice to improve instruction and guide professional growth
1, 4	ICC9S12	Engage in professional activities that benefit individuals with exceptional learning needs, their families, and one's colleagues
6, 8, 9, 10	ICC9S13	Demonstrate commitment to engage in evidence-based practices

Chps Standard 10 Collaboration

		Knowledge
4, 5, 6, 7, 9, 10, 11	ICC10K1	Models and strategies of consultation and collaboration
4, 5, 6, 9, 10, 11	ICC10K2	Roles of individuals with exceptional learning needs, families, and school and community personnel in planning of an individualized program
1, 2, 3, 4, 6, 11	ICC10K3	Concerns of families of individuals with exceptional learning needs and strategies to help address these concerns
4	ICC10K4	Culturally responsive factors that promote effective communication and collaboration with individuals with exceptional learning needs, families, school personnel, and community members
2, 6, 7, 9, 10, 11	DDA10.K1	Services, networks, and organizations for individuals, professionals, and families with developmental disabilities/autism spectrum disorders
		Skills
2, 4	ICC10S1	Maintain confidential communication about individuals with exceptional learning needs
5	ICC10S2	Collaborate with families and others in assessment of individuals with exceptional learning needs
4	ICC10S3	Foster respectful and beneficial relationships between families and professionals
4, 6	ICC10S4	Assist individuals with exceptional learning needs and their families in becoming active participants in the educational team
4, 6	ICC10S5	Plan and conduct collaborative conferences with individuals with exceptional learning needs and their families
8, 9, 10, 11	ICC10S6	Collaborate with school personnel and community members in integrating individuals with exceptional learning needs into various settings
4	ICC10S7	Use group problem-solving skills to develop, implement, and evaluate collaborative activities
4	ICC10S8	Model techniques and coach others in the use of instructional methods and accommodations

4, 6	ICC10S9	Communicate with school personnel about the characteristics and needs of individuals with exceptional learning needs
4, 6, 9, 10	ICC10S10	Communicate effectively with families of individuals with exceptional learning needs from diverse backgrounds
4	ICC10S11	Observe, evaluate, and provide feedback to paraeducators
11	DDA10S1	Collaborate with team members to plan transition to adulthood that encourages full community participation

GLOSSARY

0–3 Infant Diagnostic Classification System: Published by the National Center for Infants, Toddlers, and Families; addresses the need for a classification system integrating developmental issues of infants and children ages 0 to 3.

Accommodations: Providing specialized support for individuals with special needs often within regular education settings.

The Ages and Stages Questionnaire, Second Edition: A structured questionnaire that elicits information from caregivers about language, personal-social, fine and gross motor, and cognitive development.

Alternative and augmentative communication: Types of communication supports to help individuals with ASD communicate, such as visual symbols, sign language, and specialized computers that provide a voice corresponding with visual icons.

Ambiguous loss: A sense of loss marked by much uncertainty. For instance, parents with a child diagnosed with ASD may not understand the cause of the disorder, nor the long-term prognosis.

Amygdala: An almond-shaped collection of nuclei located beneath the temporal lobe; part of the limbic system, which is associated with motivation and emotion, and is particularly involved in emotional responses of fear and aggression.

Antecedents package: Interventions that include strategies for manipulating and modifying events that occur prior to the target behavior.

Authentic caring: Actions and behaviors that parents identified as genuine, voluntary, child focused, and benefitting children or the parents themselves.

Autism Comorbidity Interview-Present and Lifetime Version: A semistructured interview for caregivers of children with ASD. The ACI-PL distinguishes core features of autism from psychiatric disorders such as mood and anxiety disorders.

Autism Diagnostic Interview-Revised: A semistructured interview designed to provide information contributing to a diagnosis of ASD for children and adults. Based on the diagnostic criteria of the *DSM-IV-TR* and ICD-10, the ADI-R includes a series of structured questions in three primary areas: reciprocal social interaction, communication and language, and restricted/stereotyped and repetitive interests and behavior.

The Autism Diagnostic Observation Scale (ADOS): A standardized assessment tools that include parent/caregiver interviews and an interactive assessment procedure that provides a context for assessing characteristics of ASD.

Autism Genome Project: Scientists from 19 countries investigating genes and gene variants contributing to the expression of ASD.

The Autism Observational Scale for Infants: Developed to monitor and screen for ASD in high-risk infants (6–18 months), such as those with siblings with ASD, by assessing developmental characteristics such as visual orienting and tracking, imitation, and sensory-motor development.

Autistic regression: Typical development followed by loss of skills such as communication and social development before age 3.

Aversive punishments: Typically involves pain such as spanking or shocks following an undesirable behavior.

Behavioral packages: A package of interventions that focus on increasing appropriate behaviors through reinforcement and decreasing inappropriate behaviors using principles of operant conditioning.

Behaviorism: The paradigm that considers psychology the science of changing behaviors through objective methods; term coined by John Watson in his classic paper *Psychology as the Behaviorist Views It.*

Bioecological theory: Offers insight into developing special education interventions and strengthening the home–school partnership.

Candida yeast: Yeastlike fungus, in children with ASD, which may be related to immune system difficulties and possibly associated with exposure to antibiotics, viruses, or other environmental toxins.

Cerebellum: The structure at the base of the brain that is part of the hindbrain.

Associated with the vestibular system and coordinates movement, balance, and equilibrium and associated with cognitive processes such as certain types of learning and memory and even emotional function.

Chaining: A technique used to teach specific skills that together allow a child to engage in a complex social interaction, such as ordering at a restaurant, playing a game, and inviting a peer to play.

Chelation: Has been used to treat individuals in cases of severe lead poisoning, introduces molecules that bond to specific metals in the body.

Childhood Autism Rating Scale, Second Edition: An interview with caregivers and teachers appropriate for children ages 2 and older. Provides ratings of mild autism, moderate autism, severe autism, or nonautism.

Chronosystem: Describes the impact of sociohistorical changes over time.

Circle of Friends: An example of peer-mediated intervention; a promising intervention for children with ASD to build skills such as increasing social initiation, reducing anxiety during social interactions, and increasing social reciprocity.

Cognitive psychology: Matter of mind and thought, and the scientific method of investigation championed by the behaviorism and the natural sciences.

Collaborative support: Support by a trained educator (such as a special education teacher or paraprofessional) is provided to a child with special needs for some portion of the school day, often with the regular education classroom.

Collateral skills: The most relevant social skills goals indirectly support a child's academic functioning by reducing anxiety and providing emotional support.

Comic strip conversations: Technique using cartooning to teach social skills to children with ASD.

Community living arrangements: Living arrangement in which support staff provides 24/7 assistance with home and community supports.

Comorbidity: Diagnosis of two or more clinical disorders.

Competitive employment: Refers to engagement in meaningful paid employment with limited supports.

Complementary and Alternative Medicine (CAM): Interventions that have limited supporting empirical research.

Comprehensive behavioral treatment for young children: Utilizes ABA and often focuses on early intervention.

Consultative support: Special education monitors progress of child and consults with regular education teacher to provide individualized support for the child.

Coteaching: A teaching relationship where often a special educator and a regular education teacher collaborate to serve the needs of children in the classroom, or specific children with special needs (often both).

Cultural reciprocity: Involves developing collaborative relationships by respecting and striving to understand differences in perspectives and values, contributes to cultural sensitive services.

Cytogenetics: Study of chromosomes.

Degree of spontaneity: Whether the child initiates communication if communication is primarily prompted by others.

Delayed echolalia: The repetition of all or part of an utterance after a delay.

Developmental, Individual-Difference, Relationship-Based Model (Floor Time): A play-based intervention in which the caregiver interacts with the child to develop trust, intimacy, and engage in reciprocal interaction.

Diagnostic and Statistical Manual of Mental Disorders (DSM): Most widely used classification system within the United States for diagnosing autism and other developmental disorders. Published by the American Psychiatric Association.

Differential reinforcement of other behavior: Procedure involving providing a child with reinforcement for the absence of self-injurious behavior.

Discourse management: Involves skills such as staying on topic, conversational turn taking, and repairing conversational breakdowns.

Discrete Trial Instruction (DTI): Uses learning trials that are individually developed to address a particular learning goal.

Discrete trial instruction: Approach built around educational trials that always contain a prompt from the teacher, a response by the child, and a consequence delivered by the teacher.

Duration: How long the behavior occurs.

Early Start Denver Model: An individualized curriculum using a combination of instructional techniques based on behavioral, developmental, and relationship theories.

Echolalia: Automatically repeating vocalizations made by another.

Ecological validity: Measuring real-life functioning.

Elopement: A child running away from adults, which can be as minor as running across the room and as major as running out of the building.

Emerging intervention: Uses practices with some limited support.

Epigenetics: Refers to heritable changes in the expression of genes (the cellular phenotype) that are not caused by changes of the underlying DNA. *Epi* refers to the outer structures (rather than underlying structures) of the cell.

Errorless learning: Uses prompts that are gradually faded to provide the child with a learning experience with minimal frustration.

Established intervention: When using evidence-based practices, has strong empirical support for treatment validity.

Evaluation of Sensory Processing: An instrument designed to assess sensory processing across all sensory domains in children ages 2 to 12.

Evidence-based practices: Interventions supported by empirical research. Ratings such as *established, emerging,* and *unestablished* help guide teachers, parents, and other professionals in choosing interventions for children with ASD.

Executive functioning: Associated with the prefrontal cortex of the brain; used to describe many higher-level skills that are necessary for learning and being successful in school.

Exosystem: A social setting not immediately impacting the child but influencing relationships.

Expressive language: The ability to express one's thoughts with language.

Extinction burst: Situation when using extinction in which the behavior gets worse before it gets better.

Family systems theory: A branch of psychotherapy that addresses issues associated with intimate relationships in the context of families and the systems that underlie those relationships.

Family-centered approach: The cornerstone of early intervention efforts, the strengths and priorities of the family are equally important as the recommendations provided by professionals.

FISH analysis (fluorescence in situ hybridization): Fluorescent probe targets a DNA-specific region to detect if there is a deletion.

Form (communication style): Considers how the child attempts to communicate.

Fragile X syndrome: Most common genetic condition known to be associated with ASD; name of disorder is due to a fragile-looking extra piece of material that hangs from the X chromosome.

Frequency of communication: Involves an analysis of how often communication occurs.

Frequency: How often a behavior occurs in a specific time period.

Functional behavioral assessment: Technique developed by behavior analysts that focuses on determining why a problem behavior is occurring.

Functional magnetic resonance imaging (fMRI): Measures change of blood flow associated with a region of the brain.

Functional play: Play involving interacting with an object in the manner in which it is intended.

G-banded chromosomal analysis: Identifying relatively large pieces of genetic material that have been deleted or added to the chromosome.

Hans Asperger: Austrian pediatrician described children in 1944, today considered to have high-functioning autism, in his paper *Autistic Psychopathology in Children*. Later the diagnosis "Asperger syndrome or disorder" was named to describe this condition.

Heterogeneous disorder: Involving many different etiologies.

Hidden curriculum: The implicit rules students need to know to be successful with teachers and peers. Often learn informally from context and observation. Children with ASD may need such "rules" explicitly presented.

Higher Education Opportunity Act (HEOA) of 2008: Provides further support for people with ASD and other developmental disabilities.

Human Genome Project: A 13-year endeavor to map out the entire sequence of human chromosomes.

Humanistic psychology: A psychological perspective that addresses aspects of the person as a whole in an effort to facilitate a personally meaningful and enriched existence.

Hyperlexic: Development of reading skills more quickly or more advanced than same-age peers.

Hypersensitivities: Overly sensitive to certain sounds, type of physical contact, or textures.

Hyposensitivities: Appears less responsive to stimuli than peers, including pain.

Immediate echolalia: The repetition of all or part of an utterance that has just been spoken.

Incidental teaching: A type of DTI that increases the generalizability of the learned skill by teaching during daily activities with highly motivating materials.

Incidental teaching: A type of DTI that takes advantage of a child's interests to guide instruction.

Individualized Education Plan (IEP): Describes individualized educational goals for the school-aged child ages 3 to 21, with focus on the child within the context of the educational setting.

Individualized Family Service Plan (IFSP): Created based on family and child needs and includes ongoing assessment of the family's priorities, expectations, goals, concerns, and their measurement of progress, as well as the child's developmental level.

Individualized transition plan: The written identification of a student's preferences for their lives after public school, including employment or further education, leisure and recreation, social/interpersonal, and residential.

The Individuals with Disabilities Education Act (IDEA): Mandates parent involvement in every phase of the special education process, including pre-referral, assessment, creating the educational plan, and monitoring progress.

Interactive sampling: Involves collecting data about communication behavior within interactive settings.

International Classification of Diseases (ICD): Classification system; published by the World Health Organization, closely aligns with the *DSM* and is used by the medical professional in Europe and many other countries.

Intervention fidelity: The valid implementation of interventions.

Job coach: Sometimes referred to as an employment specialist or consultant, this individual helps identify a job that fits the individual's interests and skills, provides supports for initial employment, and gradually reduces the coaching role as the individual adjusts to the job setting.

Joint attention intervention: Teaches the subskills needed to learn the skill of maintaining joint attention with others.

Joint attention: Coordinated by the infant and is the basis of engaging in shared experiences involving behaviors such as gazing and pointing.

Joint attention: Joining in the gaze or focus on something with another individual; may use pointing, gesturing, or eye gaze.

Leo Kanner: An American psychiatrist who described a disorder he called "Early Infantile Autism" as distinctly different from schizophrenia in his 1943 paper *Autistic Disturbances of Affective Contact.*

Latency: How much time it takes for the behavior to occur after a stimulus is presented.

Leaky gut theory: Theory that some children with ASD experience severe inflammation in the gut membrane, causing irregular metabolic pathways.

Least restrictive environment (LRE): A learning environment that allows optimal interaction with same-age typically developing peers.

Ivar O. Lovaas: Used the principle of chaining simple skills together to create interventions that addressed more complex skills.

Macrosystem: An institution or aspect of the greater culture that influences the microsystem.

Mand: In ABA, a mand is a request for something the child wants. After communicating with a mand, the child is reinforced by receiving what they requested. Manding is considered a natural way for teaching spontaneous speech.

Measles, mumps, and rubella (MMR) vaccine: Vaccination to prevent measles, mumps, and rubella given at approximately 1 year of age, and a second shot given at about 4 years of age. A great deal of controversy surrounds the association of MMR to autism, with leading research and medical establishments asserting no association between the two.

Mesosystem: A relationship between microsystems (school and family).

Microsystem: Involves day-to-day interactions.

Modeling interventions: Individuals are encouraged to repeat target behaviors modeled by adults or peers.

Modified Checklist for Autism in Toddlers (M-CHAT): A popular screening tool for detecting characteristics of autism in infants and toddlers 16 to 30 months of age.

Monarch program: An inclusion program to transition children to elementary school inclusive experiences.

Morphology: Utilizing the smallest unit of meaning for a word.

Multiplex families: Refers to families with at least two siblings diagnosed with ASD.

Multisystem developmental disorder: Found under the category of Disorders of Relating and Communicating, can diagnose children under the age of 3; associated with delays in language, social development, motor planning, and sensory processing.

The National Standards Report: Produced by the National Autism Center in 2009, provides a guide to the most current evidence-based interventions for ASD.

Naturalistic teaching strategies: Interacting with a student to teach content in a natural setting such as the playground.

Neobehaviorism: Expands the behaviorist perspective, resulting in an explosion of research and later application to a wide range of clinical and educational interventions.

Neurotypical: Individuals experiencing normal development for their chronological age.

Nonsyndromic: Having no identifiable medical disorder associated with ASD; idiopathic.

Occupational therapist: May conduct assessments of fine motor skills and sensory integration functioning.

Operant behavior: Behavior shaped by its consequences.

Overextension: The tendency to overgeneralize and use a word to refer to many different things.

Peer-mediated intervention: Involves identifying and training peers as mentors to initiate and respond to their peers with ASD.

Peer-training packages: A package of interventions that involve having students with ASD interact with their typically developing peers who have undergone training, often to enhance social skills.

Person-centered planning: An approach to determining and setting goals that focuses on the hopes, dreams, and desires of the individual and his or her family.

Phenotypes: Expression of the disorder; observational traits.

Phonology: Pronunciation and articulation of the sounds in words.

Pivotal response teaching: Approach that focuses on teaching children important skills that will exponentially improve their ability to learn and interact with others.

Pivotal response training (PRT): A type of DTI that utilizes incidental teaching; PRT teaches responses to *multiple cues* increasing the likelihood that the learned skill with be generalized to multiple settings.

Pragmatics: The social convention of language in which the verbal and nonverbal language is used appropriately.

Prompt: Anything that offers additional support to the child during the intervention.

Prompting: Used to provide support to the child during learning, ensuring success.

Protodeclarative pointing: Using the index finger to identify something of interest.

Pseudoscience: Undermines the scientific process and often is rooted in ulterior motives such as personal gain; falsely purports to be based on scientific principles.

Psychoanalysis: A complex theory based on the belief that unconscious forces impact a significant degree of human behavior and that personality development is most significantly impacted by early parenting practices.

Psychoeducational Profile, Third Edition (PEP-3): Assesses developmental skills in children 6 months to 7 years with ASD.

Rate: How often a behavior occurs per unit of time (i.e., rate per hour).

Receptive language: Understanding language.

Reinforcers: Reinforcing consequences; increases the future probability that the behavior that came before the consequence

will be repeated again sometime in the future.

Relationship Development Intervention (RDI): A parent-based, cognitive-developmental intervention approach.

Respite care: A short-term child care service.

Response blocking: A form of extinction that involved not allowing the child to complete the self-injurious behavior, thus removing the consequence.

Response to Intervention (RTI): Used to provide educational support within general education before considering special education services.

Retrospective studies: Analysis of data about past behavior to explain current behavior.

Bernard Rimland: A research psychologist and father of a son with autism; published *Infantile Autism: The Syndrome and Its Implications for a Neural Theory of Behavior.* The book presented a convincing rationale asserting that autism was a cognitive disorder with neurobiological origins.

Risperidone: Atypical antipsychotic medication that is sometimes prescribed to reduce aggressive, self-injurious, or excessively repetitive behaviors.

Scaffold: Supporting learning by offering reduced support as the child gets closer to mastery.

Schedules: Use of a series of pictures, words, or a photograph to communicate a task's requirements.

School psychologist: Generally writes a psychoeducational report based on a battery of tests and interviews. Often skilled in developing and assessing IEP goals. Often part of the multidisciplinary team in an educational setting.

Secretin: Gastrointestinal hormone used to diagnose digestive difficulties.

Section 504 of the Rehabilitation Act and the Americans with Disabilities Act: Federal laws that protect rights of individuals with disabilities in the United States.

Selective serotonin reuptake inhibitors (SSRIs): Abnormal levels of serotonin appear implicated in ASD; SSRIs seem to prevent certain nerve cells in the brain from reabsorbing serotonin, which is associated with elevated mood.

Self-determination: Refers to making meaningful decisions about one's life based on an understanding of one's self and real-world experiences, and without undue influences or interferences. Self-determination is also understood to be the ability to make choices about one's life. It is considered a fundamental human right and is formally recognized on a federal and international level.

Self-management: Skills enabling an individual to monitor their own behavior and promote independence.

Semantics: The content of language, including the use of vocabulary to express meaning.

Sensory integration therapy: Designed to help the child organize sensory stimuli by exposure to increased and reduced levels of sensory stimuli.

Sensory integration therapy: Therapy that targets sensory issues, often used in occupational therapy and within educational settings.

Service dogs: The use of pet therapy, specifically dogs, provides individuals with ASD the opportunity to experience pleasure in having a relationship with a pet and learning to care for their pet.

Shape: Behaviors can be shaped using reinforcement to reward approximations of target behavior.

Shape: Using reinforcement to reward approximations of target behaviors.

Sib shops: Provides a forum for siblings of children with disabilities to connect with their peers and discuss meaningful topics such as feeling embarrassed by a sibling's behaviors and concerns about their sibling's long-term care needs.

Skill acquisition deficits: Absence of a skill, has not learned the skill.

Skill performance deficits: Difficulties performing a particular skill.

B. F. Skinner: Developed the theory of operant conditioning based on research with animals on which the many variants of ABA are based.

Social cognition: Refers to the way in which individuals perceive, process, and understand social information.

Social Communication Emotional Regulation Transactional Supports (SCERTS): Addresses the development of social communication skills such as joint attention, symbolic behavior, sharing emotions, and expressing emotions.

Social Communication Questionnaire: A screening tool for children ages 4 and older based on items from the Autism Diagnostic Interview-Revised (ADI-R) addressing social communication skills such as expressing empathy and peer relationships.

Social Communication/Emotional Regulation/Transactional Supports: A family-centered educational approach that systematically identifies the child's needs, determines supports that are meaningful and purposeful, and monitors progress.

Social competence: Describes the ability to interact with others in an appropriate manner based on age and context.

Social referencing: Referring to others to gather information about events.

Social stories: A visual technique using a story format for teaching children with autism how to read the intricacies of the social environment.

Social story: Provides a brief story with specific information about a particular social experience using text, pictures, or both.

Social validity: Social importance.

Social-emotional reciprocity: The give-and-take of social interactions.

Socio-dramatic play: Imaginary play involving role-playing such as playing school.

Spectrum disorder: Individuals with ASD express a diverse range of functioning on each of the core deficits; a continuum or spectrum reflects the wide range

of strengths and weaknesses within the population.

Speech-generating device: Communication technology that provides an understandable message through preset phrases typically used in conversation.

Speech-language pathologist: Specialized in conducting thorough evaluations of difficulties with communication and voice, and provide therapy to address a variety of disorders related to communication deficits for individuals with ASD.

Stereotypies: Behaviors such as hand or finger flapping, body rocking, and other stereotyped motor mannerisms; sometimes called self-stimulatory behaviors.

Stimulus generalization: Occurs when a behavior is learned in one setting, and then is demonstrated, without further training, by the same individual, in a different setting.

Story-based intervention package: Using individualized stories to explain a series of behaviors needed to be successful in a specific event, and provide a framework of what to expect during the event. Often uses pictures or text to visually present this information.

Supportive employment: For individuals who require some degree of support while employed, supportive employment helps individuals with ASD work within their community. Many individuals with ASD benefit from on-the-job supports, which allow them to participate in meaningful and sometimes paid employment.

Supportive living: With use of appropriate supports, supportive living is living outside of one's family's home and within the community.

Symbolic play: Substituting one object for another during play. For instance, pretending that a brush is a microphone.

Syndromic: Having an identifiable medical disorder.

Syntax: The rules of how language is put together.

Theory of mind (TOM): One's theory about the mental state of someone else.

Theory of Mind: The understanding that others bring a unique perspective to problem-solving situations based on their experiences and knowledge.

Thinning the schedule of reinforcement: As the child continues to learn and engage in more appropriate behavior he or she will gradually need less and less of the reinforcement to engage in the desired behavior.

Treatment and Education of Autistic and Communication-Handicapped Children (TEACCH): Program developed by Eric Schopler that blends behavioral components firmly rooted in ABA with cognitive components, integrated alongside a multitiered education program designed to empower parents and teachers to create environments that allow children with autism to grow and develop throughout the life span. Also emphasizes a visual approach to learning and communication.

Triad of core deficits: Significant deficits as compared with same-age peers in three core areas: socialization, communication (both verbal and nonverbal), and restricted, repetitive, and stereotyped patterns of behaviors and interests.

Tuberous sclerosis: The most frequently occurring genetic disorder caused by a single gene associated with ASD; causes benign tumors to grow throughout the body, including within the brain, and is associated with a variety of physical and cognitive difficulties, including seizures, developmental delays, and ASD in many individuals with the disorder.

Underextension: Involves limiting a word to refer to only one particular person, place, or thing.

Unestablished practices: Have virtually no empirical support.

Vestibular input: Activities such as swinging that can provide sensory stimulation to the vestibular system. May have a calming effect in children with ASD. Sensory input associated with movement and balance.

Video modeling: An intervention using video of a social behavior to model an appropriate social skill.

Video self-modeling: A type of video modeling in which the child, the target of the intervention, is filmed exhibiting the pro-social behavior.

Vocational rehabilitation: The opportunity for individuals with ASD to participate in the employment benefits that are available to non-ASD peers. In addition to financial benefits, employment offers social opportunities, promotes personal dignity that is associated with a high quality of life and may enhance cognitive skills.

Voice output communication aid (VOCA): Assistive technology that supports communication.

Vygotsky's social-cultural theory: Considers the impact of culture on learning and overall development.

Weak central coherence theory (or central coherence theory): Describes a trend of many individuals with ASD of demonstrating strengths in recognizing details, but more difficulty seeing the whole or "big picture."

Weak central coherence: A theory explaining a deficit found in many individuals with ASD involving an overfocus on extraneous details at the expense of understanding the big picture.

Wechsler Intelligence Scale for Children-Fourth Edition: One of the most widely used tests to assess cognitive ability in children. Provides a full-scale score along with four Index Scores, including Verbal Comprehension, Perceptual Reasoning, Working Memory, and Processing Speed.

Whole gene microarray: Identification of even smaller details of DNA segments.

Zone of proximal development (ZPD): Captures a point at which the child can almost master a skill alone but still requires some support.

Index

About the Authors

Dr. Michelle Haney is an Associate Professor of Psychology at Berry College in Mount Berry, Georgia. She also teaches in the Education and Graduate Education Departments at Berry College. Dr. Haney is the Director of the Berry College Psychology Lab and coordinates the George Scholar program, an endowed undergraduate research program. Dr. Haney earned her Ph.D. from Georgia State University in School Psychology with a cognate in developmental learning disorders. She earned her Master's and Educational Specialist degrees at the University of Georgia, also in School Psychology. Her undergraduate degree is from Oglethorpe University with a major in Psychology and a minor in Biology. Dr. Haney spent a decade working in the public school system as a school psychologist and specialized in working with children on the Autism Spectrum, their teachers, and their families. Currently, Dr. Haney enjoys mentoring undergraduate students interested in conducting research in ASD and working in careers supporting children with ASD and their families. In addition, Dr. Haney is a representative for the Georgia Human Rights Council of Developmental Disabilities, an advisory review board for the state of Georgia. Her professional and research interests include collaborating with and supporting families of children with developmental disabilities, gender differences in ASD, postsecondary education for individuals with developmental disabilities, and supporting self-determination in people with ASD and other developmental disabilities.

Contributing Author

Dr. Cynthia Golden is a psychologist and the principal of an educational and therapeutic program serving students with severe emotional and behavioral needs and autism. She has served as special education supervisor in the public school system, supervising the county autism and emotional/behavioral disorders programs. Dr. Golden has an undergraduate degree in Special Education from the University of West Florida; Master's and Educational Specialist degrees in School Psychology from Georgia State University; a certificate in Educational Leadership; and an Educational Specialist degree and an Educational Doctorate in Inclusive Education from Kennesaw State University. She has most recently published *The Special Educator's Toolkit: Everything You Need to Organize, Manage, and Monitor Your Classroom* (Brookes, 2012).

⬤SAGE research**methods**

The essential online tool for researchers from the world's leading methods publisher

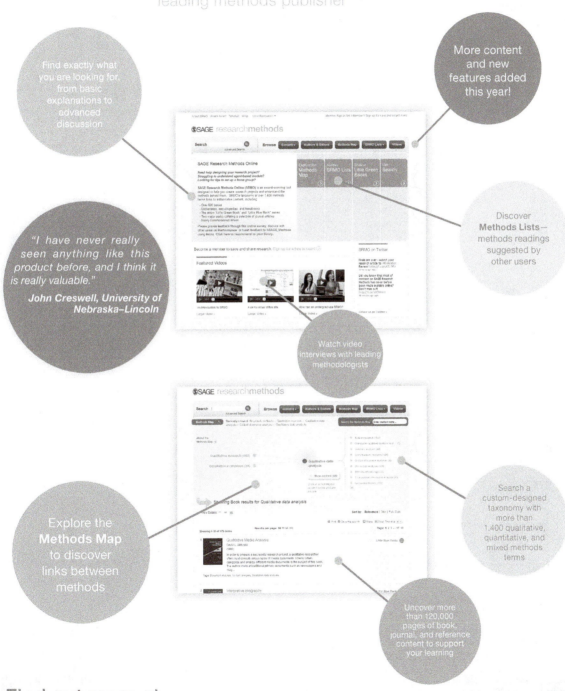

Find exactly what you are looking for, from basic explanations to advanced discussion

More content and new features added this year!

"I have never really seen anything like this product before, and I think it is really valuable."

John Creswell, University of Nebraska–Lincoln

Discover **Methods Lists**— methods readings suggested by other users

Watch video interviews with leading methodologists

Explore the **Methods Map** to discover links between methods

Search a custom-designed taxonomy with more than 1,400 qualitative, quantitative, and mixed methods terms

Uncover more than 120,000 pages of book, journal, and reference content to support your learning

Find out more at
www.sageresearchmethods.com

CPSIA information can be obtained
at www.ICGtesting.com
Printed in the USA
LVHW062000240721
693235LV00008B/5